ABBOT SUGER

Corpore, gente brevis, gemina brevitate coactus,
In brevitate sua noluit esse brevis.

ABBOT SUGER

ON THE ABBEY CHURCH OF ST.-DENIS

AND ITS ART TREASURES

EDITED, TRANSLATED AND ANNOTATED

BY ERWIN PANOFSKY

SECOND EDITION
BY GERDA PANOFSKY-SOERGEL

PRINCETON UNIVERSITY PRESS
PRINCETON, NEW JERSEY

Published by Princeton University Press, Princeton, New Jersey
In the United Kingdom: Princeton University Press,
Oxford

ALL RIGHTS RESERVED

This book has been composed in Linotype Caslon Old Face
Clothbound editions of Princeton University Press books
are printed on acid-free paper, and binding materials are chosen
for strength and durability.

The thirteenth-century seal of St.-Denis on the title-page
is after the reproduction in *Trésor de Numismatique et de
Glyptique*, XIII, Paris, 1858, pl. II, no. 4

PRINTED IN THE UNITED STATES OF AMERICA
BY PRINCETON UNIVERSITY PRESS, PRINCETON, NEW JERSEY

15 14 13 12 11 10 9 8

To Booth Tarkington

(1869–1946)

PREFACE TO THE SECOND EDITION

AFTER the second printing of this book was exhausted some twenty years ago, the author resisted the requests for still another reprinting, because, as he wrote in a letter to his publisher, "so much of it has become untenable by the progress of scholarship," especially as far as the commentary was concerned. Yet, that Erwin Panofsky was not on principle opposed to a second edition at some future date, is not only attested by the same letter but by the fact that in the intervening years he had recorded some of his intended revisions. Encouraged by these, but nevertheless with great hesitation, I decided to accept the responsibility of preparing the present new edition after my husband's death.

Of Erwin Panofsky's own additions and emendations, some account is in order here: About a year after the publication of the first edition, the author learned that of the medieval manuscripts of Suger's *De Consecratione*, which he had assumed to be lost, two were still extant and had been identified by Luchaire as early as 1899. Thus Luchaire's readings of these manuscripts could be compared with the proposed conjectures against Lecoy de la Marche's edition of Suger's *Œuvres Complètes* (1867), on which the author's translation had relied. Meanwhile, the manuscripts of Suger's *De Rebus Administratione Sua Gestis* and of his *Ordinatio* of 1140/41, inaccessible to the author during World War II, had again become available for study; and in 1947 he collated therefore a long list of variants and other observations (see Bib. 132), which are now incorporated in the section entitled TEXTS AND TRANSLATIONS, superseding the remarks on p. 146 ff. of the first edition.

With regard to the COMMENTARY, this section has been augmented by all of the author's addenda and corrigenda as previously printed on p. 243 f., and as left in handwritten or typed notes entered in his personal copy of the book. Wherever references to more recent scholarship have seemed appropriate, I have inserted these, together with any necessary explanation, distinguishing them from the author's text by angular brackets.

The BIBLIOGRAPHY, provided in this new edition, reflects the wealth of literature that has been published on St.-Denis in the last thirty years. Unfortunately, the publication that the author

would have wished most to precede our venture—Sumner Mc-
Knight Crosby's *The Abbey of St.-Denis*, vol. ii—has not yet
been completed. However, Crosby's interim publications on his
numerous excavations and investigations (see Bib. 21 ff., especially
Bib. 26) have answered many questions, and I am grateful for his
generous replacement of two outdated text figures, the section of
the choir and the plan, both newly drawn under his supervision.

A brief glance at the new entries will reveal that those on
Suger's stained-glass windows contribute most extensively to revisions as the pertinent paragraphs of the earlier Commentary
have become outdated not only by the postwar restorations and
re-installations of the glass but even more so by the important
findings of Louis Grodecki, Paris. I am immensely indebted to
Mr. Grodecki for having checked my draft of this difficult chapter
and for having provided me in the most devoted and selfless way
with an unlimited amount of unpublished information of his own
for his forthcoming two volumes of the *Corpus Vitrearum Medii
Aevi* (see Bib. 93).

Willibald Sauerländer, Munich, has been kind enough to read
through my bibliographical items concerning the St.-Denis sculpture, while Hugo Buchthal, New York and London, took the
trouble of verifying for me the Montfaucon drawings at the
Bibliothèque Nationale, Paris.

For the venerated liturgical objects, restored or commissioned
by Suger, students may now consult Florentine Mütherich's excellent catalogue (see Bib. 153) as well as Peter Lasko's Pelican
volume (see Bib. 111). Comte Blaise de Montesquiou-Fezensac's
exemplary edition of the inventory of the St.-Denis treasury (see
Bib. 125), taken in 1634 before most of the medieval goldsmith-
works were destroyed, ought henceforth to elucidate Suger's
descriptions, at times so puzzling. Here, though tempting, it
would have been beyond my competence to try my hand at novel
reconstructions of lost monuments. I want to thank Philippe
Verdier, Montreal, for his gracious correspondence, often accompanied by offprints, on Sugerian enamels, and I deeply appreciate
the alacrity with which John D. Cooney, Cleveland, sent me his
still unpublished paper on the agate cup of Suger's chalice (see
Bib. 20).

Suger's complete writings will soon be available in a modern reprint of Lecoy de la Marche's edition (see p. 262). Philippe Verdier has announced an ambitious multilingual translation of these (see *Gazette des Beaux-Arts*, sér. 6, LXXIII, 1969, p. 28), and at least one of Suger's texts, the *De Consecratione*, has been translated into French (see Bib. 112). Georg Misch has analyzed Suger's accounts within the literary tradition of the autobiography (see Bib. 116 f.), whereas Paul Frankl's survey of the treatises dwells solely on passages containing the abbot's "personal conception of Gothic" (see Bib. 59).

Various sections of the first edition of Erwin Panofsky's book have been reprinted, and there has appeared an Italian, French, and Polish translation of the Introduction, p. 1 ff. (for all of which see Bib. 131). Suger's fascinating personality has invited another biography (see Bib. 5) and even a charming book for children (see Bib. 144). Much has been written on his philosophy and aesthetics (see Bib. 72, 80, 86, 133, 154 f., 157 f.) as well as on his political goals (see Bib. 9, 52 f., 68 ff., 73, 105, 115, 158), while the 1960's focused on the aspect of his patronage of the arts (see Bib. 6, 19, 29 f., 76, esp. 97). In this vast field of literature, I acknowledge many helpful references from Lester Little, Northampton, Mass., and above all from Konrad Hoffmann, Tübingen, who was untiring in bringing to my attention publications which I should otherwise have missed.

Those familiar with the first edition, will find various changes in the ILLUSTRATIONS: New photographs have been obtained throughout, occasionally replacing the former ones by more recent views. The inclusion of additional illustrations (see Figs. 10, 18, 21, 25, 27), and the omission of the former Fig. 14, have also prompted a revision of the sequence. Instead of following Suger's narration as before, the Abbey Church and its treasures are now unfolded systematically, beginning with the architecture and ending with the minor arts. I wish to express my gratitude to Messrs. Jean Adhémar, Sumner McKnight Crosby (whose replacement of two text figures has already been noted above), Louis Grodecki, Konrad Hoffmann, and Pierre Verlet for their assistance and generosity in procuring some of the new photographs for me, and for the courtesy of the many institutions mentioned in the List of Illustrations.

Finally, I want to say that the basic decisions on how to arrange the later material and how to handle the ensuing scholarly problems would have been an overwhelming task, had I not been so fortunate as to be able to depend on the unfailing advice of our friend Richard Krautheimer, formerly of New York and now living in Rome. My warmest thanks go to him for having guided me through what seemed a "selva oscura."

In presenting this new edition of *Abbot Suger*, I ask the indulgence of medievalists for any shortcomings, and I hope that the ADDITIONAL BIBLIOGRAPHY may prove useful to students, including my own and those my husband loved to teach.

G.P.-S.

Princeton, New Jersey, October 9, 1976

PREFACE TO THE FIRST EDITION

THE texts reprinted and translated in this volume have long
been familiar to every student of medieval art and civiliza-
tion. They are concerned with what still deserves to be called the
parent monument of all Gothic cathedrals. They were composed
by a man not only famed and much beloved in his day but also
recognized as one who helped to shape the course of European
history. They abound in concrete information as to archaeological
facts, liturgical customs, and social habits. They reflect the varied
and often conflicting tendencies and attitudes of a period that is
related to the subsequent phases of the Middle Ages much as the
Florentine Quattrocento is to the Modern Era. They constitute a
human document as well as a historical source; and they contain
some real gems of medieval oratory both in prose and verse.

Yet these well-known texts have never been translated *in extenso*. An unabridged translation into French planned by Henri
Waquet some fifteen years ago has not appeared so far as can be
ascertained. Selections in English and German have been printed
in Arthur Kingsley Porter's *Medieval Architecture*, New Haven,
vol. II, 1912, pp. 158, 194-199; and in Ernst Gall's *Die Gotische
Baukunst in Frankreich und Deutschland*, I, Leipzig, 1925, pp.
93-101, 103 f. But these translations, in addition to their fragmentary character, contain too many errors really to be helpful;
even such isolated passages as have been adduced by various other
scholars in the discussion of special archaeological problems have
not always been correctly rendered and interpreted.

An attempt to fill this gap is a hazardous undertaking. Suger,
praised by his admirers as a "second Tullius," writes with Ciceronian verve and eloquence but not with Ciceronian lucidity. Without ever being confused, he can be confusing by his irrepressible
love of word-play, quotation, paraphrase, and circumlocution, and
by his delight in long, involved periods composed with a strong
feeling for sound and rhythm rather than with due reverence for
grammar. He is prolix where we would wish him to be brief, and
all too laconic, especially in his references to technical or administrative detail, where we would wish him to be more circumstantial.
For, with all his apostrophes to "future generations," Suger writes
under the silent assumption that his readers are metropolitan

Frenchmen of the twelfth century, and this presents much greater difficulties than *recherché* expressions and questionable syntax. While emulating the style of the Roman classics, while borrowing phrases from the Bible, the Fathers and John the Scot, the house-philosopher of St.-Denis, he speaks of contemporary personages, local landmarks, and national institutions much as the *New Yorker* speaks of Mayor La Guardia, Lord and Taylor, and the Fuller Brush Man.

It is therefore impossible to translate Suger without commenting upon him, and to make such a commentary really adequate would require the combined efforts of four or five specialists. As an art historian, this writer has naturally paid especial attention to those passages that bear directly upon Suger's enterprises in the fields of architecture, sculpture, glass painting and the so-called minor arts; and he has tried to elucidate these passages by a sketch-map and a selection of pictures that illustrate such objects of Suger's descriptions as have come down to us in the original or in reliable renderings. He wishes to express his gratitude to Dr. G. Schön-berger, Dr. H. Swarzenski, and the Misses D. Miner and A. Mongan for their kind assistance in procuring suitable photographs. Further he wishes to thank Dr. P. Frankl for the design of text illustration p. 221 and Mr. J. H. MacFadyen for the execution of the sketch-map; the Trustees of the Walters Art Gallery for permission to republish the photographs reproduced in *figs.* 4 and 5; Professor W. F. Stohlman for permission to publish a photograph by the late Clement Heaton (now in the possession of the Princeton Department of Art and Archaeology) reproduced in *fig.* 18, and for the generous communication of his personal notes concerning the stained glass in St.-Denis; Professor C. Ward for permission to reproduce, in *fig.* 7, his private print of an unpublished photograph by Mr. Princehorn; Father Q. F. Beckley, O.P., Dr. R. Ettinghausen, Dr. E. A. Lowe, and Miss R. J. Dean for valuable advice in liturgical, historical, and palaeographical matters; Mr. G. H. Forsyth, Jr., for aid and comfort in several emergencies, especially for executing the excellent original of text illustration p. 172 f. and for redesigning the cover stamp from the thirteenth-century seal of St.-Denis as reproduced in *Trésor de Numismatique et de Glyptique*, XIII (*Sceaux des Communes,*

Communautés, Evêques, Barons, et Abbés), Paris, 1858, pl. II, no. 4; and Miss Elizabeth Trotter for her kind help in revising the English.

Above all, however, the writer wishes to acknowledge his great indebtedness to S. McK. Crosby's monograph *The Abbey of St.-Denis*, I, New Haven, 1942. The sketch-map as well as the text illustration p. 221 depend, so far as architectural features are concerned, entirely on Professor Crosby's plans and reconstructions; and even where the writer disagrees with him on certain points he would not have been able to do so without basing himself upon Professor Crosby's researches and findings.

In spite of all this help the writer does not flatter himself that he has avoided inaccuracies and palpable errors. But, to quote from Suger himself, "quia sicut voluimus non potuimus, quam melius potuimus voluimus."

E.P.

Princeton, New Jersey, June 11, 1944

CONTENTS

LIST OF TEXT FIGURES

LIST OF ILLUSTRATIONS

Following p. 285

St.-Denis, Plan of the Carolingian nave and transept as reconstructed by S. McK. Crosby, and of Suger's still extant narthex and choir (drawing lent by S. McK. Crosby)

1. St.-Denis, Former Abbey Church. West Façade prior to 1837. Engraving by Adolphe and Emile Rouargue (after Crosby, Frontispiece)

2. St.-Denis, Former Abbey Church. Interior of Narthex, viewed from north-west to south-east (Phot. Archives Photographiques, Paris)

3. St.-Denis, Former Abbey Church. West Façade, central portal (Phot. Archives Photographiques, Paris)

4. Destroyed Jamb Figure (so-called Clothaire III), formerly on the West Façade of the Abbey Church of St.-Denis. Drawing, published as engraving in Bernard de Montfaucon, 1729. Paris, Bibliothèque Nationale, MS Fr. 15.634, fol. 51 (Phot. Courtesy of the Bibliothèque Nationale, Paris)

5. Head of a Jamb Figure (so-called Clothaire III), formerly on the West Façade of the Abbey Church of St.-Denis. Baltimore, Md., The Walters Art Gallery (Phot. Courtesy of the Walters Art Gallery, Baltimore, Md.)

6. St.-Denis, Former Abbey Church. West Façade, southern portal, reliefs on the left doorpost showing November and December (Phot. Archives Photographiques, Paris)

7. St.-Denis, Former Abbey Church. West Façade, southern portal, reliefs on the right doorpost showing February and January (Phot. Archives Photographiques, Paris)

8. St.-Denis, Former Abbey Church. Exterior of Chapels on Ambulatory (Phot. Archives Photographiques, Paris)

9. St.-Denis, Former Abbey Church. Interior of Choir, viewed from north-west to south-east (Phot. Archives Photographiques, Paris)

10. Statue of a King, formerly in the Cloister of the Abbey of St.-Denis. New York, The Metropolitan Museum of Art (Phot. The Metropolitan Museum of Art, Purchase, 1920. Joseph Pulitzer Bequest)

11. St.-Denis, Former Abbey Church. Chapel of the Virgin, Life of the Virgin (Infancy of Christ) Window in northern bay (Phot. Archives Photographiques, Paris)

12. St.-Denis, Former Abbey Church. Chapel of the Virgin, Tree of Jesse Window in southern bay (Phot. Archives Photographiques, Paris)

[xvii]

SUGER, ABBOT OF ST.-DENIS, Detail of Fig. 15

INTRODUCTION

R ARELY—in fact, all but never—has a great patron of the
arts been stirred to write a retrospective account of his inten-
tions and accomplishments. Men of action, from Caesars to country
doctors, have recorded the deeds and experiences they felt would
not attain deserved permanence save by grace of the written word.
Men of expression, too, from writers and poets to painters and
sculptors (once artistry had been promoted to Art by the Renaissance), have resorted to autobiography and self-interpretation
whenever they feared that their works alone, being but isolated
and crystallized products of a continuous process of creation, might
not convey a unified and living message to posterity. Not so with
the patron, the man whose prestige and initiative summons other
men's work into being: the prince of the Church, the secular ruler,
the aristocrat and the plutocrat. From his point of view the work
of art should render praises unto the patron, but not the patron
unto the work of art. The Hadrians and Maximilians, the Leos
and Juliuses, the Jean de Berrys and Lorenzo de' Medicis decided
what they wanted, selected the artists, took a hand in devising the
program, approved or criticized its execution and paid—or did not
pay—the bills. But they left it to their court officials or secretaries
to draw up the inventories, and to their historiographers, poets
and humanists to write the descriptions, eulogies and explanations.

A special concatenation of circumstances and a unique blend of
personal qualities were needed to bring into existence the documents produced by Suger, Abbot of St.-Denis, and preserved by
time's mercy.

As THE HEAD AND REORGANIZER of an abbey that in political significance and territorial wealth surpassed most bishoprics, as the
Regent of France during the Second Crusade, and as the "loyal
adviser and friend" of two French kings at a time when the Crown
began to reassert its power after a long period of great weakness,
Suger (born 1081 and Abbot of St.-Denis from 1122 until his
death in 1151) is an outstanding figure in the history of France;
not without reason has he been called the father of the French
monarchy that was to culminate in the state of Louis XIV. Combining the shrewdness of a great business man with a natural sense

of equity and a personal rectitude (*fidelitas*) recognized even by those who did not really like him, conciliatory and averse to violence yet never infirm of purpose and not lacking physical courage, restlessly active yet a past master in the art of biding his time, a genius for detail yet capable of seeing things in perspective, he placed these contradictory gifts at the service of two ambitions; he wanted to strengthen the power of the Crown of France, and he wanted to aggrandize the Abbey of St.-Denis.

To Suger these ambitions did not conflict with each other. On the contrary, they appeared to him as aspects of but one ideal which he believed to correspond both to natural law and to the Will Divine. For he was convinced of three basic truths. First, a king, and most particularly the king of France, was a "vicar of God," "bearing God's image in his person and bringing it to life"; but this fact, far from implying that the king could do no wrong, entailed the postulate that the king must do no wrong ("it disgraces a king to transgress the law, for the king and the law—*rex et lex*—are receptacles of the same supreme power of government"). Second, any king of France, but quite especially Suger's beloved master, Louis le Gros, who at his coronation in 1108 had divested himself of the secular sword and had been girded with the sword spiritual "for defense of the Church and the poor," had both the right and the sacred duty to subdue all forces conducive to internal strife and obstructive to his central authority. Third, this central authority and, therefore, the unity of the nation were symbolized, even vested, in the Abbey of St.-Denis which harbored the relics of the "Apostle of all Gaul," the "special and, after God, unique protector of the realm."[1]

Founded by King Dagobert in honor of Saint Denis and his legendary Companions, Sts. Rusticus and Eleutherius (usually referred to by Suger as "the Holy Martyrs" or "our Patron Saints"), St.-Denis had been the "royal" abbey for many centuries. "As though by natural right" it housed the tombs of the French kings; Charles the Bald and Hugh Capet, the founder of the ruling dynasty, had been its titular abbots; and many princes of the blood received their early education there (it was indeed in the school of St.-Denis-de-l'Estrée that Suger, as a boy, had formed

[1] ⟨Cf. now Glaser, Bib. 69.⟩

his lifelong friendship with the future Louis le Gros). In 1127 St. Bernard summed up the situation fairly correctly when he wrote: "This place had been distinguished and of royal dignity from ancient times; it used to serve for the legal business of the Court and for the soldiery of the king; without hesitation or deceit there were rendered unto Caesar the things which are his, but there were not delivered with equal fidelity to God the things which are God's."

In this much-quoted letter, written in the sixth year of Suger's abbacy, the Abbot of Clairvaux congratulates his worldlier *con-frère* on having successfully "reformed" the Abbey of St.-Denis. But this "reform," far from diminishing the Abbey's political importance, invested it with an independence, prestige and prosperity that permitted Suger to tighten and to formalize its traditional ties with the Crown. Reform or no reform, he never ceased to promote the interests of St.-Denis and the Royal House of France with the same naive, and in his case not entirely unjustified, conviction of their identity with those of the nation and with the Will of God as a modern oil or steel magnate may promote legislation favorable to his company and to his bank as something beneficial to the welfare of his country and to the progress of mankind. For Suger the friends of the Crown were and remained the "partisans of God and Saint Denis" just as an enemy of St.-Denis was and remained a "man with no regard for either the king of the Franks or the King of the Universe."

Constitutionally peace-loving, Suger tried to achieve his ends, wherever possible, by negotiation and financial settlement rather than by military force. From the inception of his career he had incessantly worked for an improvement of the relations between the Crown of France and the Holy See, which had been worse than strained under Louis le Gros's father and predecessor, Philip I. Suger was entrusted with special missions to Rome long before his elevation to the abbacy; it was on one of these missions that he received the news of his election. Under his skillful management the relations between the Crown and the Curia developed into so firm an alliance that it not only strengthened the internal position of the king but also neutralized his most dangerous external enemy, the German Emperor Henry V.

No diplomacy could prevent a series of armed conflicts with Louis's other great foe, the proud and gifted Henry I Beauclerc of England. A son of William the Conqueror, Henry very naturally refused to renounce his continental heritage, the Duchy of Normandy, while Louis, just as naturally, tried to transfer it to his less powerful and more reliable vassals, the Counts of Flanders. Yet Suger (who had a genuine admiration for Henry's military and administrative genius) miraculously managed to acquire and to retain his confidence and private friendship. Time and again he acted as an intermediary between him and Louis le Gros; and it is in this connection that Suger's special protégé and devoted biographer, the monk Willelmus of St.-Denis (relegated to the Priory of St.-Denis-en-Vaux as soon as his protector had died) produced one of those happy formulae that are at times granted to simple-minded affection rather than to critical acumen: "Has not Henry, the mighty King of England," he writes, "prided himself on this man's friendship and enjoyed the intercourse with him? Has he not chosen him as his mediator with Louis, King of France, and as a tie of peace?"[2]

Mediator et pacis vinculum: these four words comprise about all that can be said about Suger's aims as a statesman, with respect to foreign as well as to interior policy. Thibaut IV (the Great) of Blois, a nephew of Henry I of England, was generally on the side of his uncle. But with him, too, Suger remained on excellent terms and finally succeeded in bringing about a lasting peace between him and the King of France, now Louis VII who had succeeded his father in 1137; Thibaut's son, Henry, was to become one of the younger Louis's most loyal supporters. When Louis VII, chivalrous and temperamental, had fallen out with his Chancellor, Algrin, it was Suger who effected a reconciliation. When Geoffroy of Anjou and Normandy, the second husband of Henry Beauclerc's only daughter, threatened war it was Suger who warded it off. When Louis VII had good reasons to wish a divorce from his wife, the beautiful Eleanor of Aquitaine, it was Suger who prevented the worst as long as he lived, so that the politically disastrous rupture did not become a fact until 1152.

It is no accident that the two great victories of Suger's public

[2] ⟨On Willelmus of St.-Denis, cf. now Glaser, Bib. 70.⟩

life were bloodless ones. One was the suppression of a *coup d'état* attempted by the brother of Louis VII, Robert de Dreux, whom Suger, then Regent and a man of sixty-eight, "put down in the name of righteousness and with the confidence of a lion." The other and still greater victory was the frustration of an invasion attempted by Emperor Henry V of Germany. Feeling himself sufficiently strong after the Concordat of Worms, he had prepared a powerful attack but was forced to retreat in the face of a "France whose forces had become united." For once, all the king's vassals, even the greatest and most recalcitrant of them, had laid aside their quarrels and grievances and followed the "call of France" (*ajuracio Franciæ*): a triumph, not only of Suger's general policy but also of his special office. While the hosts were assembling, the relics of Saint Denis and his Companions were laid out on the main altar of the Abbey, later to be restored to the crypt "on the shoulders of the king himself." The monks said offices day and night. And Louis le Gros accepted from the hands of Suger, and "invited all France to follow it," the banner known as the "Oriflamme"—that famous "Oriflamme" that was to remain the visible symbol of national unity for almost three centuries yet, at the same time, to proclaim the king of France a vassal of St.-Denis; for the "Oriflamme" was in reality the banner of Vexin, a possession the king held in fief of the Abbey.[3]

In only one contingency did Suger advise and even insist on the use of force against his countrymen: when "rebels" appeared to violate what Louis le Gros had promised to protect, the rights of the Church and of the poor. Suger could look with reverence upon Henry Beauclerc, and with wistful respect upon Thibaut of Blois who opposed the king on almost equal terms; but he was unremitting in his hatred and contempt for such "serpents" and "wild beasts" as Thomas de Marle, Bouchart de Montmorency, Milon de Bray, Matthieu de Beaumont or Hugues du Puiset (many of them members of the minor nobility), who had established themselves as local or regional tyrants, attacked their loyal neighbors, ravaged the towns, oppressed the peasants and laid their hands on ecclesiastical property—even on the possessions of St.-Denis.

[3] ⟨For the supposed identification of the banner of Vexin with the "Oriflamme," see below, p. 252.⟩

Against these Suger recommended, and helped to enforce, the strongest possible measures, favoring the oppressed not only for reasons of justice and humanity (though he was, by instinct, a just and humane man) but also because he was intelligent enough to know that a bankrupt merchant could not pay taxes and that a farmer or wine-grower subject to constant pillage and extortion was likely to abandon his fields or vineyards. When Louis VII came home from the Holy Land Suger was able to turn over to him a country as peaceful and unified as it had seldom been before; and, still more miraculously, a well-filled treasury. "From then on," writes Willelmus, "the people and the prince called him the Father of the Fatherland"; and (with a special reference to the loss of Aquitaine resulting from the divorce of Louis VII): "No sooner had he been taken from our midst than the scepter of the realm suffered great damage owing to his absence."

WHAT SUGER COULD REALIZE only in part within the macrocosm of the kingdom, he could realize in full within the microcosm of his Abbey. Even if we deduct a little from the high-minded condemnation of St. Bernard who likened the unreformed St.-Denis to a "workshop of Vulcan" and a "synagogue of Satan," and if we somewhat discount the bitter invectives of poor, disgruntled Abelard who speaks of "intolerable obscenities" and calls Suger's predecessor, Adam, "a man as much the more corrupt of habits and renowned for infamy as he was the others' superior by his prelacy," even then we cannot fail to see that the conditions at St.-Denis previous to Suger were far from satisfactory. Suger himself tactfully refrains from any personal indictment of Adam, his "spiritual father and foster parent." But he tells us of gaping fissures in the walls, of damaged columns and of towers "threatening ruin"; of lamps and other furnishings falling to pieces for want of repair; of valuable ivories "moldering away under the chests of the treasury"; of altar vessels "lost as pawns"; of unfulfilled obligations toward princely benefactors; of tithes handed over to laymen; of outlying possessions either not brought under cultivation at all or deserted by the tenants on account of oppression from nearby squires and barons; and, worst of all, of constant trouble with the "bailiffs" (*advocati*) who held the hereditary right to certain revenues from the Abbey's domains in return for protection against outside enemies (*advocationes*), but were often unable or unwilling to fulfill this office and even more often abused it by arbitrary taxation, conscription and corvée.

Long before Suger became the head of St.-Denis he had a first-hand experience of these unhappy conditions. Having served for about two years as Abbot's Deputy (*præpositus*) at Berneval-le-Grand in Normandy, where he had occasion to become familiar with and to be greatly impressed by the administrative innovations of Henry Beauclerc, he was transferred, in the same capacity, and at the age of twenty-eight, to one of the Abbey's most cherished possessions, Toury-en-Beauce, not far from Chartres. But he found it avoided by pilgrims and merchants and almost empty of tenants, owing to persecutions on the part of his *bête noire*, Hugues du Puiset: "Those who had remained could hardly live under the burden of so nefarious an oppression." After enlisting both the moral support of the Bishops of Chartres and Orléans and the manual aid of the local priests and parishioners, he asked protection from the king himself and fought, with considerable bravery and varying success, until the castle of Le Puiset succumbed to the last of three sieges within two years and was destroyed, or at least put out of commission, in 1112. The wicked Hugues managed to hold onto his possession for another ten or fifteen years, but seems to have left his castle in charge of a Provost and ultimately disappeared into the Holy Land. Suger, however, began to restore the domain of Toury "from sterility to fecundity," and no sooner had he been elected abbot than he stabilized the situation for good. He built sturdy, "defensible" houses, fortified the whole place with palisades, a solid fort and a new tower above the entrance gate; arrested, "when he happened to be in the neighborhood with an armed force," Hugues's Provost who had begun "to take revenge for past misfortunes"; and settled the question of the *advocatio* in thoroughly characteristic fashion. The *advocatio*, it turned out, had descended by inheritance to a young girl, the granddaughter of one Adam de Pithiviers, who could not do much good but very much harm in case she were to marry the wrong person. So Suger arranged to "give the maiden together with the *advocatio*" to a nice young man of his own entourage, put up one hundred pounds to be divided between the newlyweds and the apparently not very prosperous parents, and everybody was happy: the young lady had a dowry and a husband; the young gentleman had a wife and a modest but steady income; the parents had a share of Suger's hundred pounds; "the unrest in the district was allayed"; "the inhabitants ceased to be afflicted by the customary annoyances"; and the Abbey's annual revenue from Toury rose from twenty pounds to eighty.

This story of one single domain is characteristic of Suger's whole method of administration. Where force was necessary he applied it with energy and no regard for personal danger; he tells of several other cases in which he had to resort to arms "in the early days of his abbacy." But it is more than professional hypocrisy—though an admixture of this element cannot be overlooked—when he professes regret on this account: had it been within his power, he would have solved all problems in much the same way as he solved that of Adam de Pithiviers's granddaughter.

Apart from obtaining numerous royal donations and privileges (the most important of which were the extension of the Abbey's local jurisdiction and the concession of the big annual fair known as the "Foire du Lendit") and from securing private benefactions of all kinds, Suger was a great hand at discovering forgotten claims to lands and feudal rights. "In the docile age of my youth," he says, "I used to thumb the documents of our possessions in the ambry and to consult the charts of our immunities in view of the dishonesty of many calumniators." He did not hesitate to push such claims for the sake of the Holy Martyrs, but he seems to have done this, on the whole, "without chicanery" (*non aliquo malo ingenio*), the only possible exception being the eviction of the nuns from the convent of Argenteuil. This eviction was demanded, not only on legal but also on moral grounds (which does cast some little doubt upon the validity of the former) and Suger has even been suspected of having been influenced by the fact that Abelard's Heloise was Prioress of Argenteuil. Certain it is, however, that the claims of St.-Denis were upheld by a synod on which was present so upright a defender of Abelard's rights as Geoffroy de Lèves, Bishop of Chartres; and from what we know of Suger it would seem doubtful whether he even thought of the old scandal in connection with the case.

In all other known instances Suger appears to have acted in perfect good faith. New property was acquired and rented at fair prices. Bothersome but legitimate liabilities were abolished by paying off the holders of the titles even if they happened to be Jews. Undesirable *advocati* were given a chance to renounce their privileges in return for a compensation either agreed upon directly or fixed by canonical procedure. And as soon as physical and legal security had been established Suger embarked upon a program of reconstruction and rehabilitation which, as in Toury, proved advantageous both to the welfare of the tenantry and the finances of the Abbey. Dilapidated buildings and implements were replaced and new ones provided. Measures were taken against reckless deforestation. New tenants were settled in many places so as to transform into cornfields and vineyards what had been waste lands. The obligations of the tenantry were conscientiously revised with careful distinction between rightful "consuetude" and arbitrary "exaction," and with due regard for individual needs and capacities. And all this was done under the personal supervision of Suger who, with all his obligations as a "prince of the Church and the realm," moved about his domains as the whirlwind, laying out plans for new settlements, indicating the most suitable places for fields and vineyards, looking after the smallest detail and seizing upon every opportunity. Of the possession of Essonnes, for instance, not much had been left, after long depredations by the Counts of Corbeil, except a ruined little chapel known as Notre-Dame-des-Champs, where "sheep and goats came to feed upon the very altar overgrown with vegetation." One fine day Suger was notified that candles had been observed to be burning in the deserted shrine and that sick people had been cured there in miraculous fashion. Seeing his chance at once, he sent down his Prior Hervée—"a man of great saintliness and admirable simplicity though not too erudite"—with twelve monks, restored the chapel, established claustral buildings, planted vineyards, provided plows, wine-presses, altar vessels, vestments, and even a little library; and within a few years the place had developed into the medieval equivalent of a flourishing and self-sufficient sanitarium.

In thus enlarging and improving the outlying domains of the Abbey, Suger created the basis for a thorough reorganization of the convent itself.

In 1127, we remember, St.-Denis was "reformed," and this "reform" elicited St. Bernard's famous letter of congratulation, already mentioned twice. This letter is, however, more than an expression of pious satisfaction. Marking the end of a whispering—or rather clamoring—campaign apparently launched by St. Bernard himself, it seals an armistice and offers peace terms. In depicting the state of affairs at St.-Denis in sinister colors and describing the indignation of the "saintly," St. Bernard makes it perfectly clear that Suger alone had been the object of this indignation: "It was at your errors, not at those of your monks, that the zeal of the saintly aimed its criticism. It was by your excesses, not by theirs, that they were incensed. It was against you, not against the Abbey, that arose the murmurs of your brothers. You alone were the object of their indictments. You would mend your ways, and nothing would remain that might be open to calumny. In fine, if you were to change, all the tumult would subside, all the clamor would be silenced. This was the one and only thing that moved us: that, if you were to continue, that pomp and circumstance of yours might appear a little too insolent. . . . Finally, however, you have satisfied your critics and even added what we can justly praise. For what shall rightly be commended in human affairs if this (although in truth a work of God) is not deemed worthy of the highest praise and admiration, this simultaneous and so sudden change of so many men? Much joy shall be in heaven over one sinner's conversion—what about that of a whole congregation?"

Thus all seems well with Suger, who—a pun scarcely pardonable in even a saint—has learned to "suck" (*sugere*) the breasts of Divine Wisdom instead of the lips of flatterers. But after so many amenities St. Bernard strongly intimates that the continuance of his good will depends upon Suger's conduct in the future, and finally he comes to the point: he wishes the elimination of Etienne de Garlande, Seneschal of Louis le Gros, who, combining a high position in the Church with an even greater influence at Court, was the most formidable barrier between the Abbot of Clairvaux and the Crown.

We do not know what Suger—St. Bernard's senior by nine years —replied to this amazing document; but we learn from the events that he understood it. By the end of the very same year, 1127, Etienne de Garlande fell from grace. Though he returned to favor afterwards he never returned to power. And on May 10, 1128, "the Abbot of Clairvaux found himself, for the first time, in direct and official relation with the King of France": Suger and St. Bernard had come to terms. Realizing how much they could hurt each other as enemies—one the adviser of the Crown and the greatest political power in France, the other the mentor of the Holy See and the greatest spiritual force in Europe—they decided to be friends.

From now on nothing but praise of Suger is heard from St. Bernard (though he retained a certain tendency to make Suger responsible for the objectionable conduct of others and on one occasion somewhat maliciously asked him, the "rich abbot," to lend assistance to a "poor one"). They addressed each other as *"vestra Sublimitas," "vestra Magnitudo"* or even *"Sanctitas vestra."* Shortly before his death, Suger expressed the wish to see Bernard's "angelic face" and was comforted by an edifying letter and a precious handkerchief; and, above all, they carefully refrained from interfering with each other's interests. Suger observed the strictest neutrality when St. Bernard persecuted his heretics or appointed bishops and archbishops almost at will, and he did nothing to prevent the Second Crusade of which he was foresighted enough to disapprove. St. Bernard, on the other hand, abstained from further fulminations against St.-Denis and never revised his optimistic interpretation of Suger's conversion and reform, no matter what they amounted to in reality.

No doubt Suger was as god-fearing a man as any other faithful churchman of his century and exhibited the proper emotions on the proper occasions, "flooding the pavement with tears" before the tomb of the Holy Martyrs (not too exceptional at a time when kings sank weeping to their knees in front of sacred relics and melted into tears at official funerals), and showing himself "devoutly festive, festively devout" on the joyous feasts of Christmas and Easter. But hardly did he ever undergo a conversion comparable to that of the German cleric Mascelinus whom St. Bernard enticed from the service of the Archbishop of Mayence into the monastery of Clairvaux, or of the Saint's own brother Guy whom he wrested from a beloved wife and two young children. No doubt Suger abolished all sorts of irregularities in the Abbey. But he most certainly did not transform it into a place where "no secular person has access to the House of God," where "the curious are not admitted to the sacred objects," where "silence and a perpetual remoteness from all secular turmoil compel the mind to meditate on celestial things."

In the first place, the reform of St.-Denis resulted, not so much from a sudden change of heart on the part of the brethren as from their skillful and considerate reeducation. Where St. Bernard speaks of the "conversion of a whole congregation" Suger, characteristically, congratulates himself on having "reinstated the purpose of the holy Order in peaceable fashion, without upheaval and disturbance of the brethren though they had not been accustomed to it." In the second place, this reform, while doing away with flagrant waste and disorderliness, was far from achieving, or even aiming at, anything like St. Bernard's austere ideal of monastic life. As has already been mentioned, St.-Denis continued to render unto Caesar the things which are Caesar's, and this the more effectively the more secure had become its possessions, the sounder its finances, and the firmer the Abbot's grip on his community; and the life of the monks, while probably more strictly supervised than before, was made as pleasant as possible.

St. Bernard conceived of monasticism as a life of blind obedience and utter self-denial with respect to personal comfort, food and sleep; he himself is said to have waked and fasted *ultra possibilitatem humanam*. Suger, on the other hand, was all for discipline and moderation, but thoroughly against subjection and asceticism. To the admiring amazement of his biographer he did not put on weight after his accession to power. But neither did he make a point of self-mortification. "Declining to be conspicuous in one way or the other," he liked his food "neither very exquisite nor very coarse"; his cell measured barely ten by fifteen feet, but his couch was "neither too soft nor too hard" and was—a very charming touch—"covered with pretty fabrics in daytime." And what he did not demand of himself he demanded even less of his monks. He held that the relationship between prelates and subordinates was prefigured by that between the priests of the Old Law and the Ark of the Covenant: as it had been the duty of those priests to protect their Ark with animals' skins lest it be damaged by wind and rain, so, he thought, was it the duty of an abbot to provide for the physical well-being of his monks "lest they break down on the road." Thus the chilly choir stalls of copper and marble—a real hardship in winter—were replaced by comfortable wooden ones. The diet of the monks was constantly improved (with a special injunction that the poor be given their proper share); and it was with obvious enthusiasm that Suger revived the discontinued ob-servances in memory of Charles the Bald which entailed, in honor of "so great an Emperor and so intimate and cordial a friend of the blessed Denis," an exceptionally good dinner every month. Where St. Bernard made a cult of silence Suger was what a French scholar terms a "causeur infatigable." "Very human and genial" (*humanus satis et jocundus*), he loved to keep his monks together until mid-night, telling of memorable events which he had "either seen or heard of" (and he had seen and heard of a great deal), narrating the deeds of whichever French king or prince was named to him, or reciting long passages of Horace from memory.

The reformed St.-Denis as realized by Suger thus differed very considerably from the reformed St.-Denis as imagined by St. Bernard; and in one essential respect there was not only a dif-ference but an irreconcilable contrast between the one and the other. Nothing could be further from Suger's mind than to keep secular persons out of the House of God: he wished to accommo-date as great a crowd as possible and wanted only to handle it without disturbances—therefore he needed a larger church. Noth-ing could seem less justified to him than not to admit the curious to the sacred objects: he wished to display his relics as "nobly" and "conspicuously" as he could and wanted only to avoid jostling and rioting—therefore he transferred the relics from the crypt and the nave to that magnificent upper choir which was to become the unsurpassed model of the Gothic cathedral chevet. Nothing, he thought, would be a graver sin of omission than to withhold from the service of God and His saints what He had empowered nature to supply and man to perfect: vessels of gold or precious stone adorned with pearls and gems, golden candelabra and altar panels, sculpture and stained glass, mosaic and enamel work, lustrous vestments and tapestries.

This was precisely what the *Exordium Magnum Ordinis Cisterciensis* had condemned and what St. Bernard had thundered against in the *Apologia ad Willelmum Abbatem Sancti Theodorici*. No figural painting or sculpture, except for wooden crucifixes, was tolerated; gems, pearls, gold and silk were forbidden; the vestments had to be of linen or fustian, the candlesticks and censers of iron; only the chalices were permitted to be of silver or silver-gilt. Suger, however, was frankly in love with splendor and beauty in every conceivable form; it might be said that his response to ecclesiastical ceremonial was largely aesthetic. For him the benediction of the holy water is a wonderful dance, with countless dignitaries of the Church, "decorous in white vestments, splendidly arrayed in pontifical miters and precious orphreys embellished by circular ornaments," walking "round and round the vessel" as a "chorus celestial rather than terrestrial." The simultaneous performance of the twenty first Masses in the new chevet is a "symphony angelic rather than human." Thus, if the spiritual preeminence of St.-Denis was Suger's conviction, its material embellishment was his passion: the Holy Martyrs, whose "sacred ashes" could be carried only by the king and took precedence over all other relics however much revered, had to have the most beautiful church in France.

From the earliest years of his abbacy Suger had begun to raise funds for the reconstruction and redecoration of the basilica, and when he died he left it "renewed from its very foundations" and filled with treasures second only—perhaps even superior—to those in Hagia Sophia. In arranging his processions, translations, foundation ceremonies and consecrations Suger foreshadowed the showmanship of the modern movie producer or promoter of world's fairs, and in acquiring pearls and precious stones, rare vases, stained glass, enamels and textiles he anticipated the unselfish rapacity of the modern museum director; he even appointed the first known ancestors of our curators and restorers.

In short, by making concessions to the zeal of St. Bernard in matters of morals and major ecclesiastical policy, Suger gained freedom and peace in all other respects. Unmolested by the Abbot of Clairvaux, he made his church the most resplendent in the Western world and raised pomp and circumstance to the level of a fine art. If his St.-Denis had ceased to be a "synagogue of Satan" it certainly became, more than it had ever been, a "workshop of Vulcan."

AFTER 1127, THEN, Suger had St. Bernard no longer at his heels; but he had him very much on his mind, and this is one of the several reasons why he became that great exception to the rule, the patron who turned *littérateur*.

There can be no doubt that the memorials reprinted in this volume are in part pointedly apologetic and that this apology is largely directed against Cîteaux and Clairvaux. Time and again Suger interrupts his enthusiastic descriptions of gleaming gold and precious jewels to counter the attacks of an imaginary opponent who is in fact not imaginary at all but identical with the man who had written: "But we who, for the sake of Christ, have deemed as dung whatever shines with beauty, enchants the ear, delights through fragrance, flatters the taste, pleases the touch—whose devotion, I ask, do we intend to incite by means of these very things?"

Where St. Bernard, in the words of "pagan Persius," indignantly exclaims: "What has gold to do in the sanctuary?" Suger requests that all the gorgeous vestments and altar vessels acquired under his administration be laid out in the church on his anniversary ("for we are convinced that it is useful and becoming not to hide but to proclaim Divine benefactions"). He deeply regrets that his Great Cross, one of the most sumptuous objects ever contrived by man, still lacks its full complement of gems and pearls; and he is keenly disappointed that he was forced to encase the new tomb of the Holy Martyrs with mere copper-gilt instead of with solid gold ("for we, most miserable men, . . . should deem it worth our effort to cover the most sacred ashes of those whose venerable spirits—radiant as the sun—attend upon Almighty God with the most precious materials we possibly can").

At the end of the description of the main altar—to the frontal of which he had added three other panels, "so that the whole altar would appear golden all the way round"—Suger goes over to the offensive: "If golden pouring vessels, golden vials, little golden mortars used to serve, by the word of God or the command of the Prophet, to collect the blood of goats or calves or the red heifer: how much more must golden vessels, precious stones, and whatever is most valued among all created things, be laid out, with continual reverence and full devotion, for the reception of the blood of Christ! . . . If, by a new creation, our substance were reformed from that of the holy Cherubim and Seraphim, it would still offer an insufficient and unworthy service for so ineffable a victim. . . . The detractors also object that a saintly mind, a pure heart, a faithful intention ought to suffice for this sacred function; and we, too, explicitly and especially affirm that it is these that principally matter. But we profess that we must do homage also through the outward ornaments of sacred vessels. . . . For it behooves us most becomingly to serve our Saviour in all things in a universal way—Him Who has not refused to provide for us in all things in a universal way and without any exception."

Remarkable in utterances like these is Suger's use of passages from Scripture as evidence against the Cistercians. In *Hebrews* St. Paul had likened the blood of Christ to that of sacrificial animals mentioned in the Old Testament (but solely in order to illustrate the superiority of spiritual over merely magical sanctification): Suger concludes from this comparison that Christian chalices should be more gorgeous than Jewish vials and pouring vessels. Pseudo-Andrew had apostrophized the Cross of Golgotha as being adorned with the members of Christ "even as with pearls": Suger infers from this poetic apostrophe that a liturgical crucifix should gleam with a profusion of real pearls. And when he finishes the description of his new chevet with a magnificent quotation from *Ephesians* containing the clause: "in Whom all the building groweth unto one holy temple in the Lord," he qualifies the word "building" by the parenthesis "whether spiritual or material," thereby twisting St. Paul's metaphor into a justification of super-resplendent architecture.

This does not mean that Suger deliberately "falsified" the Bible and the *Apocrypha*. Like all medieval writers he quoted from memory and failed to make a sharp distinction between the text and his personal interpretation; so that his very quotations—and this is the reward for verifying them—reveal to us his own philosophy.

To speak of Suger's philosophy may seem surprising. As one of those who, to quote his own phrase, "are men of action by virtue of their prelacies" (and whose relation to the "contemplative" life is merely one of benevolent patronage), Suger had no ambitions as a thinker. Fond of the classics and the chroniclers, a statesman, a soldier and a jurisconsult, an expert in all that which Leone Battista Alberti was to sum up under the heading of *La Cura della Famiglia*, and apparently not without interest in science, he was a proto-humanist rather than an early scholastic. Nowhere does he evince the slightest interest in the great theological and epistemological controversies of his time, such as the dispute between the realists and the nominalists, the bitter argument about the nature of the Trinity, or that great issue of the day, the case of faith *vs.* reason; and his relations with the protagonist of this intellectual drama, Peter Abelard, were, characteristically, of a strictly official and entirely impersonal nature.

Abelard was a genius, but a genius of that paranoiac sort that repels affection by overbearance, invites real persecution by constantly suspecting imaginary conspiracies, and, feeling oppressed by any kind of moral indebtedness, tends to convert gratitude into resentment. After the cruel events that had ruined his life he had found refuge at St.-Denis during the gay and inefficient administration of Abbot Adam. Soon Abelard indulged in criticism which, warranted or not, seldom endears a newcomer to an established community, and finally he "facetiously" announced a discovery that, from the point of view of St.-Denis, amounted to *lèse-majesté*: he had chanced upon a passage in Bede according to which the titular Saint of the Abbey was not the same person as the famous Dionysius the Areopagite mentioned in the *Acts of the Apostles* and held to have been the first bishop of Athens, but was identical with the more recent and far less famous Dionysius of Corinth. Abelard was accused as a traitor to the Crown, was thrown into prison, managed to escape, and sought shelter in the territory of Thibaut of Blois. This was the state of affairs when Suger became Adam's successor, and presently the problem was solved:

after some calculated hesitation Suger consented to drop the whole matter and permitted Abelard to live in peace wherever he pleased, under the sole condition that he would not enter another monastery—this sole condition being imposed, according to Abelard, because "the Abbey did not want to forfeit the glory that it used to derive from myself," but much more probably because Suger, considering Abelard a good riddance, was nevertheless reluctant to see an ex-monk of St.-Denis subjected to the authority of another and therefore, in his estimation, inferior abbot. He did not object when Abelard, some two or three years later, became a (very unhappy) abbot himself; he took no part in St. Bernard's savage and carefully prepared attack that led to Abelard's condemnation by the Synod of Sens in 1140; and no one knows whether or not Suger even opened one of those books in which the Abbot of Clairvaux had detected sheer paganism flavored with the combined heresies of Arius, Nestorius and Pelagius.

What Suger did read, however, were the writings ascribed to the very man whose semilegendary personality had caused the rift between Abelard and St.-Denis. That Dionysius the Areopagite, of whom nothing is known except that he "clave unto St. Paul and believed," had been identified, not only with the actual Saint Denis, Apostle of the Gauls, but also with a most important theological writer—to us a nameless Syrian of ca. 500—whose works had thus become no less revered a patrimony of the Abbey than were the "Oriflamme" and the relics of the Holy Martyrs. A manuscript of the Greek texts, obtained by Louis the Pious from the Byzantine Emperor Michael the Stammerer, had been immediately deposited at St.-Denis; after an earlier, not quite successful attempt these texts had been brilliantly translated and commented upon by John the Scot, the honored guest of Charles the Bald; and it was in these translations and commentaries that Suger discovered—somewhat ironically in view of Abelard's fate—not only the most potent weapon against St. Bernard but also a philosophical justification of his whole attitude toward art and life.[4]

[4] (For the "Oriflamme," cf. below, p. 252; for the ninth century Byzantine manuscript of the works of Dionysius the Pseudo-Areopagite, formerly at St.-Denis, now Paris, Bibliothèque Nationale, MS Grec. 437, see Mütherich, in Schramm-Mütherich, Bib. 153, p. 120 f. no. 19. For the legend of St. Denis, see Moretus Plantin, S. J., Bib. 126; and for the saint's identification with the Areopagite, see Loenertz, Bib. 113.)

Fusing the doctrines of Plotinus and, more specifically, Proclus with the creeds and beliefs of Christianity, Dionysius the Pseudo-Areopagite—whose "negative theology," defining the Superessential One as eternal darkness and eternal silence, and thus identifying ultimate knowledge with ultimate ignorance, can concern us here no more than it concerned Suger—combined the neo-Platonic conviction of the fundamental oneness and luminous aliveness of the world with the Christian dogmas of the triune God, original sin and redemption. According to the Pseudo-Areopagite, the universe is created, animated and unified by the perpetual self-realization of what Plotinus had called "the One," what the Bible had called "the Lord," and what he calls "the superessential Light" or even "the invisible Sun"—with God the Father designated as "the Father of the lights" (*Pater luminum*), and Christ (in an allusion to *John* III, 19 and VIII, 12) as the "first radiance" (φωτοδοσία, *claritas*) which "has revealed the Father to the world" ("Patrem clarificavit mundo"). There is a formidable distance from the highest, purely intelligible sphere of existence to the lowest, almost purely material one (almost, because sheer matter without form could not even be said to exist); but there is no insurmountable chasm between the two. There is a hierarchy but no dichotomy. For even the lowliest of created things partakes somehow of the essence of God—humanly speaking, of the qualities of truth, goodness and beauty. Therefore the process, by which the emanations of the Light Divine flow down until they are nearly drowned in matter and broken up into what looks like a meaningless welter of coarse material bodies, can always be reversed into a rise from pollution and multiplicity to purity and oneness; and therefore man, *anima immortalis corpore utens*, need not be ashamed to depend upon his sensory perception and sense-controlled imagination. Instead of turning his back on the physical world, he can hope to transcend it by absorbing it.

Our mind, says the Pseudo-Areopagite at the very beginning of his major work, the *De Cælesti Hierarchia* (and consequently John the Scot at the very beginning of his commentary), can rise to that which is not material under only the "manual guidance" of that which is (*materiali manuductione*). Even to the prophets the Deity and the celestial virtues could appear only in some visible form. But this is possible because all visible things are "material lights" that mirror the "intelligible" ones and, ultimately, the *vera lux* of the Godhead Itself: "Every creature, visible or invisible, is a light brought into being by the Father of the lights. . . . This stone or that piece of wood is a light to me. . . . For I perceive that it is good and beautiful; that it exists according to its proper rules of proportion; that it differs in kind and species from other kinds and species; that it is defined by its number, by virtue of which it is 'one' thing; that it does not transgress its order; that it seeks its place according to its specific gravity. As I perceive such and similar things in this stone they become lights to me, that is to say, they enlighten me (*me illuminant*). For I begin to think whence the stone is invested with such properties . . . ; and soon, under the guidance of reason, I am led through all things to that cause of all things which endows them with place and order, with number, species and kind, with goodness and beauty and essence, and with all other grants and gifts."

Thus the whole material universe becomes a big "light" composed of countless small ones as of so many lanterns (". . . universalis hujus mundi fabrica maximum lumen fit, ex multis partibus veluti ex lucernis compactum"); every perceptible thing, manmade or natural, becomes a symbol of that which is not perceptible, a steppingstone on the road to Heaven; the human mind, abandoning itself to the "harmony and radiance" (*bene compactio et claritas*) which is the criterion of terrestrial beauty, finds itself "guided upward" to the transcendent cause of this "harmony and radiance" which is God.

This ascent from the material to the immaterial world is what the Pseudo-Areopagite and John the Scot describe—in contrast to the customary theological use of this term—as the "anagogical approach" (*anagogicus mos*, literally translated: "the upward-leading method"); and this is what Suger professed as a theologian, proclaimed as a poet, and practiced as a patron of the arts and an arranger of liturgical spectacles. A window showing subjects of an allegorical rather than typological character (e.g. The Prophets Carrying Grain to a Mill Turned by St. Paul, or The Ark of the Covenant Surmounted by the Cross) "urges us on from the material to the immaterial." The twelve columns supporting the high vaults of the new chevet "represent the number of the Twelve Apostles" while the columns in the ambulatory, likewise twelve in number, "signify the [minor] Prophets." And the consecration ceremony of the new narthex was carefully planned to symbolize the idea of the Trinity: there was "one glorious procession of three men" (one archbishop and two bishops) that performed three distinct motions, leaving the building by a single door, passing in front of the three principal portals and, "thirdly," reentering the church by another single door.

These instances may be interpreted as normal medieval symbolism without specifically "Dionysian" connotations. But the deservedly famous passage in which Suger relates his experience in contemplating the precious stones that glowed on the main altar and its ornaments, the "Cross of St. Eloy" and the "*Escrin de Charlemagne*," is full of direct reminiscences: "When—out of my delight in the beauty of the house of God—the loveliness of the many-colored stones has called me away from external cares, and worthy meditation has induced me to reflect, transferring that which is material to that which is immaterial, on the diversity of the sacred virtues: then it seems to me that I see myself dwelling, as it were, in some strange region of the universe which neither exists entirely in the slime of the earth nor entirely in the purity of Heaven; and that, by the grace of God, I can be transported from this inferior to that higher world in an anagogical manner." Here Suger gives a vivid picture of that trancelike state which can be induced by gazing upon such shining objects as crystal balls or precious stones. But he describes this state, not as a psychological but as a religious experience, and his description is principally in the words of John the Scot. The term *anagogicus mos*, explained as a transition from the "inferior" to the "higher" world, is as literal a quotation as is the phrase *de materialibus ad immaterialia transferendo*; and the "diversity of the sacred virtues," which reveals itself in the divers properties of the gems, recalls both the "celestial virtues" appearing to the Prophets "in some visible form" and the spiritual "illumination" to be derived from any physical object.

Yet even this splendid piece of prose is nothing as compared to the orgy of neo-Platonic light metaphysics to which Suger abandons himself in some of his poetry. He was intensely fond of inscribing everything accomplished under his administration, from the parts of the building itself to the stained-glass windows, altars and vases, with what he calls *versiculi*: hexameters or elegiac couplets not always very classical in meter but full of original, at times very witty, conceits and on occasion verging upon the sublime. And when his aspirations were the highest he had recourse not only to the still neo-Platonic language of the *tituli* of Early Christian mosaics but also to the phraseology of John the Scot:

"Pars nova posterior dum jungitur anteriori,

"Once the new rear part is joined to the part in front,

Aula micat medio clarificata suo.

The church shines with its middle part brightened.

Claret enim claris quod clare concopulatur,

For bright is that which is brightly coupled with the bright,

Et quod perfundit lux nova, claret opus

And bright is the noble edifice which is pervaded by the new light."

Nobile. . . ."

Literally interpreted, this inscription, commemorating the consecration of the new chevet and describing its effect upon the rest of the church once the rebuilding of its "middle part" would be completed, seems to paraphrase a purely "aesthetic" experience: the new, transparent choir, which had replaced the opaque Carolingian apse, would be matched by an equally "bright" nave, and the whole building would be pervaded by a light more brilliant than before. But the words are deliberately chosen so as to be intelligible on two different levels of meaning. The formula *lux nova* makes perfect sense with reference to the improvement of the actual lighting conditions brought about by the "new" architecture; but at the same time it recalls the light of the New Testament as opposed to the darkness or blindness of the Jewish Law. And the insistent play upon the words *clarere, clarus, clarificare*, which almost hypnotizes the mind into the search for a significance hidden beneath their purely perceptual implications, reveals itself as metaphysically meaningful when we remember that John the Scot, in a remarkable discussion of the principles he proposed to follow in his translation, had explicitly decided for *claritas* as the most adequate rendering of the numerous Greek expressions with which the Pseudo-Areopagite denotes the radiance or splendor emanating from the "Father of the lights."

In another poem Suger explains the doors of the central west portal which, shining with gilded bronze reliefs, exhibited the "Passion" and the "Resurrection or Ascension" of Christ. In reality these verses amount to a condensed statement of the whole theory of "anagogical" illumination:

"Portarum quisquis attollere quæris honorem,

Aurum nec sumptus, operis mirare laborem.

Nobile claret opus, sed opus quod nobile claret

Clarificet mentes, ut eant per lumina vera

Ad verum lumen, ubi Christus janua vera.

Quale sit intus in his determinat aurea porta:

Mens hebes ad verum per materialia surgit,

Et demersa prius hac visa luce resurgit."

"Whoever thou art, if thou seekest to extol the glory of these doors,

Marvel not at the gold and the expense but at the craftsmanship of the work.

Bright is the noble work; but, being nobly bright, the work

Should brighten the minds so that they may travel, through the true lights,

To the True Light where Christ is the true door.

In what manner it be inherent in this world the golden door defines:

The dull mind rises to truth through that which is material

And, in seeing this light, is resurrected from its former submersion."

This poem states explicitly what the other merely implies: the physical "brightness" of the work of art will "brighten" the minds of the beholders by a spiritual illumination. Incapable of attaining to truth without the aid of that which is material, the soul will be guided by the "true," though merely perceptible "lights" (*lumina vera*) of the resplendent reliefs to the "True Light" (*verum lumen*) which is Christ; and it will thus be "raised," or rather "resurrected" (*surgit, resurgit*), from terrestrial bondage even as Christ is seen rising in the "*Resurrectio vel Ascensio*" depicted on the doors. Suger would not have ventured to designate reliefs as *lumina* had he not been familiar with those passages which demonstrate that every created thing "is a light to me"; his "Mens hebes ad verum per materialia surgit" is nothing but a metrical condensation of John the Scot's ". . . impossibile est nostro animo ad immaterialem ascendere cælestium hierarchiarum et imitationem et contemplationem nisi ea, quæ secundum ipsum est, materiali manuductione utatur" (". . . it is impossible for our mind to rise to the imitation and contemplation of the celestial hierarchies unless it relies upon that material guidance which is commensurate to it"). And it is from phrases such as: "Materialia lumina, sive quæ naturaliter in cælestibus spatiis ordinata sunt, sive quæ in terris humano artificio efficiuntur, imagines sunt intelligibilium luminum, super omnia ipsius veræ lucis" ("The material lights, both those which are disposed by nature in the spaces of the heavens and those which are produced on earth by human artifice, are images of the intelligible lights, and above all of the True Light Itself") that the lines: ". . . ut eant per lumina vera Ad verum lumen . . ." are derived.

One can imagine the blissful enthusiasm with which Suger must have absorbed these neo-Platonic doctrines. In accepting what he took for the *ipse dixits* of Saint Denis, he not only did homage to the Patron Saint of his Abbey but also found the most authoritative confirmation of his own innate beliefs and propensities. Saint Denis himself seemed to sanction Suger's conviction (which found its practical expression in his role as *mediator et pacis vinculum*) that "the admirable power of one unique and supreme reason equalizes the disparity between things human and Divine"; and that "what seems mutually to conflict by inferiority of origin and contrariety of nature is conjoined by the single, delightful concordance of one superior, well-tempered harmony." Saint Denis himself seemed to justify Suger's partiality to images and his insatiable passion for everything lustrously beautiful, for gold and enamel, for crystal and mosaic, for pearls and precious stones of all descriptions, for the sardonyx in which "the sard's red hue, by varying its property, so strongly contrasts with the blackness of the onyx that one property seems to be bent on trespassing upon the other," and for stained glass designed "by the exquisite hands of many masters from different regions."

St. Bernard's contemporary eulogists assure us—and his modern biographers seem to agree—that he was simply blind to the visible world and its beauty. He is said to have spent a whole year in the noviciate of Cîteaux without noticing whether the ceiling of the dormitory was flat or vaulted and whether the chapel received its light from one window or from three; and we are told that he rode a whole day on the shores of the Lake of Geneva without casting a single glance upon the scenery. However, it was not a blind or insensitive man who wrote the *Apologia ad Willelmum*: "And further, in the cloisters, under the eyes of the brethren engaged in reading, what business has there that ridiculous monstrosity, that amazing mis-shapen shapeliness and shapely mis-shapenness? Those unclean monkeys? Those fierce lions? Those monstrous centaurs? Those semi-human beings? Those spotted tigers? Those fighting warriors? Those huntsmen blowing their horns? Here you behold several bodies beneath one head; there again several heads upon one body. Here you see a quadruped with the tail of a serpent; there a fish with the head of a quadruped. There an animal suggests a horse in front and half a goat behind; here a horned beast exhibits the rear part of a horse. In fine, on all sides there appears so rich and so amazing a variety of forms that it is more delightful to read the marbles than the manuscripts, and to spend the whole day in admiring these things, piece by piece, rather than in meditating on the Law Divine."

A modern art historian would thank God on his knees for the ability to write so minute, so graphic, so truly evocatory a description of a decorative ensemble in the "Cluniac manner"; the one phrase *deformis formositas ac formosa deformitas* tells us more about the spirit of Romanesque sculpture than many pages of stylistic analysis. But in addition the whole passage reveals, especially in its remarkable conclusion, that St. Bernard disapproved of art, not because he did not feel its charms but because he felt them too keenly not to consider them dangerous. He banished art, like Plato (only that Plato did it "regretfully"), because it belonged on the wrong side of a world that he could see only as an unending revolt of the temporal against the eternal, of human reason against faith, of the senses against the spirit. Suger had the good fortune to discover, in the very words of the thrice blessed Saint Denis, a Christian philosophy that permitted him to greet material beauty as a vehicle of spiritual beatitude instead of forcing him to flee from it as though from a temptation; and to conceive of the moral as well as the physical universe, not as a monochrome in black and white but as a harmony of many colors.

IT WAS NOT ONLY against Cistercian puritanism that Suger had to defend himself in his writings. Some of the opposition, it seems, came from the ranks of his own monks.

In the first place, there were the fastidious who objected to Suger's taste or, if "taste" be defined as a sense of beauty tempered by reticence, lack of taste. Both as a writer and as a patron of the arts he aimed at gorgeousness rather than unobtrusive refinement. As his ear delighted in a kind of medieval euphuism, involved though not always grammatical, bristling with word-play, quotation, metaphor and allusion, and thundering with oratory (the almost untranslatable first chapter of the *De Consecratione* is like an organ prelude filling the room with magnificent sound before the appearance of a discernible theme), so did his eye demand what his more sophisticated friends apparently considered ostentatious and flamboyant. One hears the echo of a faint and futile protest when Suger refers to the mosaic incongruously combined with the sculpture of an already proto-Gothic portal as having been installed there "on his orders and contrary to modern custom." When he exhorts the admirer of his door reliefs "not to marvel at the gold and the expense but at the craftsmanship of the work" he seems to make a good-natured allusion to those who kept reminding him that, according to Ovid, the perfection of "form" should be valued more highly than precious material. Suger aims at the same critics—and here quite clearly in a spirit of friendly irony—when he admits that the new golden back of the main altar was indeed somewhat lavish (chiefly, he claims, because it had been executed by foreigners) but hastens to add that its reliefs —just as the frontal of the new "Autel des Reliques"—were admirable for their workmanship as well as for their costliness; so that "certain people" might be able to apply their favorite quotation: "Materiam superabat opus."

In the second place, there was the more serious dissatisfaction of those who objected to Suger's enterprises in the name of sacred traditions. The Carolingian church of St.-Denis was held, until quite recently, to have been built by the original founder of the Abbey, King Dagobert; according to legend it had been consecrated by Christ in person; and modern scholarship has confirmed the tradition that the old structure was never touched until Suger's accession to power. But when Suger wrote his report "On What Was Done under His Administration" he had torn down the old apse and the old west front (including the porch protecting the tomb of Pepin the Short), had constructed a brand-new narthex and a brand-new chevet, and had just started operations that would eliminate the last remaining part of the ancient basilica, the nave. It was as if a President of the United States were to have had the White House rebuilt by Frank Lloyd Wright.

In justifying this destructively creative enterprise—which was to set the course of Western architecture for more than a century— Suger untiringly stresses four points. First, whatever had been done had been done upon due deliberation with the brethren "whose hearts burned for Jesus while He talked with them by the way," and many of them had even explicitly requested it. Second, the work had manifestly found grace in the eyes of God and the Holy Martyrs who had miraculously disclosed the presence of suitable building materials where nothing of the kind had been believed to exist, who had protected unfinished vaults from a terrible storm, and had promoted the work in many other ways so that the chevet could be constructed in the incredibly brief—and symbolically significant—space of three years and three months. Third, care had been taken to save as much as possible of the sacred old stones "as though they were relics." Fourth, the rebuilding of the church was an indisputable necessity because of its dilapidated condition and, more important, because of its relative smallness which, coupled with an insufficient number of exits, had led to riotous and dangerous disorders on feast days; Suger, free from "any desire for empty glory" and entirely uninfluenced by "the reward of human praise and transitory compensation," would never have "presumed to set his hand to such a work, nor even to think of it, had not so great, so necessary, so useful and honorable an occasion demanded it."

All these assertions are entirely correct—so far as they go. No doubt Suger discussed his plans with those of the brethren whom he found interested and cooperative, and he was careful to have his decisions formally approved by the general chapter. But a lack of unanimity becomes at times apparent even from his own narrative (as when he tells us how, after the completion of the narthex and chevet, "some people" had persuaded him to finish the towers before rebuilding the nave, but how "Divine inspiration" had urged him to reverse the process); and the formal approval of the general chapter seems to have been obtained *ex post-facto* rather than beforehand (as when the construction and consecration of the new narthex, and the laying of the foundations for the new chevet, were solemnly placed on record in an *"Ordinatio"* enacted afterwards).

No doubt the operations proceeded with unusual speed and smoothness. But to what extent the discovery of stones and timber in unexpected places and the survival of the "isolated and newly made arches tottering in mid-air" required the personal intercession of the Holy Martyrs in addition to Suger's own ingenuity and to the skill of his workmen is a matter of surmise.

No doubt Suger rebuilt the basilica a part at a time and thereby saved the "sacred stones" at least provisionally, as it were. His very eulogists praised him for having remade the church from top to bottom. And the fact remains that in the end nothing was left except the remodelled substructures of the chevet.

No doubt the old building was worn with age and no longer able to accommodate without grave inconvenience the crowds attracted by the Fair and the relics. But one cannot help feeling that Suger is a little overemphatic in depicting these tribulations, all the more so because the fearsome stories of the pious women who could reach the altar only "by walking upon the heads of the men as though upon a pavement," or had to be carried into the cloisters "in a half-dead condition," are told alternately to prove the need of a new narthex and the need of a new chevet. One thing is certain: the main incentive to Suger's artistic activity—and to his writing about it—must be sought within himself.

THERE IS NO DENYING, in spite (or, rather, because) of his persistent protestations to the contrary, that Suger was animated by a passionate will to self-perpetuation. To put it less academically: he was enormously vain. He requested the honor of an anniversary —not without a wistful admonition to future Cellarers not to be angry because of the additional expense for food and drink but to remember that it was he, Suger, who had increased the budget of their department—and thereby placed himself on the same footing as King Dagobert, Charles the Bald and Louis le Gros, the only persons previously thus honored. He frankly thanked God for having reserved the task of rebuilding the church to "his life time and labors" (or, as he puts it in another place, to "so small a man who was the successor to the nobility of such great kings and abbots"). At least thirteen of the *versiculi* with which he covered every available space on walls and liturgical objects mention his name; and numerous donors' portraits of him were strategically disposed on the main axis of the basilica: two in the principal entrance (one in the tympanum, the other on the doors), a third one at the foot of the Great Cross that commanded the opening arch of the new upper choir and could be seen from almost every point in the church, and one in the windows adorning the central chapel of the ambulatory. When we read of Suger's huge, gold-lettered inscription above the west portals ("O may it not be obscured!"), when we observe him constantly preoccupied with the memory of future generations and alarmed by the thought of "Oblivion, the jealous rival of Truth," when we hear him speak of himself as the "leader" (*dux*) under whose guidance the church had been enlarged and ennobled, we feel as though we listened to some of Jacob Burckhardt's evidence for "the modern form of glory," and not to the words of an abbot of the twelfth century.

Yet there is a fundamental difference between the Renaissance man's thirst for fame and Suger's colossal but, in a sense, profoundly humble vanity. The great man of the Renaissance asserted his personality centripetally, so to speak: he swallowed up the world that surrounded him until his whole environment had been absorbed by his own self. Suger asserted his personality centrifugally: he projected his ego into the world that surrounded him until his whole self had been absorbed by his environment.

To understand this psychological phenomenon, we have to remember two things about Suger that again place him in diametrical contrast to the highborn convert, St. Bernard. First, Suger entered the monastery, not as a novice devoting himself to monastic life of his own free will, or at least with the comprehension of a relatively mature intelligence, but as an oblate dedicated to Saint Denis when a boy of nine or ten. Second, Suger, the schoolmate of young noblemen and princes of the blood, was born—no one knows where—of very poor and very lowly parents.

Many a boy would have developed into a shy or bitter person under such circumstances. The future abbot's extraordinary vitality resorted to what is known as overcompensation. Instead of either yearningly clinging to or drastically breaking away from his natural relatives, Suger kept them at a friendly distance and, later on, made them participate, in a small way, in the life of the Abbey.[5] Instead of either concealing or resenting his humble birth, Suger almost gloried in it—though only to glory all the more in his adoption by St.-Denis. "For who am I, or what is my father's house?" he exclaims with young David. And his literary works as well as his official documents fairly bristle with such phrases as: "I, insufficient with regard to family as well as knowledge"; or: "I, who succeeded to the administration of this church against the prospects of merit, character and family"; or (in the words of Hannah, mother of Samuel): "I, the beggar, whom the strong

[5] The names of Suger's father, Helinandus, and of one brother and sister-in-law, Radulphus and Emmelina, figure in the obituary of the Abbey. Another brother, Peter, accompanied Suger to Germany in 1125. One of his nephews, Gerard, paid to the Abbey an annual amount of fifteen shillings, five shillings as rent and ten for reasons unknown. Another nephew, John, died on a mission to Pope Eugenius III who wrote a very cordial letter of condolence to Suger. A third one, Simon, witnessed an Ordinance of his uncle in 1148 and became embroiled with the latter's successor, Odon de Deuil (who was a protégé of St. Bernard and looked with disfavor upon everyone close to Suger). None of these instances seems to involve illegitimate favoritism.

hand of the Lord has lifted up from the dunghill." But the strong
hand of the Lord had operated through the Abbey of St.-Denis.
In taking him away from his natural parents, He had given to
Suger another "mother"—an expression persistently recurring in
his writings—who had made him what he was. It was the Abbey
of St.-Denis which had "cherished and exalted him"; which had
"most tenderly fostered him from mother's milk to old age";
which "with maternal affection had suckled him as a child, had
held him upright as a stumbling youth, had mightily strengthened
him as a mature man and had solemnly set him among the princes
of the Church and the realm."

Thus Suger, conceiving of himself as the adopted child of St.-
Denis, came to divert to the Abbey the whole amount of energy,
acumen and ambition nature had bestowed upon him. Completely
fusing his personal aspirations with the interests of the "mother
church," he may be said to have gratified his ego by renouncing
his identity: he expanded himself until he had become identical
with the Abbey. In spreading his inscriptions and portraits all over
the church, he took possession of it but at the same time divested
himself, to some extent, of his existence as a private individual.
When Peter the Venerable, Abbot of Cluny, saw Suger's narrow
little cell he is said to have exclaimed, with a sigh: "This man puts
all of us to shame; he builds, not for himself, as we do, but only
for God." But for Suger there was no difference between the one
and the other. He did not need much private space and luxury
because the space and luxury of the basilica was no less his than
was the modest comfort of his cell; the Abbey Church belonged to
him because he belonged to the Abbey Church.

Nor did this process of self-affirmation through self-effacement
stop at the borders of St.-Denis. To Suger, St.-Denis meant
France, and so he developed a violent and almost mystical na-
tionalism as apparently anachronistic as was his vaingloriousness.
He whom all contemporary writers praise as a man of letters at
home in all subjects, one who could write boldly, brilliantly and
"almost as fast as he could speak," never felt moved to make use
of this gift except in honor of the Abbey of which he was the head,
and of the two French kings whom he had served—according to
his eulogists, had ruled. And in the *Life of Louis le Gros* we find

[31]

sentiments that foreshadow the specific form of patriotism best characterized by the French word *chauvinisme*. According to Suger, the English are "destined by moral and natural law to be subjected to the French, and not contrariwise"; and what he thought of the Germans, whom he loved to describe as "gnashing their teeth with Teutonic fury," appears from the following: "Let us boldly cross their border lest they, withdrawing, bear with impunity what they have arrogantly presumed against France, the mistress of the earth. Let them feel the reward of their affront, not in our land but in theirs which, often conquered, is subject to the Franks by the royal right of the Franks."

In Suger's case this urge to grow by metempsychosis, if one may say so, was further sharpened by an apparently irrelevant circumstance which he himself does not mention at all (perhaps he had even ceased to be conscious of it) but which appeared noteworthy to all his admirers: he was uncommonly small of stature. "He had been allotted a short and spare body," says Willelmus, and goes on to marvel how such a "weak little frame" (*imbecille corpusculum*) could stand the strain of so "vigorous and lively a mind." And an anonymous encomiast writes:

> "I am amazed at the huge spirit in such a body,
> And how so many and so great good qualities have room
>   in a small vessel.
> But by this one man nature wanted to prove
> That virtue can be hidden under any kind of skin."

An exceptionally small physique seems to be insignificant in the eyes of history; and yet it has been an essential factor in determining the character of many a well-remembered historical figure. More effectively than any other handicap can it be turned into an asset if the victim of this handicap is able to outbalance his physical inferiority by what is perhaps most graphically described as "pluck," and if he can break down the psychological barrier separating him from the average-sized group of men with whom he lives by a more-than-average aptitude and willingness to identify his own self-interest with theirs. It is this combination of pluck and will-to-fellowship (often coupled with a naive, innocuous vanity) that places such "great little men" as Napoleon, Mozart,

Lucas van Leyden, Erasmus of Rotterdam or General Mont-
gomery in a class by themselves and endows them with a special
charm or fascination. The evidence seems to show that Suger had
some of this peculiar charm and that his tiny stature was as much
of an incentive to his great ambitions and accomplishments as was
his lowly origin. A Canon Regular of St.-Victor, bearing the
curious name of Simon Chièvre d'Or (Simon Capra Aurea),
showed remarkable insight into the character of his dead friend
when he included in his obituary the couplet found on the title
page of this volume:

> "Small of body and family, constrained by twofold smallness,
> He refused, in his smallness, to be a small man."

It is amusing and, at times, almost a little pathetic to note how
far Suger's unselfish selfishness would go where the prestige and
splendor of St.-Denis were concerned. How he put on a shrewd
little show to prove to one and all the authenticity of certain relics
given by Charles the Bald. How he induced "by his example" the
royal, princely and episcopal visitors of the Abbey to donate the
stones of their very rings for the adornment of a new altar frontal
(apparently by divesting himself of his own ring in their presence
and thereby forcing them to do likewise). How members of those
ill-advised Orders that had no use for pearls and gems except to
convert them into money for alms, offered him theirs for sale, and
how he, thanking God for the "merry miracle," gave them four
hundred pounds for the lot "though they were worth much more."
How he would corner travelers from the East until they assured
him that the treasures of St.-Denis surpassed those of Constantinople; how he tries to gloss over his disappointment if a more
obtuse or less obliging visitor failed to give him such satisfaction;
and how he finally consoles himself with a quotation from St.
Paul: "Let every man abound in his own sense" which he takes
to mean (or pretends to take to mean): "Let every man believe
himself to be rich."

As a "beggar lifted up from the dunghill" Suger was naturally
not free from that arch-weakness of the parvenu, snobbery. He
wallows in the names and titles of all the kings, princes, popes,
and high ecclesiastics who had visited the Abbey and shown him

their personal esteem and affection. He looks with a certain condescension upon the mere counts and nobles, not to mention the "ordinary troops of knights and soldiers," who flocked to the Great Consecration of June 11, 1144; and it is not without boastfulness that he twice enumerates the nineteen bishops and archbishops whom he had brought together on this glorious day: had only one more been able to attend, each of the twenty new altars would have been consecrated by a different dignitary—while, as it was, the Bishop of Meaux had to officiate at two. But again it is impossible to draw a sharp line between personal and what may be called institutional self-satisfaction. When speaking of himself, Suger makes no distinction, even in one and the same sentence, between "I" and "we"; at times he uses the "we" much as a sovereign would, but more often than not he does it in the spirit of a genuinely "pluralistic" feeling: "we, the community of St.-Denis." While taking enormous pride in the little private presents he occasionally received from royalty, he never failed to offer them afterwards to the Holy Martyrs; and his abbatial dignity did not prevent him from personally supervising the purchase of food for grand occasions or from rummaging in chests and cupboards in order to recover long-forgotten *objets-d'art* that might be reused.

For all his airs, Suger had never lost touch with the "common man" whom he had come to know so well in the long years at Berneval and Toury, and whose immortal ways of thought and speech he occasionally sketches with a few masterly strokes. We almost hear the ox-drivers at the quarry near Pontoise as they grumble about "having nothing to do" and "the laborers standing around and losing time" when part of the help had run away in a violent rainstorm. We almost see the sheepish yet supercilious grin of the woodmen in the *Forêt de Rambouillet* when the great Abbot had asked them what they considered a stupid question. Some exceptionally long beams were needed for the roofing of the new west part and could nowhere be found in the nearer vicinity; "But on a certain night, when I had returned from celebrating Matins, I began to think in bed that I myself should go through all the forests in these parts. . . . Quickly disposing of other duties and hurrying up in the early morning, we hastened with our carpenters, and with the measurements of the beams, to the forest called Iveline. When we traversed our possession in the Valley of Chevreuse we summoned . . . the keepers of our own forests as well as those who knew about the other woods, and questioned them under oath whether we could find there, no matter with how much trouble, any timbers of that measure. At this they smiled, or rather would have laughed at us if they had dared; they wondered whether we were quite ignorant of the fact that nothing of the kind could be found in the entire region. . . . But we . . . began, with the courage of our faith as it were, to search through the woods; and toward the first hour we had found one timber adequate to the measure. Why say more? By the ninth hour or sooner we had, through the thickets, the depths of the forests and the dense, thorny tangles, marked down twelve timbers (for so many were necessary). . . ."

There is something engaging, even touching, about this picture of the little man, nearer sixty than fifty, how he cannot sleep after midnight service, still worrying about his beams; how he is struck with the idea that he ought to look after things himself; how he dashes off in the early morning, at the head of his carpenters and with the measurements in his pocket; how he scrambles through the wilderness "with the courage of his faith"—and ultimately gets precisely what he wants. However, setting aside all "human interest," this small incident gives perhaps the final answer to our initial question: Why was it that Suger, in contrast to so many other patrons of the arts, felt compelled to commit his exploits to writing?

As we have seen, one of his motives was a desire for self-justification, possibly sharpened by the fact that he, unlike the popes, princes and cardinals of later centuries, still felt a kind of democratic responsibility to his chapter and Order. A second motive was, unquestionably, his personal and, as we have termed it, institutional vanity. But both these impulses, strong though they were, might not have become articulate had it not been for Suger's well-founded conviction that his had been a role quite different from that of one who, to quote the *Oxford Dictionary*'s definition of a "patron," "countenances or protects or deigns to employ a person, cause or art."

A man who takes his carpenters into the woods in quest of beams and personally picks the right trees, a man who sees to it that his new chevet is properly aligned with the old nave by means of "geometrical and arithmetical instruments," is still more closely akin to the amateur or gentleman architect of the earlier Middle Ages—and, by the way, of colonial America—than to the great patrons of the High Gothic and Renaissance periods who would appoint an architect-in-chief, pass judgment on his plans and leave all technical details to him. Devoting himself to his artistic enterprises "both with mind and body," Suger may be said to record them, not so much in the capacity of one who "countenances or protects or deigns to employ" as in the capacity of one who supervises or directs or conducts. To what extent he was responsible or co-responsible for the very design of his structures is for others to decide. But it would seem that very little was done without at least his active participation. That he selected and invited the individual craftsmen, that he ordered a mosaic for a place where apparently nobody wanted it, and that he devised the iconography of his windows, crucifixes and altar panels is attested by his own words; but also an idea such as the transformation of a Roman porphyry vase into an eagle suggests a whim of the abbot rather than the invention of a professional goldsmith.

Did Suger realize that his concentration of artists "from all parts of the kingdom" inaugurated that great selective synthesis of all French regional styles in the hitherto relatively barren Isle-de-France which we call Gothic? Did he suspect that the rose in his west façade—so far as we know the first appearance of this motif in this place—was one of the great innovations in architectural history, destined to challenge the inventiveness of countless masters up to Bernard de Soissons and Hugues Libergier? Did he know, or sense, that his unreflecting enthusiasm for the Pseudo-Areopagite's and John the Scot's light metaphysics placed him in the van of an intellectual movement that was to result in the proto-scientific theories of Robert Grosseteste and Roger Bacon, on the one hand, and in a Christian Platonism ranging from William of Auvergne, Henry of Ghent and Ulric of Strassburg to Marsilio Ficino and Pico della Mirandola, on the other? These questions, too, will have to be left unanswered. Certain it is, however, that Suger was acutely conscious of the stylistic difference that existed between his own, "modern" structures (*opus novum* or even *mo-*

dernum) and the old Carolingian basilica (*opus antiquum*). So long as parts of the old building were still in existence he clearly perceived the problem of harmonizing (*adaptare et coæquare*) the "modern" work with the "ancient." And he was fully aware of the new style's distinctive aesthetic qualities. He felt, and makes us feel, its spaciousness when he speaks of his new chevet as being "ennobled by the beauty of length and width"; its soaring verticalism when he describes the central nave of this chevet as being "suddenly (*repente*) raised aloft" by the supporting columns; its luminous transparency when he depicts his church as "pervaded by the wonderful and uninterrupted light of most luminous windows."

IT HAS BEEN SAID that Suger was harder to visualize as an individual than were the great cardinals of the seventeenth century of whom he was the historical ancestor. Yet it would seem that he steps out of the pages of history as a figure surprisingly alive and surprisingly French: a fierce patriot and a good householder; a little rhetorical and much enamored of grandeur, yet thoroughly matter-of-fact in practical affairs and temperate in his personal habits; hard-working and companionable, full of good nature and *bon sens*, vain, witty, and irrepressibly vivacious.

In a century unusually productive of saints and heroes Suger excelled by being human; and he died the death of a good man after a life well spent. In the fall of 1150 he fell ill of a malarial fever and was past hope before Christmas. In the effusive and somewhat theatrical way of his period he asked to be led into the convent and weepingly implored the monks to be forgiven for everything in which he might have failed the community. But he also prayed to God to be spared until the end of the festive season "lest the joy of the brethren be converted into sorrow on his account." This request, too, was granted. Suger died on January 13, 1151, the octave of Epiphany that ends the Christmas holidays. "He did not tremble in the sight of the end," says Willelmus, "because he had consummated his life before his death; nor was he loath to die because he had enjoyed to live. He departed willingly because he knew that better things were in store for him after his passing, and he did not hold that a good man should leave like one who is ejected, who is thrown out against his will."

TEXTS AND TRANSLATIONS

Arabic numerals in brackets refer to the pages in A. Lecoy de la Marche, *Œuvres Complètes de Suger*, Paris, 1867.

Roman numerals in brackets and words or letters in brackets have been added by the translator for clarification.

Footnotes in angular brackets were provided
by G.P.-S.

SUGERII ABBATIS
SANCTI DIONYSII LIBER

DE REBUS
IN ADMINISTRATIONE SUA GESTIS

I

ANNO administrationis nostræ vicesimo tertio, cum in capitulo generali, quadam die, conferendo cum fratribus nostris tam de hominibus[1] quam de privatis negotiis consederemus, iidem charissimi fratres et filii obnixe *in charitate*[2] sup-
5 plicare cœperunt, ne fructum tanti laboris nostri præteriri silentio sustinerem: quin potius ea quæ larga Dei omnipotentis munificentia contulerat huic ecclesiæ prælationis nostræ tempore incrementa, tam in novarum acquisitione quam in amissarum recuperatione, emendatarum etiam possessionum mul-
10 tiplicatione, ædificiorum constitutione, auri, argenti et pretiosissimarum gemmarum, necnon et optimorum palliorum repositione, calamo et atramento posteritati memoriæ reservare; ex hoc uno nobis duo repromittentes, tali notitia fratrum succedentium omnium jugem orationum pro salute animæ
15 nostræ mereri instantiam, et circa ecclesiæ Dei cultum hoc exemplo eorum excitare bene zelantem sollicitudinem. Nos igitur tam devote quam devotis et rationabilibus eorum petitionibus assensum [156] exhibentes, nullo inanis gloriæ appetitu, nullam laudis humanæ aut retributionis transitoriæ
20 exigendo retributionem, ne post decessum nostrum quacumque aut cujuscumque defraudatione redditibus ecclesia minuatur, ne copiosa, quæ tempore amministrationis nostræ larga Dei munificentia contulit, silentio malis successoribus depereant incrementa: sicut a corpore ecclesiæ beatissimorum
25 martyrum Dionysii, Rustici et Eleutherii, quæ nos quam dulcissime a mamilla usque in senectam fovit, de ædificiorum institutione et thesaurorum augmentatione loco suo incipere dignum duximus, ita etiam a castello suo, videlicet prima

---

[1] Should read *communibus*; cf. below, p. 147.
[2] *I Corinthians* IV, 21; XVI, 14. *Ephesians* I, 4; III, 17; IV, 2; IV, 16. *Colossians* II, 2. I *Thessalonians* V, 13. II *Thessalonians* III, 5. Here translated according to Douai Version.

THE BOOK OF
SUGER, ABBOT OF ST.-DENIS

ON WHAT WAS DONE UNDER HIS ADMINISTRATION

I

IN the twenty-third year of our administration, when we sat on a certain day in the general chapter, conferring with our brethren about matters both common and private, these very beloved brethren and sons began strenuously to beseech me *in charity* that I might not allow the fruits of our so great labors to be passed over in silence; and rather to save for the memory of posterity, in pen and ink, those increments which the generous munificence of Almighty God had bestowed upon this church, in the time of our prelacy, in the acquisition of new assets as well as in the recovery of lost ones, in the multiplication of improved possessions, in the construction of buildings, and in the accumulation of gold, silver, most precious gems and very good textiles. For this one thing they promised us two in return: by such a record we would deserve the continual fervor of all succeeding brethren in their prayers for the salvation of our soul; and we would rouse, through this example, their zealous solicitude for the good care of the church of God. We thus devoutly complied with their devoted and reasonable requests, not with any desire for empty glory nor with any claim to the reward of human praise and transitory compensation; and lest, after our demise, the church be diminished in its revenue by any or anyone's roguery and the ample increments which the generous munificence of God has bestowed in the time of our administration be tacitly lost under bad successors, we have deemed it worthy and useful, just as we thought fitting to begin, in its proper place, our tale about the construction of the buildings and the increase of the treasures with the body of the church of the most blessed Martyrs Denis, Rusticus, and Eleutherius (which [church] has most tenderly fostered us from mother's milk to old age), so to inform present and future readers about the

ejus sede, et in vicinia circumquaque, de reddituum augmentatione tam præsentium quam futurorum notitiæ significare honestum et utile proposuimus. ....
....

XXIV

De ecclesiæ ornatu

5 HIS igitur reddituum incrementis taliter assignatis, ad ædificiorum institutionem memorandam manum reduximus, ut et ex hoc ipso Deo omnipotenti tam a [186] nobis quam a successoribus nostris grates referantur, et eorum affectus ad hoc ipsum prosequendum et, si necesse sit, peragendum bono exemplo animetur. Neque enim aut penuria aliqua aut 10 quodcumque impedimentum cujuscumque potestatis timendum erit, si ob amorem sanctorum Martyrum de suo sibi secure serviatur. Primum igitur quod Deo inspirante hujus ecclesiæ incœpimus opus, propter antiquarum maceriarum vetustatem et aliquibus in locis minacem diruptionem, ascitis 15 melioribus quos invenire potui de diversis partibus pictoribus, eas[3] aptari et honeste depingi tam auro quam preciosis coloribus devote fecimus. Quod, quia etiam in scholis addiscens hoc facere si unquam possem appetebam, libentius complevi.

XXV

De ecclesiæ primo augmento

20 VERUM, cum jam hoc ipsum multo sumptu compleretur, inspirante divino nutu propter eam quam sæpe diebus festis, videlicet in festo beati Dionysii et in Indicto et in aliis quamplurimis, et videbamus et sentiebamus importunitatem (exigebat enim loci angustia ut mulieres super capita virorum, tanquam super pavimentum, ad altare dolore multo et cla- 25 moso tumultu currerent), ad augmentandum et amplifican-

---

3 ⟨For this variant, see Panofsky, Bib. 132, p. 120.⟩

increase of the revenue [by starting] from his own little town, that is to say, his first resting-place, and its vicinity on all sides

....

XXIV

Of the Church's Decoration

HAVING assigned these increases of the revenue in this manner, we turned our hand to the memorable construction of buildings, so that by this thanks might be given to Almighty God by us as well as by our successors; and that by good example their ardor might be roused to the continuation and, if necessary, to the completion of this [work]. For neither any want nor any hindrance by any power will have to be feared if, for the love of the Holy Martyrs, one takes safely care of oneself by one's own resources. The first work on this church which we began under the inspiration of God [was this]: because of the age of the old walls and their impending ruin in some places, we summoned the best painters I could find from different regions, and reverently caused these [walls] to be repaired and becomingly painted with gold and precious colors. I completed this all the more gladly because I had wished to do it, if ever I should have an opportunity, even while I was a pupil in school.

XXV

Of the First Addition to the Church

HOWEVER, even while this was being completed at great expense, I found myself, under the inspiration of the Divine Will and because of that inadequacy which we often saw and felt on feast days, namely the Feast of the blessed Denis, the Fair, and very many others (for the narrowness of the place forced the women to run toward the altar upon the heads of the men as upon a pavement with much anguish and noisy confusion), encouraged by the counsel of wise men and by the prayers of many monks (lest it displease God and the Holy Martyrs) to enlarge and amplify

dum nobile manuque divina consecratum monasterium virorum sapientum consilio, religiosorum multorum precibus, ne
Deo sanctisque Martyribus displiceret, adjutus, hoc ipsum incipere aggrediebar; [187] tam in capitulo nostro quam in
5 ecclesia divinæ supplicans pietati, ut qui *initium est et finis, id
est Alpha et Omega*,[4] bono initio bonum finem salvo medio
concopularet, ne *virum sanguinum*[5] ab ædificio templi refutaret, qui hoc ipsum toto animo magis quam Constantinopolitanas gazas obtinere præoptaret. Accessimus igitur ad priorem
10 valvarum introitum; et deponentes augmentum quoddam,
quod a Karolo Magno factum perhibebatur honesta satis
occasione (quia pater suus Pipinus imperator extra in introitu
valvarum pro peccatis patris sui Karoli Martelli prostratum
se sepeliri, non supinum, fecerat), ibidem manum apposui
15 mus; et, quemadmodum apparet, et in amplificatione corporis ecclesiæ, et introitus et valvarum triplicatione, turrium
altarum et honestarum erectione, instanter desudavimus.

XXVI

De dedicatione

ORATORIUM sancti Romani ad famulandum Deo sanctisque ejus angelis dedicari a venerabili viro Rothoma
20 gensi archiepiscopo Hugone et aliis quamplurimis episcopis
obtinuimus. Qui locus quam secretalis, quam devotus, quam
habilis divina celebrantibus, qui ibidem Deo deserviunt, ac si
jam in parte dum sacrificant eorum in cœlis sit habitatio, cognorunt. Eadem etiam dedicationis celebritate in inferiori tes
25 tudine[6] ecclesiæ dedicata sunt hinc et inde duo oratoria, ex
una parte sancti Hippoliti sociorumque ejus et ex altera sancti
Nicolai, a venerabilibus viris Manasse [188] Meldensi episcopo et Petro Silvanectensi. Quorum trium una et gloriosa
processio, cum per ostium sancti Eustachii egrederetur, ante
30 principales portas transiliens cum ingenti cleri decantantis et
populi tripudiantis turba, episcopis præeuntibus et sanctæ in

---

[4] *Revelation* XXI, 6; cf. *ibidem*, I, 8 and XXII, 13.
[5] *II Kings* XVI, 7: "Egredere, egredere, *vir sanguinum*"; cf. also *ibidem*,
8. Further *Psalms* XXV, 9; LIV, 24; LVIII, 3; CXXXVIII, 19.
[6] *testitudine* has been corrected to *testudine*.

the noble church consecrated by the Hand Divine; and I set out
at once to begin this very thing. In our chapter as well as in
church I implored Divine mercy that He Who is the One, *the
beginning and the ending, Alpha and Omega*, might join a good
end to a good beginning by a safe middle; that He might not repel
from the building of the temple a *bloody man* who desired this
very thing, with his whole heart, more than to obtain the treasures
of Constantinople. Thus we began work at the former entrance
with the doors. We tore down a certain addition asserted to have
been made by Charlemagne on a very honorable occasion (for his
father, the Emperor Pepin, had commanded that he be buried,
for the sins of his father Charles Martel, outside at the entrance
with the doors, face downward and not recumbent); and we set
our hand to this part. As is evident we exerted ourselves incessantly with the enlargement of the body of the church as well
as with the trebling of the entrance and the doors, and with the
erection of high and noble towers.

XXVI

Of the Dedication

WE brought about that the chapel of St. Romanus be dedicated to the service of God and His Holy Angels by the
venerable man Archbishop Hugues of Rouen and very many other
bishops. How secluded this place is, how hallowed, how convenient
for those celebrating the divine rites has come to be known to those
who serve God there as though they were already dwelling, in a
degree, in Heaven while they sacrifice. At the same solemn dedication ceremony, there were dedicated in the lower nave of the
church two chapels, one on either side (on one side that of St. Hippolytus and his Companions, and on the other that of St. Nicholas),
by the venerable men Manasseh, Bishop of Meaux, and Peter,
Bishop of Senlis. The one glorious procession of these three men
went out through the doorway of St. Eustace; it passed in front
of the principal doors with a huge throng of chanting clergy and
exulting people, the bishops walking in front and performing the
holy consecration; and, thirdly, they reentered through the single

sistentibus consecrationi, per singularem atrii portam de antiquo in novum opus transpositam tertio ingrediebantur. Et ad honorem omnipotentis Dei festivo opere completo, cum in superiore parte elaborare accingeremur, aliquantulum fatiga-
5 tos recreabant, et ne laboris aut penuriæ alicujus timore deprimeremur gratantissime sollicitabant.

XXVII

De portis fusilibus et deauratis

VALVAS siquidem principales, accitis fusoribus et electis sculptoribus, in quibus passio Salvatoris et resurrectio vel ascensio continetur, multis expensis, multo sumptu in earum
10 deauratione, ut nobili porticui conveniebat, ereximus; necnon et alias in dextera parte novas, in sinistra vero antiquas sub musivo, quod et novum contra usum hic fieri et in arcu portæ imprimi elaboravimus. Turrim etiam et superiora frontis propugnacula, tam ad ecclesiæ decorem quam et utilitatem, si op-
15 portunitas exigeret, variari condiximus; litteris etiam cupro deauratis consecrationis annum intitulari, ne oblivioni traderetur, præcepimus hoc modo:

> Ad decus ecclesiæ, quæ fovit et extulit illum,
> Suggerius[7] studuit ad decus ecclesiæ.
20 > [189] Deque tuo tibi participans martyr Dionysi,
> Orat ut exores fore participem Paradisi.
> Annus millenus et centenus quadragenus
> Annus erat Verbi, quando sacrata fuit.

Versus etiam portarum hi sunt:

25 > Portarum quisquis attollere quæris honorem,
> Aurum nec sumptus, operis mirare laborem,
> Nobile claret opus, sed opus quod nobile claret
> Clarificet mentes, ut eant per lumina vera

---

[7] ⟨See Panofsky, Bib. 132, p. 120.⟩

door of the cemetery which had been transferred from the old building to the new. When this festive work had been completed in the honor of Almighty God, and when we were girding ourselves to officiate in the upper part, [the visiting bishops] invigorated us, as we were a little tired, and most graciously exhorted us not to be discouraged by the fear of labor or of any want.

XXVII

Of the Cast and Gilded Doors

BRONZE casters having been summoned and sculptors chosen, we set up the main doors on which are represented the Passion of the Saviour and His Resurrection, or rather Ascension, with great cost and much expenditure for their gilding as was fitting for the noble porch. Also [we set up] others, new ones on the right side and the old ones on the left beneath the mosaic which, though contrary to modern custom, we ordered to be executed there and to be affixed to the tympanum of the portal. We also committed ourselves richly to elaborate the tower[s] and the upper crenelations of the front, both for the beauty of the church and, should circumstances require it, for practical purposes. Further we ordered the year of the consecration, lest it be forgotten, to be inscribed in copper-gilt letters in the following manner:

"For the splendor of the church that has fostered and exalted him,
Suger has labored for the splendor of the church.
Giving thee a share of what is thine, O Martyr Denis,
He prays to thee to pray that he may obtain a share of Paradise.
The year was the One Thousand, One Hundred, and Fortieth
Year of the Word when [this structure] was consecrated."

The verses on the door, further, are these:

"Whoever thou art, if thou seekest to extol the glory of
    these doors,
Marvel not at the gold and the expense but at the
    craftsmanship of the work.
Bright is the noble work; but, being nobly bright, the work
Should brighten the minds, so that they may travel,
    through the true lights,

Ad verum lumen, ubi Christus janua vera.
Quale sit intus in his determinat aurea porta:
Mens hebes ad verum per materialia surgit,
Et demersa prius hac visa luce resurgit.

5   Et in superliminari:

Suscipe vota tui, judex districte, Sugeri;
Inter oves proprias fac me clementer haberi.

XXVIII

De augmento superioris partis

EODEM vero anno, tam sancto et tam fausto opere exhilarati, ad inchoandam in superiori parte divinæ propi-
10 tiationis cameram, in qua jugis et frequens redemptionis nostræ hostia absque turbarum molestia secreto immolari debeat,
acceleravimus. Et quemadmodum in scripto consecrationis
ejusdem superioris operis invenitur, Deo cooperante et nos et
nostra prosperante, cum fratribus et conservis nostris tam
15 sanctum, tam gloriosum, tam famosum opus ad bonum per-
duci finem misericorditer obtinere meruimus; tanto Deo
sanctisque Martyribus obnoxii, quanto nostris temporibus et
laboribus tam diu differendo [190] agenda reservavit. *Quis
enim ego sum, aut quæ domus patris mei,*[8] qui tam nobile, tam
20 gratum ædificium vel inchoasse præsumpserim, vel perfecisse
speraverim, nisi, divinæ misericordiæ et sanctorum auxilio
Martyrum fretus, totum me eidem operi et mente et corpore
applicuissem? Verum qui dedit velle, dedit et posse; et quia
bonum opus fuit in voluntate, ex Dei adjutorio stetit in per-
25 fectione. Quod quidem gloriosum opus quantum divina manus in talibus operosa protexerit, certum est etiam argumentum, quod in tribus annis et tribus mensibus totum illud
magnificum opus, et in inferiore cripta et in superiore voltarum sublimitate, tot arcuum et columnarum distinctione

---

[8] Freely quoted from *I Kings* XVIII, 18: "*Quis ego sum, aut quæ* est vita
mea, aut cognatio *patris mei* in Israel, ut fiam gener regis?"

To the True Light where Christ is the true door.
In what manner it be inherent in this world the golden
  door defines:
The dull mind rises to truth through that which is
  material   ·
And, in seeing this light, is resurrected from its
  former submersion."

And on the lintel:

"Receive, O stern Judge, the prayers of Thy Suger;
Grant that I be mercifully numbered among Thy own sheep."

XXVIII

Of the Enlargement of the Upper Choir

IN the same year, cheered by so holy and so auspicious a work,
we hurried to begin the chamber of divine atonement in the
upper choir where the continual and frequent Victim of our redemption should be sacrificed in secret without disturbance by the
crowds. And, as is found in [our] treatise about the consecration
of this upper structure, we were mercifully deemed worthy—God
helping and prospering us and our concerns—to bring so holy, so
glorious, and so famous a structure to a good end, together with
our brethren and fellow servants; we felt all the more indebted
to God and the Holy Martyrs as He, by so long a postponement,
had reserved what had to be done for our lifetime and labors. *For
who am I, or what is my father's house*, that I should have presumed to begin so noble and pleasing an edifice, or should have
hoped to finish it, had I not, relying upon the help of Divine
mercy and the Holy Martyrs, devoted my whole self, both with
mind and body, to this very task? But He Who gave the will also
gave the power; because the good work was in the will therefore
it stood in perfection by the help of God. How much the Hand
Divine Which operates in such matters has protected this glorious
work is also surely proven by the fact that It allowed that whole
magnificent building [to be completed] in three years and three
months, from the crypt below to the summit of the vaults above,
elaborated with the variety of so many arches and columns, includ-

variatum, etiam operturæ integrum supplementum admiserit. Unde etiam epitaphium prioris consecrationis, una sola sublata dictione, hujus etiam annalem terminum concludit, hoc modo:

5   Annus millenus et centenus quadragenus
               Quartus erat Verbi, quando sacrata fuit.

Quibus etiam epitaphii versibus hos adjungi delegimus:

           Pars nova posterior dum jungitur anteriori,
               Aula micat medio clarificata suo.
10   Claret enim claris quod clare concopulatur,
               Et quod perfundit lux nova, claret opus
           Nobile, quod constat auctum sub tempore nostro,
               Qui Suggerus[9] eram, me duce dum fieret.

Promptus igitur urgere successus meos, cum nihil mallem 15 sub cœlo quam prosequi matris ecclesiæ honorem, quæ puerum materno affectu lactaverat, juvenem offendentem sustinuerat, ætate integrum poten-[191]ter roboraverat, *inter* Ecclesiæ et regni *principes* solemniter *locaverat,*[10] ad executionem operis nos ipsos contulimus, et cruces collaterales 20 ecclesiæ ad formam prioris et posterioris operis conjungendi attolli et accumulari decertavimus.

XXIX

De continuatione utriusque operis

QUO facto, cum quorumdam persuasione ad turrim anterioris partis prosecutionem studium nostrum contulissemus, jam in altera parte peracta, divina, sicut credimus, 25 voluntas ad hoc ipsum nos retraxit, ut mediam ecclesiæ testudinem,[11] quam dicunt navim, innovare et utrique innovato operi conformare et coæquare aggrederemur; reservata tamen quantacumque portione de parietibus antiquis, quibus summus pontifex Dominus Jesus Christus testimonio antiquorum 30 scriptorum manum apposuerat, ut et antiquæ consecrationis

---

[9] ⟨Cf. above, p. 46, line 19.⟩
[10] Freely quoted from *I Kings* II, 8: "elevat pauperem, ut sedeat cum principibus."
[11] ⟨See Panofsky, Bib. 132, p. 120.⟩

ing even the consummation of the roof. Therefore the inscription of the earlier consecration also defines, with only one word eliminated, the year of completion of this one, thus:

"The year was the One Thousand, One Hundred, Forty and Fourth of the Word when [this structure] was consecrated."

To these verses of the inscription we choose the following ones to be added:

"Once the new rear part is joined to the part in front,
The church shines with its middle part brightened.
For bright is that which is brightly coupled with the bright,
And bright is the noble edifice which is pervaded by the new light;
Which stands enlarged in our time,
I, who was Suger, being the leader while it was being accomplished."

Eager to press on my success, since I wished nothing more under heaven than to seek the honor of my mother church which with maternal affection had suckled me as a child, had held me upright as a stumbling youth, had mightily strengthened me as a mature man, and had solemnly *set me among the princes* of the Church and the realm, we devoted ourselves to the completion of the work and strove to raise and to enlarge the transept wings of the church [so as to correspond] to the form of the earlier and later work that had to be joined [by them].

XXIX

Of the Continuation of Both Works

THIS done, when under the persuasion of some we had devoted our efforts to carrying on the work upon the front tower[s] (already completed on one side), the Divine will, as we believe, diverted us to the following: we would undertake to renew the central body of the church, which is called the nave, and harmonize and equalize it with the two parts [already] remodelled. We would retain, however, as much as we could of the old walls on which, by the testimony of the ancient writers, the Highest Priest, our Lord Jesus Christ, had laid His hand; so that the

reverentia et moderno operi juxta tenorem cœptum congrua cohærentia servaretur. Cujus immutationis summa hæc fuit, quod, si interpolate in navi ecclesiæ occasione turrium ageretur, aut temporibus nostris aut successorum nostrorum, tardius
5 aut nunquam quocumque infortunio, sicut dispositum est, perficeretur. Nulla enim rerum importunitas rerum auctores urgeret, quin novi et antiqui operis copula longam sustineret expectationem. Sed quia jam incœptum est in alarum extensione, aut per nos aut per quos Dominus elegerit, ipso auxili
10 ante, perficietur. Præteritorum enim recordatio futurorum est exhibitio. Qui enim inter alia majora etiam admirandarum vitrearum operarios, materiem saphirorum locupletem, [192] promptissimos sumptus fere septingentarum librarum aut eo amplius administraverit, peragendorum supplementis
15 liberalissimus Dominus deficere non sustinebit. Est etenim *initium et finis.*[12]

XXX

De ornamentis ecclesiae

ORNAMENTORUM etiam ecclesiæ descriptionem, quibus manus divina administrationis nostræ tempore ecclesiam suam sponsam vocatam exornavit, ne veritatis æmula
20 subrepat oblivio et exemplum auferat agendi, intitulare dignum duximus. Dominum nostrum ter beatum Dionysium tam largum, tam benignum et confitemur et prædicamus, ut tot et tanta credamus apud Deum effecisse, tot et tanta impetrasse, ut centupliciter quam fecerimus ecclesiæ illius profecisse po
25 tuissemus, si fragilitas humana, si varietas temporum, si mobilitas morum non restitisset. Quæ tamen ei, Deo donante, reservavimus, hæc sunt.

[12] *Revelation* XXI, 6; cf. *ibidem*, I, 8.

reverence for the ancient consecration might be safeguarded, and yet a congruous consistency [might be assured] to the modern work in accordance with the course embarked upon. The chief reason for this change was this: if, in our own time or under our successors, work on the nave of the church would only be done betweenwhiles, whenever the towers would afford the opportunity, the nave would not be completed according to plan without much delay or, in case of any unlucky development, never. For no difficulty would ever embarrass those [then] in power but that the link between the old and the new work would suffer long postponement. However, since it has already been started with the extension of the side-aisles, it will be completed either through us or through those whom the Lord shall elect, He Himself helping. The recollection of the past is the promise of the future. For the most liberal Lord Who, among other greater things, has also provided the makers of the marvelous windows, a rich supply of sapphire glass, and ready funds of about seven hundred pounds or more will not suffer that there be a lack of means for the completion of the work. For He is the *beginning and the ending*.

XXX

Of the Church's Ornaments

WE have thought it proper to place on record the description of the ornaments of the church by which the Hand of God, during our administration, has adorned His church, His Chosen Bride; lest Oblivion, the jealous rival of Truth, sneak in and take away the example for further action. Our Patron, the thrice blessed Denis, is, we confess and proclaim, so generous and benevolent that we believe him to have prevailed upon God to such an extent, and to have obtained from Him so many and so great things, that we might have been able to do for his church a hundred times more than we have done, had not human frailty, the mutability of the times, and the instability of manners prevented it. What we, nevertheless, have saved for him by the grace of God is the following.

[53]

XXXI

De tabula aurea superiori

IN tabula illa, quæ ante sacratissimum corpus ejus assistit,
circiter quadraginta duas marcas auri posuisse nos æsti-
mamus, gemmarum preciosarum multiplicem copiam, jacinctorum, rubetorum, saphirorum, smaragdinum, topaziorum
5 necnon et opus discriminantium unionum, quantam nos re-
perire nunquam præ-[193]sumpsimus. Videres reges et principes multosque viros præcelsos imitatione nostra digitos
manuum suarum exanulare, et anulorum aurum et gemmas
margaritasque preciosas, ob amorem sanctorum Martyrum
10 eidem tabulæ infigi præcipere. Nec minus etiam archiepiscopi
et episcopi, ipsos suæ desponsationis anulos ibidem sub tuto
reponentes, Deo et Sanctis ejus devotissime offerebant. Ven-
ditorum etiam gemmariorum tanta de diversis regnis et
nationibus ad nos turba confluebat, ut non plus emere quærere-
15 mus quam illi vendere sub amministratione omnium festina-
rent. Versus etiam ejusdem tabulæ hi sunt:

> Magne Dionysi, portas aperi Paradisi,
> Suggeriumque piis protege præsidiis.
> Quique novam cameram per nos tibi constituisti,
20 In camera cœli nos facias recipi,
> Et pro præsenti cœli mensa satiari.
> Significata magis significante placent.

Quia igitur sacratissima dominorum nostrorum corpora in
volta superiore quam nobilius potuimus locari oportuit, qua-
25 dam de collateralibus tabulis sanctissimi eorum sarcofagi
nescimus qua occasione erepta, quindecim marcas auri reponendo, ulteriorem frontem ejusdem et operturam superiorem undique inferius et superius deaurari quadraginta ferme
unciis elaboravimus. Tabulis etiam cupreis fusilibus et deau-
30 ratis, atque politis lapidibus impactis propter interiores lapideas voltas, necnon et januis continuis ad arcendos populorum

XXXI

Of the Golden Altar Frontal
in the Upper Choir

INTO this panel, which stands in front of his most sacred body, we have put, according to our estimate, about forty-two marks of gold; [further] a multifarious wealth of precious gems, hyacinths, rubies, sapphires, emeralds and topazes, and also an array of different large pearls—[a wealth] as great as we had never anticipated to find. You could see how kings, princes, and many outstanding men, following our example, took the rings off the fingers of their hands and ordered, out of love for the Holy Martyrs, that the gold, stones, and precious pearls of the rings be put into that panel. Similarly archbishops and bishops deposited there the very rings of their investiture as though in a place of safety, and offered them devoutly to God and His Saints. And such a crowd of dealers in precious gems flocked in on us from diverse dominions and regions that we did not wish to buy any more than they hastened to sell, with everyone contributing donations. And the verses on this panel are these:

"Great Denis, open the door of Paradise
And protect Suger through thy pious guardianship.
Mayest thou, who hast built a new dwelling for thyself through us,
Cause us to be received in the dwelling of Heaven,
And to be sated at the heavenly table instead of at the
    present one.
That which is signified pleases more than that which signifies."

Since it seemed proper to place the most sacred bodies of our Patron Saints in the upper vault as nobly as we could, and since one of the side-tablets of their most sacred sarcophagus had been torn off on some unknown occasion, we put back fifteen marks of gold and took pains to have gilded its rear side and its superstructure throughout, both below and above, with about forty ounces. Further we caused the actual receptacles of the holy bodies to be enclosed with gilded panels of cast copper and with polished stones, fixed close to the inner stone vaults, and also with continuous gates

tumultus, ita tamen ut venerabiles personæ, sicut decuerit, ipsa sanctorum corporum continentia vasa cum magna devotione et lacrymarum profusione [194] videre valeant, circumcingi fecimus. Eorumdem vero sanctorum tumulorum hi
5 sunt versus:

> Sanctorum cineres ubi cœlicus excubat ordo,
> Plebs rogat et plorat, clerus canit in decachordo.
> Spiritibus quorum referuntur vota piorum;
> Cumque placent illis, mala condonantur eorum.
10 Corpora Sanctorum sunt hic in pace sepulta,
> Qui post se rapiant nos orantes prece multa.
> Hic locus egregium venientibus extat asylum;
> Hic fuga tuta reis, subjacet ultor eis.

XXXII
De Crucifixo aureo

ADORANDAM vivificam crucem, æternæ victoriæ Sal-
15 vatoris nostri vexillum salutiferum, de quo dicit Apostolus: *Mihi autem absit gloriari nisi in cruce Domini mei Jesu Christi,*[13] quanto gloriosum non tantum hominibus quantum etiam ipsis *angelis filii hominis signum apparens* in extremis *in cœlo,*[14] tanto gloriosius ornatum iri tota mentis devotione si
20 possemus inniteremur, jugiter eam cum apostolo Andrea[15] salutantes: *Salve crux, quæ in corpore Christi dedicata es, et ex membris ejus tanquam margaritis ornata.*[16] Verum quia sicut voluimus non potuimus, quam melius potuimus voluimus, et perficere Deo donante elaboravimus. Hinc est quod precio-
25 sarum margaritarum gemmarumque copiam circumquaque per nos et per nuncios nostros quæritantes, quam preciosiorem in auro et gemmis tanto ornatui materiam invenire potuimus præparando, artifices peritiores de diversis parti-[195]bus convocavimus, qui et diligenter et morose fabricando crucem
30 venerabilem ipsarum ammiratione gemmarum retro attolle-

---

[13] *Galatians* VI, 14; the Vulgate text has *nostri* instead of *mei.*

[14] *Matthew* XXIV, 30: "Et tunc parebit signum Filii hominis in cælo"; *ibid.,* 31: "Et mittet angelos suos . . ." (kind communication of Prof. W. S. Heckscher).

[15] ⟨See Panofsky, Bib. 132, p. 120.⟩

[16] *Passio Andreæ* X (*Acta Apostolorum Apocrypha,* R. A. Lipsius and M. Bonnet eds., II, 1, Leipzig, 1898, p. 24); the text printed in this edition reads, after the comma, *et ex membrorum eius margaritis ornata.*

to hold off disturbances by crowds; in such a manner, however, that reverend persons, as was fitting, might be able to see them with great devotion and a flood of tears. On these sacred tombs, however, there are the following verses:

"Where the Heavenly Host keeps watch, the ashes
   of the Saints
Are implored and bemoaned by the people, [and] the
   clergy sings in ten-voiced harmony.
To their spirits are submitted the prayers of the devout,
And if they please them their evil deeds are forgiven.
Here the bodies of the Saints are laid to rest in peace;
May they draw us after them, us who beseech them with fervent
   prayer.
This place exists as an outstanding asylum for those who come;
Here is safe refuge for the accused, here the avenger is
   powerless against them."

XXXII

Of the Golden Crucifix

WE should have insisted with all the devotion of our mind—had we but had the power—that the adorable, life-giving cross, the health-bringing banner of the eternal victory of Our Saviour (of which the Apostle says: *But God forbid that I should glory, save in the cross of our Lord Jesus Christ*), should be adorned all the more gloriously as the *sign of the Son of Man*, which *will appear in Heaven* at the end of the world, will be glorious not only to men but also to the very *angels*; and we should have perpetually greeted it with the Apostle Andrew: *Hail Cross, which art dedicated in the body of Christ and adorned with His members even as with pearls.* But since we could not do as we wished, we wished to do as best we could, and strove to bring it about by the grace of God. Therefore we searched around everywhere by ourselves and by our agents for an abundance of precious pearls and gems, preparing as precious a supply of gold and gems for so important an embellishment as we could find, and convoked the most experienced artists from diverse parts. They would with diligent and patient labor glorify the venerable cross on its reverse

rent, et ante, videlicet in conspectu sacrificantis sacerdotis, adorandam Domini Salvatoris imaginem in recordatione passionis ejus tanquam et adhuc patientem in cruce ostentarent. Eodem sane loco beatus Dionysius quingentis annis et eo am-

5 plius, videlicet a tempore Dagoberti usque ad nostra tempora, jacuerat. Unum jocosum, sed nobile miraculum,[17] quod super his ostendit nobis Dominus, sub silentio præterire nolumus. Cum enim hærerem penuria gemmarum, nec super hoc sufficienter mihi providere valerem (raritas enim eas cariores

10 facit), ecce duorum ordinum trium abbatiarum, videlicet Cistellensis et alterius abbatiæ ejusdem ordinis et Fontis Ebraldi, camerulam nostram ecclesiæ inhærentem intrantes, gemmarum copiam, videlicet jacinctorum, saphirorum, rubetorum, smaragdinum, topaziorum, quantam per decennium invenire

15 minime sperabamus, emendam nobis obtulerunt. Qui autem eas habebant, a comite Theobaldo sub eleemosyna obtinuerant, qui a thesauris avunculi sui regis Henrici defuncti, quas in mirabilibus cuppis toto tempore vitæ suæ congesserat, per manum Stephani fratris sui regis anglici receperat. Nos autem

20 onere quærendarum gemmarum exonerati, gratias Deo referentes, quater centum libras, cum plus satis valerent, pro eis dedimus.

Nec eas solum, verum etiam multam et sumptuosam [196] aliarum gemmarum et unionum copiam ad perfectionem tam

25 sancti ornamenti apposuimus. De auro vero obrizo circiter quater viginti marcas nos posuisse, si bene recordor, meminimus. Pedem vero quatuor Evangelistis comptum, et columnam cui sancta insidet imago subtilissimo opere smaltitam, et Salvatoris historiam cum antiquæ legis allegoriarum testi-

30 moniis designatis, et capitello superiore mortem Domini cum suis imaginibus ammirante, per plures aurifabros Lotharingos, quandoque quinque, quandoque septem, vix duobus annis perfectam habere potuimus. Tanti igitur et tam sancti instrumenti ornatum altius honorare et exaltare misericordia Salvatoris

35 nostri accelerans, domnum papam Eugenium ad celebrandum sanctum Pascha, sicut mos est Romanis pontificibus in Galliis demorantibus ob honorem sancti apostolatus beati Dionysii,

---

[17] *jocosum, sed miraculum nobile* has been corrected to *jocosum, sed nobile miraculum.*

side by the admirable beauty of those gems; and on its front—that
is to say in the sight of the sacrificing priest—they would show the
adorable image of our Lord the Saviour, suffering, as it were, even
now in remembrance of His Passion. In fact the blessed Denis had
rested on this very spot for five hundred years or more, that is to
say, from the time of Dagobert up to our own day. One merry but
notable miracle which the Lord granted us in this connection we do
not wish to pass over in silence. For when I was in difficulty for
want of gems and could not sufficiently provide myself with more
(for their scarcity makes them very expensive): then, lo and behold, [monks] from three abbeys of two Orders—that is, from
Cîteaux and another abbey of the same Order, and from Fontevrault—entered our little chamber adjacent to the church and
offered us for sale an abundance of gems such as we had not hoped
to find in ten years, hyacinths, sapphires, rubies, emeralds, topazes.
Their owners had obtained them from Count Thibaut for alms;
and he in turn had received them, through the hands of his brother
Stephen, King of England, from the treasures of his uncle, the
late King Henry, who had amassed them throughout his life in
wonderful vessels. We, however, freed from the worry of searching for gems, thanked God and gave four hundred pounds for the
lot though they were worth much more.

We applied to the perfection of so sacred an ornament not only
these but also a great and expensive supply of other gems and
large pearls. We remember, if memory serves, to have put in about
eighty marks of refined gold. And barely within two years were we
able to have completed, through several goldsmiths from Lorraine
—at times five, at other times seven—the pedestal adorned with
the Four Evangelists; and the pillar upon which the sacred image
stands, enameled with exquisite workmanship, and [on it] the
history of the Saviour, with the testimonies of the allegories from
the Old Testament indicated, and the capital above looking up,
with its images, to the Death of the Lord. Hastening to honor and
extol even more highly the embellishment of so important and
sacred a liturgical object, the mercy of our Saviour brought to us
our Lord Pope Eugenius for the celebration of holy Easter (as
is the custom of Roman Pontiffs, when sojourning in Gaul, in
honor of the sacred apostolate of the blessed Denis, which we have

quod etiam de Calixto et Innocentio illius prædecessoribus vi-
dimus, ad nos adduxit; qui eundem crucifixum ea die solenni-
ter consecravit. De titulo "veræ crucis Domini, quæ omnem et
universalem excedit margaritam," de capella sua portionem in
5 eo assignavit; publice coram omnibus, quicumque inde aliquid
raperent, quicumque ausu temerario in eum manum inferrent,
mucrone beati Petri et gladio Spiritus sancti anathematizavit.
Nos autem idem anathema inferius in cruce intitulari fecimus.

XXXIII

PRINCIPALE igitur beati Dionysii altare, cui tantum
10 anterior tabula a Karolo Calvo imperatore tertio speciosa
et preciosa habebatur, quia eidem ad monasticum propositum
oblati fuimus, ornatum iri [197] acceleravimus, et utrique
lateri aureas apponendo tabulas, quartam etiam preciosiorem,
ut totum circumquaque altare appareret aureum, attollendo
15 circumcingi fecimus. Collateralibus quidem candelabra viginti
marcarum auri regis Ludovici Philippi, ne quacumque occasione raperentur, ibidem deponentes, jacinctos, smaragdines,
quascumque gemmas preciosas apposuimus, et apponendas diligenter quæritare decrevimus. Quorum quidem versus hi
20 sunt.

In dextro latere:

> Has aræ tabulas posuit Suggerius[18] abbas,
>
> Præter eam quam rex Karolus ante dedit.
> Indignos venia fac dignos, Virgo Maria.
25 > Regis et abbatis mala mundet fons pietatis.

In sinistro latere:

> Si quis præclaram spoliaverit impius aram,
> Æque damnatus pereat Judæ sociatus.

Ulteriorem vero tabulam miro opere sumptuque profuso,
30 quoniam barbari et profusiores nostratibus erant artifices, tam
forma quam materia mirabili anaglifo opere, ut a quibusdam

---

[18] ⟨Cf. above, p. 46, line 19.⟩

also experienced with his predecessors, Callixtus and Innocent);
and he solemnly consecrated the aforesaid crucifix on that day.
Out of the title "The True Cross of the Lord Surpassing All
and Every Pearl" he assigned to it a portion from his chapel; and
publicly, in the presence of all, he anathematized, by the sword
of the blessed Peter and by the sword of the Holy Ghost, whosoever would steal anything therefrom and whosoever would raise
his hand against it in reckless temerity; and we ordered this ban
to be inscribed at the foot of the cross.

XXXIII

WE hastened to adorn the Main Altar of the blessed Denis
where there was only one beautiful and precious frontal
panel from Charles the Bald, the third Emperor; for at this
[altar] we had been offered to the monastic life. We had it all
encased, putting up golden panels on either side and adding a
fourth, even more precious one; so that the whole altar would
appear golden all the way round. On either side, we installed there
the two candlesticks of King Louis, son of Philip, of twenty marks
of gold, lest they might be stolen on some occasion; we added
hyacinths, emeralds, and sundry precious gems; and we gave
orders carefully to look out for others to be added further. The
verses on these [panels] are these.

On the right side:

"Abbot Suger has set up these altar panels
In addition to that which King Charles has given before.
Make worthy the unworthy through thy indulgence, O Virgin Mary.
May the fountain of mercy cleanse the sins both of the King and
the Abbot."

On the left side:

"If any impious person should despoil this excellent altar
May he perish, deservedly damned, associated with Judas."

But the rear panel, of marvelous workmanship and lavish sump-
tuousness (for the barbarian artists were even more lavish than
ours), we ennobled with chased relief work equally admirable for
its form as for its material, so that certain people might be able to

dici possit *Materiam superabat opus*,[19] extulimus. Multa de
acquisitis, plura de quibus ecclesiæ ornamentis quæ perdere
timebamus, videlicet pede decurtatum calicem aureum et
quædam alia, ibidem configi fecimus. Et quoniam tacita visus
5 cognitione materiei diversitas, auri, gemmarum, unionum,
absque descriptione facile non cognoscitur, opus quod solis
patet litteratis, quod allegoriarum jocundarum jubare re-
splendet, apicibus litterarum mandari fecimus. Versus etiam
[198] idipsum loquentes, ut enucleatius intelligantur, ap-
10 posuimus:

> Voce sonans magna Christo plebs clamat: Osanna!
> Quæ datur in cœna tulit omnes hostia vera.
> Ferre crucem properat qui cunctos in cruce salvat.
> Hoc quod Abram pro prole litat, Christi caro signat.
15   Melchisedech libat quod Abram super hoste triumphat.
> Botrum vecte ferunt qui Christum cum cruce quærunt.

Hæc igitur tam nova quam antiqua ornamentorum discri-
mina ex ipsa matris ecclesiæ affectione crebro considerantes,
dum illam ammirabilem sancti Eligii cum minoribus crucem,
20 dum incomparabile ornamentum, quod vulgo "crista" vocatur,
aureæ aræ superponi contueremur, corde tenus suspirando:
Omnis, inquam, *lapis preciosus operimentum tuum, sardius,
topazius, jaspis, crisolitus, onix et berillus, saphirus, carbuncu-
lus et smaragdus.*[20] De quorum numero, præter solum car-
25 bunculum, nullum deesse, imo copiosissime abundare, gemmarum proprietatem cognoscentibus cum summa ammiratione
claret. Unde, cum ex dilectione decoris domus Dei aliquando
multicolor, gemmarum speciositas ab exintrinsecis[21] me curis
devocaret, sanctarum etiam diversitatem virtutum, de materi-
30 alibus ad immaterialia transferendo, honesta meditatio insistere persuaderet, videor videre me quasi sub aliqua extranea

---

[19] Ovid, *Metamorphoses* II, 5.
[20] *Ezekiel* XXVIII, 13; here translated according to the Douai Version.
[21] Should read *extrinsecis*.

say: *The workmanship surpassed the material.* Much of what had been acquired and more of such ornaments of the church as we were afraid of losing—for instance, a golden chalice that was curtailed of its foot and several other things—we ordered to be fastened there. And because the diversity of the materials [such as] gold, gems and pearls is not easily understood by the mute perception of sight without a description, we have seen to it that this work, which is intelligible only to the literate, which shines with the radiance of delightful allegories, be set down in writing. Also we have affixed verses expounding the matter so that the [allegories] might be more clearly understood:

> "Crying out with a loud voice, the mob acclaims Christ:
> 'Osanna.'
> The true Victim offered at the Lord's Supper has carried
> all men.
> He Who saves all men on the Cross hastens to carry the
> cross.
> The promise which Abraham obtains for his seed is sealed by
> the flesh of Christ.
> Melchizedek offers a libation because Abraham triumphs over
> the enemy.
> They who seek Christ with the Cross bear the cluster of
> grapes upon a staff."

Often we contemplate, out of sheer affection for the church our mother, these different ornaments both new and old; and when we behold how that wonderful cross of St. Eloy—together with the smaller ones—and that incomparable ornament commonly called "the Crest" are placed upon the golden altar, then I say, sighing deeply in my heart: *Every precious stone was thy covering, the sardius, the topaz, and the jasper, the chrysolite, and the onyx, and the beryl, the sapphire, and the carbuncle, and the emerald.* To those who know the properties of precious stones it becomes evident, to their utter astonishment, that none is absent from the number of these (with the only exception of the carbuncle), but that they abound most copiously. Thus, when—out of my delight in the beauty of the house of God—the loveliness of the many-colored gems has called me away from external cares, and worthy meditation has induced me to reflect, transferring that

orbis terrarum plaga, quæ nec tota sit in terrarum fæce nec
tota in cœli puritate, demorari, ab hac etiam inferiori ad illam
superiorem anagogico more Deo donante posse transferri.
Conferre consuevi cum Hierosolymitanis et gratantissime ad-
5 discere, quibus Constantinopolitanæ patuerant gazæ [199]
et Sanctæ Sophiæ ornamenta, utrum ad comparationem illorum hæc aliquid valere deberent. Qui cum hæc majora fate-
rentur, visum est nobis quod timore Francorum ammiranda
quæ antea audieramus caute reposita essent, ne stultorum
10 aliquorum impetuosa rapacitate Græcorum et Latinorum
ascita familiaritas in seditionem et bellorum scandala subito
moveretur; astucia enim præcipue Græcorum est. Unde fieri
potuit ut majora sint quæ hic sub tuto reposita apparent, quam
ea quæ non tuto propter scandala ibidem relicta apparuerunt.
15 Ammiranda siquidem et fere incredibilia a viris veridicis
quampluribus, et ab episcopo Laudunensi Hugone, in celebra-
tione missæ de Sanctæ Sophiæ ornamentorum prærogativa,
necnon et aliarum ecclesiarum audieramus. Quæ si ita sunt,
imo quia eorum testimonio ita esse credimus, tam inæstima-
20 bilia quam incomparabilia multorum judicio exponerentur.
Abundet unusquisque in suo sensu.[22] Mihi fateor hoc potissimum placuisse, ut quæcumque cariora, quæcumque carissima,
sacrosanctæ[23] Eucharistiæ amministrationi super omnia deservire debeant. *Si* libatoria aurea, si fialæ aureæ, et si mortariola
25 aurea ad collectam *sanguinis hircorum aut vitulorum aut vac-
cæ ruffæ*, ore Dei aut prophetæ jussu, deserviebant: *quanto
magis ad susceptionem sanguinis Jesu Christi*[24] vasa aurea,
lapides preciosi, quæque inter omnes creaturas carissima, continuo famulatu, plena devotione exponi debent. Certe nec nos
30 nec nostra his deservire sufficimus. Si de sanctorum Cherubim
et Seraphim substantia nova creatione nostra mutaretur, in-

[22] *Romans* XIV, 5 ("Unusquisque in suo sensu abundet"); here translated
according to the Douai Version.
[23] *sacrosantæ* has been corrected to *sacrosanctæ*.
[24] *Hebrews* IX, 13, 14; cf. below, p. 193.

which is material to that which is immaterial, on the diversity of
the sacred virtues: then it seems to me that I see myself dwelling,
as it were, in some strange region of the universe which neither
exists entirely in the slime of the earth nor entirely in the purity of
Heaven; and that, by the grace of God, I can be transported from
this inferior to that higher world in an anagogical manner. I used
to converse with travelers from Jerusalem and, to my great delight, to learn from those to whom the treasures of Constantinople
and the ornaments of Hagia Sophia had been accessible, whether
the things here could claim some value in comparison with those
there. When they acknowledged that these here were the more
important ones, it occurred to us that those marvels of which we
had heard before might have been put away, as a matter of pre-
caution, for fear of the Franks, lest through the rash rapacity of a
stupid few the partisans of the Greeks and Latins, called upon the
scene, might suddenly be moved to sedition and warlike hostilities;
for wariness is preeminently characteristic of the Greeks. Thus it
could happen that the treasures which are visible here, deposited
in safety, amount to more than those which had been visible there,
left [on view] under conditions unsafe on account of disorders.
From very many truthful men, even from Bishop Hugues of
Laon, we had heard wonderful and almost incredible reports
about the superiority of Hagia Sophia's and other churches' ornaments for the celebration of Mass. If this is so—or rather because
we believe it to be so, by their testimony—then such inestimable
and incomparable treasures should be exposed to the judgment of
the many. *Let every man abound in his own sense.* To me, I confess, one thing has always seemed preeminently fitting: that every
costlier or costliest thing should serve, first and foremost, for the
administration of the Holy Eucharist. *If* golden pouring vessels,
golden vials, golden little mortars used to serve, by the word of
God or the command of the Prophet, to collect the *blood of goats
or calves or the red heifer: how much more* must golden vessels,
precious stones, and whatever is most valued among all created
things, be laid out, with continual reverence and full devotion, for
the reception of the *blood of Christ*! Surely neither we nor our

sufficientem tamen et indignum tantæ et tam ineffabili hostiæ
exhiberet famulatum. Tantam tamen propi-[200]ciationem
pro peccatis nostris habemus. Opponunt etiam qui derogant,
debere sufficere huic amministrationi mentem sanctam, ani-
5 mum purum, intentionem fidelem. Et nos quidem hæc interesse præcipue proprie, specialiter approbamus. In exterioribus
etiam sacrorum vasorum ornamentis, nulli omnino æque ut
sancti sacrificii servitio, in omni puritate interiori, in omni no-
bilitate exteriori, debere famulari profitemur. In omnibus
10 enim universaliter decentissime nos oportet deservire Re-
demptori nostro, qui in omnibus universaliter absque excep-
tione aliqua nobis providere non recusavit; qui naturæ suæ
nostram sub uno et ammirabili individuo univit, qui *nos in
parte dexteræ suæ locans, regnum suum veraciter possidere*[25]
15 promisit, Dominus noster qui *vivit et regnat per omnia secula
seculorum.*[26]

[XXXIII A]

ALTARE etiam quod testimonio antiquorum "sanctum"
nominatur altare (sic enim consuevit dicere gloriosus rex
Ludovicus Philippi ab infantia sua, dum hic nutriretur, se a
20 senioribus loci didicisse), quia cum vetustate, tum defectu
fidelis custodiæ, tum etiam propter frequentem motionem
quæ fit nobilissimi apparatus occasione, qui diversi diversis,
excellentes excellentioribus festis apponuntur, minus honeste
comptum apparebat, ob reverentiam sanctarum reliquiarum
25 renovare excepimus. Sacratus siquidem lapis porphireticus
qui superest aræ, non minus qualitativo colore quam quanti-
tativa magnitudine satis aptus, concavo ligno auro operto,
ipsa vetustate interpolata admodum disrupto cingebatur.
Cujus concavi faceta [201] compositione in anteriori parte
30 locatum brachium sancti Jacobi apostoli, idipsum litteris
interius attestantibus pervia candidissimi cristalli apertione,
credebatur. Nec minus in dextera parte, uniformiter littera-

---

[25] *Matthew* XXV, 33 f.; here translated according to the Douai Version.
[26] *Tobit* IX, 11. *Revelation* I, 18; V, 14; XI, 15; XV, 7.

possessions suffice for this service. If, by a new creation, our substance were re-formed from that of the holy Cherubim and Seraphim, it would still offer an insufficient and unworthy service for so great and so ineffable a victim; and yet we have so great a propitiation for our sins. The detractors also object that a saintly mind, a pure heart, a faithful intention ought to suffice for this sacred function; and we, too, explicitly and especially affirm that it is these that principally matter. [But] we profess that we must do homage also through the outward ornaments of sacred vessels, and to nothing in the world in an equal degree as to the service of the Holy Sacrifice, with all inner purity and with all outward splendor. For it behooves us most becomingly to serve Our Saviour in all things in a universal way—Him Who has not refused to provide for us in all things in a universal way and without any exception; Who has fused our nature with His into one admirable individuality; Who, *setting us on His right hand*, has promised us in truth *to possess His kingdom*; our Lord Who *liveth and reigneth for ever and ever*.

[XXXIII A]

WE also undertook to renew, out of reverence for sacred relics, the altar which, by the testimony of the ancients, is called "The Holy Altar" (for so the glorious King Louis, son of Philip, had learned it, as he used to say, from the older residents of this place from early childhood while he was brought up here); for, partly on account of old age, partly for want of faithful care, and partly also on account of the frequent movement occurring on the occasion of solemn decoration—of which [decorations] different ones are set up for different feasts, the important for the more important ones—it did not appear to be in very good condition. The sacred porphyry stone on top of this altar, very appropriate no less by the quality of its color than by the quantity of its size, was set into a hollow [frame of] wood covered with gold and very ruined by the lapse of so much time. It was believed that in the front part of this hollow [frame] there was placed, with artful contrivance, an arm of the Apostle St. James, a document inside attesting this through clear disclosure by a most limpid crystal. In the right part, too, there was hidden, as an inside inscription pro-

rum apparitione, brachium prothomartyris Stephani recondi, in sinistra vero æque sancti Vincentii levitæ et martyris brachium titulus interius perorabat. Nos igitur tantarum et tam sanctarum reliquiarum protectione muniri appetentes, 5 eas videre, eas deosculari, si Deo displicere non timerem, gratantissime multo temporum processu rapiebar. Assumens igitur ex devotione audaciam, et antiquitati honorem veritatis conservans, modum et diem detegendi ipsas sanctas reliquias elegimus, sacratissima videlicet die martyrii[27] beatorum 10 Martyrum dominorum nostrorum, octavo scilicet idus octobris. Aderant siquidem diversarum provinciarum archiepiscopi et episcopi, qui gratantissime, quasi ex debito apostolatus Galliarum, ad tantæ solemnitatis celebrationem pia vota deferre accesserant: archiepiscopi scilicet Lugdunensis, Remensis, Tu-15 ronensis et Rothomagensis; episcopi vero Suessionensis, Belvacensis, Silvanectensis, Meldensis, Redonensis, Aletensis et Venetensis; abbatum etiam et monachorum, sive clericorum, atque optimatum conventus; sed et populi promiscui sexus turba innumerabilis. Decantata igitur, eadem solemnitatis die, 20 Tertia, cum jam in conspectu omnium assistentium celeberrima tantæ diei ordinaretur processio, tanta certæ rei veritatis fiducia, solo patrum testimonio et titulo referti, ac si jam omnia vidissemus, archiepi-[202]scopos et episcopos, abbates et autenticas assistentes personas ad efferendam aram ascivi-25 mus; quod eam aperire, quod sanctissimarum reliquiarum thesaurum videre vellemus, exposuimus. Dicebant ergo quidam ex familiaribus nostris, consulte quidem, quod et personæ et ecclesiæ famæ tutius fuisset, si secreto utrum ita esset ut litteræ loquebantur videretur. Quibus ilico, fidei fervore 30 excitus, responsum reddidi, magis mihi placere, si ita est ut legitur, ab omnibus contuentibus scire,[28] quam, si secreto inspexissem, omnes non contuentes dubitare. Deferentes igitur in medium præfatam aram, ascitis aurifabris qui locellos illos quibus sanctissima brachia continebantur, ubi super-35 sedebant cristallini lapides titulos eorum offerentes, diligenter

---

[27] ⟨See Panofsky, Bib. 132, p. 120.⟩
[28] Should read *sciri*.

claimed through the appearance of a document in the same form, an arm of the Proto-Martyr Stephen; and, likewise, in the left part an arm of St. Vincent, Levite and Martyr. Anxious to be fortified by the protection of so important and sacred relics, I had for a long time joyfully longed to see and to kiss them had I not feared to incur the displeasure of God. Thus, taking courage from our devotion and saving the honor of truth for antiquity, we selected the manner and date for the disclosure of these sacred relics, namely, on the day of the martyrdom of our blessed Patron Saints, viz., the eighth day before the Ides of October. There were present archbishops and bishops from diverse Provinces who, as though paying a debt to the apostolate of all Gaul, had most joyfully come hither to bring pious prayers to the celebration of so great a solemnity, namely: the Archbishops of Lyons, Reims, Tours, and Rouen; the Bishops of Soissons, Beauvais, Senlis, Meaux, Rennes, St.-Malo, and Vannes; further, a conflux of abbots and monks or clerics as well as of noblemen; but also an innumerable crowd of people of both sexes. On the day of this solemnity then, after the offices of Tierce had been sung, and when the most solemn procession of so great a day was already being formed before the eyes of all, we, filled as we were—on the mere testimony and writ of our forebears—with so much confidence in the certain truth of the matter as though we had already seen everything, convoked the archbishops, bishops, abbots and the attending personages of high rank to the altar which we proposed to lift from its place; and we explained that we wanted to open it, that we wanted to see the treasure of the most sacred relics. Some of our intimates said, deliberately, that it would have been safer for the reputation of our person and of the church if it had been secretly ascertained whether in truth it were as the documents said. To these I answered on the spot, aroused with the fervor of faith, that, if it was as written, I would prefer that all those who had seen it would know it, than that—in case I had investigated the matter in secret—all those who had not seen it would doubt it. Thus we took down the aforesaid altar into our midst; summoned goldsmiths who would carefully open those little compartments, which contained the most sacred arms, where the pieces of crystal that offered their inscriptions to the eye were superimposed upon them; and, God granting,

aperirent, sicut sperabamus, omnia plenarie, Deo annuente,
videntibus cunctis, invenimus.

Causam etiam repositionis reliquiarum in eisdem locellis
invenimus, videlicet quod Karolus imperator tertius, qui
5 eidem altari subjacet gloriose sepultus, ad tuitionem animæ
et corporis de theca imperiali eas sibi assumi et penes se
reponi imperiali edicto assignaverit. Argumentum etiam,
anuli sui depressione signatum, quod valde omnibus placuit,
ibidem reperimus. Nec enim sine causa ante "sanctum" illud
10 altare septem lampades in vasis argenteis, quæ nos quidem
dissoluta refecimus, incessanter tam die quam nocte in sempiternum ardere constituisset, nisi maximam spem et corporis
et animæ in sanctarum reliquiarum repositione credidisset.
Sumptibus enim illarum et anniversarii sui, et suorum refec-
15 tioni, possessionem [203] suam quæ dicitur Ruoilum, cum
appendiciis, sigillis aureis confirmavit. Hinc est etiam quod
in solemnitatibus diversis fere sexaginta magni et honesti
cerei sex, quales alibi in ecclesia aut raro aut nunquam apponuntur, circa idem altare accenduntur. Hinc est etiam quod
20 quotiens altare beati Dionysii, totiens et idem altare nobili
apparatu adornatur.

Crucem etiam mirabilem quantitatis suæ, quæ superposita
est inter altare et tumulum ejusdem Karoli, in cujus medio
fama retinuit confixum nobilissimum monile Nantildis re-
25 ginæ, uxoris Dagoberti regis ecclesiæ fundatoris, aliud vero
in frontem sancti Dionysii (tamen huic minori nullum æqui-
pollere peritissimi artifices testantur), erigi fecimus, maxime
ob reverentiam sanctissimæ boiæ ferreæ, quæ, in carcere
Glaucini sacratissimo collo beati Dionysii innexa, cultum et
30 venerationem tam a nobis quam ab omnibus promeruit.

Ea etiam parte abbas venerabilis Corbeiæ bonæ memoriæ
Robertus, hujus sanctæ ecclesiæ professus et ab infantia nutri-
tus, quem eidem Corbeiensi monasterio abbatem præesse Deo
donante exhibuimus, tabulam argenteam optime deauratam,

we found everything as we had hoped, all complete and before the eyes of everyone.

We also discovered the reason why the relics had been placed in said little compartments, namely, because Charles the third Emperor who, gloriously buried, lies in front of this altar had ordered by Imperial decree that they be taken out for him from the Imperial repository and be placed near him for the protection of his soul and body. We also found there the evidence, sealed with the impression of his ring, by which everyone was exceedingly pleased. Not without reason would he have ordered that seven lamps in silver vessels—which we had remade because they had gone to pieces—should perpetually burn forever, day and night, before this "Holy Altar," had he not placed the highest hopes for his body and soul in this deposition of the sacred relics; inasmuch, for the expense of these and of [the services on] his anniversary, and for the repast of his friends [on this occasion], he allocated, under his golden seals, his possession Rueil with its dependencies. This is also why, at about sixty different celebrations, six big and stately wax candles, such as are rarely or never set up elsewhere in the church, are lit round this altar. And this is also why this altar is decked out with noble ornaments as often as is the altar of the blessed Denis.

We further erected the cross, admirable for its size, which is set up between the altar and the tomb of the same Charles, and to the middle of which is fastened, according to tradition, the most noble necklace of Queen Nanthilda, wife of King Dagobert, the founder of the church (another one, however, [we fastened] to the brow of Saint Denis, and this, though smaller, is equaled by none according to the testimony of the most competent artists); [we did this] chiefly out of reverence for the most sacred Iron Collar which, having circled the most sacred neck of the blessed Denis in the "Prison de Glaucin," has deserved worship and veneration from us and all.

Also, in the same part [of the church] the venerable Abbot Robert of Corbie, of blessed memory, professed in this sacred church and brought up here from childhood—whom we, God granting, had proposed to be placed at the head of said Monastery of Corbie as abbot—has caused to be set up a silver panel, very

pro recognitione professionis suæ et multorum ecclesiæ bene-
ficiorum gratiarum actione, fieri fecit.

XXXIV

CHORUM etiam fratrum, quo valde gravabantur qui
assidue ecclesiæ insistebant servitio, frigiditate marmoris
5 et cupri aliquantisper infirmum in hanc quæ nunc apparet
formam, laboribus eorum compatientes, mutavimus, et propter conventus augmentationem, Deo auxiliante, augmentare
elaboravimus.

[204] Pulpitum etiam antiquum, quod, ammirabile tabu-
10 larum eburnearum subtilissima nostrisque temporibus inre-
parabili sculptura, et antiquarum historiarum descriptione
humanam æstimationem excedebat, recollectis tabulis quæ in
arcarum et sub arcarum repositione diutius fœdabantur, refici,
dextraque parte restitutis animalibus cupreis, ne tanta tamque
15 mirabilis deperiret materia, ad proferendam superius sancti
Evangelii lectionem erigi fecimus. In novitate siquidem ses-
sionis nostræ impedimentum quoddam, quo medium ecclesiæ
muro tenebroso secabatur, ne speciositas ecclesiæ magnitudinis
talibus fuscaretur repagulis, de medio sustolli feceramus.

20 Nec minus nobilem gloriosi regis Dagoberti cathedram, in
qua, ut perhibere solet antiquitas, reges Francorum, suscepto
regni imperio, ad suscipienda optimatum suorum hominia
primum sedere consueverant, tum pro tanti excellentia officii,
tum etiam pro operis ipsius precio, antiquatam et disruptam
25 refici fecimus.

Aquilam vero in medio chori ammirantium tactu frequenti
dedeauratam reaurari fecimus.

Vitrearum etiam novarum præclaram varietatem, ab ea
prima quæ incipit a *Stirps Jesse* in capite ecclesiæ usque ad
30 eam quæ superest principali portæ in introitu ecclesiæ, tam
superius quam inferius magistrorum multorum de diversis

well gilded, in recognition of his profession and as an act of gratitude for many benefactions from this church.

XXXIV

WE also changed to its present form, sympathizing with their discomfort, the choir of the brethren, which had been detrimental to health for a long time on account of the coldness of the marble and the copper and had caused great hardship to those who constantly attended service in church; and because of the increase in our community (with the help of God), we endeavored to enlarge it.

We also caused the ancient pulpit, which—admirable for the most delicate and nowadays irreplaceable sculpture of its ivory tablets—surpassed human evaluation also by the depiction of antique subjects, to be repaired after we had reassembled those tablets which were moldering all too long in, and even under, the repository of the money chests; on the right side we restored to their places the animals of copper lest so much and admirable material perish, and had [the whole] set up so that the reading of Holy Gospels might be performed in a more elevated place. In the beginning of our abbacy we had already put out of the way a certain obstruction which cut as a dark wall through the central nave of the church, lest the beauty of the church's magnitude be obscured by such barriers.

Further, we saw to it, both on account of its so exalted function and of the value of the work itself, that the famous throne of the glorious King Dagobert, worn with age and dilapidated, was restored. On it, as ancient tradition relates, the kings of the Franks, after having taken the reins of government, used to sit in order to receive, for the first time, the homage of their nobles.

Also we had regilded the Eagle in the middle of the choir which had become rubbed bare through the frequent touch of admirers.

Moreover, we caused to be painted, by the exquisite hands of many masters from different regions, a splendid variety of new windows, both below and above; from that first one which begins [the series] with the *Tree of Jesse* in the chevet of the church to that which is installed above the principal door in the church's

nationibus manu exquisita depingi fecimus. Una quarum de materialibus ad immaterialia excitans, Paulum apostolum molam ver-[205]tere, prophetas saccos ad molam apportare repræsentat. Sunt itaque ejus materiæ versus isti:

5
    Tollis agendo molam de furfure, Paule, farinam.
       Mosaicæ legis intima nota facis.
    Fit de tot granis verus sine furfure panis,
       Perpetuusque cibus noster et angelicus.

Item in eadem vitrea, ubi aufertur velamen de facie
10 Moysi:

    Quod Moyses velat, Christi doctrina revelat.
    Denudant legem qui spoliant Moysen.

In eadem vitrea, super arcam fœderis:

15
    Fœderis ex arca Christi cruce sistitur ara;
       Fœdere majori vult ibi vita mori.

Item in eadem, ubi solvunt librum leo et agnus:

    Qui Deus est magnus, librum Leo solvit et Agnus.
    Agnus sive Leo fit caro juncta Deo.

In alia vitrea, ubi filia Pharaonis invenit Moysen in fiscella:

20
    Est in fiscella Moyses Puer ille, puella
       Regia mente pia quem fovet Ecclesia.

In eadem vitrea, ubi Moysi Dominus apparuit in igne rubi:

25
    Sicut conspicitur rubus hic ardere, nec ardet,
    Sic divo plenus hoc ardet ab igne, nec ardet.

[206] Item in eadem vitrea, ubi Pharao cum equitatu suo in mare demergitur:

    Quod baptisma bonis, hoc militiæ Pharaonis
    Forma facit similis, causaque dissimilis.

entrance. One of these, urging us onward from the material to the immaterial, represents the Apostle Paul turning a mill, and the Prophets carrying sacks to the mill. The verses of this subject are these:

> "By working the mill, thou, Paul, takest the flour out
> of the bran.
> Thou makest known the inmost meaning of the Law of
> Moses.
> From so many grains is made the true bread without bran,
> Our and the angels' perpetual food."

Also in the same window, where the veil is taken off the face of Moses:

> "What Moses veils the doctrine of Christ unveils.
> They who despoil Moses bare the Law."

In the same window, above the Ark of the Covenant;

> "On the Ark of the Covenant is established the altar
> with the Cross of Christ;
> Here Life wishes to die under a greater covenant."

Also in the same [window], where the Lion and Lamb unseal the Book:

> "He Who is the great God, the Lion and the Lamb, unseals
> the Book.
> The Lamb or Lion becomes the flesh joined to God."

In another window, where the daughter of Pharaoh finds Moses in the ark:

> "Moses in the ark is that Man-Child Whom the maiden
> Royal, the Church, fosters with pious mind."

In the same window, where the Lord appeared to Moses in the burning bush:

> "Just as this bush is seen to burn yet is not burned,
> So he who is full of this fire Divine burns with it yet
> is not burned."

Also in the same [window], where Pharaoh is submerged in the sea with his horsemen:

> "What Baptism does to the good, that does to the
> soldiery of Pharaoh
> A like form but an unlike cause."

Item in eadem, ubi Moyses exaltat serpentem æneum:

Sicut serpentes serpens necat æneus omnes,
Sic exaltatus hostes necat in cruce Christus.

In eadem vitrea, ubi Moyses accipit legem in monte:

5   Lege data Moysi, juvat illam gratia Christi.
       Gratia *vivificat, littera mortificat.*[29]

Unde, quia magni constant mirifico opere sumptuque profuso vitri vestiti et saphirorum materia,[30] tuitioni et refectioni
earum ministerialem magistrum, sicut etiam ornamentis
10 aureis et argenteis peritum aurifabrum, constituimus, qui et
præbendas suas et quod eis super hoc visum est, videlicet ab
altari nummos et a communi fratrum horreo annonam, suscipiant, et ab eorum providentia numquam se absentent.

Septem quoque candelabra, quoniam ea quæ Karolus
15 imperator beato Dionysio contulerat sua vetustate dissipata
apparebant, opere smaltito et optime deaurato componi fecimus.

[XXXIV A]

VASA etiam, tam de auro quam preciosis lapidibus, ad
Dominicæ mensæ servicium, præter illa quæ reges Fran-
20 corum et devoti ecclesiæ eidem officio deputaverunt,[31] beato
Dionysio debita devotione adquisivimus; magnum videlicet
calicem aureum septies viginti [207] unciarum auri, gemmis
preciosis, scilicet jacinthis et topaziis ornatum, pro alio, qui
tempore antecessoris nostri vadimonio perierat, restitui ela-
25 boravimus.

Aliud etiam vas preciosissimum de lapide prasio ad formam navis exsculptum, quod rex Ludovicus Philippi per
decennium fere vadimonio amiserat, cum nobis ad videndum
oblatum fuisset, ejusdem regis concessione sexaginta marcis
30 argenti comparatum cum quibusdam floribus coronæ imperatricis beato Dionysio obtulimus. Quod videlicet vas, tam pro

[29] Cf. *II Corinthians* III, 6: "nam littera occidit et spiritus vivificat."
[30] Should probably read *materiæ*.
[31] ⟨See Panofsky, Bib. 132, p. 120.⟩

Also in the same [window], where Moses raises the brazen serpent:

> "Just as the brazen serpent slays all serpents,
> So Christ, raised on the Cross, slays His enemies."

In the same window, where Moses receives the Law on the mount:

> "After the Law has been given to Moses the grace of
>   Christ invigorates it.
> Grace *giveth life, the letter killeth*."

Now, because [these windows] are very valuable on account of their wonderful execution and the profuse expenditure of painted glass and sapphire glass, we appointed an official master craftsman for their protection and repair, and also a skilled goldsmith for the gold and silver ornaments, who would receive their allowances and what was adjudged to them in addition, viz., coins from the altar and flour from the common storehouse of the brethren, and who would never neglect their duty to look after these [works of art].

We further caused to be composed seven candlesticks of enamelled and excellently gilded [metal] work, because those which Emperor Charles had offered to the blessed Denis appeared to be ruined by age.

[XXXIV A]

ALSO, with the devotion due to the blessed Denis, we acquired vessels of gold as well as of precious stones for the service of the Table of God, in addition to those which the kings of the Franks and those devoted to the church had donated for this service. Specifically we caused to be made a big golden chalice of 140 ounces of gold adorned with precious gems, viz., hyacinths and topazes, as a substitute for another one which had been lost as a pawn in the time of our predecessor.

We also offered to the blessed Denis, together with some flowers from the crown of the Empress, another most precious vessel of prase, carved into the form of a boat, which King Louis, son of Philip, had left in pawn for nearly ten years; we had purchased it with the King's permission for sixty marks of silver when it had been offered to us for inspection. It is an established fact that this

preciosi lapidis qualitate quam integra sui quantitate miri-
ficum, inclusorio sancti Eligii opere constat ornatum, quod
omnium aurificum judicio preciosissimum æstimatur.

Vas quoque aliud, quod instar justæ berilli aut cristalli
5 videtur, cum in primo itinere Aquitaniæ regina noviter de-
sponsata domino regi Ludovico dedisset, pro magno amoris
munere nobis rex, nos vero sanctis Martyribus dominis nostris
ad libandum divinæ mensæ affectuosissime contulimus. Cujus
donationis seriem in eodem vase, gemmis auroque ornato,
10 versiculis quibusdam intitulavimus:

> Hoc vas sponsa dedit Aanor regi Ludovico,
> Mitadolus avo, mihi rex, Sanctisque Sugerus.

Comparavimus etiam præfati altaris officiis calicem preciosum, de uno et continuo sardonice (quod est de *"sardio"* et
15 *"onice"*), quo uno usque adeo sardii rubor a nigredine onichini
proprietatem variando discrimi-[208]nat, ut altera in al-
teram proprietatem usurpare inniti æstimetur.

Vas quoque aliud, huic ipsi materia, non forma persimile,
ad instar amphoræ adjunximus, cujus versiculi sunt isti:

20
> Dum libare Deo gemmis debemus et auro,
> Hoc ego Suggerius[32] offero vas Domino.

Lagenam quoque præclaram, quam nobis comes Blesensis
Theobaldus in eodem vase destinavit, in quo ei rex Siciliæ
illud transmiserat, et aliis in eodem officio gratanter apposui-
25 mus.

Vascula etiam cristallina, quæ in capella nostra quotidiano
servitio altaris assignaveramus, ibidem reposuimus.

Nec minus porphyriticum vas sculptoris et politoris manu
ammirabile factum, cum per multos annos in scrinio vacasset,
30 de amphora in aquilæ formam transferendo auri argentique
materia altaris servicio adaptavimus, et versus hujusmodi
eidem vasi inscribi fecimus:

> Includi gemmis lapis iste meretur et auro.
> Marmor erat, sed in his marmore carior est.

[32] ⟨Cf. above, p. 46, line 19.⟩

vessel, admirable for the quality of the precious stone as well as for the latter's unimpaired quantity, is adorned with "verroterie cloisonnée" work by St. Eloy which is held to be most precious in the judgment of all goldsmiths.

Still another vase, looking like a pint bottle of beryl or crystal, which the Queen of Aquitaine had presented to our Lord King Louis as a newly wed bride on their first voyage, and the King to us as a tribute of his great love, we offered most affectionately to the Divine Table for libation. We have recorded the sequence of these gifts on the vase itself, after it had been adorned with gems and gold, in some little verses:

> "As a bride, Eleanor gave this vase to King Louis,
> Mitadolus to her grandfather, the King to me, and
>   Suger to the Saints."

We also procured for the services at the aforesaid altar a precious chalice out of one solid sardonyx, which [word] derives from "sardius" and "onyx"; in which one [stone] the sard's red hue, by varying its property, so keenly vies with the blackness of the onyx that one property seems to be bent on trespassing upon the other.

Further we added another vase shaped like a ewer, very similar to the former in material but not in form, whose little verses are these:

> "Since we must offer libations to God with gems and gold,
> I, Suger, offer this vase to the Lord."

We also gladly added to the other vessels for the same office an excellent gallon vase, which Count Thibaut of Blois had conveyed to us in the same case in which the King of Sicily had sent it to him.

Also we deposited in the same place the little crystal vases which we had assigned to the daily service in our [private] chapel.

And further we adapted for the service of the altar, with the aid of gold and silver material, a porphyry vase, made admirable by the hand of the sculptor and polisher, after it had lain idly in a chest for many years, converting it from a flagon into the shape of an eagle; and we had the following verses inscribed on this vase:

> "This stone deserves to be enclosed in gems and gold.
> It was marble, but in these [settings] it is more precious than marble."

Pro quibus omnibus Deo omnipotenti et sanctis Martyribus grates referimus, quod sanctissimo altari, cui sub præceptione sanctæ regulæ nos a puero offerri voluit, unde ei honorifice serviremus copiose largiri non renuit.

5 [209] Quia ergo divina beneficia non occultare, sed prædicare utile et honestum cognovimus, palliorum quod divina manus tempore amministrationis nostræ huic sanctæ ecclesiæ contulit augmentum designavimus; implorantes ut in anniversario, ad propiciandam divinæ majestatis excellentiam et

10 fratrum devotionem ampliandam, et successorum abbatum exemplum, exponantur. Nec enim pro tot et tantis commissis, vel enormitate scelerum meorum, tam sera quam rara satisfacere pœnitentia sufficit, nisi universalis Ecclesiæ suffragiis innitamur.

For all this we thank Almighty God and the Holy Martyrs, since He has not refused abundantly to bestow upon the most sacred altar, at which He willed us to be offered as a child under the precepts of our holy rule, that with which we may serve Him in worthy manner.

And since we are convinced that it is useful and becoming not to hide but to proclaim Divine benefactions, we have destined [for this purpose] that increase in textiles which the Hand Divine has granted to this sacred church in the time of our administration; we urge that they be laid out on our anniversary in order to propitiate the supreme power of Divine Majesty and to enhance the devotion of the brethren, and as an example for the succeeding abbots. For late and scanty penance cannot atone for so many and so great [sins] as I have committed, nor for the enormity of my crimes, unless we rely upon the intercession of the Universal Church.

LIBELLUS ALTER
DE CONSECRATIONE ECCLESIÆ
SANCTI DIONYSII

I

DIVINORUM humanorumque disparitatem unius et
singularis summæque rationis vis admirabilis contem-
perando coæquat; et quæ originis inferioritate et naturæ con-
trarietate invicem repugnare videntur, ipsa sola unius supe-
5 rioris moderatæ armoniæ convenientia grata concopulat.
Cujus profecto summæ et æternæ rationis participatione qui
gloriosi effici innituntur, crebro in solio mentis argutæ quasi
pro tribunali residentes, de concertatione continua similium et
dissimilium, et contrariorum inventioni et judicio insistunt; in
10 æternæ sapientiæ rationis fonte, charitate ministrante, unde
bello intestino et seditioni interiori obsistant, salubriter exhau-
riunt, spiritualia corporalibus, æterna deficientibus præpo-
nentes. Corporeæ sensualitatis, exteriorum sensuum molestias
et gravissimas angarias postponunt; ab earum oppressione
15 seipsos sublevantes, solidissimam mentis aciem in spem æternæ infigentes remunerationis, æternitati tantum studiose obse-
quuntur. Carnalia desideria in admirationem et spectaculum
aliorum obliviscuntur; summæ rationis hoc modo et æternæ
beatitudinis consortio, promittente unigenito Dei filio: *In*
20 *patientia possidebitis animas vestras,*[1] se gloriosæ conscien-
[214]tiæ merito uniri gratulantur. Quod tamen conditionis
primæ corruptione depressa et graviter sauciata humanitas,
præsentia potius amplectens quam futura expectans, nullo
modo sustineret, si non etiam rationis et intelligentiæ humanæ
25 rationabilis summæ et divinæ caritatis copiosa administratio
hoc ipsum effectui mancipare misericorditer suppeditaret.
Unde legitur: *Misericordia ejus super omnia opera ejus.*[2] Ex
quo quidem cum aliis audacter et veraciter profitemur, quod,
quanto sola misericordia salvos nos facit per lavacrum regene-

---

[1] *Luke* XXI, 19.
[2] *Psalm* CXLIV, 9; the Vulgate text has *miserationes*.

THE OTHER LITTLE BOOK ON
THE CONSECRATION OF THE CHURCH
OF ST.-DENIS

I

THE admirable power of one unique and supreme reason equalizes by proper composition the disparity between things human and Divine; and what seems mutually to conflict by inferiority of origin and contrariety of nature is conjoined by the single, delightful concordance of one superior, well-tempered harmony. Those indeed who crave to be glorified by a participation in this supreme and eternal reason often devote their attention to this continual controversy of the similar and dissimilar, and to the trial and sentence of the litigant parties, sitting on the throne of the acute mind as though on a tribunal. With the aid of loving-kindness, whereby they may withstand internal strife and inner sedition, they drink wholesomely from the fountain of the reason of eternal wisdom, preferring that which is spiritual to that which is corporeal, that which is eternal to that which is perishable. They set aside the vexations and most grievous anxieties of corporal sensuality and of the exterior senses; elevating themselves from the oppression by these, focusing the undivided vision of their mind upon the hope of eternal reward, they zealously seek only that which is eternal. They forget carnal desires to the admiration and amazement of others; thus, through communion with supreme reason and eternal bliss, they rejoice—according to the promise of the only-begotten Son of God: *In your patience possess ye your souls*—in being deservedly united with the Glorious Consciousness. Yet human nature, debased and gravely impaired by the corruption of its first condition, embracing the present rather than expecting the future, would in no wise be strong enough for this, were it not for the fact that the abundant aid given to human reason and rational intelligence by supreme and Divine lovingkindness mercifully enables us to carry it into effect. Hence we read: *His tender mercies are over all His works.* Therefore we and others profess boldly and truthfully that, the more Mercy alone

rationis et renovationis Spiritus sancti, tanto nos gratissimo
purificatæ mentis holocausto pro toto velle et posse justitiam
nostram, quantumcumque et ipse dederit, supplici ei devotione offerre elaboremus: ut ipse qui potest ut Deus, qui debet
5 ut creator, si non resistimus disparitatem istam periculosam in
nobis parificet, contrarietatis intestinæ inimicitias, quas in
amicitiæ ejus amissione prima prævaricatione incurrimus, ea
ineffabili caritate qua divinitatem suam captivatæ humanitati
nostræ ineffabiliter et inseparabiliter univit, dissolvat, sopita
10 carnalitatis gravissima molestia, tumultuque vitiorum sedato,
pacato habitaculo interiora repugnantia pacificet; ut mente et
corpore expediti, gratam ei offerentes servitutem, beneficio-
rum etiam immensorum ejus circa nos et nobilem cui nos
præferri sustinuit ecclesiam replicare et prædicare valeamus
15 largitatem; ne, si muti in laudem ejus extiterimus, beneficio-
rum ejus ob hoc defectum incurramus et vocem illam terribiliter audiamus: *Non est inventus qui rediret et daret gloriam
Deo.*[3]

[215] *Justificati igitur ex fide*, pace nostra interiori, secun-
20 dum Apostolum, *pacem apud Deum habentes,*[4] unum et inter
multos singulare divinæ largitatis beneficium, more eorum qui
ad gratificandum impertita dona donatoribus suis ultro refe-
runt, in medium proferentes, gloriosam et Deo[5] dignam sanctæ hujus ecclesiæ consecrationem, pretiosissimorum marty-
25 rum dominorum et apostolorum nostrorum[6] Dionysii, Rustici
et Eleutherii, et aliorum sanctorum quorum prompto inniti-
mur patrocinio, sacratissimam translationem ad successorum
notitiam stylo assignare elaboravimus; qua de causa, quo
ordine, quam solemniter, quibus etiam personis ad ipsum[7]
30 actum sit reponentes, ut et divinæ propitiationi pro tanto
munere condignas pro posse nostro gratiarum actiones refera-
mus, et sanctorum protectorum nostrorum, tam pro impensa
tanti operis cura quam pro tantæ solemnitatis adnotatione,
opportunam apud Deum obtineamus intercessionem.

[3] *Luke* XVII, 18.
[4] *Romans* V, 1; the Vulgate text has *ad Deum.*
[5-6] (See Panofsky, Bib. 132, p. 119.)
[7] *idipsum* has been corrected to *ad ipsum.*

saves us by the bath of regeneration and renovation through the Holy Spirit, the more we must endeavor, with all our will and power, to offer to Him with humble devotion, as the most acceptable burnt offering of a purified mind, our own righteousness, however much He Himself may have given [to us]. So that He Who can inasmuch as He is God, and must inasmuch as He is the Creator, may equalize (unless we resist) that perilous inequality within ourselves; so that He may resolve, with that ineffable loving-kindness by which He has ineffably and inseparably united His Divinity with our enslaved humanity, those conflicts of internal strife in which we have become involved by the loss of His friendship through our first prevarication; so that He, having becalmed the most grievous vexations of carnality and stilled the turmoil of vices, may appease the inner struggles in a pacified dwelling; so that we, unfettered in mind and body [and] offering to Him our joyful servitude, may be able to reveal and to proclaim the generosity of His immeasurable beneficence in regard to ourselves and to the glorious church of which He has suffered us to become the head; lest, if we were standing mute at His praise, we might therefore incur a diminution of His benefactions and hear that terrible voice *There are not found that returned to give glory to God.*

Therefore, being justified by faith, according to the Apostle, *we have peace with God* through our own inner peace; and in the manner of those who, out of gratitude, return of their own accord the gifts bestowed to those who have bestowed them, we make publicly known that one favor, singular among many, of Divine generosity: we have endeavored to commit to writing, for the attention of our successors, the glorious and worthy consecration of this church sacred to God [and] the most solemn translation of the most precious martyrs Denis, Rusticus and Eleutherius, our Patrons and Apostles, as well as of the other saints upon whose ready tutelage we rely. We have put down why, in what order, how solemnly and also by what persons this was performed, in order to give thanks as worthy as we can to Divine grace for so great a gift, and to obtain, both for the care expended on so great an enterprise and for the description of so great a celebration, the favorable intercession of our Holy Protectors with God.

II

GLORIOSUS et famosus rex Francorum Dagobertus, vir etsi in regni administratione magnanimitate regia conspicuus, nihilominus tamen Ecclesiæ Dei devotus, cum ad declinandam patris sui Clotharii magni[8] intolerabilem iram
5 Catulliacum vicum aufugisset, et sanctorum Martyrum ibidem quiescentium effigies venerandas, tanquam pulcherrimos viros niveis vestibus comptos, servitium suum requirere et auxilium promittere incunctanter voce et opere comperisset, basilicam Sanctorum regia munificentia fabricatum iri affectu
10 mirabili imperavit. Quam cum mirifica mar-[216]morearum columnarum varietate componens, copiosis purissimi auri et argenti thesauris inæstimabiliter locupletasset, ipsiusque parietibus et columnis et arcubus auro textas[9] vestes margaritarum varietatibus multipliciter exornatas suspendi fecisset,
15 quatinus aliarum ecclesiarum ornamentis præcellere videretur et, omnimodis incomparabili nitore vernans et omni terrena[10] pulchritudine compta, inæstimabili decore splendesceret: hoc solum ei defuit quod quam oporteret magnitudinem non admisit. Non quod aliquid ejus devotioni aut voluntati deesset,
20 sed quod forsitan tunc temporis in primitiva Ecclesia nulla adhuc aut major aut æqualis existeret, aut quod brevior fulgorantis auri et splendorem gemmarum propinquitati arridentium oculorum acutius delectabiliusque refundendo, ultra satis quam si major fabricaretur irradiaret.
25 Hujus brevitatis egregiæ grata occasione, numerositate fidelium crescente et ad suffragia Sanctorum crebro confluente, tantas præfata basilica sustinere consuevit molestias, ut sæpius, in solemnibus videlicet diebus, admodo plena per omnes valvas turbarum sibi occurrentium superfluitatem refunderet, et
30 non solum intrantes non intrare, verum etiam qui jam intraverant præcedentium expulsus exire compelleret. Videres aliquando (mirabile visu), quod innitentibus ingredi ad venerationem et deosculationem sanctarum reliquiarum, Clavi et Coronæ Domini, tanta congestæ multitudinis opponebatur

---

[8] ⟨See Panofsky, Bib. 132, p. 119.⟩
[9] *tectas* has been corrected to *textas*, a reading attested by the *Gesta Dagoberti* (see below, p. 225).
[10] ⟨See Panofsky, Bib. 132, p. 119.⟩

II

WHEN the glorious and famous King of the Franks, Dagobert, notable for his royal magnanimity in the administration of his kingdom and yet no less devoted to the Church of God,
had fled to the village of Catulliacum in order to evade the intolerable wrath of his father Clothaire the Great, and when he had
learned that the venerable images of the Holy Martyrs who rested
there—appearing to him as very beautiful men clad in snow-white
garments—requested his service and unhesitatingly promised him
their aid with words and deeds, he decreed with admirable affection
that a basilica of the Saints be built with regal magnificence. When
he had constructed this [basilica] with a marvelous variety of
marble columns he enriched it incalculably with treasures of purest
gold and silver and hung on its walls, columns and arches tapestries
woven of gold and richly adorned with a variety of pearls, so that
it might seem to excel the ornaments of all other churches and,
blooming with incomparable luster and adorned with every terrestrial beauty, might shine with inestimable splendor. Only one thing
was wanting in him: that he did not allow for the size that was
necessary. Not that anything was lacking in his devotion or good
will; but perhaps there existed thus far, at that time of the Early
Church, no [church] either greater or [even] equal in size; or
perhaps [he thought that] a smallish one—reflecting the splendor
of gleaming gold and gems to the admiring eyes more keenly and
delightfully because they were nearer—would glow with greater
radiance than if it were built larger.

Through a fortunate circumstance attending this singular smallness—the number of the faithful growing and frequently gather-
ing to seek the intercession of the Saints—the aforesaid basilica had
come to suffer grave inconveniences. Often on feast days, completely filled, it disgorged through all its doors the excess of the
crowds as they moved in opposite directions, and the outward
pressure of the foremost ones not only prevented those attempting
to enter from entering but also expelled those who had already
entered. At times you could see, a marvel to behold, that the
crowded multitude offered so much resistance to those who strove
to flock in to worship and kiss the holy relics, the Nail and Crown

repugnantia, ut inter innumera populorum millia ex ipsa sui compressione nullus pedem movere valeret, nullus aliud ex ipsa sui constrictione quam sicut statua marmorea stare, stupere, quod unum supererat, vociferare. Mulierum autem
5 tanta et tam in-[217]tolerabilis erat angustia, ut in commixtione virorum fortium sicut prelo depressæ, quasi imaginata morte exsanguem faciem exprimere, more parturientium terribiliter conclamare, plures earum miserabiliter decalcatas, pio virorum suffragio super capita hominum exaltatas, tan-
10 quam pavimento abhorreres[11] incedere, multas etiam extremo singultantes spiritu in prato fratrum, cunctis desperantibus, anhelare. Fratres etiam insignia Dominicæ passionis adventantibus exponentes, eorum angariis et contentionibus succumbentes, nullo divertere habentes, per fenestras cum reliquiis
15 multoties effugerunt. Quod cum scholaris puer inter fratres erudirer audiebam, extra juvenis dolebam, maturus corrigi affectuose appetebam. *Cum autem placuit illi, qui me segregavit ex utero matris meæ, et vocavit per gratiam suam,*[12] meritis etiam repugnantibus, parvitatem meam hujus sanctæ
20 ecclesiæ tantæ præficere administrationi, sola Dei omnipotentis ineffabili misericordia præfatæ molestiæ correctioni sanctorum Martyrum dominorum nostrorum suffragio raptus, ad augmentationem præfati loci toto animo, tota mentis affectione accelerare proposuimus: qui nunquam, si tanta, tam
25 necessaria, tam utilis et honesta non exigeret opportunitas, manum supponere vel cogitare præsumeremus.

Quia igitur in anteriori parte, ab aquilone, principali ingressu principalium valvarum porticus artus hinc [218] et inde gemellis, nec altis, nec aptis multum, sed minantibus
30 ruinam, turribus angebatur, ea in parte inito directæ testudinis[13] et geminarum turrium robusto valde fundamento materiali, robustissimo autem spirituali, de quo dicitur: *Fundamentum aliud nemo potest ponere præter id quod positum est, quod est Christus Jesus,*[14] laborare strenue Deo cooperante in-
35 cœpimus. Cujus inæstimabili freti consilio et irrefragabili auxilio, usque adeo in tanto tamque sumptuoso opere profeci-

---

[11] ⟨See Panofsky, Bib. 132, p. 119.⟩   [12] *Galatians* I, 15.
[13] *testitudinis* has been corrected to *testudinis*.   [14] *I Corinthians* III, 11.

of the Lord, that no one among the countless thousands of people because of their very density could move a foot; that no one, because of their very congestion, could [do] anything but stand like a marble statue, stay benumbed or, as a last resort, scream. The distress of the women, however, was so great and so intolerable that you could see with horror how they, squeezed in by the mass of strong men as in a winepress, exhibited bloodless faces as in imagined death; how they cried out horribly as though in labor; how several of them, miserably trodden underfoot [but then] lifted by the pious assistance of men above the heads of the crowd, marched forward as though upon a pavement; and how many others, gasping with their last breath, panted in the cloisters of the brethren to the despair of everyone. Moreover the brethren who were showing the tokens of the Passion of Our Lord to the visitors had to yield to their anger and rioting and many a time, having no place to turn, escaped with the relics through the windows. When I was instructed by the brethren as a schoolboy I used to hear of this; in my youth I deplored it from without; in my mature years I zealously strove to have it corrected. *But when it pleased Him who separated me from my mother's womb, and called me by His grace*, to place insignificant me, although my merits were against it, at the head of the so important administration of this sacred church; then, impelled to a correction of the aforesaid inconvenience only by the ineffable mercy of Almighty God and by the aid of the Holy Martyrs our Patron Saints, we resolved to hasten, with all our soul and all the affection of our mind, to the enlargement of the aforesaid place—we who would never have presumed to set our hand to it, nor even to think of it, had not so great, so necessary, so useful and honorable an occasion demanded it.

Since in the front part, toward the north, at the main entrance with the main doors, the narrow hall was squeezed in on either side by twin towers neither high nor very sturdy but threatening ruin, we began, with the help of God, strenuously to work on this part, having laid very strong material foundations for a straight nave and twin towers, and most strong spiritual ones of which it is said: *For other foundation can no man lay than that is laid, which is Jesus Christ*. Leaning upon God's inestimable counsel and irrefragable aid, we proceeded with this so great and so sumptuous

mus, ut, cum primum pauca expendendo multis, exinde multa expendendo[15] nullis omnino indigeremus, verum etiam habundando fateremur: *Sufficientia nostra ex Deo est.*[16] Materiæ autem validissimæ nova quadraria qualis et quanta
5 nunquam in partibus istis inventa fuerat, Deo donante, occurrit. Cementariorum, lathomorum, sculptorum, et aliorum operariorum solers succedebat frequentia, ut ex hoc et aliis Divinitas ab hoc quod timebamus absolveret, et voluntatem suam nobis confortando et inopinata suppeditando ministra-
10 ret. Conferebam de minimis ad maxima, non plus Salomonianas opes templo quam nostras huic operi sufficere posse, nisi idem ejusdem operis auctor ministratoribus copiose præpararet. Identitas auctoris et operis sufficientiam facit operantis.
15   In agendis siquidem hujusmodi, apprime de convenientia et cohærentia antiqui et novi operis sollicitus, unde marmoreas aut marmoreis æquipollentes habe-[219]remus columnas, cogitando, speculando, investigando per diversas remotarum partium[17] regiones, cum nullam offenderemus, hoc solum
20 mente laborantibus et animo supererat, ut ab urbe (Romæ enim in palatio Diocletiani et aliis termis sæpe mirabiles conspexeramus) ut[18] per mare Mediterraneum tuta classe, exinde per Anglicum, et per tortuosam fluvii Sequanæ reflexionem, eas magno sumptu amicorum, inimicorum etiam Sarraceno-
25 rum proximorum conductu haberemus. Multis annis, multis temporibus cogitando, quæritando angebamur: cum subito larga Omnipotentis munificentia, laboribus nostris condescendens, quod nec cogitare nec opinari liceret, decentes et peroptimas in admirationem omnium sanctorum Martyrum merito
30 revelavit. Unde quanto contra spem et humanam opinionem apto, et nullibi nobis gratiori loco miseratio divina dignata est conferre, tanto majores gratiarum actiones pro tanti remedio laboris operæ pretium duximus rependendo referre. Locus quippe quadrariæ admirabilis prope Pontisaram, castrum

[15] (See Panofsky, Bib. 132, p. 119.)
[16] *II Corinthians* III, 5.
[17] (See Panofsky, Bib. 132, p. 119.)
[18] This second *ut* should be deleted or corrected into *et*.

work to such an extent that, while at first, expending little, we lacked much, afterwards, expending much, we lacked nothing at all and even confessed in our abundance: *Our sufficiency is of God*. Through a gift of God a new quarry, yielding very strong stone, was discovered such as in quality and quantity had never been found in these regions. There arrived a skillful crowd of masons, stonecutters, sculptors and other workmen, so that—thus and otherwise—Divinity relieved us of our fears and favored us with Its goodwill by comforting us and by providing us with unexpected [resources]. I used to compare the least to the greatest: Solomon's riches could not have sufficed for his Temple any more than did ours for this work had not the same Author of the same work abundantly supplied His attendants. The identity of the author and the work provides a sufficiency for the worker.

In carrying out such plans my first thought was for the concordance and harmony of the ancient and the new work. By reflection, by inquiry, and by investigation through different regions of remote districts, we endeavored to learn where we might obtain marble columns or columns the equivalent thereof. Since we found none, only one thing was left to us, distressed in mind and spirit: we might obtain them from Rome (for in Rome we had often seen wonderful ones in the Palace of Diocletian and other Baths) by safe ships through the Mediterranean, thence through the English Sea and the tortuous windings of the River Seine, at great expense to our friends and even by paying passage money to our enemies, the near-by Saracens. For many years, for a long time, we were perplexed, thinking and making inquiries—when suddenly the generous munificence of the Almighty, condescending to our labors, revealed to the astonishment of all and through the merit of the Holy Martyrs, what one would never have thought or imagined: very fine and excellent [columns]. Therefore, the greater acts of grace, contrary to hope and human expectation, Divine mercy had deigned to bestow by a suitable place where it could not be more agreeable to us, the greater [acts of gratitude] we thought it worth our effort to offer in return for the remedy of so great an anguish. For near Pontoise, a town adjacent to the confines of our territory, there [was found] a wonderful quarry [which] from ancient times had offered a deep chasm (hollowed out, not by

terrarum nostrarum confinio collimitans, vallem profundam
non natura, sed industria concavam, molarum cæsoribus sui
quæstum ab antiquo offerebat; nihil egregium hactenus pro-
ferens, exordium tantæ utilitatis tanto et tam divino ædificio,
5 quasi primitias Deo sanctisque Martyribus, ut arbitramur,
reservabat. Quotiens autem columnæ ab imo declivo funibus
innodatis extrahebantur, tam nostrates quam loci affines bene
devoti, nobiles et innobiles, brachiis, pectoribus et [220]
lacertis funibus adstricti, vice trahentium animalium educe-
10 bant; et per medium castri declivium diversi officiales, relictis
officiorum suorum instrumentis, vires proprias itineris diffi-
cultati offerentes obviabant, quanta poterant ope Deo sanctisque Martyribus obsequentes. Unde nobile quoddam et
dignum relatione contigit miraculum, quod nos ipsi ab assi-
15 stentibus addiscentes ad laudem Omnipotentis Sanctorumque
suorum calamo et atramento adsignare decrevimus.

III

QUADAM itaque die, cum imbrium refusione turbatum
aera tenebrosa obtexisset opacitas, adventantibus ad quadrariam plaustris, qui adjutores esse consueverant operandi
20 pro impluvii infestatione seipsos absentaverunt. Bubulcis[19]
vero querentibus et reclamantibus se otio vacare, operarios
præstolantes suspendere, usque adeo clamando institerunt,
quod quidam imbecilles et debiles cum pueris aliquibus numero decem et septem, præsente, nisi fallor, sacerdote, ad
25 quadrariam acceleraverunt, unamque cordarum assumentes,
columnæ innectentes, aliam sudem in terra jacentem dimise-
runt. Neque enim erat qui ea[20] trahere inniteretur. Animatus
itaque grex pusillus pio zelo: "Sancte," inquiunt, "Dionysi,
pro teipso vacantem accipiens sudem, si placet, nos adjuva.
30 Non enim nobis, si non poterimus, imputare poteris." Moxque fortiter impingentes, quod centum quadraginta aut minus
centum graviter ab ima valle extrahere consueverant, ipsi non
per se, quod impossibile esset, sed voluntate Dei et Sanctorum
quos invocabant suffragio [221] extraxerunt, eamque ec-

[19] (See Panofsky, Bib. 132, p. 119.)
[20] Should read *eam.*

nature but by industry) to cutters of millstones for their liveli-
hood. Having produced nothing remarkable thus far, it reserved,
we thought, the beginning of so great a usefulness for so great and
divine a building—as a first offering, as it were, to God and the
Holy Martyrs. Whenever the columns were hauled from the
bottom of the slope with knotted ropes, both our own people and
the pious neighbors, nobles and common folk alike, would tie their
arms, chests, and shoulders to the ropes and, acting as draft animals,
drew the columns up; and on the declivity in the middle of the
town the diverse craftsmen laid aside the tools of their trade and
came out to meet them, offering their own strength against the
difficulty of the road, doing homage as much as they could to God
and the Holy Martyrs. There occurred a wonderful miracle
worthy of telling which we, having heard it ourselves from those
present, have decided to set down with pen and ink for the praise
of the Almighty and His Saints.

III

ON a certain day when, with a downpour of rain, a dark opacity
had covered the turbid air, those accustomed to assist in
the work while the carts were coming down to the quarry went
off because of the violence of the rain. The ox-drivers complained
and protested that they had nothing to do and that the laborers
were standing around and losing time. Clamoring, they grew so
insistent that some weak and disabled persons together with a few
boys—seventeen in number and, if I am not mistaken, with a
priest present—hastened to the quarry, picked up one of the ropes,
fastened it to a column and abandoned another shaft which was
lying on the ground; for there was nobody who would undertake
to haul this one. Thus, animated by pious zeal, the little flock
prayed: "O Saint Denis, if it pleaseth thee, help us by dealing for
thyself with this abandoned shaft, for thou canst not blame us if we
are unable to do it." Then, bearing on it heavily, they dragged
out what a hundred and forty or at least one hundred men had
been accustomed to haul from the bottom of the chasm with difficulty—not alone by themselves, for that would have been impossible, but through the will of God and the assistance of the

clesiæ ad²¹ fabricam in plaustro destinaverunt. Unde per totam propalatum est viciniam Deo omnipotenti hoc opus admodum placere, cum ad laudem et gloriam nominis sui his et
hujusmodi intersignis²² ejus operatoribus elegerit opem de-
5 ferre.

Secundatur et aliud nobile factum memoria dignum, relatione conspicuum, auctoritate prædicandum. Peracto siquidem
magna ex parte opere et compactis novi et antiqui ædificii tabulatis, magnoque deposito quem diu habueramus timore
10 propter illas patulas antiquarum maceriarum rimas, magno-
rum capitellorum et basium columnas deportantium disrup-
tionem exhilarati deaptare sollicitabamur. Cumque pro
trabium inventione tam nostros quam Parisienses lignorum
artifices consuluissemus, responsum nobis est pro eorum existi-
15 matione verum, in finibus istis propter silvarum inopiam minime inveniri posse, vel ab Autissiodorensi pago necessario
devehi oportere. Cumque omnes in hoc ipso consonarent, nos-
que super hoc tam pro laboris magnitudine quam pro operis
longa delatione gravaremur, nocte quadam, a matutinarum
20 obsequio regressus, lecto cogitare cœpi meipsum per omnes
partium istarum silvas debere procedere, circumquaque perlustrare, moras istas et labores, si hic inveniri possent, alleviare. Moxque rejectis curis aliis, summo mane arripiens, cum
carpentariis et trabium mensuris ad silvam quæ dicitur Ivilina
25 acceleravimus. Cumque per terram nostram Capreolensis
vallis transiremus, accitis servientibus nostris nostrarum
[222] custodibus et aliarum silvarum peritis, adjurando fide
et sacramento eos consuluimus, si ejus mensuræ ibidem trabes
invenire quocumque labore valeremus. Qui subridentes, si
30 auderent, potius deriderent; admirantes si nos plane nescire-
mus in tota terra nihil tale inveniri posse, maxime cum Milo
Capreolensis castellanus homo noster, qui medietatem silvæ a
nobis cum alio feodo habet, cum sustinuisset tam a domino
rege quam ab Amalrico de Monte Forti longo tempore guer-

²¹ ⟨See Panofsky, Bib. 132, p. 119.⟩
²² ⟨See Panofsky, Bib. 132, p. 119.⟩

Saints whom they invoked; and they conveyed it to the site of the church on a cart. Thus it was made known throughout the neighborhood that this work pleased Almighty God exceedingly, since for the praise and glory of His name He had chosen to give His help to those who performed it by this and similar signs.

As a second instance there is related another notable event worthy of remembrance, remarkable to tell and deserving to be set forth with authority. When the work had been finished in great part, when the stories of the old and the new building had been joined, and when we had laid aside the anxiety we had long felt because of those gaping cracks in the old walls, we undertook with new confidence to repair the damages in the great capitals and in the bases that supported the columns. But when we inquired both of our own carpenters and those of Paris where we might find beams we were told, as was in their opinion true, that such could in no wise be found in these regions owing to the lack of woods; they would inevitably have to be brought hither from the district of Auxerre. All concurred with this view and we were much distressed by this because of the magnitude of the task and the long delay of the work; but on a certain night, when I had returned from celebrating Matins, I began to think in bed that I myself should go through all the forests of these parts, look around everywhere and alleviate those delays and troubles if [beams] could be found here. Quickly disposing of other duties and hurrying up in the early morning, we hastened with our carpenters, and with the measurements of the beams, to the forest called Iveline. When we traversed our possession in the Valley of Chevreuse we summoned through our servants the keepers of our own forests as well as men who knew about the other woods, and questioned them under oath whether we could find there, no matter with how much trouble, any timbers of that measure. At this they smiled, or rather would have laughed at us if they had dared; they wondered whether we were quite ignorant of the fact that nothing of the kind could be found in the entire region, especially since Milon, the Castellan of Chevreuse (our vassal, who holds of us one half of the forest in addition to another fief) had left nothing unimpaired or untouched that could be used for building palisades and bulwarks while he was long subjected to wars both

ras, ad tristegas et propugnacula facienda nihil tale illibatum
vel intactum præteriisset. Nos autem quicquid dicebant res-
puentes quadam fidei nostræ audacia silvam perlustrare cœpimus, et versus quidem primam horam trabem unam mensuræ
5 sufficientem invenimus. Quid ultra? usque ad nonam aut citius
per fruteta, per opacitatem silvarum, per densitatem spina-
rum, duodecim trabes (tot enim necessariæ erant) in admirationem omnium, præsertim circumstantium, assignavimus et
ad basilicam sanctam deportatas cum exultatione novi operis
10 operturæ superponi fecimus, ad laudem et gloriam Domini
Jesu, qui sibi sanctisque Martyribus, a manibus raptorum pro-
tegens, sicut facere voluit, reservaverat. Nec igitur superflua
neque minus continens id circa divina extitit largitio, quæ *in
pondere et mensura*[23] omnia moderari, omnia dare constituit,
15 cum ultra quam oportuit nulla ulterius invenire[24] potuerit.

IV

TANTIS itaque et tam manifestis tantorum ope-[223]
rum intersignis[25] constanter animati, ad præfati perfectionem ædificii instanter properantes, quomodo et quibus personis et quod valde solemniter Deo omnipotenti consecrare-
20 tur deliberantes, accito egregio viro Hugone Rothomagensi
archiepiscopo et aliis venerabilibus episcopis, Odone Belvacensi, Petro Silvanectensi, ad id peragendum multimodam
laudem, magnoque diversarum personarum ecclesiasticarum,
cleri et populi maximo conventu, decantabamus. Qui in medio
25 novi incrementi priorem in consistente[26] dolio benedicentes
aquam, per oratorium sancti Eustachii cum processione exe-
untes per plateam quæ "Panteria," eo quod inibi omnia emp-
tioni et venditioni[27] teruntur, antiquitus vocitatur, per aliam,
quæ in sacro cimeterio aperitur, æream portam revertentes, in
30 æternæ benedictionis et sanctissimi chrismatis delibutione,
veri corporis et sanguinis summi pontificis Jesu-Christi ex-
hibitione, quicquid tanto et tam sancto convenit ædificio devotissime compleverunt: pulcherrimum et angelica mansione
dignum superius oratorium, in honore sanctæ Dei Genitricis

[23] Cf. *Book of Wisdom* XI, 21. [24] Should read *inveniri*.
[25-26] ⟨See Panofsky, Bib. 132, p. 119.⟩
[27] Should read *emptione et venditione* as kindly suggested by Prof. R. Salomon.

by our Lord the King and Amaury de Montfort. We however—scorning whatever they might say—began, with the courage of our faith as it were, to search through the woods; and toward the first hour we found one timber adequate to the measure. Why say more? By the ninth hour or sooner we had, through the thickets, the depths of the forests and the dense, thorny tangles, marked down twelve timbers (for so many were necessary) to the astonishment of all, especially those on the spot; and when they had been carried to the sacred basilica, we had them placed, with exultation, upon the ceiling of the new structure, to the praise and glory of our Lord Jesus, Who, protecting them from the hands of plunderers, had reserved them for Himself and the Holy Martyrs as He wished to do. Thus in this matter Divine generosity, which has chosen to limit and to grant all things *according to weight and measure*, manifested itself as neither excessive nor defective; for not one more [timber] than was needed could be found.

IV

THUS continually encouraged in so great enterprises by so great and manifest signs, we immediately hastened to the completion of the aforesaid building. Having deliberated in what manner, by what persons, and how truly solemnly the church should be consecrated to Almighty God, and having summoned the excellent man, Hugues, Archbishop of Rouen, and the other venerable Bishops, Eudes of Beauvais [and] Peter of Senlis, we chanted in celebration of this ceremony a polyphonic praise amidst a great throng of diverse ecclesiastical personages and an enormous one of clergy and laity. These [three dignitaries] blessed, in the central nave of the new addition, the first water in a vat standing there; they then went out with the procession through the chapel of St. Eustace [and] across the square which from ancient times is called "Panetière" (because everything is worn down there by buying and selling); they returned through the other bronze door which opens onto the sacred cemetery; and they performed with the greatest devotion—by bestowing the unction of the eternal blessing and the most holy chrism, and by exhibiting the true body and blood of the High Priest Jesus Christ—whatever is fitting

semperque[28] virginis Mariæ et sancti Michaelis archangeli omniumque Angelorum, sancti Romani ibidem quiescentis aliorumque multorum sanctorum quorum ibi nomina subtitulata habentur, dedicantes; inferius vero in dextro latere ora-
5 torium in honore sancti Bartholomæi multorumque aliorum sanctorum; in sinistro autem, ubi sanctus requiescere perhibetur Hippolitus, oratorium in honore ejusdem et sanctorum Laurentii, Sixti, Felicissimi, Agapiti aliorumque multorum ad laudem et gloriam Dei omnipotentis. Nos autem tantæ bene-
10 dictionis pro fructu impensi laboris Dei dono [224] participes effici toto affectu desiderantes, quasi pro dote, sicut solet fieri, ad expensas emendorum luminariorum, plateam quandam cimeterio collimitantem juxta ecclesiam sancti Michaelis, quam quater viginti libris a Willelmo Cornillonensi[29] emera-
15 mus, eisdem[30] contulimus oratoriis, ut in sempiternum censum inde[31] habeant. De termino vero hæc est veritatis consistentia, sicut legitur—si tamen non obscuretur!—in aureo super portas, quas ad honorem Dei et Sanctorum deauratas fieri fecimus, epitaphio:

20   Annus millenus[32] centenus et quadragenus
        Annus erat Verbi, quando sacrata fuit.

Igitur post illam, quæ majestatis summæ opitulatione in anteriore parte de oratorio sancti Romani et aliorum celebrata est, consecrationem, nostra qua tam ex ipsa sui prosperitate
25 animabatur devotio, quam ipsa circa Sanctum Sanctorum[33] tanto tempore tam intolerabiliter opprimebat coarctatio, votum nostrum illo convertit: ut præfato vacantes operi, turriumque differendo prosecutionem in superiori parte, augmentationi matris ecclesiæ operam et impensam pro toto posse, pro
30 gratiarum actione eo quod tantillo tantorum regum et abbatum nobilitati succedenti tantum opus divina dignatio reservasset, quam decentius, quam gloriosius rationabiliter effici posset, fieri inniteremur. Communicato siquidem cum fratribus nostris bene devotis consilio, quorum *cor ardens erat de*

---

[28] *semper* has been corrected to *semperque.*
[29] *Corneilensi* has been corrected to *Cornillonensi* (see below, p. 237 f.).
[30-32] (See Panofsky, Bib. 132, p. 119.)
[33] The unintelligible *circa Sanctorum* has been completed into *circa Sanctum Sanctorum* (see below, p. 238).

for so great and so sacred an edifice. They dedicated the upper
chapel, most beautiful and worthy to be the dwelling place of
angels, in honor of the Holy Mother of God, the eternal Virgin
Mary, of St. Michael the Archangel, of All the Angels, of St.
Romanus (who rests in that very place), and of many other saints
whose names are inscribed there. The lower chapel on the right
[they dedicated] in honor of St. Bartholomew and many other
saints; the lower chapel on the left, however, where St. Hippolytus is said to rest, in honor of him and of Sts. Lawrence, Sixtus,
Felicissimus, Agapitus, and many others, to the praise and glory
of Almighty God. But we, desiring with all our heart to be made,
God granting, the participant in so great a blessing as in a fruit
of the expended labor, conferred upon these chapels—as though
for a dowry, as the custom is, to meet the expense of buying lights
—a certain property adjacent to the cemetery, hard by the church
of St. Michael, which we had bought from Guillaume de Cornillon for eighty pounds, so that they might have the rent therefrom in perpetuity. Concerning the date of completion, however,
this is the established truth as it can be read—oh, may it not be obscured!—in the golden inscription above the gilded doors which
we have caused to be made in honor of God and the Saints:

"The year was the One Thousand, One Hundred, and Fortieth
Year of the Word when [this structure] was consecrated."

After the consecration of the Chapel of St. Romanus and others
which, with the help of the Highest Majesty, had been celebrated
in the front part [of the church], our devotion—so much invigorated by its own success, and so long and intolerably distressed by
that congestion around the Holy of Holies—directed our inten-
tions toward another goal: free from the aforesaid work, and
through postponing the completion of the towers in their upper
portions, we would strive with all our might to devote labor and
expense, as fittingly and nobly as it could reasonably be done, to
the enlargement of the church our mother—as an act of gratitude
because Divine condescension had reserved so great a work to so
small a man who was the successor to the nobility of such great
kings and abbots. We communicated this plan to our very devoted
brethren, *whose hearts burned for Jesus while He talked with*

Jesu dum loqueretur eis in via,[34] hoc Deo inspirante [225]
deliberando elegimus, ut propter eam quam divina operatio,
sicut veneranda scripta testantur, propria et manuali extensione ecclesiæ consecrationi antiquæ imposuit benedictionem,
5 ipsis sacratis lapidibus tanquam reliquiis deferremus, illam
quæ tanta exigente necessitate novitas inchoaretur, longitudi-
nis et latitudinis pulchritudine inniteremur nobilitare. Consulte siquidem decretum est illam altiori inæqualem, quæ
super absidem sanctorum dominorum nostrorum corpora reti-
10 nentem operiebat, removeri voltam usque ad superficiem
criptæ cui adhærebat; ut eadem cripta superioritatem sui
accedentibus per utrosque gradus pro pavimento offerret, et
in eminentiori loco Sanctorum lecticas auro et preciosis gemmis adornatas adventantium obtutibus designaret. Provisum
15 est etiam sagaciter ut superioribus columnis et arcubus mediis,
qui in inferioribus in cripta fundatis superponerentur, geometricis et aritmeticis instrumentis medium antiquæ testudinis[35] ecclesiæ augmenti novi medio æquaretur, nec minus
antiquarum quantitas alarum novarum quantitati adaptare-
20 tur; excepto illo urbano et approbato in circuitu oratoriorum
incremento, quo tota clarissimarum[36] vitrearum luce mirabili
et continua interiorem perlustrante pulchritudinem eniteret.

  Ut autem sapienti consilio, dictante Spiritu sancto cujus
unctio de omnibus docet, luculento ordine designatum est quid
25 prosequi proponeremus, collecto virorum illustrium tam episcoporum quam abbatum conventu, accita etiam domini ac
serenissimi regis Francorum Ludovici præsentia,[37] pridie idus
julii, die [226] dominica, ordinavimus ornamentis decoram,
personis celebrem processionem. Quin etiam manibus episco-
30 porum et abbatum insignia Dominicæ Passionis, videlicet
clavum et coronam Domini, et brachium sancti senis Simeonis,
et alia sanctarum reliquiarum patrocinia præferentes, ad de-
fossa faciendis[38] fundamentis præparata loca[39] humiliter ac[40]
devote descendimus. Dein[41] paraclyti Spiritus sancti consola-

---

[34] *Luke* XXIV, 32; the words *de Jesu* and *eis* are absent from the Vulgate
text.
[35-36] ⟨See Panofsky, Bib. 132, p. 119.⟩   [37-39] Cf. below, p. 142, note 4.
[40] ⟨See Panofsky, Bib. 132, p. 119.⟩   [41] Cf. below, p. 142, note 4.

them by the way. Deliberating under God's inspiration, we choose
—in view of that blessing which, by the testimony of venerable
writings, Divine action had bestowed upon the ancient consecration
of the church by the extension of [Christ's] own hand—to respect
the very stones, sacred as they are, as though they were relics;
[and] to endeavor to ennoble the new addition, which was to be
begun under the pressure of so great a need, with the beauty of
length and width. Upon consideration, then, it was decided to remove that vault, unequal to the higher one, which, overhead,
closed the apse containing the bodies of our Patron Saints, all the
way [down] to the upper surface of the crypt to which it adhered;
so that this crypt might offer its top as a pavement to those approaching by either of the two stairs, and might present the chasses
of the Saints, adorned with gold and precious gems, to the visitors'
glances in a more elevated place. Moreover, it was cunningly provided that—through the upper columns and central arches which
were to be placed upon the lower ones built in the crypt—the
central nave of the old nave should be equalized, by means of geometrical and arithmetical instruments, with the central nave of the
new addition; and, likewise, that the dimensions of the old side-
aisles should be equalized with the dimensions of the new side-
aisles, except for that elegant and praiseworthy extension, in [the
form of] a circular string of chapels, by virtue of which the whole
[church] would shine with the wonderful and uninterrupted light
of most luminous windows, pervading the interior beauty.

Thus, when, with wise counsel and under the dictation of the
Holy Ghost Whose unction instructs us in all things, that which
we proposed to carry out had been designed with perspicuous order,
we brought together an assembly of illustrious men, both bishops
and abbots, and also requested the presence of our Lord, the Most
Serene King of the Franks, Louis. On Sunday, the day before the
Ides of July, we arranged a procession beautiful by its ornaments
and notable by its personages. Carrying before ourselves, in the
hands of the bishops and the abbots, the insignia of Our Lord's
Passion, viz., the Nail and the Crown of the Lord, also the arm
of the aged St. Simeon and the tutelage of other holy relics, we
descended with humble devotion to the excavations made ready
for the foundations. Then, when the consolation of the Comforter,

tione invocata, ut bonum domus Dei principium bono fine con-
cluderet, cum primum ipsi episcopi ex aqua benedicta dedicationis factæ proximo quinto idus junii propriis confecissent
manibus cementum, primos lapides imposuerunt, hymnum
5 Deo dicentes, et *Fundamenta ejus*[42] usque ad finem psalmi
solemniter decantantes. Ipse enim serenissimus rex intus de-
scendens propriis manibus suum imposuit; nos quoque, et
multi alii tam abbates quam religiosi viri lapides suos imposuerunt; quidam etiam gemmas, ob amorem et reverentiam Jesu
10 Christi, decantantes: *Lapides preciosi omnes muri tui.*[43] Nos
igitur tanta et tam festiva tam sancti fundamenti positione
exhilarati, de peragendo solliciti, varietatem temporum, dimi-
nutionem personarum et mei ipsius defectum pertimescentes,
communi fratrum consilio, assistentium persuasione, domini
15 regis assensu, annalem redditum his explendis constituimus,
videlicet: centum quinquaginta libras de gazofilacio (id est de
oblationibus altaris et reliquiarum, centum in Indicto et quinquaginta in festo sancti Dionysii); quinquaginta etiam de
possessione sita in Belsa, quæ dicitur Villana, prius inculta, sed
20 auxilio Dei et nostro labore [227] composita et ad valens
quater viginti aut centum librarum singulis annis adaptata.
Quæ si quocumque infortunio his explendis deficeret, alia
Belsa nostra, quam dupliciter aut tripliciter in redditibus aug-
mentavimus, suppleret. Has autem ducentas libras, præter ea
25 quæ ad arcam gazofilacii devotione fidelium deportabuntur,
vel quæcumque ipsi utrique operi offerentur, tantum continuari ipsis operibus firmavimus, donec totaliter absque ulla[44]
quæstione et ipsa ædificia, et anteriora et superiora, cum suis
turribus omnino honorifice compleantur.

[42] *Psalm* LXXXVI.
[43] *Roman Breviary, Commune Dedicationis Ecclesiæ*, 5th Antiphon, con-
tinuing: "et turres Jerusalem gemmis ædificabuntur" ("and the towers of
Jerusalem shall be built of gems").
[44] ⟨See Panofsky, Bib. 132, p. 119.⟩

the Holy Spirit, had been invoked so that He might crown the good beginning of the house of God with a good end, the bishops—having prepared, with their own hands, the mortar with the blessed water from the dedication of the previous fifth day before the Ides of June—laid the first stones, singing a hymn to God and solemnly chanting the *Fundamenta ejus** to the end of the Psalm. The Most Serene King himself stepped down [into the excavation] and with his own hands laid his [stone]. Also we and many others, both abbots and monks, laid their stones. Certain persons also [deposited] gems out of love and reverence for Jesus Christ, chanting: *Lapides preciosi omnes muri tui*.† We, however, exhilarated by so great and so festive a laying of so holy a foundation, but anxious for what was still to be done and fearful of the changes of time, the diminution of persons and my own passing away, ordained in a common council of the brethren, at the advice of those present and by the consent of our Lord the King, an annual revenue for completing this work; namely, one hundred and fifty pounds from the treasury, that is, from the offerings at the altars and at the Relics; one hundred [from the offerings] at the Fair, and fifty [from the offerings] at the Feast of Saint Denis. In addition, fifty from the possession called Villaine in the district of Beauce, previously uncultivated but with the help of God and by our labors brought under cultivation and developed to an annual revenue of eighty or a hundred pounds. If, through any mischance, this possession should fall short of its full contribution, our other [possessions in] Beauce, the revenue of which we had doubled or trebled, would supply the balance. And we decreed that these two hundred pounds, in addition to anything which will be brought to the collection box through the devotion of the faithful or might be offered specifically for the two structures, be applied to the continuation of these works until, without any question, these edifices, the front part as well as the upper choir, will be entirely and honorably completed throughout, including their towers.

* *The foundations thereof [are in the holy mountains]* (Douai Version).
† *All thy walls are precious stones.*

V

INSISTENTES igitur per triennium multo sumptu, populoso operariorum conventu, æstate et hieme, operis perfectioni, ne nobis conqueri Deo *Imperfectum meum viderunt oculi tui*[45] jure oporteret, admodum ipso cooperante proficie-
5 bamus; instarque divinorum fundabatur *exultationi universæ terræ mons Syon, latera aquilonis, civitas Regis magni,*[46] cujus in *medio Deus non commovebitur,*[47] sed peccatorum incitamentis *commotus,* odorifero pœnitentium holocausto placari et propitiari non dedignabitur. *Medium* quippe duodecim
10 columnæ duodenorum[48] Apostolorum exponentes numerum, secundario vero totidem alarum columnæ Prophetarum numerum significantes, altum[49] repente subrigebant ædificium, juxta Apostolum spiritualiter ædificantem: *Jam non estis,* inquit, *hospites et advenæ; sed estis cives sanctorum et domes-*
15 *tici Dei, superædificati super fundamentum Apostolorum et Prophetarum, ipso summo angulari lapide Christo Jesu,* qui utrumque conjungit parietem, *in quo omnis ædificatio,* sive spi-[228]ritualis, sive materialis, *crescit in templum sanctum in Domino. In quo et nos* quanto altius, quanto aptius ma-
20 terialiter ædificare instamus, tanto per nos ipsos spiritualiter *coædificari in habitaculum Dei in Spiritu*[50] sancto edocemur.

Interea siquidem potissimum de dominorum nostrorum sanctissimorum Martyrum et aliorum sanctorum, qui per ecclesiam sparsi diversis colebantur oratoriis, translatione sol-
25 liciti, sacratissimas eorum lecticas, præcipue dominorum, ornatum iri votive animabamur; et ubi gloriosius adventantium obtutibus et conspicabilius transferrentur eligentes, aurifabrorum eleganti sive artis industria, sive[51] auri gemmarumque pretiosarum copia illustrem valde[52] fieri Deo cooperante ela-
30 boravimus. Et deforis quidem his et hujusmodi pro ornatu nobilem, pro tuto vero intus fortissimorum lapidum muro non ignobilem circumquaque muniri; extra vero econtra, ne lapi-

---

[45] *Psalm* CXXXVIII, 16.
[46] *Psalm* XLVII, 3.
[47] *Psalm* XLV, 6.
[48] ⟨See Panofsky, Bib. 132, p. 119.⟩
[49] Before *altum* supply *in.*
[50] *Ephesians* II, 19-22; cf. below, p. 241 f.
[51] ⟨See Panofsky, Bib. 132, p. 119.⟩
[52] After *valde* supply *tumulum, sepulturam,* or the like.

V

FOR three years we pressed the completion of the work at great expense, with a numerous crowd of workmen, summer and winter, lest God have just cause to complain of us: *Thine eyes did see my substance yet being unperfect*; we made good progress with His own cooperation and, in the likeness of the things Divine, there was established to *the joy of the whole earth mount Zion, on the sides of the north, the city of the Great King*, in the *midst* of which *God will not be moved*, but will not disdain, *moved* by the entreaties of the sinners, to be placated and propitiated by the sweet-smelling burnt offerings of the penitent. The *midst* of the edifice, however, was suddenly raised aloft by twelve columns representing the number of the Twelve Apostles and, secondarily, by as many columns in the side-aisles signifying the number of the [minor] Prophets, according to the Apostle who buildeth spiritually. *Now therefore ye are no more strangers and foreigners*, says he, *but fellow citizens with the saints and of the household of God; and are built upon the foundation of the apostles and prophets, Jesus Christ Himself being the chief cornerstone* which joins one wall to the other; *in Whom all the building*—whether spiritual or material—*groweth unto one holy temple in the Lord. In Whom we, too*, are taught *to be builded together for an habitation of God through the* Holy *Spirit* by ourselves in a spiritual way, the more loftily and fitly we strive to build in a material way.

Meanwhile—chiefly solicitous for the translation of our Patron Saints the most Holy Martyrs and also of the other saints who, scattered about the church, were worshiped in the different chapels —we felt devoutly moved to embellish their most sacred chasses, especially those of the Patrons; and selecting [a place] to which they might be transferred [so as to present themselves] to the visitors' glances in more glorious and conspicuous manner, we endeavored, God helping, to build [a tomb] very illustrious both by the exquisite industry of the goldsmiths' art and by a wealth of gold and precious stones. We made preparations to fortify it all round, outwardly noble for ornament by virtue of these and similar [precious materials], yet inwardly not ignoble for safety by virtue of a masonry of very strong stones; and on

dum materia apparentium locus vilesceret, cupreis tabulis
fusilibus et deauratis decorari, non tamen sicut deceret, præparavimus. Exigit enim tantorum patrum experta nobis et
omnibus magnificentia, ut quorum venerandi spiritus Deo
5 omnipotenti sicut sol fulgentes assistunt, nos miserrimi, qui
eorum patrocinia et sentimus et indigemus, sacratissimos
cineres eorum pretiosiori qua possemus materia, videlicet
auro obrizo, jacinthorum, et smaragdinum, et aliarum gemmarum copia operæ pretium liquet[53] operiri. Hoc autem unum
10 egregie fieri elegimus, ut ante corpora Sanctorum cele-[229]
berrimam[54] ad libandum Deo, quæ nunquam ibidem fuerat,
erigeremus aram, ubi Summi Pontifices et personæ autenticæ
suffragio eorum, qui seipsos holocaustum odoriferum Deo
obtulerunt,[55] placabiles et Deo acceptabiles hostias offerre me-
15 reantur. Cui etiam cum tabulam auream, mediocrem tamen
defectus pusillanimitate præponere proposuissem, tantam auri, tantam gemmarum pretiosissimarum inopinatam et vix
ipsis regibus existentem copiam ipsi sancti Martyres nobis
propinaverunt, ac si nobis ore ad os loquerentur: "Velis nolis,
20 optimam eam volumus"; ut eam aliter quam mirabilem et
valde pretiosam tam opere quam materia efficere aut non au-
deremus aut non valeremus. Neque enim ipsi pontifices, qui
his egregie pro officii sui dignitate potiuntur, annulos etiam
pontificales mirabili pretiosorum lapidum varietate gemmatos
25 eidem imponere tabulæ præsentes abnegabant, verum absentes
a transmarinis etiam partibus, sanctorum Martyrum amore
invitati, ultro delegabant. Ipse etiam rex inclytus perlucidas
et maculis distinctas smaragdines, comes Theobaldus jacin-
thos, rubetos, optimates et principes diversorum colorum et
30 valitudinum pretiosas margaritas ultro offerentes, nos ipsos ad
peragendum gloriose invitabant. Præterea tot venales ab omnibus pene terrarum partibus nobis afferebantur, et unde eas
ememus Deo donante offerebantur, ut eas sine pudore magno et Sanctorum offensa dimittere nequiremus. Hic et alibi
35 experiri potuimus: sit bonum opus in voluntate, ex Dei adju-

53 Should read *libeat*.
54-55 (See Panofsky, Bib. 132, p. 119.)

the exterior—lest the place be disfigured by the substance of un-concealed stones—to adorn it (yet not [so handsomely] as would be proper) with gilded panels of cast copper. For the gener-osity of so great Fathers, experienced by ourselves and all, de-mands that we, most miserable men who feel as well as need their tutelage, should deem it worth our effort to cover the most sacred ashes of those whose venerable spirits, radiant as the sun, attend upon Almighty God with the most precious material we possibly can: with refined gold and a profusion of hyacinths, emeralds and other precious stones. One thing, however, we did choose to have done resplendently: we would erect in front of the bodies of the Saints what had never been there before—the very famous altar for the sacrificial worship of God, where popes and persons of high rank might worthily offer the propitiatory Hosts, acceptable to God, with the intercession of those who offered themselves to God as a fragrant burnt offering. While we, overcome by timidity, had planned to set up in front of this [altar] a panel golden but modest, the Holy Martyrs themselves handed to us such a wealth of gold and most precious gems—unexpected and hardly to be found among kings—as though they were telling us with their own lips: "Whether thou wantst it or not, we want it of the best"; so that we would neither have dared, nor have been able to, make it other than admirable and very precious in workmanship as well as ma-terial. For not only did the very pontiffs—who wear them espe-cially on account of the dignity of their office—consent, if they were present, to assign their pontifical rings, set with a wonderful variety of precious stones, to this panel; they even, if they were absent in lands overseas, sent them of their own accord, incited by the love of the Holy Martyrs. Also the illustrious King himself, offering of his own accord emeralds, pellucid and distinguished by markings—Count Thibaut, hyacinths and rubies—peers and princes, precious pearls of diverse colors and properties: [all these] invited us to complete the work in glorious fashion. In addition, so many [gems and pearls] were brought to us for sale from nearly all the parts of the world (and, by the grace of God, we were also offered wherewith to buy them) that we should have been unable to let them go without great shame and offense to the Saints. Here and elsewhere we could find by experience: let there be a good

torio erit in perfectione. Hoc itaque ornamentum [230] tantorum devotione, tantis protectoribus commodatum si quis temerario ausu auferre aut scienter minuere præsumpserit, domni Dionysii offensam et Spiritus sancti mucrone perfodi
5 mereatur.

Nec illud etiam silere dignum duximus, quod dum præfatum novi augmenti opus capitellis et arcubus superioribus[56] ad altitudinis cacumen produceretur, cum necdum principales arcus singulariter voluti[57] voltarum cumulo cohærerent, terri-
10 bilis et pene intolerabilis[58] obnubilatione nubium, inundatione imbrium, impetu validissimo ventorum subito tempestatis exorta est procella; quæ usque adeo invaluit, ut non solum validas domos, sed etiam lapideas turres et ligneas tristegas concusserit. Ea tempestate, quadam die, anniversario gloriosi
15 Dagoberti regis, cum venerabilis Carnotensis episcopus Gaufredus missas gratiarum pro anima ejusdem in conventu ad altare principale festive celebraret, tantus oppositorum ventorum impetus præfatos arcus nullo suffultos[59] podio, nullis renitentes suffragiis impingebat, ut miserabiliter tremuli, et
20 quasi hinc et inde fluctuantes, subito pestiferam minarentur ruinam. Quorum quidem operturarumque impulsionem cum episcopus expavesceret, sæpe manum benedictionis in ea parte extendebat, et brachium sancti senis Simeonis signando instanter opponebat, ut manifeste nulla sui constantia, sed sola Dei
25 pietate et Sanctorum merito ruinam evadere appareret. Sicque cum multis in locis firmissimis, ut putabatur, ædificiis multa ruinarum incommoda intulisset, virtute repulsa divina titubantibus in alto solis et recentibus arcubus nihil proferre prævaluit incommodi.
30 Secutum est aliud dignum memoria factum, quod [231] non ex accidenti (sicut de talibus judicant qui illi consentiunt sectæ, videlicet quod

Fors incerta vagatur,
Fertque refertque vices, et habent mortalia casus),[60]

[56] The *et* between *superioribus* and *ad altitudinis* has been deleted on the evidence of Bibl. Nat., MS Lat. 5949 A.
[57] ⟨See Panofsky, Bib. 132, p. 119.⟩
[58] *tolerabilis* has been corrected to *intolerabilis* ⟨cf. above, note 56⟩.
[59] ⟨See Panofsky, Bib. 132, p. 120.⟩
[60] Lucanus, *Pharsalia* II, 13 f. The better manuscripts have *habet* instead of *habent*, but all have of course *Fors* and not *Foris* as in Lecoy.

work in the will—then, with the aid of God, will it be in perfection. Thus, should anyone presume to take away with rash temerity, or knowingly to diminish, this ornament presented by the devotion of such great men to such great Protectors: may he deserve the wrath of our Lord Denis and to be pierced by the sword of the Holy Ghost.

Nor do we think it proper to be silent in regard to the following fact: when the work on the new addition with its capitals and upper arches was being carried forward to the peak of its height, but the main arches—vaulted independently—were not yet held together by the bulk of the severies, there suddenly arose a terrible and almost unbearable storm with an obfuscation of clouds, an inundation of rain, and a most violent rush of wind. So mighty did this [storm]become that it blew down, not only well-built houses but even stone towers and wooden bulwarks. At this time, on a certain day (the anniversary of the glorious King Dagobert), when the venerable Bishop of Chartres, Geoffroy, was solemnly celebrating at the main altar a conventual Mass for the former's soul, such a force of contrary gales hurled itself against the aforesaid arches, not supported by any scaffolding nor resting on any props, that they threatened baneful ruin at any moment, miserably trembling and, as it were, swaying hither and thither. The Bishop, alarmed by the strong vibration of these [arches] and the roofing, frequently extended his blessing hand in the direction of that part and urgently held out toward it, while making the sign of the cross, the arm of the aged St. Simeon; so that he escaped disaster, manifestly not through his own strength of mind but by the grace of God and the merit of the Saints. Thus [the tempest], while it brought calamitous ruin in many places to buildings thought to be firm, was unable to damage these isolated and newly made arches, tottering in mid-air, because it was repulsed by the power of God.

There followed another memorable event which happened, not by accident (as is believed of such matters by those agreeing with that doctrine according to which

Chance wanders aimlessly,
Brings and brings back events; and Accident
rules all that is mortal),

sed divina largitione, quæ in se sperantibus magnis et parvis
in omnibus providet affluenter, et quæ novit profutura ad-
ministrat. Cum enim quadam die de apparatu proximæ consecrationis curiæ, quia maximam fore præstolabamur, et cum
5 amicis et ministerialibus et villicis nostris ageremus, et pro
temporum gravitate (mense enim junio pene omnia victualia
cara erant) de aliis fauste satis providissemus, hoc nos solum
graviter offendebat, quod carnes arietinas, propter ovium quæ
eodem anno extiterant morticinia, Aurelianensium[61] pago et
10 versus Burgundiam quæritare oporteret. Cumque mille solidos, aut quantum oporteret, ob hoc illuc pergentibus dari
graviter, ne tarde redirent quia sero incœperant, præcepissem,
sequente mane, cum de camerula nostra ad sancti sacrificii ex
consuetudine accelerarem celebrationem, subito quidam de
15 fratribus albis monachus renitentem ad cameram me retrahit.
In quem aliquantisper, quia nos a tanto impediebat opere,
commotus, cum minus bene respondissem: "Audivimus," inquit, "domine Pater, vos ad instantem consecrationis vestræ
solemnitatem arietinis carnibus indigere; et inde a fratribus
20 nostris missus arietum gregem maximum Paternitati vestræ
adduco, ut quod vobis placuerit retineatis, et quod non placuerit nobis dimittatis." Quo audito, ut post [232] missas nos
expectaret præcepimus,[62] et quod offerebat[63] eo præsente, fini-
ta missa, nostris retulimus; qui hoc ipsum divinæ ascribebant
25 largitioni, eo quod hoc solum quod deerat, quod quærendo
fatigaremur, inopinate religiosorum fratrum deportatione de-
legasset.

VI

URGEBAT deinceps novæ fieri consecrationem ecclesiæ
tam operis laboriosa consummatio quam nostra, quæ ad
30 hoc diu anhelaverat, suspensa devotio. Et quoniam tam ipsam
quam sanctorum dominorum nostrorum, velut pro gratiarum
actione et laboris nostri gratissimo fructu, translationem fieri
celeberrimam optando affectaremus, regiæ majestatis serenissimi regis Francorum Ludovici placido favore (desiderabat
35 enim sanctos Martyres suos protectores ardentissime videre),

[61-63] (See Panofsky, Bib. 132, p. 119 f.)

but by Divine Generosity Which abundantly provides for those who place their hope in It in all things great and small, and administers what It knows to be beneficial. On a certain day we conferred with our friends, servants and stewards about the provisions for the court [to be held on the occasion] of the imminent consecration, because we anticipated it would be very great; and, considering the difficulty of the times (for in June almost all victuals were scarce), we had fairly well provided for all other things. Only one thing worried us grievously: because of a plague among the sheep born in that year we would have to search for mutton in the district of Orléans and toward Burgundy. I had reluctantly ordered to give 1,000 shillings, or whatever was necessary, to those who would go there for this purpose, lest they should take too long in returning inasmuch as they had started so late. But on the following morning, when I, according to custom, hurried from our little chamber to the celebration of Holy Mass, a Premonstratensian monk suddenly drew me back to my room in spite of my protests. When I—a little irritated because he detained me from so great a task—had answered him without too much civility, he said: "We have heard, Lord Father, that you need mutton for the impending celebration of your consecration; therefore, sent by our brethren, I bring to your Paternal Grace a very great flock of rams so that you may keep what you like and send us back what you do not like." When we had heard this we requested him to wait for us until after Mass, and after Mass we informed our brethren in his presence of what he had offered to us. They ascribed this to Divine Generosity because It had unexpectedly furnished, through the pious brethren's bringing it hither, the only thing which we were lacking and should have found tiresome to search for.

VI

NOW the laborious consummation of the work and our own suspended devotion, which had been panting for this a long time, demanded the consecration of the new church. And since we fervently wished this consecration as well as the translation of our Patron Saints to be a most solemn event—as an act of gratitude, as it were, and as a most welcome fruit of our labors—we fixed,

diem agendi secunda junii dominica, videlicet III idus, quod
est Barnabæ Apostoli, consulte assignavimus.

Invitatorias itaque nuntiis multis, etiam cursoribus et præ-
ambulis pene per universas Galliarum regiones litteras dele-
5 gavimus; archiepiscopos, episcopos, ex parte Sanctorum et
debito apostolatus eorum tantæ interesse solemnitati votive
sollicitavimus. Quorum cum multos et diversos ad hoc peragendum gratanter, gratantius omnes, si fieri posset, excepis-
semus. Ipse dominus rex Ludovicus, et regina conjux ejus
10 Aanor, et mater ejus, et regni optimates perendie adventa-
runt. De diversis nationum et regnorum proceribus, [233]
nobilibus, et gregariis militum et peditum turmis, nulla sup-
petit computatio. Archiepiscoporum vero et episcoporum assistentium hæc intitulata sunt nomina: Samson Remensis ar-
15 chiepiscopus, Hugo Rothomagensis archiepiscopus, Guido[64]
Senonum archiepiscopus, Gaufredus Burdegalensis archiepiscopus,[65] Theobaldus Cantuariensis archiepiscopus, Gaufredus
Carnoti episcopus, Joslenus Suessorum episcopus, Simon No-
viomi episcopus, Elias Aurelianis episcopus, Odo Belvaci
20 episcopus, Hugo Autissiodori episcopus, Alvisus Atrebati
episcopus, Guido Catalaunis episcopus, Algarus Constantiarum episcopus, Rotrocus Ebroicensis episcopus, Milo Teru-
anensis episcopus, Manasses Meldis episcopus, Petrus Silva-
nectis episcopus. Qui omnes cum gloriose ex altioribus ecclesiæ
25 suæ personis pro tanta et tam nobili actione tanto spectaculo
accessissent, interiorem mentis et corporis intentionem cultus
et habitus exterior designavit. Nos autem non tantum[66] exterioribus (ea enim affluenter sine querela exhiberi præcepera-
mus), die sabbati proxima, sanctorum corpora de suis assu-
30 mentes oratoriis, ex consuetudine in palliatis tentoriis in exitu
chori decentissime reponendo locavimus. Sacramentalia consecrationis instrumenta devote tantum gaudium præstolantes
præparabamus, quo intenta tantarum personarum, tam sancta
expedite ecclesiam intus et extra perlustrare posset processio,
35 componebamus. Unde cum gloriosum et humillimum Francorum regem Ludovicum ut per optimates et nobiles suos ab
ipsa processione obviantem arceret turbam hu-[234]militer

---

[64] The Bishop's real name was *Hugo*; cf. below, pp. 118 and 245.
[65] ⟨See Panofsky, Bib. 132, p. 119.⟩
[66] Between *tantum* and *exterioribus* supply *intenti* or *instantes*.

upon deliberation and with the gracious consent of his Royal
Majesty Louis the Most Serene King of the Franks (for he ar-
dently wished to see the Holy Martyrs, his protectors), the date
of the ceremony for the second Sunday in June, that is to say the
third day before the Ides, the day of the Apostle Barnabas.

We sent invitations by many messengers, also by couriers and
envoys, through almost all the districts of Gaul and urgently requested the archbishops and bishops, in the name of the Saints
and as a debt to their apostolate, to be present at so great a solemnity. Numerous and different ones of these [we welcomed] joyfully to this celebration; more joyfully we would have welcomed
all of them had that been possible. Our Lord King Louis himself
and his spouse Queen Eleanor, as well as his mother, and the peers
of the realm arrived on the third day. Of the diverse counts and
nobles from many regions and dominions, of the ordinary troops
of knights and soldiers there is no count. But of the archbishops
and bishops who were present the names are placed on record as
follows: Samson, Archbishop of Reims; Hugues, Archbishop of
Rouen; Guy, Archbishop of Sens; Geoffroy, Archbishop of Bordeaux; Theobald, Archbishop of Canterbury; Geoffroy, Bishop of
Chartres; Jocelin, Bishop of Soissons; Simon, Bishop of Noyon;
Elias, Bishop of Orléans; Eudes, Bishop of Beauvais; Hugues,
Bishop of Auxerre; Alvise, Bishop of Arras; Guy, Bishop of
Châlons; Algare, Bishop of Coutances; Rotrou, Bishop of Evreux;
Milon, Bishop of Térouanne; Manasseh, Bishop of Meaux; Peter,
Bishop of Senlis. Since all of these had come to so noble a ceremony
and so great a spectacle in state, in their capacity of higher dignitaries of their church, their outward apparel and attire indicated
the inward intention of their mind and body. We, however, were
not so much [intent upon] external matters (for these we had
already ordained to be provided in affluence without argument),
but on the preceding Saturday took the bodies of the saints out of
their chapels and, according to custom, placed them most honorably in draped tents at the exit of the [monks'] choir. Devoutly
looking forward to so great a joy, we prepared the sacramental
implements for the consecration and made arrangements by which
the eager and so sacred procession of so many persons might
smoothly wend its way throughout the church, within and without.

[113]

rogassemus, humilius satis per seipsum et per suos hoc se libenter facturum respondit.

Pernoctantes itaque tota nocte vespertina matutinorum synaxi in laudem Divinitatis, Jesum Christum Dominum 5 nostrum propitiationem pro peccatis nostris factum, quatinus pro suo honore et Sanctorum suorum amore sanctum locum misericorditer visitare et sacris actionibus non tantum potentialiter, sed etiam personaliter adesse dignaretur, devotissime flagitabamus. Igitur summo mane archiepiscopi, episcopi, de 10 propriis hospitiis cum archidiaconis et abbatibus et aliis honestis personis ad ecclesiam accedentes, episcopaliter se componebant, et ad dolium pro consecratione aquarum superius, inter sanctorum Martyrum sepulturas et sancti Salvatoris altare, satis decenter, satis venerabiliter assistebant. Videres, et qui 15 aderant non sine devotione magna videbant, tot tantorum choream pontificum vestibus albis decoram, mitris pontificalibus et circinatis aurifrisiis pretiosis admodum comatam, pastorales virgas manibus tenere, circumcirca dolium ambire, nomen Domini exorcizando invocare; tam gloriosos et admi- 20 rabiles viros æterni sponsi nuptias tam pie celebrare, ut potius chorus cœlestis quam terrenus, opus divinum quam humanum, tam regi quam assistenti nobilitati videretur apparere. Populus enim pro intolerabili magnitudinis suæ impetu foris agebatur, et dum chorus præfatus aquam benedictam extra, hysopo 25 ecclesiæ parietes virtuose aspergendo, projiciebat, rex ipse ejusque decuriones tumultuosum impetum arcebant, et virgis et baculis regredientes ad portas protegebant.

VII

UT autem, peractis ordinarie sanctæ consecra-[235]tionis mysteriis, ventum est ad sanctarum reliquiarum reposi- 30 tionem, ad sanctorum dominorum nostrorum antiquos et venerandos tumulos accessimus (neque enim adhuc de loco

Then, when we had humbly asked the glorious and most humble
Louis, King of the Franks, to keep away, through his peers and
nobles, the impeding crowd from the procession itself, he answered, more humbly by far, that he would gladly do this in
person as well as through his retinue.

Spending the whole preceding night in reading the office of
Matins in praise of God, we devoutly implored our Lord Jesus
Christ Who was made the Propitiator for our sins that, for His
own honor and for love of His Saints, He might deign mercifully
to visit the holy place and to participate in the holy ceremonies,
not only potentially but also in person. In the early morning,
then, the archbishops and bishops came with the archdeacons,
abbots and other honorable persons from their respective guest-
quarters to the church, arranged themselves in episcopal manner,
and very solemnly, very venerably assumed, for the consecration
with the [holy] water, their places near the vat, [namely,] in the
upper choir between the tombs of the Martyrs and the altar of
the Saviour. You might have seen—and those present did see not
without great devotion—how so great a chorus of such great pontiffs, decorous in white vestments, splendidly arrayed in pontifical
miters and precious orphreys embellished by circular ornaments,
held the crosiers in their hands, walked round and round the vessel
and invoked the name of God by way of exorcism; how so glorious
and admirable men celebrated the wedding of the Eternal Bride-
groom so piously that the King and the attending nobility believed
themselves to behold a chorus celestial rather than terrestrial, a
ceremony divine rather than human. The populace milled around
outside with the drive of its intolerable magnitude; and when the
aforesaid chorus sprinkled the holy water onto the exterior, com-
petently aspersing the walls of the church with the aspergillum,
the King himself and his officials kept back the tumultuous impact
and protected those returning to the doors with canes and sticks.

VII

WHEN the mysteries of the holy consecration had been performed in proper manner we proceeded to the translation of
the sacred Relics and approached the ancient and venerable tombs
of our Patron Saints; for thus far they had not been moved from

suo mota erant). Prosternentes autem se tam ipsi pontifices
quam dominus rex, et nos omnes, quantum pro loci angustia
permittebamur, inspectis isto aperto[67] venerandis scriniis rege
Dagoberto fabricatis, in quibus sanctissima et Deo chara eo-
5 rum continebantur corpora, gaudio inæstimabili psallebant et
flebant, regemque tam devotum quam humilem accersientes:
"Vade," inquiunt, "et tu ipse manibus tuis dominum et apostolum et protectorem nostrum huc afferre adjuva, ut sacratissimos cineres veneremur, sacratissimas urnas amplectamur,
10 toto tempore vitæ nostræ eas suscepisse, eas tenuisse gratule-
mur. Hi sunt enim sancti viri, qui pro testamento Dei sua
corpora tradiderunt, qui pro salute nostra, charitatis igne
accensi, terram suam et cognationem exierunt, qui fidem Jesu
Christi apostolica auctoritate omnem Galliam edocuerunt, pro
15 eo viriliter certaverunt, nudi virgas, ligati feroces et famelicas
bestias compescuerunt, equulei extensionem, clibani succensionem illæsi, demumque hebetatis securibus decapitationem
felicem sustinuerunt. Age igitur, rex christiane,[68] beatum
suscipiamus susceptorem nostrum Dionysium, suppliciter fla-
20 gitantes ut pro nobis petat ab eo qui fideliter promisit; dilectio
et benignitas quam habes semper pro quibuscumque petieris
impetrabit." Protinus lacerti moventur, [236] brachia exten-
duntur, tot et tantæ manus iniiciuntur,[69] quod nec etiam
septima manus ipsa sancta scrinia attingere valeret. Eapropter
25 ipse dominus rex se medium eis ingerens, lecticam argenteam
specialis patroni de manu episcoporum, sicut videtur, de manu
Remensis archiepiscopi, Senonensis, Carnotensis et aliorum
assumens, tam devote quam honeste prævius egrediebatur.
Mirabile visu! Nunquam talem, præter illam quæ in antiqua
30 consecratione cœlestis exercitus visa est, processionem aliquis
videre potuit, cum sanctorum corpora martyrum et confes-
sorum de tentoriis palliatis, humeris et collis episcoporum et
comitum et baronum, sanctissimo Dionysio sociisque ejus ad
eburneum ostium occurrerunt; per claustrum cum candelabris
35 et crucibus et aliis festivis ornamentis, cum odis et laudibus
multis processerunt; dominos suos tam familiariter quam

67 (See Panofsky, Bib. 132, p. 120, and) cf. below, p. 247.
68-69 (See Panofsky, Bib. 132, p. 119 f.)

their place. After prostrations, the pontiffs as well as our Lord the
King, and all of us so far as we could in view of the narrowness of
the room, inspected—when it had been opened—the venerable
shrines, executed under King Dagobert, which contained their most
sacred bodies dear to God; chanted and wept with immeasurable
joy; and said, inviting a king as devout as humble: "Come, help
thyself with thy own hands to carry hither our Lord, Apostle and
Protector, so that we may revere the most sacred ashes, embrace
the most sacred urns, rejoice throughout our lives at having received and held them. For these are the holy men who gave over
their bodies as a testimony to God; who for our salvation, burning
with the fire of charity, left their land and kin; who with apostolic
authority taught the faith of Jesus Christ to all Gaul; who fought
for Him like men; who, naked, conquered scourges and, fettered,
[conquered] wild and famished beasts; who sustained, unscathed,
extension on the rack and the fire of the furnace, and finally blissful
decapitation by blunted axes. Onward, then, Christian King, let us
receive him who will receive us, our blessed Denis, humbly en-
treating him to pray for us to Him who promised truthfully; the
love and benevolence which thou hast will always obtain its end
for whomsoever thou wilt pray." Forthwith muscles are moved,
arms are thrust out, so many and so important hands are laid on
that not even the seventh hand was able to reach the sacred shrines
themselves. Therefore, our Lord the King himself, injecting
himself into their midst, received the silver chasse of our special
Patron from the hand of the bishops—I believe, from the hand of
the Archbishops of Reims and Sens, the Bishop of Chartres and
others—and led the way out as devoutly as nobly. A marvel to
behold! never could anyone see such a procession, apart from that
which had been seen on the occasion of the old consecration by the
Heavenly Host: when the bodies of the holy martyrs and confes-
sors, out of the draped tents and on the shoulders and necks of
bishops, counts and barons, went forth to meet the most holy Denis
and his Companions at the ivory door; when [those in the pro-
cession] proceeded through the cloisters with candlesticks, crosses
and other festive ornaments and with many odes and hymns; when

præ gaudio lacrymabiliter deportaverunt. Nullo unquam
majori in omnibus potuerunt gaudio sublimari.

Revertentes igitur ad ecclesiam, et per gradus ad altare
superius quieti Sanctorum destinatum ascendentes, super anti-
5 quum altare pignoribus Sanctorum repositis, de nova ante
novam eorum sepulturam consecranda agebatur principali
ara, quam domino Remensi archiepiscopo Samsoni imposuimus consecrandam. Agebatur etiam de aliis tam gloriose quam
solemniter aris viginti consecrandis: quarum illam quæ in
10 medio Salvatori nostro et sanctorum choro Angelorum et
sanctæ Cruci assignatur, domino Can-[237]tuariensi archiepiscopo Theobaldo; beatæ semperque virginis Dei Genitricis
Mariæ, domino Hugoni Rotomagensi archiepiscopo; sancti
Peregrini, domino Hugoni Autissiodorensi episcopo; sancti
15 Eustachii, domino Widoni⁷⁰ Catalaunensi episcopo; sanctæ
Osmannæ, domino Petro Silvanectensi episcopo; sancti In-
nocentii, domino Simoni Noviomensi episcopo; sancti Cucu-
phatis, domino Alviso Atrebatensi episcopo; sancti Eugenii,
domino Algaro Constantiarum episcopo; sancti Hilari, do-
20 mino Rotroco Ebroicensi episcopo; sancti Johannis Baptistæ
et sancti Johannis Evangelistæ, domino Nicolao Cameracensi
episcopo sacrandam imposuimus. In crypta vero inferius ma-
jus altare in honore sanctæ Dei Genitricis Mariæ virginis,
domino Gaufredo Burdegalensi archiepiscopo; in dextra
25 parte, altare sancti Christophori martyris, domino Heliæ
Aurelianensi episcopo; sancti Stephani protomartyris, domino
Gaufredo Carnotensi episcopo; sancti Eadmundi regis, domino Widoni⁷¹ Senonensi archiepiscopo; sancti Benedicti,
domino Josleno Suessionensi episcopo. In sinistra parte, sanc-
30 torum Sixti, Felicissimi et Agapiti, domino Miloni Taruanensi
episcopo; sancti Barnabæ apostoli, domino Manassæ Meldensi
episcopo; item et sancti Georgii martyris et Gauburgis virginis, eidem episcopo; sancti Lucæ evangelistæ, domino Odoni Belvacensi episcopo consecrandam assignavimus.
35 [238] Qui omnes tam festive, tam solemniter, tam diversi,

⁷⁰ The Bishop's real name was *Guido*; cf. above, p. 112, and below, p. 245.
⟨cf. Panofsky, Bib. 132, p. 119.⟩
⁷¹ The Bishop's real name was *Hugo*. ⟨cf. *ibid.*⟩

they carried their Patrons amicably yet, for joy, weepingly. No greater joy in the world could ever have exalted them.

When the [procession] had returned to the church and had ascended by the stairs to the upper altar, destined for the rest of the Saints (while the Relics of the Saints had been deposited on the old altar) the rites were performed at the new main altar which was to be consecrated in front of their new tomb; the consecration of this [new main altar] we entrusted to the Lord Archbishop of Reims, Samson. The rites were also splendidly and solemnly performed at the other twenty altars that were to be consecrated. The consecration of that which, in the central nave, is dedicated to Our Saviour, the Host of the Holy Angels and the Holy Cross, we entrusted to Theobald, Archbishop of Canterbury; that of the blessed eternal Virgin Mary, Mother of God, to Lord Hugues, Archbishop of Rouen; that of St. Peregrinus, to Lord Hugues, Archbishop of Auxerre; that of St. Eustace, to Lord Guido, Bishop of Châlons; that of St. Osmanna, to Lord Peter, Bishop of Senlis; that of St. Innocent, to Lord Simon, Bishop of Noyon; that of St. Cucuphas, to Lord Alvise, Bishop of Arras; that of St. Eugene, to Lord Algare, Bishop of Coutances; that of St. Hilary, to Lord Rotrou, Bishop of Evreux; that of St. John the Baptist and St. John the Evangelist, to Lord Nicholas, Bishop of Cambrai. In the crypt, however, we assigned for consecration: the lower main altar in honor of the Holy Virgin, Mary, Mother of God, to Lord Geoffroy, Archbishop of Bordeaux; on the right, the altar of St. Christopher, Martyr, to Lord Elias, the Bishop of Orléans; that of St. Stephen, Proto-Martyr, to Lord Geoffroy, Bishop of Chartres; that of St. Edmund, King, to Lord Guido, Archbishop of Sens; that of St. Benedict, to Lord Jocelin, Bishop of Soissons. On the left [we assigned for consecration the altar] of Sts. Sixtus, Felicissimus and Agapitus, to Lord Milon, Bishop of Térouanne; that of St. Barnabas, Apostle, to Lord Manasseh, Bishop of Meaux; further, that of St. George, Martyr, and St. Walburga, Virgin, to the same Bishop; and that of St. Luke the Evangelist, to Lord Eudes, Bishop of Beauvais.

After the consecration of the altars all these [dignitaries] performed a solemn celebration of Masses, both in the upper choir and in the crypt, so festively, so solemnly, so different and yet

tam concorditer, tam propinqui, tam hilariter ipsam altarium
consecratione missarum solemnem celebrationem superius in-
feriusque peragebant, ut ex ipsa sui consonantia et cohærente
harmoniæ[72] grata melodia potius angelicus quam humanus
5 concentus æstimaretur, et ab omnibus corde et ore acclamare-
tur: *"Benedicta gloria Domini de loco suo*,[73] benedictum et
laudabile et superexaltatum[74] nomen tuum, Domine Jesu
Christe, quem summum Pontificem unxit Deus Pater oleo
exsultationis præ participibus tuis. Quæ sacramentali sanc-
10 tissimi Chrismatis delibutione[75] et sanctissimæ Eucharistiæ
susceptione materialia immaterialibus, corporalia spiritualibus, humana divinis uniformiter concopulas, sacramentaliter
reformas ad suum puriores principium; his et hujusmodi
benedictionibus visibilibus invisibiliter restauras, etiam præ-
15 sentem in regnum cœleste mirabiliter transformas, ut, *cum
tradideris regnum Deo et Patri*,[76] nos et angelicam creaturam,
cœlum et terram, unam rempublicam potenter et misericorditer efficias; qui *vivis et regnas* Deus *per omnia secula seculorum*.[77] Amen."

[72] Should probably read *harmonia*.
[73] *Ezekiel* III, 12.
[74] *Daniel* III, 52 ff.; here translated according to Douai Version.
[75] ⟨See Panofsky, Bib. 132, p. 120.⟩
[76] *I Corinthians* XV, 24.
[77] See above, p. 66, note 26.

so concordantly, so close [to one another] and so joyfully that their song, delightful by its consonance and unified harmony, was deemed a symphony angelic rather than human; and that all exclaimed with heart and mouth: *"Blessed be the glory of the Lord from His place.* Blessed and *worthy of praise and exalted above all* be Thy name, Lord Jesus Christ, Whom God Thy Father has anointed the Highest Priest with the oil of exultation above Thy fellows. By this sacramental unction with the most holy chrism and by the susception of the most holy Eucharist, Thou uniformly conjoinest the material with the immaterial, the corporeal with the spiritual, the human with the Divine, and sacramentally reformest the purer ones to their original condition. By these and similar visible blessings, Thou invisibly restorest and miraculously transformest the present [state] into the Heavenly Kingdom. Thus, when Thou *shalt have delivered up the kingdom to God, even the Father,* mayest Thou powerfully and mercifully make us and the nature of the angels, Heaven and earth, into one State; Thou Who *livest and reignest* as God *for ever and ever.* Amen."

[ORDINATIO A.D. MCXL°
VEL MCXLI° CONFIRMATA]

IN nomine Patris et Filii et Spiritus sancti. Amen.

Sugerius, Beati Dionysii qualiscumque[1] abbas, Dei omnipotentis servitio mancipatis providere, labores et certaminum sudores quibuscumque seu spiritualium seu temporalium re-

5 mediis alleviare, victualibus, ne deficiant in via, sustentare, cum omnibus fidelibus tum præcipue prælatis Ecclesiæ coram Deo et honestum et utile arbitramur. His siquidem signatum est, Domino præcipiente, quomodo confovere et contegere eos oporteat bovinis et vaccinis coriis Arcam fœderis Domini,

10 ad [350] repellendos imbres tumultuosos et quæcumque molesta; in quo idem ipsi exprimuntur,[2] qui prælationibus actuales ex debito officii ex seipsis habent loco coriorum et confovere et contra omnem molestiam protegere contemplativos, qui vere sunt arca divinæ propitiationis. Eapropter ego Su-

15 gerius, Dei patientia ter beati Dionysii vocatus abbas, mandatorum Dei prævaricator, ad cor Dei miseratione redire festinans, unde venerim, quid fecerim, et quo ire debeam, in timore et amaritudine animæ meæ recogitans, ad servorum Dei tutelam tremulus confugio; et qui irreligiosus existo, re-

20 ligionem eorum toto animo amplectens, religiosorum suffragia suppliciter imploro, et ut devotius et efficacius nobis in spiritualibus sustentando provideant, et in temporalibus eis providendo eos sustentare victualibus confovere devotissime accuramus.

25 DE PRÆPOSITURA SIQUIDEM VILCASSINI, quæ olim ante nos adeo destituta erat, ut vix posset quinque solidos ad cotidianum fratrum generale sufficere, quam in novitate prælationis nostræ, Dei auxilio, multo sumptu, valida et (quod etiam conscientiam meam gravat) militari manu, ab oppressione ad-

30 vocatorum et aliorum malefactorum eam[3] excussimus, et,

[1-2] ⟨See Panofsky, Bib. 132, p. 120.⟩

[3] *eam* should be deleted; as it stands, the sentence is an anacoluthon.

[ORDINANCE ENACTED IN THE YEAR 1140 OR IN THE YEAR 1141]

IN the name of the Father, the Son, and the Holy Ghost, Amen. We, Suger, undistinguished Abbot of the Blessed Denis, believe it proper and useful in God's sight for all the faithful, especially for the prelates of the Church, to provide for those committed to the service of Almighty God; to alleviate their labors and the toil of their struggles by all possible means, spiritual or temporal, and to sustain them with the necessities of life lest they break down on the road. For to these [prelates] it has been betokened, under the command of God, how it behooved them to take care of and protect the Ark of the Covenant of the Lord with the skins of oxen and cows in order to ward off violent rainstorms and all kinds of damage; wherein are typified those very men who, being men of action by virtue of their prelacies, have it within their power, as a duty of their office, to take care of and to protect from all damage—as though with skins—the men of contemplation who are in truth the Ark of Divine Propitiation. Therefore, I, Suger—by the patience of God chosen Abbot of the thrice blessed Denis, prevaricator of God's commands, hastening to return by mercy to the heart of God, and recognizing in the fear and anguish of my soul whence I have come, what I have done, and where I must go—tremblingly flee to the protection of the servants of God; I, clearly being an irreligious man, embrace their religion with all my heart and humbly crave the intercession of the religious; and, providing for them in matters temporal, we devoutly endeavor to sustain and comfort them with the necessities of life so that they may all the more devoutly and effectively provide for us in matters spiritual.

FROM THE DOMAIN LE VEXIN—which before our time had been in such decay that it could hardly contribute five shillings to the main course of the brethren's daily dinner; which we, God helping, have rescued in the early days of our prelacy with great expense, and with a strong and (a fact now aggravating my conscience) armed hand, from the oppression of the bailiffs and other

sicut nobis videtur, dupliciter aut tripliciter augmentando in melius composuimus, generali fratrum quinque solidos diebus quinque in omni hebdomada apponimus, ut in illis semper decem habeant solidos. Aliis siquidem duobus diebus, videlicet
5 feria[4] quinta et septima, ob reverentiam nostrarum memoriarum, sanctæ Dei Genitricis et sanctorum Martyrum, qua-
[351]tuordecim solidos in alia ordinatione constituimus. Quicquid tamen et in hac et in alia ordinatione ultra quinque solidos consistit, nostro labore ob amorem Dei et sanctæ
10 regulæ observationem amplificato fratrum numero, per Dei misericordiam constare dinoscitur. Hanc autem augmentationis cartam communi fratrum nostrorum consensu minui aut in aliquo defraudari perpetuo anatemate, perpetua maledictione prohibemus. Hæc de generali.
15 De pulmento autem, quia nescio qua occasione fratribus ab Indicto usque ad octabas beati Dionysii subtrahebatur, volumus et constituimus deinceps per totum anni circulum, per manus ministrorum monachorum aut laicorum, continuatim suppleri; et ne materia his deficiat, censum novum novorum
20 quos hospitari feci in vacua horti terra, quinquaginta videlicet solidos aut amplius, huic apposuimus incremento. Hanc etiam pulmenti regulam firmissime teneri, tam pro ipsis fratribus quam pro exteriorum pauperum supportatione qui his et aliis indigent, sine interpellatione sanctiendo firmamus. Hæc
25 itaque de prima.
De secunda vero, quæ cœna dicitur, tertium confecimus capitulum: quæ, ut convenientius et solito decentius fœcundior fiat, quibusdam olim a nobis aucta est incrementis, videlicet Sancti Luciani decimis, quæ ad nos pertinebant, viginti
30 solidorum largitione, qui nobis de superabundante ab ipsis hortolanis solvebantur, annona etiam quæ nobis de Petraficta reddebatur. Inpræsentiarum vero, ob amorem et reverentiam sanctæ religionis et fratrum nostrorum devotionem, censum
[352] etiam ejusdem villæ, videlicet centum solidos aut si

---

[4] (See Panofsky, Bib. 132, p. 120.)

malefactors; and which we have improved, we believe, by a two-fold or threefold increase—we add to the main course of the brethren's dinner five shillings for five days in each week; so that they may always have ten shillings on these [five days]. For the other days, that is to say, the Thursdays and Saturdays, we have already allocated, in another Ordinance, fourteen shillings in honor of our memorial days, viz., those of the Mother of God and the Holy Martyrs. And whatever in this and that other Ordinance is fixed in excess of five shillings is herewith recognized as permanently valid by the mercy of God, even though the number of brethren has been increased through our labors for the love of God and the observance of our holy rule. With the common consent of the brethren we forbid under perpetual ban and perpetual malediction to diminish or in any fraudulent way to detract from this document of increase. This as regards the main course of the dinner.

Concerning the additional course—for it, I know not for what reason, had come to be withheld from the brethren from the Fair until the octave of the Feast of the blessed Denis—we wish and ordain that it hereafter be supplied continually throughout the whole year by the hands of the attendant monks or lay brothers. And lest the means for this be lacking, we have assigned to this increase the new rent from the new [tenants] whom I have settled in the vacant garden land, that is to say, fifty shillings or more. We establish by solemn decree, without objection, that this rule of the additional course, too, be most strictly observed, both for the brethren themselves and for the sustenance of the outside poor who are in want of this and other things. This, then, as regards the dinner.

Concerning the second meal, which is called supper, we have laid down a third article. So as to be more nourishing in more fitting and becoming manner than before, this [second meal] has previously been enlarged by us out of certain increases, namely, the tithe of Saint-Lucien which belonged to us; the contribution of twenty shillings which was paid to us by the gardeners there out of their surplus; and the grain which was surrendered to us from Pierrefitte. Now, out of love and reverence of holy religion, and in view of the devotion of our brethren, we have, in addition,

amplior fuerit, et contulimus et perpetuo anathemate indisso-
lubiliter confirmavimus; hoc tamen retento, quod ejusdem
monachi cœnatoris deliberatione et testificatione vinearum
nostrarum de eodem censu ibidem, quantum ad nos pertinet,
5 collectio fiat; medietas etenim expensarum ad mediatores
pertinet vinearum.

Præterea operibus pietatis insistere, infirmorum curam
gerere quanti constet, ore sacratissimo ipsius audivimus, qui
dicturus est in illa universali et admirabili auditione: *Infirmus*
10 *fui et visitastis me*,[5] et contraria contrariis. Quod autem ad
prælatos potissimum spectet enucleatius edocuit, qui ovem
morbidam ad gregem in humeris reportavit. Hac siquidem
sollicitudine votiva angariatus, fratres hujus ministerii officiales, tam præsentes quam successuros, in hoc ipso vicarios
15 nostros, auctoritate Dei commonemus et præcipimus, quatenus
hylariter, pie et mansuete, fratribus ægrotantibus, senibus,
quibuscumque debilibus, secundum diversas infirmitates diversis illorum appetitibus condescendant et *ministrent* tanquam *angelis*[6] Dei, quoniam charitas est summa monasticæ
20 religionis; et his quidem primo, sed animo uno illis ordinarie
serviant, qui quacumque de causa jussu custodis Ordinis in
domibus infirmorum cesserint, videlicet uno ferculo in omni
mensa, præter illud quod eis a refectorio deportabitur. Ut
autem hoc possit semper continuari, antiquis ejusdem præposi-
25 turæ redditibus sex libras addidimus, quos[7] labore nostro in
burgo adquisivimus, non aliquo malo inge-[353]nio, sed
emptione cujusdam domus et positione stallorum, de quibus
hic census irrefragabiliter debetur. Commonemus autem et
consulimus fratribus in hoc[8] officio agentibus, quatinus, præter
30 ea quæ ad exteriorem terrarum curam pertinere oportet,
usumfructum totius præposituræ fratrum necessitatibus ex-
pendat,[9] nec aliqua ei occasio aut emendorum palliorum aut
aliorum ornamentorum subrepat, sed totum[10] totaliter fratrum necessitatibus reservetur. Quibus etiam debilitati et se-
35 niorum condescendendo, ad calefaciendum eos, quo valde ege-

---

[5] *Matthew* XXV, 36; the Vulgate text has *eram*. Cf. below, p. 255.
[6] Should read *angeli*. Prof. R. Salomon kindly referred the translator to
Matthew IV, 11: "angeli accesserunt, et ministrabant ei," and *Mark* I, 13: "et
angeli ministrabant illi."
[7] Should read *quas*.   [8] (See Panofsky, Bib. 132, p. 120.)
[9] Should read *expendant*.   [10] (See Panofsky, Bib. 132, p. 120.)

allocated [for this], and unshakably confirmed under perpetual ban, the rent from the aforesaid possession, viz., one hundred shillings or, if it so happens, more; with the reservation, however, that, upon consideration and testimony of the brother *cœnator*, there shall be collected there, out of that rent, the yield of our vineyards to the extent as it belongs to us (for the moiety of the produce belongs to the métayers of the vineyards).

Furthermore we have heard, from the most sacred lips of Him Who shall say, at that universal and wonderful hearing: *I was sick and ye visited me* (and contrariwise), how valuable it is to devote oneself to works of charity and to take care of the sick. And what affects the prelates in particular has been more clearly taught by Him Who on His shoulders brought back the ailing sheep to the flock. Compelled by this pious solicitude, we admonish and enjoin, under the authority of God, the brethren in charge of this office (and our deputies therein), both present and future, cheerfully, piously, and tenderly to condescend to the ailing brethren, to the aged and to the weak of all kinds, to [gratify] their diverse appetites according to their diverse illnesses, and to *minister unto* them even as *angels* of God; for charity is the essence of monastic religion. They shall regularly serve—in the first place to these but in the same spirit also to those who for one reason or another may walk about the infirmaries on orders of the Sub-Prior—one portion at every meal over and above that which will be brought to them from the refectory; and in order that it may always be possible to continue this, we have added to the old revenue from that domain six pounds which we have acquired by our labors in the village, not through any chicanery but by the purchase of a certain house and by the erection of stalls from which this rent is irrevocably due. However, we admonish and advise the brethren in charge of this office to spend—apart from what necessarily belongs to the external upkeep of the lands—the revenue of the entire domain for the needs of the brethren; never should there creep in an opportunity of purchasing textiles or other ornaments, but all should be wholly reserved for the needs of the brethren. Sympathizing with these and with the debility of the Seniors, we have—in order to keep them warm, which they very much needed—confirmed for this purpose under perpetual ban

bant, tensamentum Garsonis Villæ nostrum, qui[11] de ipsa villa eorum erat, ei perpetuo anatemate confirmavimus.

PORRO, QUONIAM parvitatis nostræ memoriam præsentium et futurorum fratrum dilectioni absque præcedentibus meritis
5 obnixe commendamus, ut saluti animæ nostræ proficiat, operæ pretium duximus imperatorum et majorum nostrorum, qui eas multa liberalitate, larga munificentia meruerunt fieri, vel multo temporum curriculo sopitas ad salutem animarum suscitare et informare memorias, inter quas inclyti et nobilis-
10 simi imperatoris Karoli tertii solemnes memorias recreare et restituere hoc modo censuimus. Modus autem idem est qui in testamento imperialis continetur majestatis, eo videlicet quo idem[12] gloriosus imperator nobilem villam Ruoilum cum appendiciis suis[13] et aquarum foreste[14] Beato Dionysio regia
15 liberalitate contulit. Constituit siquidem nobile, et quod imperatorem decebat mandatum: quod quidem[15] apud alios et de aliis regibus solet recoli singulis annis dies deposi-[354]tionis anniversarius, ipse suum sibi singulis mensibus pridie nonas mensis fieri decrevit, in capitulo pronuntiari, in monasterio
20 celebrari, in refectorio de præfatæ villæ redditibus fratribus honestam refectionem adaptari. Nec illa ignobilior tanti imperatoris prædicatur præceptio, quod de usufructu[16] præfatæ villæ septem luminaria septem lampadarum ante sacrosanctum altare sanctæ Trinitatis indeficienter per successiva secula
25 ardere sancivit. Et quoniam in administratione regni, quocumque[17] terrarum eum imperii necessitas devocaret, semper tamen pleno animi affectu et pernoctabat et designabat ibidem sepeliri, ipsum sepulturæ suæ locum tutissimis sanctarum reliquiarum munivit præsidiis, de theca imperiali capellæ sibi re-
30 tinens et in anteriori parte benedicti altaris reponens os brachii sancti Jacobi apostoli fratris Domini, in dextra brachium sancti protomartyris Stephani, in sinistra vero beati martyris et

[11] Should read *quod*.
[12-17] (See Panofsky, Bib. 132, p. 120.)

our protection tax of Garsonis Villa, which pertained to them from this possession.

FURTHER, WHILE—for want of outstanding merits—we humbly commend the memory of our insignificant self to the affection of present and future brethren, we have thought it worth our effort, in order to help the salvation of our soul, to revive and to reconstitute, for the salvation of their souls, the memorial observances, discontinued on account of the very great elapse of time, of our Emperors and forebears who by their great liberality and generous munificence have well deserved that these [observances] be held. Of these, we have decided to renew and to restore the memorial observances for the most famous Emperor Charles the Third in the following manner. The manner, however, is that which is contained in the testament of his Imperial Majesty, viz., the one by which this glorious Emperor donated to the blessed Denis the noble possession of Rueil with its dependencies and fisheries. He laid down a noble command, and one which befitted an Emperor: inasmuch as elsewhere, and with other kings, the anniversary of their exequies is usually commemorated every year, he decreed that his [anniversary] be observed every month, on the day before the Nones; that it be announced in the chapter and celebrated in the convent; that from the revenue of the aforesaid possession a worthy repast be served to the brethren in the refectory. Nor can that [other] injunction of so great an Emperor be called less excellent whereby he solemnly decreed that from the revenue of the aforesaid possession seven lights in seven lamps should uninterruptedly burn before the sacred altar of the Holy Trinity throughout the successive centuries. And, since, throughout the administration of his kingdom [and] to whichever part of the world the needs of the Empire might call him, he always yearned and planned, in the full affection of his mind, to be buried there, he fortified the place of his grave with the very safe protection of sacred relics, reserving for himself from the Imperial repository in the Chapel, and depositing in the front part of the blessed altar: an arm bone of the Apostle St. James, Brother of the Lord; in the right part, an arm of the Proto-Martyr St. Stephen; and in the left part, an arm of the blessed Vincent, Martyr and Levite—

levitæ Vincentii; quemadmodum oculis nostris nos ipsi vidi-
mus, cum venerabilibus viris archiepiscopis Lugdunensi, Remensi, Turonensi, Rothomagensi, et episcopis Suessionensi,
Belvacensi, Redonensi, Silvanectensi, Aletensi, Meldensi,
5 Venetensi, et anuli ejus impressionem in argumento veritatis
tenuimus, ut prope altare sepultus, circumquaque sanctorum
pignoribus circumseptus, omnem et spiritualem et tempora-
lem evitare[18] molestiam; quæ quidem sanctorum pignora hi
nobiscum populo Dei ad patrocinandum exposuerunt, et re-
10 parato altari eodem auro pretioso et opere approbato, ibidem
honorifice [355] reposuerunt. Verum, quoniam hæ tanti imperatoris præceptiones, licet auro bullatis cartis sancirentur,
emula longevi temporis varietate quædam tepuerant, quædam
omnino defecerant, nos ob amorem et honorem Dei et sanc-
15 tarum reliquiarum, nec minus ad remedium animæ domni et
serenissimi augusti Karoli, communicato cum fratribus nostris
consilio eas suscitare et reformare studiose laboravimus; luminaria septem lampadarum quæ deperierant jugiter ardere
decrevimus; decrepita vasa ipsarum lampadarum argentea
20 honeste restituimus; cereum ibidem jugiter ardentem illi
qui solus ante altare beati Dionysii ardebat, ut indeficienter
duo ardeant, concopulavimus, quemadmodum jam ante ipsa
Sanctorum corpora duo jugiter ardere constituimus; singulis
mensibus, pridie nonas anniversarii ejus exequia solito solem-
25 nius celebrari firmissime determinavimus; refectionem his-
dem diebus in refectorio irrefragabiliter restituimus. Ut autem et continuis luminaribus et determinatis refectionibus
convenientia deesse non valeant alimenta, de supradicta villa
Ruoilo, quam his apposuit testamento, decem libras in octabis
30 beati Dionysii assumi inviolabiliter assignavimus. Capiciario
sacristæ per manum magistri prioris dari instituimus, qui et
luminaribus oleum præparare provideat, et exequiarum refectionibus singulis mensibus decem solidos incessanter sub-
ministret. Quid est enim quod tantus imperator, et tam famili-
35 aris et præcordialis beati Dionysii amicus, promereri non
valeat, qui ejus ecclesiam tot et tantis possessionibus nobilita-

[18] Should read *evitaret*.

as we have seen ourselves with our own eyes together with the venerable Archbishops of Lyons, Reims, Tours and Rouen, and the Bishops of Soissons, Beauvais, Rennes, Senlis, St.-Malo, Meaux and Vannes. And we held [in our hands] the impression of his ring as evidence of the truth: that he [wished to] avoid all spiritual and temporal vexation, buried near the altar and surrounded on all sides by the relics of the saints. Together with ourselves those [dignitaries] showed these relics of the saints to the people of God for protection, and honorably restored them to their places after the altar had been repaired with gold and praiseworthy [gold-smith's] work. But, since these injunctions of so great an Emperor, though sanctioned by documents sealed with the golden seal, had partly cooled off owing to the envious mutability of hoary time, and partly fallen into disuse altogether, we zealously endeavored, after having deliberated our intention with our brethren, to revive and to restore them for the love and honor of God and of the sacred relics, and also for the salvation of the soul of our Lord the Most Serene and August Charles. We decreed that the lights in the seven lamps, which had gone out, burn in perpetuity. We decently restored the silver vessels of these lamps. To that ever-burning wax candle which used to burn alone before the altar of the blessed Denis we added another so that two might burn [there] uninter-ruptedly; just as we had already decreed that two burn perma-nently before the bodies of the Saints themselves. We most strictly ordained that the offices of [Charles's] anniversary be celebrated, more solemnly than had been usual, every month on the day before the Nones. We irrevocably restored the repast in the refectory on these days. And in order that proper food can never be lacking for either the perpetual lights or the appointed repasts, we inviolably decreed that on the octave of the Feast of the blessed Denis ten pounds be taken out of the revenue from the aforesaid possession of Rueil which he had assigned to these [observances] in his testament. We ordered that these be handed, through the hand of the Grand Prior, to the Sacristan-Treasurer who shall see to it that oil be ready for the lamps, and shall continually supply ten shillings for the funeral repasts in every month. For what should not so great an Emperor, and so intimate and cordial a friend of the blessed Denis, deserve? He who glorified the latter's

vit, tot auri et pretiosarum gemmarum ornamentis declaravit,
insuper ad cumulum omnium bonorum insignibus Dominicæ
passionis, [356] videlicet clavo et corona Domini, et brachio
sancti senis Symeonis, tanquam splendidissimo veri Solis
5 jubare irradiantem, celeberrime insignivit? His ergo et hujus-
cemodi bene devoti, in capitulo nostro convenientes, hanc renovationis cartam morose et discrete conferentes, auctoritate
Dei omnipotentis et beatorum martyrum Dionysii sociorumque ejus, communi etiam et concordi capituli nostri confirma-
10 tione, approbavimus et lege inconvulsa sancivimus, obtestan-
tes, et per eum quem effudit Jesus Christus in cruce sanguinem
adjurantes, ne quacumque occasione hæc institutio destituatur,
ne præsens carta, quacumque persona, quacumque occasione,
instar defectus antiquarum recidivam sustineat calamitatem,
15 sed sana et illibata suis institutionibus et capitulis semper et
per inconvulsa *seculorum secula*[19] firmissime consistat.

Matriculariis etiam quatuor clericis in eadem ecclesia ibidem jugiter desudantibus, ut nostri memoriam habeant, deci-
mam quandam, quam, quia de feodo nostro erat, a Pagano
20 de Gisortio in Francorum Villa comparavimus, quoniam
præbendæ eorum copia aliquantum tepuerat, donavimus tam
in pane quam in vino, excepta illa parte quæ de clauso proprio
vinearum ecclesiæ assumitur.

SUPEREST SIQUIDEM ET ALIUD probabile capitulum, quod, licet
25 exsecutione[20] rerum pollicitarum terminabile appareat, tamen,
quia ad æternitatis nobis proficere et optamus et speramus
retributionem, huic scripto interserere dignum duximus. Nono
decimo administrationis[21] nostræ anno, cum novo operi in anteriori ecclesiæ parte libenter et fideliter desudassemus, ipso-
30 que novo antiquo operi pulchra nova-[357]rum columnarum
et arcuum convenientia apte unito, superius sancti Romani
oratorium, inferius sancti Hyppoliti, et ex alia parte sancti
Bartholomæi, cum eadem nova ecclesia a venerabili Rothomagensi archiepiscopo Hugone et aliis venerabilibus epi-
35 scopis consecrari fecissemus, ipsisque tribus oratoriis pro dote

[19] Should read *inconvulsa per* as kindly suggested by Prof. R. Salomon. For
seculorum secula cf. above, p. 66, note 26.
[20-21] (See Panofsky, Bib. 132, p. 120.)

church by so many and important possessions; who brightened it with so many ornaments of gold and precious stones; who, as the crown of all benefactions, most nobly distinguished it by the insignia of the Lord's Passion, viz., the Nail and the Crown of the Lord, and by the arm of the aged St. Simeon, so that it shines as with the most brilliant radiance of the true Sun? Devoutly concerned with these and similar matters, convening in our chapter, and diligently and prudently discussing this document of renewal, we have approved and established it by unshakable law under the authority of Almighty God and the blessed Martyrs Denis and his Companions, and also with the common and united confirmation of our chapter. We have sworn, by the blood which Jesus Christ has shed upon the Cross, that under no circumstances shall this Ordinance be abrogated; that through no person, and under no circumstances, shall the present document suffer the recurrence of a calamity like the lapse of the old ones; but that it shall most firmly stand, sound and inviolate in its regulations and articles, and always unshakable *for ever and ever.*

Also to the four "Marguilliers" of this church, who are constantly at work there, we have given—so that they may remember us—a certain tithe both in bread and wine (for the amount of their allowances had fallen off somewhat) which we had bought in Franconville from Payen de Gisors because it was of our [own] fief; except for that part which is collected from the private vineyard of the church.

THERE REMAINS ONE OTHER important article which we have deemed proper to include in this record; though it is evidently predicated upon the performance of promises, we wish and hope that it may benefit us in regard to eternal retribution. In the nineteenth year of our administration, we had willingly and faithfully labored on the new structure in the front part of the church. After the old structure had been fitly united with this new one by the concordance of new columns and arches, we had caused to be consecrated by Hugues, the venerable Archbishop of Rouen, and other venerable bishops, together with this new church: upstairs, the Chapel of St. Romanus; downstairs, [the Chapel] of St. Hippolytus and, on the other side, [the Chapel] of St. Bartholomew.

catholica terram regiæ domus, quam quater viginti libris a
Willelmo Cornillonensi favore filiorum et parentum locandam et hospitandam²² comparavimus, ad luminaria ipsorum
oratoriorum in perpetuum confirmassemus, subito sanctorum
5 Martyrum domnorum et protectorum nostrorum amor et
devotio nos ad augmentandam et amplificandam superioris
ecclesiæ partem capitalem rapuit. Nec nos ab hujus inceptione
illius potuit imperfectio devocare, sperantes in Domino quod
Dei omnipotentia et illi priori et huic operi sequenti, aut per
10 nos aut per quos ei placuerit, plenum poterit adaptare supplementum. Huc accessit nostram rapiendo devotionem, quoniam
infra Sancti Sanctorum locus ille divinitati idoneus, sanctorum
frequentationi angelorum gratissimus, tanta sui angustia arta-
batur, ut nec hora sancti sacrificii in solemnitatibus fratres
15 sacratissimæ eucharistiæ communicantes ibidem demorari possent, nec adventantium peregrinorum molestam frequentiam
multociens sine magno periculo sustinere valerent. Videres
alios ab aliis graviter conculcari, et, quod multi discrederent,
promtas²³ mulierculas, super capita virorum tanquam super
20 pavimentum incedendo, niti ad altare concurrere, pulsas
[358] aliquando et repulsas et pene semimortuas virorum²⁴
miserantium auxilio in claustrum ad horam retrocedentes,
pene extremo spiritu anhelare. His igitur et hujusmodi in-
festationibus toto animi fervore refragari maturantes, col-
25 lecto virorum illustrium . . . .
[359] . . . donec . . . et ipsa edificia . . . cum suis turribus
omnino honorifice compleantur.²⁵

22 Doublet, Félibien and Migne have *locandas et hospitandas*; cf. below, p.
258.
23 (See Panofsky, Bib. 132, p. 120, and) cf. below, p. 259.
24 (See Panofsky, Bib. 132, p. 120.)
25 The section from *collecto virorum illustrium* to *cum suis turribus omnino
honorifice compleantur*—that is to say, the whole remainder of the document
except for the conclusion—is literally identical with *Cons.* IV, p. 100, line 25,
p. 102, line 29. The few variants have been indicated on p. 142, note 4.

And we had forever allocated to these three chapels, as a Catholic dowry for their lights, the property in the Royal Domain which we had bought for eighty pounds from Guillaume de Cornillon, with the approval of his sons and parents, for the purpose of leasing and renting it. But suddenly the love and devotion to the Holy Martyrs our Patrons and Protectors roused us to enlarge and amplify the chevet of the upper church. Nor could the unfinished state of the former [structure] restrain us from beginning the latter; for we hoped to the Lord that the omnipotence of God, either through us or through those whom He would please [to choose], would be able to provide sufficient resources for that earlier structure as well as for this later one. To this was added, so as to incite our devotion, the fact that in the lower church that place of the Holy of Holies, worthy of the Deity, inviting visits of the holy angels, was so much cramped by its narrowness that, on the hour of the Holy Sacrifice, the brethren partaking of the most holy Eucharist could not stay there, and that they were oftentimes unable to withstand the unruly crowd of visiting pilgrims without great danger. You could see how people grievously trod down one another; how—what many would not believe—eager little women struggled to advance toward the altar marching upon the heads of the men as upon a pavement; how at times, pushed back and forth and almost half-dead, they escaped in the nick of time into the cloisters with the aid of merciful men, and stayed there gasping almost with their last breath. Hastening with all the ardor of our soul to put an end to these and other outrages, we brought together an assembly of illustrious men . . . . until . . . these edifices . . . will be entirely and honorably completed, including their towers.

ACTUM IN COMMUNI CAPITULO Beati Dionysii, præsentibus personis quæ subterscribuntur, quarum auctoritas sub anathemate confirmavit prædicta capitula.

Signum Milonis, Morinorum episcopi.
5   Signum Guarini, Ambianensis episcopi.
Signum Gaufredi, Carnotensis[26] episcopi.
Signum Hugonis, Turonensis archiepi-[360]scopi.
Signum Sansonis, Remorum archiepiscopi.
Signum Gosleni, Suessionis episcopi.
10   Signum Odonis, Belvacensis episcopi.
Signum Roberti, abbatis Corbeiæ.

[26] *Carnotensi* has been corrected to *Carnotensis*.

ENACTED IN THE GENERAL CHAPTER of the Blessed Denis, in the presence of the personages that are inscribed below, [and] whose authority has confirmed the foregoing articles under the ban.

> Signature of Milon, Bishop of Térouanne.
> Signature of Guérin, Bishop of Amiens.
> Signature of Geoffroy, Bishop of Chartres.
> Signature of Hugues, Archbishop of Tours.
> Signature of Samson, Archbishop of Reims.
> Signature of Jocelin, Bishop of Soissons.
> Signature of Eudes, Bishop of Beauvais.
> Signature of Robert, Abbot of Corbie.

COMMENTARY

PRELIMINARY REMARKS

THE TEXTS: DATES, TRANSMISSION, AND READINGS

OUR texts have been singled out from Suger's writings because of their interest to art historians and archaeologists, but care has been taken not to disrupt their literary composition.

Suger's general account of his activities as Abbot of St.-Denis, the *Liber de Rebus in Administratione Sua Gestis*[1] (hereafter quoted as "*Adm.*"), was conceived by himself as a report in two parts of nearly equal length, the first dealing with the improvement of the Abbey's economical condition, the second with the remodelling and interior embellishment of the church. It seemed therefore justifiable to include only the Introduction, in which this plan is set forth (chapter I, first half), and the Second Part, beginning with chapter xxiv (p. 42 ff.).

Suger's less comprehensive but more detailed report on the construction and consecration of his new narthex and chevet, the *Libellus Alter de Consecratione Ecclesiæ Sancti Dionysii*[2] (hereafter quoted as "*Cons.*"), has been reprinted and translated in full (p. 82 ff.).

One of the *Ordinationes*[3] formulated by Suger and approved by the general chapter of the Abbey (hereafter quoted as "*Ord.*") has been included because about two-thirds of it parallel and in several ways elucidate the corresponding sections of *Adm.* (chapters xxv, xxvi, and xxxiii A) and *Cons.* (chapter iv); about fifty lines were literally incorporated in *Cons.* Except for this passage, which differs so little from that in *Cons.* that it seemed

---

[1] This is the title affixed to the work by its first editor, François Duchesne (cf. below, p. 143. Doublet, who quotes from it extensively though not always correctly, called it, more simply, *Gesta Suggeri Abbatis* (p. 230).

[2] This title was apparently devised by Lecoy. As pointed out by Luchaire, Duchesne entitled the report *Sugerii abbatis S. Dionysii libellus alter de consecratione ecclesiæ a se ædificatæ et translatione corporum S. Dionysii ac sociorum ejus facta anno MCXL.*

[3] This is Suger's own term for a document which would today be called a "Rule" or "Regulation." In their entirety, these documents are usually summed up under the heading of *Sugerii Constitutiones*.

unnecessary to print it twice,[4] the *Ordinatio* has been reprinted and translated in full (p. 122 ff.).

THE DATES of these three texts can be ascertained with some accuracy.

By Suger's own testimony the composition of *Adm.* was begun as the result of a meeting of the general chapter held "in the twenty-third year of his administration." Since he was ordained Abbot on March 12, 1122, this meeting must have taken place between March 12, 1144 and March 11, 1145, in all probability after the consecration of the chevet on June 11, 1144, which was the crowning achievement of Suger's abbacy. The treatise was, however, not completed, or was at least subject to corrections, until the end of 1148 or the beginning of 1149 because reference is made to the death of Evrard de Breteuil "qui in expeditione Hierosolymitana occubuit."[5]

The composition of *Cons.* postdates, of course, the consecration of June 11, 1144, but must precede the composition of *Adm.* because *Cons.* is already referred to in *Adm.* as "scriptum consecrationis."[6] It can therefore be dated in the second half of 1144 at the earliest, and in the years 1146-1147 at the latest.

Ord., on the other hand, precedes *Cons.* by at least three years. It gives a detailed description of the laying of the foundation stones of the chevet and must therefore postdate July 14, 1140; but it is witnessed, among others, by Abbot Robert of Corbie who died

---

[4] Apart from slight differences in spelling the variants are the following:

ORD.	CONS.
Lecoy, p. 358, line 8 f.: *præsentia, quemadmodum in capitulo nostro consultum fuerat, pridie idus julii.*	Lecoy, p. 225, last line from bottom (our p. 100, line 27): the clause from *quemadmodum* to *fuerat* is omitted.
Lecoy, p. 358, line 15: *jaciendis.*	Lecoy, p. 226, line 6 (our p. 100, line 33): *faciendis.*
Lecoy, p. 358, line 16: *loca* omitted.	Lecoy, p. 226, line 7 (our p. 100, line 33): *præparata loca humiliter.*
Lecoy, p. 358, line 17: *Deinde.*	Lecoy, p. 226, line 7 (our p. 100, line 34): *Dein.*

[5] *Adm.* XIV (Lecoy, p. 174; Migne, col. 1221 C). This terminus was pointed out by Cartellieri, p. 81, note 4.

[6] *Adm.* XXVIII, p. 48. This terminus was pointed out by Lecoy, p. xi.

on January 22, 1142.[7] It must therefore fall into the period between July 14, 1140 and the end of 1141.

The chronological sequence of our three texts is thus: *Ord.*, *Cons.*, *Adm.* They have, however, been printed in the opposite order because *Adm.* gives a complete and systematic picture of the whole building and its contents whereas *Cons.* and *Ord.* deal only with special features and events. It is therefore much easier to interpret *Adm.* without a previous discussion of *Cons.* and *Ord.* than to interpret *Cons.* and *Ord.* without a previous discussion of *Adm.* Even so a certain amount of anticipatory references could not be avoided.

SETTING ASIDE innumerable quotations and the fragmentary selections in Schlosser[8] and Kingsley Porter,[9] our three texts are available in the following manuscripts and publications:

(1) *Adm.* exists in a manuscript of the twelfth century, Paris, Bibliothèque Nationale, MS Lat. 13835, which apparently comes from St.-Denis itself. It was first published by François Duchesne in *Historiæ Francorum Scriptores*, IV, Paris, 1641, p. 281 ff. On the basis of this edition it was reprinted *in extenso* by Félibien, p. clxxii ff., and Migne, col. 1211 ff.; a partial reprint with critical notes was included, in 1781 (not 1763), in *Rerum Gallicarum et Francarum Scriptores* (*Recueil des Historiens des Gaules et de la France*) edited by the Benedictines of St.-Maur, vol. XII (Martin Bouquet, ed.), new edition, Paris, 1877, p. 96 ff. In 1867, A. Lecoy de la Marche published what may be called the Authorized Version, based upon a collation of the only existing manuscript with the earlier editions, in his *Œuvres Complètes de Suger*, p. 155 ff.

(2) *Cons.* was first published by Duchesne, *l.c.*, p. 350 ff. from a manuscript of ca. 1200, formerly in the possession of C.-A. Petau (identified by Luchaire in the Vatican Library, Cod. Reg. 571, fols. 119 r-129 v) of which, however, the two last pages were

---

[7] U. Chevalier, *Répertoire des Sources Historiques du Moyen-Age*, 2nd ed., Paris, 1907, col. 3989; cf. *Gallia Christiana*, X, Paris, 1751, col. 1275.

[8] J. von Schlosser, *Quellenbuch zur Kunstgeschichte des Abendländischen Mittelalters* (Quellenschriften für Kunstgeschichte, new series, vol. VII), Vienna, 1896, pp. 268-290; the text is based on Duchesne's edition.

[9] Quoted above, p. xi; the text is full of typographical errors.

missing. These were supplied, on the basis of a fifteenth-century manuscript then in the Abbey of St.-Victor (identified by Luchaire in the Bibliothèque de l'Arsenal, MS 1030, fols. 81 r-82 v, 137 r-143 v), by Jean Mabillon in his *Vetera Analecta*, Paris, 1675-1685 (in the edition of 1723, p. 463 f.). Thus Félibien, p. clxxxvii ff., and Migne, col. 1239 ff., were able to print the complete text, whereas the Benedictines, *l.c.*, vol. xiv (M.-J.-J. Brial, ed.), new edition, Paris, 1877, p. 312 ff., again limited themselves to reprinting and annotating a portion of the text. The final version is found in Lecoy, p. 213 ff., except for the corrections found in Luchaire, and a few others made by the same author ("Une Très Ancienne Histoire de la France," *Revue Historique*, 1887, p. 271); the latter are based on some quotations from *Cons.* which occur in a historical compilation of the fourteenth century preserved in the manuscript Bibliothèque Nationale, MS Lat. 5949 A, and are apparently independent of the redaction available to Duchesne.[10]

(3) *Ord.* has come down to us as an original document (Archives Nationales, K 23 no. 5) which was first published by Doublet, p. 871 ff. It was subsequently reprinted by Félibien, p. cii ff., and Migne, col. 1453 ff., and was finally edited by Lecoy, p. 349 ff.

APART FROM SUCH typographical matters as punctuation, capitalization, paragraphing, and the subdivision of the last two chapters of *Adm.*, our text follows the version established by Lecoy de la Marche.

When preparing the first edition, the translator (like many other scholars) had overlooked the fact that the manuscripts of *Cons.* used by Duchesne and Mabillon and thought to be lost had been rediscovered by Luchaire.[11] With the additional aid of these manuscripts Lecoy's text has now been emended.

Though the original of *Ord.* was not accessible to the translator, he has felt entitled to reinstate the readings of Doublet and Félibien wherever Lecoy's text is obviously at fault, either through misprint or through the accidental omission of words the original presence of which is evidenced by the context.

After the first edition had been published, Mr. Harry Bober

[10] ⟨Cf. Panofsky, Bib. 132, p. 119.⟩
[11] ⟨Cf. Panofsky, Bib. 132, p. 119.⟩

was kind enough to check the translator's conjectural corrections with the original in the Archives Nationales. It was found that the original bears out, not only those conjectures which were based upon the readings of Doublet and Félibien but also several of those which had been proposed independently of the earlier editions. These, too, are now incorporated in the text which thus— apart from a few insignificant corrections in spelling—shows only the deviations from the version of Lecoy de la Marche indicated in the footnotes.

QUOTATIONS are indicated by italics and identified in footnotes. Passages from the Bible have been rendered according to the King James Version unless a remark to the contrary is made. However, the appellation of *I Samuel* and *II Samuel* as *I Kings* and *II Kings* (and consequently of *I Kings* and *II Kings* as *III Kings* and *IV Kings*), as well as the numeration of the Psalms and versicles, follows the Vulgate tradition. The translator has identified as many quotations as he could, but he wishes to repeat what Lecoy de la Marche wrote in 1867: "J'ai relevé avec attention les différents emprunts, que les éditeurs précédents n'ont pas toujours distingués; mais je ne répondrais pas de n'en avoir laissé échapper aucun."

PERSONS AND PLACES;
UNITS OF WEIGHT AND CURRENCY

INFORMATION as to the personages mentioned in the texts is normally limited to dates. So far as archbishops and bishops are concerned, these have been taken from P. B. Gams, *Series Episcoporum Ecclesiæ Catholicæ*, Ratisbon, 1873, occasionally supplemented by *Gallia Christiana* (several editions) and H. Fisquet, *La France Pontificale*, Paris, n.d. For secular personages and for localities the reader is referred to Lecoy de la Marche (Index); Cartellieri (especially "Regesten," p. 127 ff.); A. Luchaire, *Louis VI le Gros, Annales de sa Vie et de son Règne*, Paris, 1890; *idem, Etudes sur les Actes de Louis VII*, Paris, 1885; and H. Waquet (tr. and ed.), *Suger, Vie de Louis VI le Gros* (Les Classiques de l'Histoire de France au Moyen Age, vol. xi), Paris, 1929.

Libra ("pound") is the *libra Gallica* (later on known as "livre poids du roi," "livre poids du marc," or "livre parisis") which amounted, in theory at least, to 489 grams. Unless specified by the addition of *auri*, it is understood to be a pound of silver the value of which in relation to a pound of gold was estimated as about one-twelfth.

Marca ("mark") is half a pound, either of silver or gold.

Uncia ("ounce") is one-twelfth of a pound, either of silver or gold.

Solidus ("shilling") is the equivalent of one-twentieth of a pound of silver.

AUTHOR'S NOTE

THE figures preceding the following notes refer to the page and line of the Latin text as printed in this volume. An analogous system of reference has been observed in the notes themselves. "*Adm.* xxv, 44, 1," for instance, refers to that passage from the twenty-fifth chapter of Suger's *Liber de Rebus in Administratione Sua Gestis* which appears in the present volume on p. 44, line 1. ⟨In the ADDITIONAL BIBLIOGRAPHY SINCE 1945 (p. 264 ff.) the entries are numbered; and throughout the COMMENTARY, the interpolations in angular brackets refer to the entries by author and number, i.e., "Crosby, Bibl. 25."⟩

COMMENTARY UPON THE "LIBER DE REBUS IN ADMINISTRATIONE SUA GESTIS"

I

40, 1. ANNO ADMINISTRATIONIS NOSTRÆ VICESIMO TERTIO. See above, p. 142.

40, 3. HOMINIBUS. Even if the word were used in the technical sense of "vassals," "retainers" or "serfs"—as, e.g., in *Cons.* III, 94, 31 f. ("Milo homo noster") or in Suger's famous Ordinance of 1125 "De hominibus villæ beati Dionysii libertati traditis" (Lecoy, pp. 319-322; Migne, cols. 1448 B-1449 D), even then a *tam . . . quam* correspondence between *hominibus* and *privatis negotiis* would be unsatisfactory both from a logical and a syntactical point of view. It has therefore been assumed that *hominibus* should read *communibus*. The error is all the more understandable as the abbreviation for *communibus* (*ɔib'*) could easily be mistaken for *ōib'* which, to a French scribe, would have suggested *hominibus* with the initial "h" omitted.

40, 11. PALLIORUM. For the translation of this word as "textiles," see below, p. 222 f.: 80,6-9.

40, 24-42, 3. SICUT A CORPORE ECCLESIÆ . . . UTILE PROPOSUIMUS. This involved sentence gives the general disposition of Suger's treatise. He proposes to divide it into two parts, the first (chapters I-XXIII) dealing with the improvement of the Abbey's economic situation by the redemption of forfeited rights or revenue and by the acquisition, reacquisition and amelioration of outlying domains; the second (chapters XXIV-end) with the remodelling and reequipment of the church. And as Suger proposes to treat, in this second part, first the edifice proper (*corpus ecclesiæ*), and afterwards its contents, so does he propose to deal, in the first part, first with the town of St.-Denis itself and its closer vicinity, and afterwards with the Abbey's more distant possessions. The first chapter continues in fact with a discussion of the revenue from local taxes (part of which had been forfeited to a Jew from Montmorency and was redeemed by Suger) and from the annual Fair. For the words *castellum* and *castrum* see Ducange, II, pp. 208, 213: in medieval Latin *castrum* denoted not only a castle but also any town which was not a *civitas*, that is to say, did not possess the *jus Episcopatus*. The word *sedes* seems to be used, as often in Roman poetry, as a synonym of "grave" or "burial ground"; the town or borough of St.-Denis was indeed the "first" resting-place of Saint Denis because his remains had originally been kept and worshiped outside the confines of the Abbey proper, most probably in St.-Denis-de-l'Estrée; see Crosby, pp. 37, 65-70, with reference to Suger's own statement (Lecoy, p. 339; Migne, col. 1443 B) that Saint Denis had rested there for three hundred years.

XXIV

42, 4-6. AD ÆDIFICIORUM INSTITUTIONEM MEMORANDAM MANUM REDUXIMUS. Grammatically, the *memorandam* can be construed with *institutionem* as well as with *manum* without changing the meaning. The first alternative has been preferred because of the analogy of the *manum reduximus* to the *manum apposuimus* in *Adm.* xxv, 44, 14 f., and the *manum supponere* in *Cons.* ii, 88, 26.

XXV

42, 21. INDICTO. For the three famous fairs held at St.-Denis, see Crosby, pp. 45 ff. and 58 f. The fair mentioned here and *Cons.* iv, 102, 17, is the "Foire du Lendit" (the word "lendit" deriving, of course, from *Indictum* and still in use for a school holiday), which began on the second Wednesday in June.

42, 23. MULIERES SUPER CAPITA VIRORUM. Cf. the still more dramatic descriptions in *Cons.* ii, 86, 31-88, 12 and *Ord.*, 134, 11-23. It should be noted, however, that the same appalling story which, in *Adm.* and *Cons.*, serves to justify the remodelling of the west front accounts, in *Ord.*, for the rebuilding of the chevet.

44, 1. MANUQUE DIVINA CONSECRATUM MONASTERIUM. For the legendary participation of Christ in the consecration of the original basilica in 636, see Crosby, pp. 43 ff., 197. From the reference to this event, as well as from the general context, it is evident that the word *monasterium* here denotes, not the monastery as a whole, but merely its church. For further instances of this usage (which corresponds to the use of "moustier" in medieval French and of "Münster" in medieval German), see Ducange, v, p. 457 f., one of the sources adduced being a somewhat later document from St.-Denis.

44, 7 f. NE VIRUM SANGUINUM AB ÆDIFICIO TEMPLI REFUTARET. Suger's self-identification with King David carries a twofold connotation. On the one hand, Suger accepts Shimei's unflattering characterization of David as a "bloody man" (*II Kings* XVI, 7, 8) because he himself, too, had had to resort to arms in his early manhood and later on looked back upon these military exploits with a feeling, or at least a show, of remorse (*Ord.*, 122, 28 f.: "et—quod etiam conscientiam meam gravat —militari manu"). On the other hand, he rejoices in the fact that he, unlike David (*II Kings* VII, 5-13), had nevertheless *not* been refused the privilege of "building an house for the Lord to dwell in."

44, 10. VALVARUM INTROITUM. This phrase (as, two lines below, *introitu valvarum*, and *ingressu principalium valvarum* in *Cons.* II, 88, 27 f.) indicates the west entrance or entrances as distinguished from subsidiary entrances on the north and south.

44, 10. AUGMENTUM QUODDAM. For this small porch in front of the Carolingian west façade, which enclosed the tomb of Pepin the Short, see Crosby, pp. 77, 93, 121 ff., figs. 37b, 38a, 89, 92.

⟨Contrary to R. Krautheimer's reconstruction (review of Crosby, in: *American Journal of Archaeology*, XLVIII, 1944, p. 218 ff., esp. p. 220 f.; XLIX, 1945, p. 117), and to Hubert (Bib. 101, p. 137 ff., esp. p. 140, who assumed a forechurch similar to Saint-Germain at Auxerre) recent excavations have suggested that the Carolingian *augmentum* was a polygonal apse, or chapel; see Crosby, Bib. 25 and Bib. 26, p. 14 f.; Smith, Bib. 159, p. 81 ff.; Formigé, Bib. 56, p. 63; Vieillard-Troïekouroff, Bib. 173, esp. p. 345.

For the traditional burial place of Carolingian rulers in front of the church entrance, cf. Folz, Bib. 52, p. 90; Smith, Bib. 159, p. 78.⟩

44, 14 f. IBIDEM MANUM APPOSUIMUS. It is worth noting that plans in this respect were under way as early as 1125 when Suger freed the inhabitants of the village of St.-Denis from certain hard and unjustified taxations because they had contributed two hundred pounds *ad introitum monasterii Beati Dionysii renovandum et decorandum* (Lecoy, p. 320; Migne, col. 1448 D). Gall, p. 102, would like to relate this passage, not to the façade of the church but to the entrance of the "eigentliche Klostergebäude" ("monastery buildings proper") because Suger uses the word *monasterium* instead of *ecclesia*. However, in *Adm.* xxv, 44, 1, *monasterium* can only mean "church" (see above, p. 148 f., and two hundred pounds would be an exorbitant sum for the renovation of a mere convent entrance when a sizable property in St.-Denis, containing five dwellings, could be bought for eighty (*Adm.* 1, Lecoy, p. 157 f.; Migne, col. 1213 c; *Cons.* IV, 98, 14; *Ord.* 134, 1; cf. below, pp. 237 and 258). ⟨Cf. Crosby, Bib. 26, p. 32.⟩

44, 15. ET IN AMPLIFICATIONE. As Crosby has shown (see, in addition to the passages quoted *sub* 44, 10, pp. 94, 118, 150-154), there was a considerable interval between the east pillars of Suger's narthex as still extant and the front wall of the Carolingian church. Suger added to the nave of this Carolingian church—counted from its western boundary to the transept—not only that interval but also the area formerly occupied by the Carolingian west structure with its entrance hall and twin towers (see pp. 225-230). This link or "addition" (*Cons.* IV, 96, 25: *incrementi*) increased the clear length of the old nave by about 40%, that is to say—assuming, with Crosby's reconstructions (except for his figs. 37b and 38a), that the number of the Carolingian columns was eighteen and not sixteen—by four bays against ten. Suger could thus rightfully claim, not only to have "trebled" the entrances but also to have "enlarged" the body of the church itself.

For the existing parts of Suger's west structure, see, pending the publication of Crosby's second volume, Crosby, pp. 6-11, 132 ff., frontispiece and fig. 92. Further, Gall, pp. 36, 48, 93-107, 164 ff.; H. Kunze, *Das Fassadenproblem der Französischen Früh- und Hochgotik*, Strassburg, 1912, p. 5 f. Our *fig.* 1 shows the façade before the unfortunate restorations by François Debret which culminated in the removal of the northern tower after it had been hit by lightning on June 9, 1837.

⟨For Suger's link or "addition" see further, Crosby, Bib. 26, p. 42; Formigé, Bib. 56, pp. 65, 68; Crosby, Bib. 37 (cf. below, p. 235 f.:96,9 f.).

For Suger's extant west structure see further, Crosby, Bib. 26, p. 34 ff., esp. p. 38 ff. (and the review thereof by Gall, Bib. 63); Frankl, Bib. 60, p. 27 ff.; v. Simson, Bib. 158, pp. 99, 108 ff., and 156 note 49 (refuting Gall's review, quoted above); Crosby, Bib. 28, and Bib. 35-36.⟩

XXVI

44, 18. ORATORIUM SANCTI ROMANI. *Oratorium* can be a regular chapel as well as a mere oratory. Here it is a chapel in the upper story of the façade, dedicated not only to St. Romanus but also to several other saints, to the Virgin Mary and to All the Angels, especially—in deference to an old tradition attached to chapels in elevated places—St. Michael (see *Cons.* IV, 98, 1, and below, p. 237).

44, 19f. ROTHOMAGENSI ARCHIEPISCOPO HUGONE. Hugues d'Amiens, Archbishop of Rouen 1130-1164.

44, 24 f. TESTUDINE. As evidenced by *Adm.* XXIX, 50, 25 f., the word *testudo*, as used by Suger, means "nave," viz., a longitudinal structure having a central nave and side-aisles. Here and in *Cons.* II, 88, 30 f., the term therefore denotes the entire new west structure minus the towers.

44, 25-27. DUO ORATORIA . . . SANCTI HIPPOLITI . . . ET . . . SANCTI NICOLAI. According to *Cons.* IV, 98, 5, as well as to *Ord.*, 132, 33, the right-hand chapel (or oratory?) was, however, dedicated to St. Bartholomew. Since *Adm.* is the latest of the three sources, and since *Ord.* has come down to us as an original document of official character, it would seem that we have to accept St. Bartholomew as the titular saint of that chapel while St. Nicholas may have been among the *multi alii sancti* mentioned in *Cons.* along with him.

As for the location of the two chapels, we can start with the assurance that Suger—except for such special considerations as governed his enumeration of the altars in the crypt, *Cons.* VI, 118, 22 ff.—used the terms *dexter* and *sinister*, not in the heraldic or liturgical but in the normal or subjective sense, that is to say, from the point of view of one who enters the church from the west. This is evident from *Adm.* XXVI, 46, 11, where he describes the old Carolingian doors—of which we know that they were in the northern portal (cf. below, p. 159)—as being installed *in sinistra parte*. The chapel of St. Bartholomew (or St. Nicholas), then, was in the southern, that of St. Hippolytus in the northern part of the structure. As to the exact location of the two chapels, we cannot be equally positive; but it is a fair assumption that they were within the area of the old west front. More than four years after the consecration of June 9, 1140 Suger records the circumstance that the remains of St. Hippolytus were resting in the chapel then dedicated to him as merely a matter of common belief, not as a positive fact: "in sinistro autem, ubi sanctus requiescere *perhibetur* Hippolitus" (*Cons.* IV, 98, 6 f.). This curious hesitation would seem to show that the relics had not been translated to the chapel—in which case Suger would have been sure of the matter—but that the chapel had been established on the spot traditionally assigned to the relics; and this spot must naturally be presumed to have been inside, not outside the Carolingian church, that is to say, in the bay beneath the former north tower. It is this apparent uncertainty as to the whereabouts of St. Hippolytus's remains that we must take into account in interpreting such later records as the so-called "*Chronicon S. Dionysii ad Cyclos Paschales*" ("Annales de Saint-Denis," *Bibliothèque de l'École des Chartes*, XI, 1879, pp. 281, 290) and the treatise on the relics of St.-Denis up to 1215 as incorporated in the *Vita et Actus Sancti Dionysii* (Ch. J. Liebman, Jr., *Étude sur la Vie en Prose de Saint Denis*, Geneva and New York, 1942, pp. XVI-XIX, 204 f. with further references). According to these records the relics of St. Hippolytus, transferred in 1236 to the new "Chapelle de St. Hippolyte" (north side, first chapel to the west of the new transept), had not been in an *oratorium* located where Suger thought them to be but in an *oratorium* which had "long been in the central nave of the church": "diu fuerat in media navi [or, according to another reading, "medio navis"] ecclesiæ." According to the *Vita et Actus* this *oratorium* was *ante majorem crucifixum*, where Abbot Fulrad had prepared a *mansio et locus decentissimus*, after having translated them, in 816, from their original resting place in Alsace.

We have thus a choice between two hypotheses. Either, the relics of St. Hippolytus were in fact where Suger supposed them to be, viz., in the bay beneath the former Carolingian north tower; in which case they would have been *transferred*—some time after Suger—to their habitat "in the central nave before the major crucifix" whence they were translated to the new "Chapelle de St. Hippolyte" in 1236. Or, the relics were in fact "in the central nave before the major crucifix" all the time, without the knowledge of Suger and his contemporaries. In this case they would have been *discovered*—again some time after Suger—in a previously undistinguished spot where nobody suspected them to be. To choose between these two alternatives is difficult, but there are two strong points in favor of the second. First, no intermediary translation is recorded between that of 816 and that of 1236. Second, the *Vita et Actus* place great emphasis on the miracles worked by the relics of St. Hippolytus, especially on one said to have occurred in 1163 when Pope Alexander III, sojourning in Paris from February to April 1163 (P. Jaffé, *Regesta Pontificum Romanorum*, Leipzig, 1885, nos. 10815-10856), originally skeptical of the relics' authenticity and repeatedly exclaiming "non credo," was convinced of it by St. Hippolytus himself who "tantum fragorem tantumque tumultum intra capsam suam concitavit, ut rugitus tonitrui putaretur" (referred to in Ch. J. Liebman, Jr., *l.c.*, p. xix) and "consecrated the altar of the saint in person." This miracle tends to confirm the assumption that the relics, long worshiped in a place where they in fact were not, had surprisingly turned up shortly before 1163 in an entirely unexpected place and were therefore badly in need of authentication before their cult in this new place could be established.

⟨Cf. Panofsky, Bib. 132, p. 121.

For the location of the *duo oratoria*, see Crosby, Bib. 26, p. 22; and Bib. 28, esp. p. 66. Regarding the relics of St. Hippolytus, Crosby suggests that they might have been venerated in an oratory subsequently incorporated in the tower of William the Conqueror (for which cf. below, p. 161: 46,11) and therefore, at Suger's time, were long hidden under the debris of that tower.⟩

44, 27 f. MANASSE MELDENSI EPISCOPO ET PETRO SILVANECTENSI. Manasseh II of Meaux reigned 1134-1158, Peter of Senlis 1134-1151. According to *Cons.* IV, 96, 21 f., it was, however, not Manasseh of Meaux but Odo II (Eudes) of Beauvais (reigned 1133-1144) who was chosen to officiate at the consecration, which—as appears from *Cons.* IV, 102, 3, and *Ord.*, Lecoy, p. 358, line 10 from bottom—took place on June 9, 1140 (this date, well known to art historians, was curiously overlooked by Cartellieri, p. 140, no. 104).

44, 28-46, 2. QUORUM TRIUM UNA ET GLORIOSA PROCESSIO . . . PER SINGULAREM ATRII PORTAM . . . TERTIO INGREDIEBANTUR. From the very words *trium una et gloriosa* it is evident that the ceremony of June 9, 1140 was deliberately arranged so as to imply a Trinitarian symbolism. The "*one* glorious procession of *three* men" (one archbishop and two bishops!) performed *one* action in *three* stages, leaving the ⟨Carolingian basilica⟩ by *one* door, passing in front of the *three* "principal" doors, and, "*thirdly*," reentering the building through another *single* door (*per singularem atrii portam*) which had been taken over from the Carolingian basilica (*de antiquo in novum opus transpositam*). This evidently explains the *tertio* (ungrammatically and not quite intelligibly rendered by "to three" in Crosby, p. 119), and it has also some bearing on the interpretation of the word *atrii*. The passage has been taken to imply that the Carolingian church had had an "atrium" as we now use the term in medieval archaeology—viz., a colonnaded courtyard in front of the west façade—which was torn down in order to make room for Suger's narthex, and from the "single entrance" of which the door was removed and reused. However, in Suger's Trinitarian context the *singularem* does not refer to the position of the door in the demolished Carolingian structure but merely stresses the fact that the procession of June 9, 1140 reentered the building, as then extant, through a single door in contradistinction to the three west portals which it had passed. Now we learn from *Cons.* IV, 96, 26 ff., that the "doorway" or "chapel" of St. Eustace, from which the procession emerged, allowed it to reach the "Place Panetière" in front of the west façade, whereas the door through which it reentered the building opened onto the *sacrum cimeterium*. Since we know from old descriptions and plans that this *sacrum cimeterium* adjoined the church in the north, the *ostium sancti Eustachii* must have faced the south. It must have led from the southern side of the Carolingian basilica to the claustral buildings whence the procession could reach the "Place Panetière" by making a right turn; whereas the *singularis atrii porta* must have led from the northern side of the new structure to the cemetery. And since the word *atrium* could denote —and in high-medieval usage mostly did denote—precisely this, that is to say, a cemetery (Ducange, I, p. 453 f.,[1] adduced by Crosby, p. 124, himself, but unfortunately without consideration of the parallel passage in *Cons.*), we must conclude that the phrase *atrii porta* is nothing but a briefer formula for what, in *Cons.*, had been more circumstantially described as *alia, quæ in sacro cimeterio aperitur, ærea porta*; far from implying the existence of a Carolingian "atrium" whence the door had come, this phrase merely refers to where it was at the time of Suger's writing. ⟨For the "door" or "chapel" of St.-Eustace, cf. below, p. 157 f.: 44, 29.⟩

It would seem, then, that the question whether or not the Carolingian basilica possessed an "atrium" at all will have to be reopened (cf. also R. Krautheimer's Review of Crosby, *American Journal of Archaeology*, XLVIII, 1944, p. 218 ff.).

---

[1] This usage may be accounted for by the early and gradually growing custom of burying persons in the actual "atrium" long before it was found necessary to establish a special "graveyard" adjacent to the church. Thus, the old "atrium" having assumed the function of a burial ground, its name could be transferred to the more recent cemetery.

Suger does not mention the demolition of such an "atrium" in connection with the remodelling of the west front, whereas he does mention the demolition of the porch protecting the tomb of Pepin the Short. The bronze door reused for the "cemetery entrance" may have come from this porch as well as from an "atrium." And the only literary source which—apart from the passage here under discussion—has been adduced in support of the "atrium" theory (Crosby, p. 119, note 119) is anything but cogent. In the ninth-century *Miracula Sancti Dionysii*, I, 19 (J. Mabillon, *Acta Sanctorum Ordinis Sancti Benedicti*, III. *sæc., pars* 2; in the Venice edition of 1734, vol. IV, p. 316) it is reported that a thief, having stolen the iron bar from the door of the basilica's *vestibulum*, was stricken with confusion and returned to the *atrium sanctorum* in the belief that he was fleeing to the city. It is difficult to say whether *atrium sanctorum* is more than a general phrase denoting the "sacred hall" of the Saints in a similar way as the Psalms speak of the *atria Domini* or the Roman poets of the *atria deorum*. But if the writer had a more definite idea in mind this idea may be inferred from another, probably somewhat earlier miracle story (apparently not yet considered in connection with the "atrium" question) which begins as follows: "Denique, cum anniversaria Parisiis sancti Dionysii martyris celebraretur passio, dum vigilia a clero caneretur in choro, egressus Eligius templo deambulabat *in atrio*, viditque eminus virum cunctis membris contractum *contra sancti sepulcrum* jacere in pavimento" (*Vita S. Eligii*, Migne, *Patrologia Latina*, vol. 87, col. 499; cf. B. Krusch in *Monumenta Germaniæ Historica, Scriptores Rerum Merovingicarum*, IV, Hanover and Leipzig, 1902, p. 645 ff.). Here we see St. Eligius stepping out of the monks' choir of St.-Denis into an *atrium*; and in this *atrium* he finds, and in due course cures, a lame man "lying against" the tomb of Saint Denis. No matter whether this account was written in the eighth or in the ninth century, and no matter what inferences, if any, may be drawn from it as to the actual location and appearance of the pre-Carolingian tomb of Saint Denis (for this moot question see Crosby, p. 71 f.): the pious writer certainly visualized this tomb—described as "towered" and occasionally referred to as *mausoleum* in still earlier sources—as a kind of memorial chapel, located outside the church proper and standing in what can best be translated as "burial ground." And he would seem to have conceived of this "burial ground" as a secluded enclosure adjoining the nave of the church, and not as a semipublic courtyard in front of its west façade.

⟨For the Carolingian "porch protecting the tomb of Pepin the Short," cf. above, p. 149: 44, 10. For the question of the *atrium monasterii*, i.e. the cemetery to the west and north of the Carolingian basilica, see in addition the short notice by Morper, Bib. 128 (cf. below, p. 248: 116, 33 f.); Hubert, Bib. 101; and further Crosby, Bib. 25, esp. p. 360 (correcting his former views of his 1942 monograph); *id.*, Bib. 26, p. 15; Formigé, Bib. 56, p. 9 ff.; Vieillard-Troïekouroff, Bib. 173, esp. pp. 342, 345 f.⟩

44, 29. PER OSTIUM SANCTI EUSTACHII. After the proof had been sent to press Professor Sumner McK. Crosby kindly called the translator's attention to an embarrassing error. The translator had mistakenly assumed that the "door of St. Eustace," by which the procession of June 9, 1140 left the church, was in the southern wall of the "link" between Suger's narthex and the Carolingian nave, whereas Professor Crosby's excavations (cf. figs. 74 and 75 of his book) have shown that this wall was continuous. In reality the "door of St. Eustace" must have been in the south wall of the basilica proper, probably (as assumed by Crosby, figs. 15, 37 and 89) giving access to the southern transept wing, in which case this southern transept wing would be identical with the "Chapel of St. Eustace" to which the door belonged (cf. *Cons.* IV, 96, 26). This assumption is confirmed by the following considerations: first, the "Chapel of St. Eustace" is not among the chapels consecrated by Suger in 1140, from which we must infer that it was in use before and must therefore have formed part of the Carolingian basilica and not of Suger's west structure; second, the procession of June 11, 1144 proceeded directly from the east part of the church into the cloisters and apparently reentered in the same way (see *Cons.* VII, 116, 34 ff., and p. 248); third, the identification of Suger's *oratorium sancti Eustachii* with the southern transept wing—and, consequently, of his *ostium sancti Eustachii* with a door leading from this southern transept wing to the cloisters —is supported by the sources connected with the famous monastery of Centula (dedicated 799), where a door fulfilling precisely this function is constantly referred to as *ostium sancti Mauritii* "because the altar of St. Maurice had its place in this part of the transept" (W. Effmann, *Centula*, Münster, 1912, pp. 59, 61, 88, 91).

XXVII

46, 7 f. ACCITIS FUSORIBUS ET ELECTIS SCULPTORIBUS. Since this ablative absolute, instead of opening the whole paragraph, is inserted into a sentence exclusively concerned with the doors proper (*valvæ*) and not with the portal as a whole, the term *sculptor* would seem to denote—as taken for granted by such early writers as Doublet, p. 240—the bronze sculptors responsible for the door reliefs rather than the stone carvers who provided the tympana, jamb figures, etc. Then the *fusores* would have been "casters" in the narrowest possible sense of the word, leaving it to the *sculptores* both to supply the models and to go over the rough casts with the chisel and burin. This distinction between mere technicians and real "artists" seems also to be expressed by the contrast between *accitis* and *electis*. "Bronze casters," Suger felt, could simply be "summoned"; "sculptors," however, had to be hand-picked for quality, no matter whether he intended the *electis* to be understood as a participle (as has been assumed by the translator) or as an adjective, in which case the translation would have to read: "Bronze casters and outstanding sculptors having been summoned."

46, 8 f. PASSIO SALVATORIS ET RESURRECTIO VEL ASCENSIO. According to Doublet, p. 240 (supplemented by Félibien, p. 534), Suger's bronze doors measured fifteen by twelve and one-half feet and showed, in addition to the inevitable portrait of the donor ("prosterné en terre" as in our *frontispiece* and *fig. 15*), "en divers cartouches l'histoire des principaux mystères de Nostre-Seigneur." Suger's *et* correctly separates the Ascension from the scenes of the Passion proper which ends with the death and entombment of the Lord.

⟨For a drawing of Suger's bronze doors by Vincenzo Scamozzi from ca. 1600, see Barbieri, Bib. 8, esp. p. 229 note 20,
and fig. 171; for the iconography of the doors, see Gerson,
Bib. 65.⟩

46, 11. [VALVAS] . . . ANTIQUAS. These were the main entrance
doors of the Carolingian basilica as opposed to the less important door reused for the cemetery entrance discussed above,
p. 154 ff. For a detailed description of these *valvæ antiquæ*,
which—contrary to Crosby's statement that their dimensions
were not known (p. 122)—are reported to have measured
fourteen by eight feet and consisted of bronze panels mounted
on wood, see Doublet, p. 241; Félibien, pp. 57, 174, 534;
and, above all, J. Mabillon, *Annales Ordinis S. Benedicti*, II,
Paris, 1704, p. 253, from whom we learn that the portal to
which Suger transferred them was the northern one. They
showed the donor and author, *Airardus monachus*, offering his
work to Saint Denis and were inscribed:

"Hoc opus Airardus cœlesti munere fretus
Offert ecce tibi, Dionysi, pectore mitis."

Mabillon and, on his authority, Félibien, identify this Airard
with one Airradus (*sic*) whose miraculous preservation is recorded in the *Miracula Sancti Dionysii*, I, 15 (quoted above,
p. 156), p. 315. When the Carolingian basilica had been completed and a bell-tower had been built, Abbot Fulrad im-
patiently told him to remove the "now useless scaffolding"
from this bell-tower. Airard went up, was hit by a plank when
the rope that held it suddenly snapped, fell to the ground in
front of St. Peter's ("Lignum . . . Airradum . . . ante basilicam sancti Petri in terram præcipitavit"), and escaped un-
harmed by courtesy of Saint Denis.[2] Since the name Airard is

---

[2] This record is, thus far, the only basis for the assumption, accepted by all recent
critics, that the Carolingian Abbey Church possessed a crossing tower (see Crosby,
pp. 137, 152 with further references). But all these critics omit the passage relating
Airard's alighting "in front of St. Peter's"—a little church well over 200 feet to the
northeast of the Abbey Church's crossing—and thus fail to explain how Airard could
have been thrown clear over the transept and more than a hundred feet beyond it; his
fall would have been almost more miraculous than his salvation. Moreover, Mabillon,
whose testimony is never to be taken lightly, seems to have interpreted Airardus' bell-
tower as a detached campanile placed somewhere between the Abbey Church and the

very uncommon, this identification is entirely convincing, all the more so as both the "Airardus" of the doors and the "Airradus" of the scaffold must have been artificers. Since the order to remove the scaffolding from a new structure would not be given to anybody but the man in charge—who, in this early period, would go up in person at the head of his crew—a further conjecture presents itself. We may assume that that "petite figure en bas-relief d'un goust fort gothique," clad in the Benedictine's working garb, the ankle-length scapular, which has been saved for posterity by an engraving in Mabillon's *Annales*, p. 254 (*text illustration*, p. 161), represented none other than the Master Carpenter, if not the leading *operarius*, of the Carolingian St.-Denis, a modest forerunner of the famous William of Sens who, almost exactly four hundred years later, met with a similar though less innocuous accident in Canterbury. In fact it is under only this assumption that we can account for the extraordinary phenomenon of a mere monk, however much sanctified by his miraculous preservation, portraying, signing and poetically commemorating himself on the principal door of the most regal church in the kingdom.

---

little church of St. Peter; he even assures us that this campanile was still extant by the end of the seventeenth century. In the *Annales, l.c.,* he refers to St. Peter's as "being very close to that tower" ("quæ turri proxima erat"), and in a footnote to his edition of the *Miracula, l.c.,* he says, explicitly, that "this tower is still extant *behind* the Abbey Church rebuilt by Suger" ("Turris hæc *post* renovatam ab Sugerio basilicam hactenus persistit"). That the *Miracula* speak of the tower as being *imposita,* which might seem to imply that it was "placed upon" something else, is no objection since the verb *imponere* can also be used in the sense of "building" or "constructing" pure and simple, as when the *Digests,* VIII, 2, 24, say "pontibus præsidiisque impositis." We learn, however, from another ninth-century source (apparently not yet adduced in this connection) that the Carolingian Church did possess some kind of bell-tower—possibly, of course, a wooden one—surmounting the crossing. In the so-called *Revelatio* of Pope Stephen II, fabricated at St.-Denis under Abbot Hilduin, the Pope is made to recount how he sought relief from a mortal sickness by invoking St. Denis and was cured by St. Peter and St. Paul who appeared to him in a vision: ". . . fui sicut in oratione in aecclesia eiusdem beati martyris *subtus campanas,* et vidi *ante altare* bonum pastorem domnum Petrum et magistrum gentium domnum Paulum" (*Monumenta Germaniae Historica, Scriptorum,* XV, 1, 1887, p. 2; M. Buchner, *Das Vizepapsttum des Abtes von St. Denis,* Paderborn, 1928, p. 250). Since the "altar of Saint Denis" can have been only the Main Altar, which was in the crossing, this passage confirms the accepted view, and we have to assume that Mabillon—who was, after all, no archaeologist— identified another tower as the one referred to in the Airardus legend. Still it would be worthwhile to check up on his statement by an excavation in the square north of the present transept and chevet.

⟨Cf. Panofsky, Bib. 132, p. 120 f. More recently, de Montesquiou-Fezensac (Bib. 118, p. 128 ff.) has questioned the identity of the Airardus mentioned by the ninth-century *Miracula* with the monk recorded on the bronze doors. For epigraphic reasons he prefers to date the doors not before the second half of the eleventh century—a conclusion based, however, on a seventeenth-century copy after the lost inscription. According to Hubert (Bib. 101, p. 137 ff.) the Airardus doors, if indeed not commissioned until around 1060, could have belonged to the so-called tower of William the Conqueror.

PORTRAIT OF AIRARDUS FROM THE LOST BRONZE DOORS OF THE CAROLINGIAN ABBEY CHURCH OF ST.-DENIS

This no longer extant structure was assumed by Hubert—and following him, by Formigé (Bib. 56, p. 52)—to be west of the Carolingian basilica, whereas Crosby excavated its alleged foundations in the north-western angle between the Carolingian transept and nave (see Crosby, Bib. 21, esp. p. 124; *id.*, Bib. 23, esp. p. 176; *id.*, Bib. 25, esp. p. 357 f. note 11; *id.*, Bib. 26, p. 20 ff.; *id.*, Bib. 28, esp. p. 66 and note 20;

Vieillard-Troïekouroff, Bib. 173, esp. p. 346; cf. further above, p. 154).⟩

46, 11 f. SUB MUSIVO, QUOD ET NOVUM CONTRA USUM. Grammatically, the *novum* might belong to *quod* as well as to *usum* (as has been assumed by the translator), and in the former case Suger would have meant to say that his mosaic, though surmounting the "old" doors of the northern portal, was nevertheless as "new" as the doors of the southern one, with the *et* referring back to the *novas* in the preceding line. The translator has made his choice, first, because it seemed to him that a pause between *novum* and *contra* would destroy the rhythm of the sentence; second, because an emphasis on the fact that the mosaic was new would have been unnecessary in a period that had no technical means of transferring an old mosaic to another place; third, because the phrase *novus usus* parallels the phrase *novum opus*, or *opus modernum*, by which Suger denotes the "modern" structures erected under his own supervision as opposed to the "old-fashioned" style of the Carolingian (in his opinion even Merovingian) basilica (*opus antiquum*). In fact the "modern"—as we would say, proto-Gothic —style of Suger's west portals required a tympanum in relief, as in the central entrance, and not one in mosaic. The selection of the latter medium, rapidly obsolescent in Northern twelfth-century art, can best be accounted for by Suger's predilection for everything that shines and glitters.

⟨For the lower part of the relief that from 1771 to 1839 replaced the mosaic above the northern portal, see Crosby, Bib. 30, esp. p. 26 note 19; *id.*, Bib. 38; and *id.*, Bib. 41, p. 8.

For the term *opus modernum*, see Freund, Bib. 61, p. 97 ff.⟩

Yet the rich mosaic pavement of the "Chapelle de St. Firmin," fragments of which are preserved in the Cluny Museum (R. de Lasteyrie, *L'Architecture Religieuse en France à l'Epoque Romane*, Paris, 1912, p. 568; P. Clemen, *Die Romanische Monumentalmalerei in den Rheinlanden*, Düsseldorf, 1916, p. 181 f., with many references), should not be adduced as "made on Suger's orders," let alone as "made on Suger's orders toward 1140" (Clemen). The "Chapelle de St. Firmin" (originally Chapel of St. Innocent, *plan*, I), was not

consecrated until June 11, 1144; its mosaic is not mentioned in Suger's writings nor is it ascribed to him by
either Doublet (p. 317) or Félibien (p. 532); and, most
important, it was given by one Albricus whose kneeling portrait, still preserved, was placed in the center of the composition. Suger, for all we know of him, would have been the
very last man to tolerate in his church a work of art inscribed
"Hoc pius Albricus nobile fecit opus" and making no reference to himself. The Obituary of St.-Denis, kept up until 1261,
lists no less than seven monks named Albericus or Albricus
(one of them Almoner, and two of them Treasurers) but gives
unfortunately no dates (*Recueil des Historiens de la France,
Obituaires de la Province de Sens*, 1, 1902, pp. 312, 315, 319,
322, 334, 348, 1024 B).

⟨For the mosaic pavement, discussed above, see further
Crosby, Bib. 26, p. 48; Formigé, Bib. 56, p. 124 ff.; Stern,
Bib. 162, esp. p. 28 f.; Crosby, Bib. 30, p. 26; the last two
authors advance the hypothesis that the mosaicist might have
been an Italian craftsman and the same who executed the tympanum above the northern portal.

In 1959, the fragments of the pavement, formerly preserved in the Cluny Museum, were re-installed in the Chapel
of St. Firminus, now dedicated to St. Michael.⟩

46, 13. TURRIM. As appears from *Adm.* XXIX, 50, 22 ff. (where
Suger says that the *turris* was already completed *in altera parte*,
that is to say, that one of the towers was already finished), the
word *turris* can mean a single tower as well as the twin-towered
superstructure as a whole.

46, 15. VARIARI. This word can mean, and means here, not "to
change" but "to elaborate in rich, diversified manner"; cf.
Adm. XXVIII, 48, 29-50, 1: *tot arcuum et columnarum distinctione variatum.*

46, 15 f. LITTERIS ETIAM CUPRO DEAURATIS. In *Cons.* IV, 98, 17,
this inscription is simply referred to as "golden."

46, 18 f. AD DECUS ECCLESIÆ . . . AD DECUS ECCLESIÆ. In the first
line of this witty distich *ecclesia* refers to St.-Denis as an ecclesiastical institution, and *decus* denotes spiritual honor or glory;
in the second line *ecclesia* refers to St.-Denis as an architectural

structure, and *decus* denotes physical beauty. Expressed without word-play, the meaning of the distich thus amounts to the following: "In order to do honor to the Abbey of St.-Denis, which has fostered and exalted him, Suger has endeavored to enhance the beauty of its basilica." For other passages referring to St.-Denis as Suger's "foster mother" and crediting it with his early education and later success, see *Adm.*, I, 40, 25 f., and xxviii, 50, 15 f.

46, 26. OPERIS MIRARE LABOREM. Here as well as elsewhere Suger aims at the more sophisticated of his critics; those, that is, who objected to his enthusiasm for art not so much as a matter of principle—as did St. Bernard—but for reasons of taste because they felt that he was inclined to overemphasize precious materials at the expense of "workmanship" or "form" (cf. *Adm.* xxxiii, 60, 30 f. ⟨see below, p. 188⟩ and *Cons.* v, 106, 21 f.).

⟨Just as in Ovid's famous passage *materiam superabat opus* (*Metamorphoses* II, 5, quoted by Suger, *Adm.* xxxiii, 62, 1) Vulcan's metal doors for the palace of Apollo are extolled for their workmanship, so even before the inscription on Suger's bronze doors, we find praise of such skill on the still extant bronze doors of Monte Sant'Angelo, executed at Constantinople in 1076: "Rogo vos omnes qui hic venitis causa orationis ut prius inspiciatis *tam pulchrum laborem* et sic intrantes precamini Dominum proni pro anima Pantaleonis qui fuit autor huius *laboris*." Suger had made a pilgrimage to the sanctuary of Monte Sant'Angelo in 1123 (*Life of Louis le Gros*, Lecoy, p. 114; cf. Swarzenski, Bib. 165, esp. p. 43), and it is perfectly possible that he remembered this inscription since he remembered those at Rome and Montecassino (cf. below, p. 169). On the use of Ovid's phrase in the Middle Ages, cf. Branner, Bib. 13, p. 59 f. For the alleged artistic antagonism between Suger and St. Bernard, see Grodecki, Bib. 80, contested by v. Simson, Bib. 158, pp. 112 f., 123.⟩

46, 27-48, 4. CLARET . . . CLARIFICET . . . LUMINA . . . LUMEN . . . LUCE. For the interpretation of these terms in connection with the neo-Platonic light metaphysics of Dionysius the Pseudo-Areopagite (supposedly identical with Saint Denis) as transmitted by the translations and commentaries of John the Scot,

see above, p. 18 ff., and Panofsky. At the same time Dr. Meyer
Schapiro has rightly pointed out that Suger's phraseology
harks back to that of the Early Christian *tituli* (cf. below,
p. 168) in which the neo-Platonic doctrines, then at the height
of their effectiveness, expressed themselves in similar fashion
and some of which were certainly familiar to Suger from his
travels to Rome.

To interpret the *lumina* in the fourth line of our hexameters
as "eyes" instead of identifying them with the reliefs is improbable in view of the context which implies a rise to the
immaterial through material objects of the senses rather than
through the organs of the human body. The translator wishes,
however, to repeat that his rendering of "Quale sit intus in
his" as "In what manner it [the light] be inherent in this
world" is only one of several possibilities.

⟨For Suger's neo-Platonic light metaphysics, see further
v. Simson, Bib. 157; Sedlmayr, Bib. 154, pp. 237 ff., 314 ff.;
Grodecki, Bib. 86, esp. p. 732 f.; Gosebruch, Bib. 72, esp. p.
252 ff. (with a different translation of "Quale sit intus in
his"); Misch, Bib. 117, pp. 374 ff., 382 f.; v. Simson, Bib.
158, pp. 50 ff., 103 ff., 114 f., 119 ff., 131; Sedlmayr, Bib.
155.⟩

48, 5. ET IN SUPERLIMINARI. The distich "on the lintel," viz.,
beneath the relief of the Last Judgment in the tympanum of
the central portal, has disappeared; but the relief itself, showing Suger's diminutive figure kneeling at the feet of the Saviour, has come down to us, however much disfigured by the
ministrations of early nineteenth-century restorers (*fig.* 3).
The sentence beginning with *Et in superliminari* is Suger's
only unequivocal reference to the monumental stone sculptures
that adorn the west façade of St. Denis; his reserve in this
respect may be accounted for by his personal preference for
the costlier and more luminous productions of the bronze
sculptor, the silk weaver, the goldsmith and the glass painter,
a preference underpropped by his belief in neo-Platonic light
metaphysics. For further information as to the stone sculptures
of St.-Denis (*figs.* 3-7), the most important of which are lost
and have come down to us only in the drawings and engravings

by Bernard de Montfaucon, see Mâle I, p. 339 ff. and II, p. 176 ff.; A. Kingsley Porter, *Romanesque Sculpture of the Pilgrimage Roads*, Boston, 1923, p. 222 ff. and *passim*, pls. 1435-1457; M. Aubert, *French Sculpture at the Beginning of the Gothic Period*, Florence, 1929, p. 4 ff. and *passim*, pls. 1-4. Three heads of the destroyed jamb figures were recently discovered and published by M. C. Ross, "Monumental Sculptures from St.-Denis," *Journal of the Walters Art Gallery*, III, 1940, p. 91 ff. (our *figs.* 4, 5). For the *Labors of the Months* on the jambs of the southern portal, which are in better condition than the rest of the sculptures (*figs.* 6, 7), cf. also J. C. Webster, *The Labors of the Months . . .*, Princeton, 1938, p. 160, pl. XLVI.

⟨For a reconstruction of the lintels, removed probably in 1771, see Gerson, Bib. 66. As for the drawings and engravings of the destroyed jamb figures, I am very much indebted to Prof. Hugo Buchthal for having checked MS Fr. 15.634 in the Bibliothèque Nationale, Paris. The manuscript contains two sets of identical drawings of which one is repeated in reverse, presumably for the benefit of the engraver (cf. Stoddard, Bib. 163, p. 7). Of the two drawings of the so-called "Clothaire III," the one on fol. 51 has been preferred for reproduction in the present edition because of the more convenient comparison with the less damaged view of the illustrated Baltimore head (*figs.* 4 and 5). The same drawing in reverse (for which see *fig.* 4 in the first edition of this book) occurs on fol. 62, and corresponds with the engraving in B. de Montfaucon, *Les Monumens de la Monarchie Françoise*, 1729, I, Pl. XVII.

For the three surviving heads of the destroyed jamb figures, now in Baltimore, Md., and Cambridge, Mass., see further Stoddard, Bib. 163, p. 7 f.; Bib. 16, p. 72 ff. no. III, 14; Bib. 141, p. 149 ff. nos. 52-53; Scher, Bib. 151, esp. p. 60 nos. 52-53. At present, samples of stone of the three heads are being tested at the Boston Museum of Fine Arts by William Young.

For some smaller heads, perhaps from the archivolts of one

of the west portals, and other fragments in the Louvre, see Aubert, Bib. 2; *id.* and Beaulieu, Bib. 136, p. 56 ff., esp. p. 57 f. nos. 52-56.

For the stone sculptures still in situ and their nineteenth-century restorations, see Crosby, Bib. 39; *id.*, Bib. 41; *id.* and Blum, Bib. 43.

For the sculptures of the west façade in general, see Stoddard, Bib. 163, pp. 1 ff., 57 ff. (and the important corrections thereof by Grodecki, Bib. 85); Crosby, Bib. 26, p. 34 ff.; v. Borries, Bib. 12; Lapeyre, Bib. 110, p. 19 ff.; v. Simson, Bib. 158, pp. 110 f., 113 ff., 148 f.; Sauerländer, Bib. 149, p. 379 ff.

For the iconography of the west portals of St.-Denis, see Vanuxem, Bib. 168, esp. p. 51 ff.; Katzenellenbogen, Bib. 103, pp. 27 ff., 83 ff.; Thérel, Bib. 167; v. Simson, Bib. 158, pp. 110 f., 148 f., esp. 113 ff.; Vieillard-Troïekouroff, Bib. 174, esp. p. 183 ff.; Gerson, Bib. 65.

For the role of the west portals at St.-Denis as they relate to the beginnings of Gothic sculpture, see Goldscheider, Bib. 71; Giesau, Bib. 67; Grodecki, Bib. 86, esp. p. 729 ff.; *id.*, Bib. 89; Kerber, Bib. 104, p. 30 ff.; Sauerländer, Bib. 148.

For the sculptures formerly decorating the cloister at St.-Denis, not mentioned by Suger, see for the limestone statue of a king, now in the Metropolitan Museum of Art, New York (*fig.* 10), Ostoia, Bib. 129; Sauerländer, Bib. 145, esp. p. 150; Kerber, Bib. 104, p. 44 ff.; Bib. 16, pp. 72 ff., 354 no. III, 15; Bib. 138, p. 5 no. 1; Sauerländer, Bib. 148, p. 37; *id.*, Bib. 149, p. 381 f. A head in the Louvre (for which see Bib. 136, p. 61 no. 66) has recently been proven not to have come from the St.-Denis cloister but from Châlons-sur-Marne; cf. Pressouyre, Bib. 139; *id.*, 140, esp. p. 20 f. The provenance of two other heads, one in storage at St.-Denis (for which see Formigé, Bib. 56, p. 19; further Bib. 138, p. 5 no. 2), and the other one in the Art Museum of Duke University, Durham, N.C. (for which see Bib. 141, p. 156 ff. no. 54; Scher, Bib. 151, p. 60 f. no. 54), is still a matter for speculation.)

XXVIII

48, 8. EODEM VERO ANNO. As recorded in *Cons.* IV, 100, 27 f., and
Ord., Lecoy, p. 358, line 9, the foundations of the chevet
were laid on July 14, 1140.

48, 9. IN SUPERIORI PARTE. Wherever Suger uses this or similar
expressions—such as *superius opus* or simply *superius*—without special reference to a part of the building other than the
chevet they denote the upper choir in contradistinction either
to the enlarged and remodelled crypt (*inferior pars, inferius
opus, inferius*) or to the nave and transept the pavement of
which was on a considerably lower level (cf. below, pp. 172,
258).

48, 12. IN SCRIPTO CONSECRATIONIS. See above, p. 142.

48, 27. IN TRIBUS ANNIS ET TRIBUS MENSIBUS. The Trinitarian
significance of this statement is obvious. As we learn from *Cons.*
VI, 112, 1, the consecration of the chevet took place on June
11, 1144, that is to say, three years and about *eleven* months
after the laying of the foundation stones. Suger may have arrived at his Trinitarian figure by counting only the purely
architectural operations, subtracting the time for the installa-
tion of the windows and interior furnishings. ⟨Cf. Aubert, Bib.
6, esp. p. 196 f.⟩

50, 9-11. AULA MICAT MEDIO CLARIFICATA SUO . . . CLARET . . .
CLARIS . . . CLARE . . . LUX NOVA . . . CLARET. See above, p. 164 f.
For the words *aula* and *micare*, cf. especially the *titulus* of the
mosaic in SS. Cosma e Damiano at Rome (J. Wilpert, *Die
Römischen Mosaiken und Malereien der Kirchlichen Bau-
ten* . . . , text vol. 1, part 2, Freiburg, 1916, p. 1072, brought
to the translator's attention by Dr. Meyer Schapiro):

"*Aula* Dei claris radiat speciosa metallis,
In qua plus fidei lux preciosa *micat*."

For a similar emphasis on light, and for the frequent use of
aula for "church," see also E. Steinmann, *Die Tituli und die
Kirchliche Wandmalerei im Abendlande* . . . , Leipzig, 1892,
passim, especially pp. 35 and 37; for *aula* cf. also below.

⟨For the Early Christian and medieval tradition of light *tituli* see further, Gosebruch, Bib. 72, esp. p. 252 ff.⟩

The term *medium* means here, not "central nave" in contradistinction to the side-aisles (as it does in *Cons.* iv, 96, 24 and 100, 17 f., *Cons.* v, 104, 7 and 9, and *Cons.* vii, 118, 10) but the entire "middle part" of the church, including the transept and most particularly the nave as a whole, in contradistinction to the west structure and the chevet. This interpretation is suggested, first, by the context itself (in that *medium* is contrasted with *pars posterior*, on the one hand, and with *pars anterior*, on the other); second, by the parallel passage in *Adm.* xxix, 50, 25 f., where the nave as a whole is referred to as "*media* ecclesiæ testudo, quam dicunt navim."

50, 13. ME DUCE DUM FIERET. It is interesting to note the contrast with respect to two dedicatory inscriptions, one modeled upon the other and both probably well-known to Suger, viz., that of Constantine on the triumphal arch in St. Peter's, and that of Abbot Desiderius on the triumphal arch of the abbey church at Montecassino:

"Quod *duce te* mundus surrexit in astra triumphans,
Hanc Constantinus victor *tibi* condidit aulam;"

and: "Ut *duce te* patria justus potiatur adepta,
Hinc Desiderius pater hanc *tibi* condidit aulam."

In both these cases (see Leo of Ostia, *Chronicon Monasterii Casinensis*, in: Migne, vol. 173, col. 749) the "dux" is God or Christ, and not a human being, least of all the builder of the edifice. One might say that, in Suger, the evolution from classical Antiquity had run full cycle; for, the *duce te* in both Constantine's and Desiderius' inscriptions is, of course, a reminiscence of Horace's "*Te duce*, Caesar" (*Carmina*, 1, 2). Suger was certainly acquainted with those two couplets; he had visited Rome on several occasions and Montecassino at least once, in 1123 (*Life of Louis le Gros*, xxviii, Lecoy, p. 114). ⟨Cf. Panofsky, Bib. 132, p. 121.⟩

50, 15-18. MATRIS ECCLESIÆ ... QUÆ ... LOCAVERAT. Again the

mater ecclesia is the church of St.-Denis, here contrasted with *Ecclesia* as Universal Church (cf. above, p. 163 f).

XXIX

50, 22. TURRIM. See above, p. 163.

50, 25 f. MEDIAM ECCLESIÆ TESTUDINEM. See above, pp. 151 and 169.

50, 28. PARIETIBUS ANTIQUIS. For the legendary participation of Christ in the consecration of the original basilica in 636, see above, p. 148 f. That as much as possible was saved of the sacred old walls is also emphasized in *Cons.* IV, 100, 1 ff. In this respect, too, Suger was on the defense against traditionally minded critics, and it is true that he tore down the old building only piecemeal. However, when he died, nothing was left of it except a few substructures in the crypt; his faithful disciple and eulogist, Willelmus of St.-Denis, especially stresses the fact that Suger had made the church *ex veteri novam* (Lecoy, p. 391; Migne, col. 1200 D), and in a poem composed shortly after his death we find the line:

"Innovat inventum pater *a fundamine* templum" (Lecoy, p. 423).

⟨More recent scholarship has asserted that of the Carolingian basilica only the narthex and the apse were torn down in Suger's time, whereas the nave was not touched until the early thirteenth century; see Crosby, Bib. 26, p. 32 f.; Grodecki, Bib. 86, p. 727; Formigé, Bib. 56, pp. 65, 99, 103; Branner, Bib. 13, pp. 45 ff., 143 ff. Cf. however below, p. 171:52, 8 f.⟩

52, 6-8. NULLA ENIM RERUM IMPORTUNITAS . . . LONGAM SUSTINERET EXPECTATIONEM. This sentence has been taken to mean that Suger wished to make things uncomfortable for his successors by leaving them with a half-finished nave which they would be forced to complete. The translation here proposed—according to which Suger was fearful that the work at the west façade, were it to proceed as originally planned, would be such a drain on the available funds that in times of stress nothing at all would be left for the nave—has been preferred, not only for linguistic but also for logical reasons. Suger's sentence parallels such phrases as Terence's "nullo modo Introire possem, quin viderent me" ("I could not have entered without being seen") etc.; *rerum importunitas* suggests general difficulties rather than a specific inconvenience; and the *interpolate* in the preceding sentence ("betweenwhiles," "intermittently") implies that the operations in the nave would have been started and pursued—as far as convenient—even if the work on the west façade had *not* been stopped.

52, 8 f. ALARUM EXTENSIONE. Gall's and Crosby's interpretation of *alæ* as side-aisles ("Seitenschiffe"), and not transept wings (Gall, p. 104; Crosby, p. 133), is not only borne out by Crosby's excavations but also by Suger's usage: in *Cons.* IV, 100, 19, and V, 104, 11, the term *alæ* is uniquely determined as meaning the side-aisles of the chevet; where he does refer to the transept wings he calls them *cruces collaterales* (*Adm.* XXVIII, 50, 19).

⟨That an extension of the side-aisles of the chevet as well as an enlargement of the transept were begun under Suger, but apparently abandoned upon his death in 1151, was also confirmed by Crosby's excavations of 1946/47. If completed, Suger's nave would have shown double side-aisles and a non-projecting transept similar to Notre-Dame of Paris. Cf. Crosby, Bib. 21-24; *id.*, Bib. 26, p. 33; Grodecki, Bib. 86, p. 729; Formigé, Bib. 56, p. 103 f.; v. Simson, Bib. 158, p. 101 f.; Crosby, Bib. 34.⟩

52, 12. MATERIEM SAPHIRORUM. For the very expensive blue glass (which up to the twelfth century had to be imported from the East and was referred to, along with Suger's term, as *vitrum sapphireum* or, simply, *sapphirum*), see W. Theobald, *Technik des Kunsthandwerks im Zehnten Jahrhundert: Des Theophilus Presbyter "Diversarum Artium Schedula,"* Berlin, 1933, pp. 34, 39, 229 f., 241. ⟨See also Bib. 166, pp. 44, 49.⟩

XXXI

54, 1. TABULA ILLA, QUÆ ANTE SACRATISSIMUM CORPUS EJUS ASSISTIT. After having described the remodelling of the building, Suger takes up the furnishings of the church which he describes in the following order: First, the altars and crosses (*Adm.* XXXI, 54-*Adm.* XXXIII A, 72, 2). Second, the monks' choir and its contents (*Adm.* XXXIV, 72, 3-27). Third, the stained-glass windows (*Adm.* XXXIV, 72, 28-76, 13, with the replacement of the seven candlesticks of Charles the Bald squeezed in as an afterthought on p. 76, lines 14-17). Fourth, the altar vessels (*Adm.* XXXIV A, 76, 18-80, 4). The altars and crosses are described from east to west and their description thus begins with the new Altar of the Relics in the "rond-point" of the chevet. This is here called *superior* ("in the upper choir") in contradistinction to the Main Altar and the "Holy Altar" (Altar of the Trinity or Matutinal Altar) both of which were on the lower level (cf. above, p. 168, and below, p. 258). The word *tabula*, when used in connection with an altar and not otherwise specified, denotes the altar frontal ("antependium").

54, 13 f. DE DIVERSIS REGNIS ET NATIONIBUS. For the translation of these two terms (cf. also *Adm.* XXXIV, 72, 31-74, 1 and *Cons.* VI, 112, 11), see Ducange, V, p. 573, and VII, p. 97; for *regnum*, see also J. H. Baxter and C. Johnson, *Medieval-Latin Word-List*, Oxford, 1934, p. 276.

54, 15. SUB AMMINISTRATIONE OMNIUM. As appears from *Cons.* V, 106, 31-34, this means that, while dealers offered pearls and gems for sale, friends of the Abbey offered the money wherewith to buy them.

54, 23 f. IN VOLTA SUPERIORE. This phrase, in which *volta* is used as a synonym of "apse" (*volta superior* meaning "apse of the upper choir"), gives the clue for the interpretation of the much discussed passage *Cons.* IV, 100, 7-14 (cf. p. 238 f.).

54, 24-56, 4. QUADAM DE COLLATERALIBUS . . . DEAURARI . . . ELABORAVIMUS. TABULIS ETIAM CUPREIS . . . CIRCUMCINGI FECIMUS. The relics of the three Patrons were enclosed in silver chasses ascribed to the period of King Dagobert (*Cons.* VII, 116, 4 f. and 25) and lost in the French Revolution. As Crosby has shown (especially p. 177 and figs. 67, 88, 91) these chasses had been kept in the "confessio" of the annular crypt beneath the apse of the Carolingian basilica (*text illustration* p. 239 until June 11, 1144 when Suger moved them to the "rond-point" of his new upper choir. Here he installed them—according to a description in Doublet, pp. 248 and 289 ff., which, though not free from obscurities and obvious errors, is circumstantial enough to explain the phrases in Suger's text —in the following manner: The three chasses—suspended from silver chains with little silver locks—were placed in a solidly built stone tomb (*Cons.* v, 104, 31 f.: *fortissimorum lapidum muro . . . circumquaque muniri*) the inner vaults of which (*interiores lapideæ voltæ*) were lined with copper-gilt. Outwardly the masonry was concealed by a revetment of black marble (*politis lapidibus impactis propter interiores lapideas voltas*), measuring seven feet in width, eight feet in depth and five and one-half feet in height, which consisted of a base molding one foot high, eight (?) square piers two and one-half feet high, and a richly molded entablature; the interstices between the piers were filled with eight (?) copper-gilt panels (*tabulis fusilibus et deauratis*) two and one-half feet wide. This tomb proper was surmounted by a tabernacle of gilded wood, which was shaped like a diminutive basilica, and the "nave" and "side-aisles" of which contained three empty coffins ("formes de cercueil"). Directly before this structure, and integrally connected with it, was the new altar (of gray porphyry), the vaults with the genuine chasses extending into its very body. The whole was—at least in Suger's time—surrounded by a series of gates (*januis continuis*) which, when closed, formed a continuous enclosure "à claire voye" (Doublet, p. 248); the back of the monument bore the inscription:

"Fecit utrumque latus, frontem, tectumque Sugerus."[3]

Whether it was Suger who placed the *"Cuve de Dagobert,"* a big Roman porphyry tub, behind the tomb of the Patron Saints (so Conway, p. 118, but neither Millet, p. 64, nor

[3] Doublet reads: "Facit vtrumque latus, frontem, lectumque Suggerus," an obviously garbled version already corrected by Labarte, *l.c.* According to Doublet this inscription was on the back of "the aforesaid *cercueil*," and since he uses this term both for the stone tomb enclosing the genuine chasses and for the empty coffin in the central nave of the tabernacle, the exact position of the inscription remains somewhat doubtful. Certain it is, however, that it refers, not to the monument as a whole but to the tabernacle only; for, the former was more emphatically glorified by the longer and more pompous inscription on the altar frontal: "Magne Dionysi . . . significante placent" (p. 54, lines 17-22).

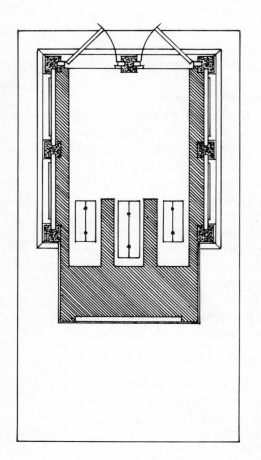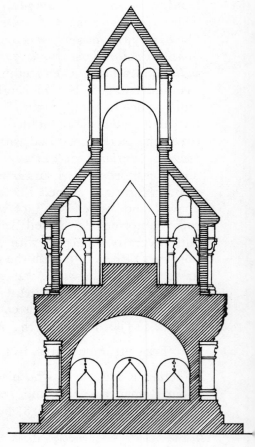

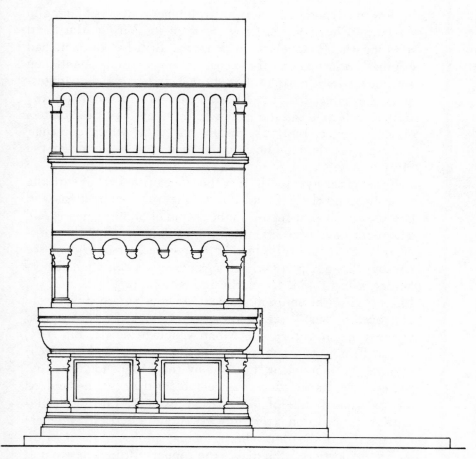

SUGER'S NEW ALTAR FOR THE RELICS OF ST.-DENIS AND HIS COMPANIONS (Reconstruction of the groundplan, cross section, and side elevation)

Félibien, pp. 20 and 532) is a matter of surmise. For further
details about the tomb itself, see Conway, p. 115; J. Labarte,
Histoire des Arts Industriels, ii, Paris, 1864, p. 252 ff. (still
indispensable); and, for a reconstruction based on Doublet,
Viollet-le-Duc, *Dictionnaire Raisonné de l'Architecture Française*, ii, Paris, 1859, p. 25 ff.

⟨For the hypothesis that the Carolingian rock crystal intaglio
showing "Christ on the Cross between the Virgin Mary and
St. John the Evangelist," now in the British Museum, had
originally adorned one of the chasses before it was mounted on
a reliquary for a portion of St. Louis' clothes, see de Montesquiou-Fezensac, Bib. 121; Lasko, Bib. 111, p. 61, plate 56;
and the relevant passage in the 1634 inventory (de Montesquiou-Fezensac, Bib. 125, p. 288 no. 345), which does not,
however, list the intaglio in connection with the tomb of the
Holy Martyrs.

For another hypothesis, that the stone carved relief with the
"Twelve Apostles," found during the 1947 excavations and
now used as an altar retable in the chapel of St. Osmanna (*plan,*
2), might have been intended as a replacement for the torn-
off side (cf. below) of Suger's "most sacred sarcophagus," see
Crosby, Bib. 42, p. 18 ff.; cf. against this assumption Sauerländer, Bib. 149, pl. 20 middle and bottom, p. 387 f.; and *id.,*
Bib. 150. For the entire monument, obviously not yet "entirely
destroyed in 1628" (cf. below), see the extensive description
in the 1634 inventory (de Montesquiou-Fezensac, Bib. 125,
p. 220 ff. nos. 199-202, p. 293 nos. 371, 372, and *passim.*)⟩

Since the monument, ravaged by the Huguenots in 1567,
was entirely destroyed in 1628, Doublet's description is indeed
our principal source of information about it. But Viollet-le-
Duc's reconstruction is certainly inaccurate. He crams two piers
into the rear of the tomb where Doublet speaks of "*le pillier du
milieu* de derriere"; he makes the copper-gilt panels two and
one-half feet high where Doublet calls them "deux & demy
pieds *de long*"; he makes the "Dagobertian" chasses, which
Doublet and Félibien saw and even measured, completely inaccessible; and he conceives of the clerestory of the little
wooden "basilica" which housed the empty coffins as of a solid

wall where Doublet describes it as consisting of twelve "colombettes a iour" (the ones at the corners shaped like little columns with bases and capitals), that is to say, as an openwork of small uprights that allowed the light to illumine the larger and "more elevated" coffin in the central nave. On the other hand, it must be admitted that Doublet's text is contradictory in itself. It is hard to see how all the piers and panels could have been of equal width if the overall dimensions were eight by seven, and how there could have been eight piers and eight panels—instead of seven piers and six panels—if the altar was attached to the front of the tomb and if one of the piers was in the center of the rear. We have thus to assume some errors in Doublet's description. Since he presumably counted and measured the features of the monument where it was accessible to the public, viz., in the rear, he would naturally set down the mathematically obvious number of eight piers and eight panels without thinking of the one pier and the two panels displaced by the altar; and it is equally understandable that he, after having taken the overall dimensions and measured the panels in the rear, overlooked the fact that those on the sides had to be one-half foot wider. But it is impossible that he should have been mistaken about the "pillier du milieu de derriere." Correcting Doublet in these two respects, we may amend Viollet-le-Duc's reconstruction as shown in the *text illustration*, p. 174 f.[4]

A still more difficult question is raised by the *sanctissimus sarcofagus* of the Patron Saints which had been deprived of one

[4] That the interior space of the tomb was divided between three small, separate vaults in the front part and a large, single vault in the rear has already been assumed by Viollet-le-Duc. The little vaults in front are indicated by Doublet's statement that the vaulted space extended "iusque soubs l'Autel" which could not have been higher than ca. three and one-half feet and thus could not have housed a large, single vault; moreover, Suger uses the plural *lapideas voltas*. The large, single vault in the rear, however, was necessary in order to make the relics accessible if necessary. Even so they could be reached only by crawling, precisely as had been the case at the time when they were kept in the old "confessio" (see Crosby, p. 177). That Suger speaks of several vaults, while Doublet uses the singular ("vne voulte"), can be accounted for by the fact that Suger describes the tomb from the point of view of a patron chiefly interested in, and probably responsible for, its technical construction; whereas Doublet describes it from the point of view of a visitor who looked into its dimly lighted interior from the rear and could see nothing but the large, single vault in front of him and the three chasses in the background.

of its *collaterales tabulæ* on some unknown occasion, and whose *ulterior frons* and *opertura superior* were gilded at an expenditure of ca. forty ounces. This "most sacred sarcophagus" cannot be identical with one of the three "Dagobertian" chasses; for, Suger explicitly states that it contained the remains of the Patron Saints (*eorum*) collectively and not those of Saint Denis, St. Rusticus or St. Eleutherius individually. Nor can it be identical with the new tomb in the upper choir; for, the incident of the abstracted *collateralis tabula* had evidently occurred in the remote past and the decoration of the new tomb, revetted as it was with marble and copper-gilt, would not have had room for a precious "side-tablet" the replacement of which required seven and one-half pounds of gold.

The only explanation seems to lie in the hypothesis that the three "Dagobertian" chasses had been kept in one large, protective receptacle before they were transferred to Suger's new tomb; and that it was this large, protective receptacle—indeed a "sarcofagus *dominorum nostrorum*"—which found its place in the central nave of the little wooden "basilica." Félibien, p. 531, informs us that the chasse of Saint Denis was only two and one-half feet long and only one foot and three inches high, while those of Sts. Rusticus and Eleutherius were still somewhat smaller. Assuming that the main chasse, placed lengthwise, occupied the center of the protective receptacle and that the two others, placed crosswise, flanked it on either side, this protective receptacle would have been a chest or coffin a little over six feet long and a little over two feet wide; it would have just about filled the little "basilica's" central nave which, as we learn from Doublet, was two and one-half feet wide and somewhat less than eight feet long. In its original place, that is to say, in the old "confessio," this *sarcofagus* would naturally have faced the worshipers with one of its sides, the chasses probably exposed to view by means of a fretwork or grill; therefore Suger could legitimately refer to the tablets then adorning the ends of the *sarcofagus* as "*collaterales tabulæ*." But when it had been placed upon the new tomb, now confronting the beholder with one of its ends—viz., the one embellished with Suger's expensive new tablet—he could equally legitimately refer to the other end—viz., the one that had merely received a new gilding—as the *sarcofagus's* "*ulterior frons.*" The little "basilica," finally, surmounting and protecting the whole, could well be called the *sarcofagus's* "*opertura superior*"; and the very fact that this wooden "superstructure" consisted of a *high* nave and *lower* aisles ("haute nef & basses voûtes," as Doublet puts it) may account for Suger's otherwise inexplicable assertion that the *opertura superior* was gilded "throughout, both *below* and *above*" ("*undique inferius* et *superius*").

The assumption that the tablet with which Suger replaced the lost *collateralis tabula* ultimately appeared on the front of the central coffin is further corroborated by Doublet's statement that this front, "ioignant ledit Autel," loomed up behind a precious panel (allegedly a gift of Bertrade, or Berthe, "au grand pied" in memory of her husband, Pepin the Short), which served as a kind of retable;[5] and that it showed a profusion of enamels, jewels and gold which would well account for an expenditure of fifteen marks. Even the curious pedantry of the inscription "Fecit utrumque latus . . ." might be explained by our hypothesis. If Suger, with characteristic respect for ancient objects, had made the old *sarcofagus* the nucleus of the elaborate contraption surmounting the new tomb—much as he had made ancient vases the nuclei of ewers and chalices—he could indeed claim credit for the *frons*, viz., the tablet substituted for the lost one and now adorning the "front" of the

[5] Doublet's assertion that Pepin himself had been the donor (repeated by Conway, p. 115) is refuted by his own rendering of the inscription: "Bertrada Deum venerans Christoque sacrata Pro Pippino Rege fœlicissimo quondam." Whether or not this inscription was authentic, the existence of so revered a panel at Suger's time would have inspired him with the wish to use it for the decoration of his new altar, and this wish may account for the excessive height (two feet) of the tomb's entablature. Doublet does not give the exact dimensions of the panel; but he does say that it was "square" ("quarrée") and that it was comparatively small, for he conjectures that it might have been "*vne partie* du derriere de l'Autel appelé le Grand Autel," in other words, a portion of one of those multipartite altar backs or altar frontals which are exemplified by the tenth-century gold antependium in Aix-la-Chapelle and the largely ninth-century "Paliotto" in Sant' Ambrogio at Milan. If so, Bertrade's panel, including its lettered frame, would have been from 1.25 to 1.75 feet square and would thus have fitted into the center of an entablature two feet high.

sarcofagus; for *utrumque latus*, viz., the side-aisles of the little
"basilica" with their less conspicuous coffins; and for the *tec-
tum*, viz., the "basilica's" high nave; but not for the *sarcofagus*
itself.

XXXII

56, 18 f. APPARENS IN EXTREMIS IN CŒLO. ⟨cf. Panofsky, Bib.
132, p. 120.⟩

58, 1-6. IN CONSPECTU SACRIFICANTIS SACERDOTIS. . . . EODEM
SANE LOCO . . . JACUERAT. According to the inventories quoted
by Conway, p. 144, Suger's Great Cross, while still extant, was
"behind the Main Altar" and "over the entrance to the vault,"
that is to say, over the central entrance to the enlarged crypt.
In other words, it stood in the center of the westernmost edge
of Suger's upper choir, and therefore in fact directly above the
old "confessio" where the relics of the Patron Saints had been
kept up to 1144 (see above, p. 172, and *text illustration*, p.
239). The phrase *in conspectu sacrificantis sacerdotis* refers to
the priest officiating at the Main Altar; but since the Cross,
including the pedestal, was more than six meters high, it was
visible from almost every point in the church.

58, 16. COMITE THEOBALDO. Thibaut IV (the Great), Count of
Blois, Chartres and Champagne, born about 1090, died 1152.
His mother, Adela, was a daughter of William the Conqueror.

58, 17. REGIS HENRICI. Henry I Beauclerc, King of England,
third son of William the Conqueror, born 1068, reigned 1100-
1135.

58, 19. STEPHANI FRATRIS. Stephen of Blois, brother of Thibaut
IV, was King of England from 1135 to 1154.

58, 27-33. PEDEM VERO . . . ET COLUMNAM . . . PERFECTAM HA-
BERE POTUIMUS. For the big, four-sided pillar or pedestal of
Suger's Great Cross—perhaps the most elaborate early example of that systematic juxtaposition of scenes from the Old and
the New Testament which had come to new life in the twelfth
century, reached a scholastic climax in the *Bible Moralisée* and
was finally summarized in the *Biblia Pauperum* and the *Speculum Humanæ Salvationis*—see Mâle I, p. 91 ff. and II, p. 153

ff.; Conway, p. 139 f.; Labarte, *l.c.*, p. 253 ff.; M. Laurent, "Godefroid de Claire et la Croix de Suger à l'Abbaye de Saint-Denis," *Revue Archéologique*, XIX, 1924, p. 79 ff. Furthermore Lutz-Perdrizet, p. 253 ff., and Cornell, p. 125 ff. As first pointed out in a still useful essay by L. Deschamps de Pas ("Le Pied de Croix de St.-Bertin," *Annales Archéologiques*, XVIII, 1858, p. 1 ff.), Suger's enormous pedestal was repeated, with many reductions and on a diminutive scale, in a pedestal, now preserved in the Museum of St.-Omer (*fig.* 23), which serves to supplement the old descriptions.

⟨For the history and reconstruction of Suger's lost Great Cross as well as for the extant pedestal at St.-Omer, see further Collon-Gevaert, Bib. 18, p. 160 ff.; Landais, Bib. 109, p. 140 f.; de Montesquiou-Fezensac, Bib. 119; Swarzenski, Bib. 164, p. 71 nos. 178-179, pl. 177-179 figs. 396-399; *id.*, Bib. 165, pp. 44, 47; de Montesquiou-Fezensac, Bib. 122; Green, Bib. 74, esp. p. 163 ff.; further Bib. 135, p. 26 f. no. 56; Verdier, Bib. 169, esp. pp. 24 ff., 32, 34, 43 notes 30, 35 f.; v. Euw, in Bib. 49, p. 257 f.; Verdier, Bib. 170 (review thereof by Gaborit-Chopin, Bib. 62); Verdier, Bib. 171; Gauthier, Bib. 64, pp. 122 f., 132, 134; Springer, Bib. 160; Kötzsche, catalogue entry in Bib. 143, I, p. 254 no. G 17; Bauch, Bib. 10, esp. pp. 158, 163; Kötzsche, Bib. 107, esp. 204 ff.; Morgan, Bib. 127, esp. pp. 263, 266, 270; Lasko, Bib. 111, pp. 188 ff., 192; the inventory description of 1634, now fully published by de Montesquiou-Fezensac, Bib. 125, p. 217 ff. nos. 195-198, and *passim.*⟩

As in the pedestal of St.-Bertin, the four busts of the capital, "looking up" (*ammirante*) to the Crucified Christ, represented the Four Elements. But it is worth noting that this amplification of the Terra-and-Oceanus group frequently seen "looking up" to the Crucified Christ in Carolingian art—an amplification required by compositional considerations and justified by cosmological doctrines vigorously revived in the twelfth century—did not affect the inscriptions. On the pedestal of St.-Bertin only *Terra* and *Mare* are explicitly identified as such (whereas the figure of Fire is characterized only by an attribute, and that of Air only by a gesture); and Suger's distich, transmitted by Doublet, p. 253, reads as follows:

"*Terra* tremit,[6] *pelagus* stupet, alta vacillat *abyssus*;
Jure dolent domini territa morte sui."

Mâle boldly translates *abyssus* by "le profond abîme de l'air" and thus obtains three "elements" out of four. But in reality the word *abyssus* can never mean "air." It is the Latin equivalent of what is rendered by "the deep" in the King James Version; and upon closer inspection Suger's cosmic lament turns out to be patterned upon *Genesis* 1, 2: "*Terra* autem erat inanis et vacua, et tenebræ erant super faciem *abyssi*, et Spiritus dei ferebatur super *aquas*."

⟨A more satisfactory interpretation of the unnamed bust pointing upward, formerly identified as "Air," is that it represents the Centurion of the Crucifixion scene; see de Montesquiou-Fezensac, Bib. 119; *id.*, Bib. 125, p. 218 no. 195, 4; cf. also Verdier, Bib. 170, esp. p. 18.⟩

From the old descriptions it appears that the *Salvatoris historia cum antiquæ legis allegoriarum testimoniis*, which was represented in enamel work on the four facets of the pillar proper, comprised no less than 68 scenes, 17 on each facet. On the evidence of the pedestal of St.-Bertin the subjects from the Old Testament can be presumed to have included the following eight scenes: (1) Moses Striking the Rock. (2) The Brazen Serpent. (3) Jacob Blessing the Sons of Joseph. (4) The Institution of Passover (*Exodus* XII, 11 ff.). (5) Isaac Carrying the Wood for his Sacrifice. (6) The Spies Returning from Canaan with the Cluster of Grapes (*Numbers* XIII, 24). (7) Elijah and the Widow of Zarephath (III *Kings* XVII, 8-17). (8) The Anointing of the Levites (*Exodus* III). All these parallels recur in the contemporary or nearly contemporary works adduced by Mâle, Lutz-Perdrizet and Cornell, and several of them are also found in Suger's windows and in the rear panel which he provided for the Main Altar (see below, pp.

[6] Doublet reads *tremuit*, an obvious error already corrected in all previous quotations.

187 and 215). At the foot of the Great Cross was a kneeling portrait of Suger himself, accompanied by the following distich:

"Rex bone, Suggeri dignare pius misereri;
De cruce protege me, pro cruce dirige me."

⟨For the various hypotheses on the iconographic program and arrangement of the enamels on Suger's lost cross pedestal as well as for recent attributions of surviving enamel plaques to this ensemble, see Kötzsche, Bib. 107, p. 205 ff., and Morgan, Bib. 127, p. 266.⟩

58, 35. PAPAM EUGENIUM. Eugene III (Bernardo Pignatelli, reigned 1145-1154) was in St.-Denis on Easter 1147, Easter Sunday falling on April 20 (see P. Jaffé, *Regesta Pontificum Romanorum*, Leipzig, 1885, nos. 9021-9023). It was on this occasion that Louis VII took the Cross, and that the Pope commanded Suger to accept the stewardship of the Kingdom during Louis's absence.

60, 1. CALIXTO. Callixtus II (Guido Count of Burgundy, reigned 1119-1124) was in St.-Denis on October 11 and November 27, 1119 (not 1121, as stated by Cartellieri, p. 11). See Jaffé, *l.c.*, nos. 6748 and 6789.

60, 1. INNOCENTIO. Innocent II (Gregorio Papareschi dei Guidoni, reigned 1130-1143) was in St.-Denis on Easter 1131, Easter Sunday falling on April 19. See Jaffé, *l.c.*, no. 7467; cf. Suger's description of this visit in the *Life of Louis le Gros*, Lecoy, p. 135 ff.; Migne, col. 1330 B ff.

60, 4 f. DE CAPELLA SUA PORTIONEM IN EO ASSIGNAVIT. The word *portio* (see Ducange, VI, p. 425) can mean, and would seem to mean here, that part of oblations offered to a church or chapel which was transferred to another ecclesiastical purpose.

⟨For a different interpretation of the above passage, cf. Verdier, Bib. 170, esp. p. 27 f. notes 1 and 13, who translates, "Il lui assigna un fragment, tiré de sa propre chapelle, du titre de la Vraie Croix du Seigneur, qui surpasse toute perle qui soit au monde."⟩

XXXIII

60, 9. PRINCIPALE IGITUR BEATI DIONYSII ALTARE. The Main Altar was always where it still is, viz., in front of the tribune in the apse of the Carolingian church, and in front of the upper choir since Suger. For its location and designations, see Crosby, pp. 92, 94, 103 f., 184; the former assumption that it was originally dedicated to Sts. Peter and Paul (Conway, p. 108) has been discarded by recent scholarship.

⟨De Montesquiou-Fezensac, Bib. 120, has pointed out an interesting fact in Doublet's description of 1610, namely, that the Main Altar was supported by four pillars of white marble, of which one carried the inscription M[illia] P[assuum] VIIII and had apparently been a Roman milestone. Since nine Roman miles corresponded to six Gaulish miles, the presence of this pillar could corroborate the Carolingian tradition that St. Denis was buried *in sexto lapide* en route from Paris.

For the assumption, that a twelfth-century wrought-iron grille, now in the central chapel of the crypt at St.-Denis, might originally have been part of Suger's Main Altar, see Formigé, Bib. 54, p. 109 f., fig. p. 108.⟩

60, 10. ANTERIOR TABULA A KAROLO CALVO IMPERATORE TERTIO. The sumptuous altar frontal given by Charles the Bald is lost but known to us through a Flemish picture of the fifteenth century published and discussed by Conway, pp. 105 ff., 134 ff., 141, 158, pls. II, XI (also *Burlington Magazine*, XXVI, 1914-1915, p. 236 ff.); *figs.* 19, 20. When the picture was painted the frontal was, however, used as a retable. For a discussion of its style and its probable relationship with Carolingian sculptures and miniatures formerly ascribed to other schools, see the literature adduced in Crosby, p. 84, note 63. The phrase *a Karolo Calvo imperatore tertio* makes us see why Suger constantly refers to Charles the Bald (823-877) as "Charles the Third." He calls him thus, not as the third Emperor named Charles but as the "third Emperor" ruling in France: a loyal Frenchman, Suger counted only Charlemagne and Louis the Pious, but not Lothaire I and Louis II (cf. also below, p. 217).

⟨For the unusual iconography of the Flemish picture "The Mass of St. Giles," which places the miracle in the Abbey Church of St.-Denis, though according to legend it occurred in the Cathedral of Ste.-Croix at Orléans, see Hinkle, Bib. 96, esp. p. 112 f.; for a detailed description and bibliography on this painting, see further Davies in Bib. 114, p. 109 ff. no. 4681.

For the lost golden altar frontal given by Charles the Bald, see now the catalogue entry by Mütherich in Bib. 153, p. 132 f. no. 48; Elbern, Bib. 46, esp. p. 119 f.; Lasko, Bib. 111, pp. 26, 62 f.; finally, the extensive inventory text of 1634, published by de Montesquiou-Fezensac, Bib. 125, p. 207 ff. no. 188.⟩

60, 11 f. QUIA EIDEM AD MONASTICUM PROPOSITUM OBLATI FUIMUS. Parents wishing to dedicate their child to a monastery as an oblate had to sign a document to this effect. This document was placed in the right hand of the child, and the hand together with the document was enveloped in the altar cloth of the monastery's main altar. Then a Mass was said at this altar so that the immolative character of the ceremony might be emphasized by the parallel with the sacrifice of Christ.

60, 12 f. UTRIQUE LATERI AUREAS APPONENDO TABULAS. According to the inventories (Conway, pp. 109, 141), each of these lateral panels showed, in conformity with the design of the frontal, an arcade of three arches; but above each arch there were circular medallions, showing the Annunciation, Visitation and Nativity on one panel, and the Lamb between Two Censing Angels on the other. As will appear from the discussion of Suger's rear panel, the panel with the Infancy scenes was probably on the right (south) side of the Altar. When Charles the Bald's antependium was transformed into a retable, the two lateral panels were put together and used as a frontal to replace the original one. In the Flemish picture this is unfortunately covered by a brocaded altar cloth.

⟨The inventory of 1634 (for which see now de Montesquiou-Fezensac, Bib. 125, p. 204 ff. no. 187) describes the two golden panels, discussed above, in the following sequence: on the right panel the medallions represented the three scenes of the Visitation, the Nativity, and the Annunciation; within the arcades below the medallions the Virgin and Child were flanked by the prophets Isaiah and Ezekiel holding scrolls with their scriptures; the left panel showed in the medallions the Lamb of God between angels with censers; in the arcades below the medallions St. Denis with the portrait of a king ("ung image de roy," perhaps mistaken for a portrait of Suger?), accompanied on the left by St. Eleutherius and on the right by "saint Ruth" (read: "St. Rusticus"?).)

60, 13. QUARTAM ETIAM PRECIOSIOREM. This fourth panel must, of course, be identical with the rear panel (*ulterior tabula*, described on pp. 60, 29-62, 16), which see.

60, 15 f. CANDELABRA . . . REGIS LUDOVICI PHILIPPI. Louis VI, known as Louis le Gros, reigned 1108-1137. The son of Philip I, he is referred to as *Ludovicus Philippi* in contradistinction to his son, King Louis VII (reigned 1137-1180). His golden candlesticks—also mentioned in Suger's *Life of Louis le Gros* (Lecoy, p. 143; Migne, col. 1337 c)—are lost.

60, 17-19. JACINCTOS, SMARAGDINES . . . QUÆRITARE DECREVIMUS. Contrary to Conway's interpretation (pp. 109, 139), it has to be assumed that these gems were destined for the new altar panels—in order to match the richly jeweled frontal of Charles the Bald—rather than for the candlesticks of Louis le Gros.

60, 29-62, 16. ULTERIOREM VERA TABULAM . . . CUM CRUCE QUÆRUNT. The rear panel of the Main Altar, matching the frontal of Charles the Bald in size and format, was lost before the inventories were drawn up (Conway, p. 141), and it has been said that nothing is known about it. However, the verses *Voce sonans magna . . . cum cruce quærunt* (p. 62, 11-15) convey a definite idea of its composition. Describing the reliefs precisely as we would describe them today—that is to say, from left to right, and giving precedence to the reliefs in the upper zone—they suggest six subjects arranged in two tiers. In logical continuation of the Infancy scenes represented on one of the lateral panels (which therefore must have been on the right, or south, side of the altar), the upper zone showed three scenes from the Public Life and Passion of Christ, while the lower exhibited the corresponding "prototypes" from the Old Testament:

1 Entry into Jerusalem	2 Last Supper	3 Bearing of the Cross
4 The Lord's Promise to Abraham (*Genesis* xii, 1 ff.)	5 Melchizedek Offering Bread and Wine to Abraham (*Genesis* xiv, 18)	6 Return of the Spies with the Cluster of Grapes (*Numbers* xiii, 24)

The correspondence of the Last Supper to the Offering of Melchizedek recurs both in the *Speculum Humanæ Salvationis* (ch. xvi, Lutz-Perdrizet, i, p. 34/35 and ii, pls. 31/32) and in the *Biblia Pauperum* (Cornell, pp. 29 f., 272, pl. 8 and others).

The correspondence of the Bearing of the Cross to the Return of the Spies recurs in the *Speculum* (Lutz-Perdrizet, i, p. 46/47 and ii, pls. 43/44), and it is alluded to in the *Bible Moralisée* (de Laborde, pl. 76), where, with an interesting parallel to Suger's *qui Christum cum cruce quærunt*, the younger of the two spies is compared to those *qui vident Christum et sequuntur eum*; he reappears in the explanatory picture under the guise of St. Andrew Carrying the Cross.

The only problem is posed by the apparently unique juxtaposition of the Entry into Jerusalem with the Promise to Abraham according to *Genesis* xii, 1 ff. (needless to say this promise cannot be the one given to him after the Sacrifice of Isaac as told in *Genesis* xxii, 17 f., first because it must precede the Melchizedek incident, and, second, because the Sacrifice of Isaac was the accepted prototype of the Crucifixion). The medium of comparison would seem to be the idea of a triumphant entry into territory to be "conquered," and, more specifically, the parallel between the *magnificabo nomen tuum, erisque benedictus* in *Genesis* XII, 2 and the *Hosanna, benedictus qui venit in nomine Domini* in *Mark* XI, 9-10 and *John* XII, 13.

60, 30. BARBARI ET PROFUSIORES NOSTRATIBUS ERANT ARTIFICES. The term *barbari* apparently refers to those artists whom Suger had imported from non-French and therefore, from his point of view, "barbarian" countries, perhaps specifically to the "goldsmiths from Lorraine" previously mentioned in connection with the Great Cross (*Adm.* XXXII, 58, 30; cf. A. Watson, *The Early Iconography of the Tree of Jesse*, London, 1934, p. 81). Suger here uses the collaboration of these "foreigners" as a defense against the same critics to whose views he also alludes in the metrical inscription of the west doors (*Adm.* XXVII, 46, 26), and he is careful to add, that, in spite of that "barbaric" lavishness, the work had turned out to be no less, nay, even more, remarkable for its artistic than for its material value (cf. also *Cons.* V, 106, 21). The reference to "certain people" who were harping on the idea that "form" should bear a stronger emphasis than "matter" has a distinctly personal and faintly ironical ring. ⟨For the interpretation of *barbari . . . artifices* as artists of the Merovingian period, cf. Verdier, Bib. 170, p. 17 note 62.⟩

60, 31. ANAGLIFO OPERE. For the specific significance of this Greek term (ἀνάγλυφος from ἀναγλύφω), see the good collection of instances in Ducange, I, p. 236.

62, 4-8. ET QUONIAM TACITA VISUS COGNITIONE . . . APICIBUS LITTERARUM. A somewhat mannered expression (originating with Aulus Gellius, *Noctes Atticæ*, XIII, 31, 10 and XVII, 9, 12) for *litteræ* pure and simple. Had Suger written a special little guide to the iconography of the reliefs or had he affixed some sort of label explaining the mysterious "virtues" of the divers precious stones, etc. (cf. *Adm.* XXXII, 62, 22-64, 3)? The latter assumption is not so odd as it might seem. According to Albrecht von Scharfenberg's *Titurel* (ca. 1270, but incorporating many reminiscences of an earlier period of architecture), samples of all the precious stones that served as materials for the Temple of the Holy Grail (which represented the Heavenly Jerusalem) were exhibited, museum fashion, before the doors of the edifice, each with a careful explanation of its name and properties:

"Mit listen man dô trahte, vor ieglîcher porten
aller steine slahte, di zů dem rîchen grôzen
                                        werk gehôrten,
di lâgen neben ein ander dâ bekennet,
*geschriben bî ieglîchem stŭnt sîn art und
                              wie er was genennet*"

(F. Zarncke, "Der Graltempel," in *Abhandlungen der Philologisch-Philosophischen Classe der Königlich Sächsischen Gesellschaft der Wissenschaften*, VII, 1879, p. 468, v. 102). The content of these explanations can be inferred from the *Titurel* itself (p. 435, v. 4-7; p. 440, v. 19-21; "Auslegung," pp. 534-538, v. 35-46), where all the stones, especially those employed for Aaron's breastplate, are described as having special and important virtues; the sardonyx, for instance, stands for and promotes chastity, the chrysolith dispels fear and protects from sinful love, the jasper cures sickness, and so on. ⟨Cf. Panofsky, Bib. 132, p. 120.⟩

62, 11-16. VOCE SONANS MAGNA . . . CUM CRUCE QUÆRUNT. For the meaning and sequence of these lines, see p. 186 f.

62, 19. SANCTI ELIGII . . . CRUCEM. For the so-called "Cross of St. Eloy"—now lost—see Félibien, pl. IV, facing p. 542, B; Conway, p. 125 f. and pl. II (also *idem, Burlington Magazine*, XXVI, 1914/15, p. 236 ff.); *figs.* 19, 20. For the peerless goldsmith St. Eloy himself (ca. 588-659, Bishop of Noyon since 640), see Thieme-Becker, *Allgemeines Lexikon der Bildenden Künstler*, X, 1914, p. 459; and, more particularly, J. J. Marquet de Vasselot, *Bibliographie de l'Orfèvrerie et de l'Emaillerie Française*, Paris, 1925, pp. 87, 100, 108, 109, 173, 176, 177, 185.

A fragment of the Cross of St. Eloy has been identified in

the Cabinet des Médailles, and published with excellent commentary by Comte B. de Montesquiou-Fezensac, "Une épave du trésor de Saint-Denis . . . ," in *Mélanges en l'honneur de François Martroye*, 1940, p. 1 ff.; our *fig.* 21.

⟨Cf. further *id.*, Bib. 118, p. 80; *id.*, Bib. 124.

For the goldsmith St. Eloy, see further Volbach, Bib. 175, and the beautiful color reproduction of the rediscovered piece *ibid.*, fig. 266. Against the identification of the jeweled cross represented in the London painting of "The Mass of St. Giles" (cf. above, p. 184 f.; *figs.* 19, 20) with the Cross of St. Eloy, see recently Elbern, Bib. 46, p. 120 f., and Lasko, Bib. 111, pp. 39, esp. 266 note 33. For the inventory description of 1634, now published by de Montesquiou-Fezensac, see Bib. 125, p. 213 ff. no. 189 and *passim.*⟩

62, 20. ORNAMENTUM, QUOD VULGO "CRISTA" VOCATUR. This splendidly useless piece of decoration, known as the *"Escrin de Charlemagne"* though it was probably a gift of Charles the Bald, is lost except for the top jewel in the Cabinet des Médailles (illustrated in Conway, fig. 2). For the whole, see Félibien, pl. IV, facing p. 542, c; Crosby, pp. 72, 163; Guibert, p. 47 ff. and pl. IX; Conway, p. 128 ff. and pl. X; our *fig.* 24.

⟨See further Hubert, de Montesquiou-Fezensac, and Grand, Bib. 100; Hubert, Bib. 102; Steingräber, Bib. 161, p. 19 ff.; Mütherich, in Bib. 153, p. 132 no. 47; Elbern, in Bib. 1, p. 381 f. nos. 562 a and b; *id.*, Bib. 46, p. 140; most explicitly, Lasko, Bib. 111, p. 24 ff., who suggests that the chasse might have been part of Charlemagne's treasure at Aix-la-Chapelle and later have been presented to St.-Denis by Charles the Bald. Detailed description of 1634 in de Montesquiou-Fezensac, Bib. 125, p. 89 ff. no. 4. The crest jewel preserved in the Cabinet des Médailles (our *fig.* 25), an aquamarine intaglio signed by a certain Evodos, shows the portrait of Julia, daughter of the Emperor Titus (A.D. 79-81), perhaps re-interpreted as an image of the Virgin. While the gold mounting with nine sapphires and six pearls is thought to be Carolingian, one of the sapphires engraved with a monogram of the Virgin in Greek and a dolphin might be of Byzantine origin.⟩

62, 21. SUPERPONI. This verb would seem to indicate that both the "Cross of St. Eloy" and the *"Escrin de Charlemagne"* were normally kept out of sight and were placed upon the Main Altar on solemn occasions only.

62, 22. OMNIS, INQUAM, LAPIS PRECIOSUS. The passage *Ezekiel* XXVIII, 13, which Suger here quotes, gives a selection from the stones in Aaron's breastplate (*Exodus* XXVIII, 17 ff.) where each stone signifies one of the tribes of Israel. In addition, precious stones were always believed to be endowed with powerful medicinal and magic qualities, a subject abundantly treated in the so-called Lapidaries and other sources (cf. the remarks on *Adm.* XXXIII, 62, 4-8) and it is these "virtues" to which Suger alludes in the following sentence.

⟨Ezekiel's selection of nine stones is commented upon by Gregory the Great as referring to the nine orders of the Angels, cf. *Moralia*, lib. XXXII, cap. XXIII, 48 (Migne, *Pat. Lat.*, vol. 76, col. 665); *Homiliæ in Evangelia*, lib. II, homilia XXXIV, 7 (*ibid.*, col. 1249 f.). By quoting Ezekiel, Suger thus pays another tribute to Dionysius the Pseudo-Areopagite, the author of *De Cælesti Hierarchia*, and in his ecstasy, he is therefore transported among the angels who dwell in that "region of the universe which neither exists entirely in the slime of the earth nor entirely in the purity of Heaven" (cf. above, p. 21). For the properties ascribed to precious stones, see Evans, Bib. 48, p. 79.⟩

62, 27-64, 3. UNDE, CUM EX DILECTIONE . . . POSSE TRANSFERRI. Owing to its misreading by Kingsley Porter, *Medieval Architecture*, II, p. 252 f., this passage has gained currency as a characterization of the emotional impact of Gothic architecture. In reality it describes only the trancelike state induced by the intense contemplation of lustrous pearls and precious stones. For the connection of this notion with the neo-Platonic doctrines of the Pseudo-Areopagite and John the Scot, see above, p. 21, and Panofsky.

64, 4-20. CONFERRE CONSUEVI . . . EXPONERENTUR. This passage exhibits a most amusing combination of wishful thinking and well-bred hypocrisy. Well-meaning travelers had assured Suger—as he of course expected them to do—that his treasures surpassed the marvels of Constantinople; whereas other, less accommodating visitors had asserted the contrary. Reluctant to give either group the lie, Suger develops—and pretends to believe in—the theory that both might be right because the ecclesiastical authorities of Constantinople might have hidden the most valuable objects for fear of being robbed, so that those who had assured him of the superiority of his own possessions would have seen only a small fraction of the Constantinopolitan marvels. But the last sentence, protesting absolute confidence in the truthfulness of the skeptics, and yet concluding with the pious wish that those "inestimable and incomparable things" in Constantinople might have been accessible to others as well, makes it perfectly clear that Suger—smilingly dismissing the subject with a nicely twisted quotation from *Romans*—preferred to believe in the superiority of his own treasures.

64, 10 f. GRÆCORUM ET LATINORUM ASCITA FAMILIARITAS. In translating this somewhat difficult passage, it has been assumed that Suger, as always, erroneously substitutes *asciscere* ("to adopt, to appropriate") for *accire* ("to call in, to summon, to invite"); cf. *Adm.* XXIV, 42, 14 f.: *ascitis . . . pictoribus*; *Adm.* XXXIII A, 68, 24 f. and 33: *personas ascivimus* and *ascitis aurifabris*; *Ord.*, Lecoy, p. 358, line 6, even: *adscita . . . Ludovici . . . præsentia*; *Life of Louis le Gros*, XXVI, Lecoy, p. 105: *absentes asciscit*. The use of the word *familiaritas* in the sense of a concrete "group or circle of friends or adherents" (instead of "friendship" in the abstract) is common in medieval as well as classical usage (cf., e.g., Tacitus, *Annales* XV, 50, 2: *Senecio e præcipua familiaritate Neronis*). In case *asciscere* had here been used in the orthodox way the translation would have to read: "lest, through the rash rapacity of a stupid few, the adscititious friendship between the Greeks and Latins might suddenly be turned into sedition and warlike hostilities," *ascita* then being understandable, as in the phrases *ascitus lepos* or *asciti milites*, as denoting something alien or acquired in contradistinction to something native or natural. This, too, makes sense; but it presupposes, as mentioned before, a use of *ascitus* otherwise foreign to Suger and, in addition, the somewhat forced interpretation of the verb *movere* as "to turn into" instead of "to move."

64, 16. ET AB EPISCOPO LAUDUNENSI HUGONE. Bishop Hugues I of Laon reigned only six months in 1112-1113, long before Suger had been elected Abbot, and is not mentioned by Suger in any other connection. Either the conversation about the treasures in Constantinople must have taken place prior to 1113 and without comparative reference to those in St.-Denis; or Suger substituted the name of Hugo for that of his famous successor, Barthélemi de Vir or Bartholomæus de Jura (reigned 1113-1151) with whom Suger was on very good terms in the earlier years of his abbacy (Cartellieri, p. 131 ff., nos. 32, 43, 50, 51).

64, 24-29. SI LIBATORIA AUREA . . . QUANTO MAGIS . . . EXPONI DEBENT. In his unfaltering effort to justify his enthusiasm for gold and precious stones Suger had the audacity to paraphrase, in this sentence, the following passage from *Hebrews* IX, 13-14: "*Si enim sanguis hircorum* et taurorum et cinis *vitulæ* aspersus inquinatos sanctificat ad emendationem carnis: *quanto magis sanguis Christi* . . . emendabit conscientiam nostram.*" ("For if the blood of bulls and of goats, and the ashes of an heifer sprinkling the unclean, sanctifieth to the purifying of the flesh: How much more shall the blood of Christ . . . purge your conscience.") The *vacca rufa*, whose ashes were used for the "water of expiation," comes from *Numbers* IX, 2. The *phialæ* and *mortariola* occur severally in the Old Testament, but in conjunction with *libatoria* only in *I Maccabees* I, 23.

64, 30-66, 3. SI DE SANCTORUM CHERUBIM ET SERAPHIM . . . FAMULATUM. TANTAM TAMEN PROPICIATIONEM . . . HABEMUS. In translating this passage, it has been assumed that *nova* is an ablative to be construed with *creatione*, and that *nostra* is a nominative to be construed with *substantia*. If *nova* were understood as a nominative to be construed with *substantia*, and *nostra* as an ablative to be construed with *creatione*, the translation would read: "If from the substance of the holy Cherubim and Seraphim a new one were derived by our [own] creation, it would still offer . . ." This version, stressing the ultimate baseness of all formable substances rather than the ultimate baseness of human nature, would make good sense with reference to what precedes ("nec nos *nec nostra*") but would be difficult to reconcile with what follows ("Tantam *tamen* propiciationem . . . habemus"). Moreover, an author of the twelfth century would have been reluctant to apply the term *creatio* to any other "creation" than that of God.

[XXXIII A]

66, 17 f. ALTARE ETIAM QUOD TESTIMONIO ANTIQUORUM "SANCTUM" NOMINATUR ALTARE. This altar, formerly known as "L'Autel Sainct," was the Altar of the Trinity, founded by Abbot Hilduin (reigned from 814 to 841) and later on mostly known as the Matutinal Altar because Mass was said there after Prime, that is to say, shortly after daybreak. Concerning its location, there is some confusion. Crosby, p. 184, has rightly rejected a theory according to which it was in a superstructure to the east of the Carolingian apse (for the very good reason that such a superstructure never existed) and has pointed out that it must have been "to the west, not to the east" of the Main Altar. But he goes too far in the other direction when he contends that it was also to the west of the monks' choir (for this, see *Adm.* xxxiv, 72, 3 ff., and below, p. 199 f.) and served the laity. The Matutinal Altar was very close to the tomb of Charles the Bald, so close in fact that Suger could speak of him as being buried "in front of" it (see p. 70, line 5, and below, p. 197); and the location of this tomb is fairly well determinable. As we know from Félibien (plate facing p. 550, AA, and plan facing p. 528), and as was already justly pointed out by Conway, p. 107, the thirteenth-century tomb slab, whose very purpose it was to mark the precise spot of Charles's original grave, was in the center of the first bay to the west of the present crossing, no more than sixty feet to the west of the Main Altar, in what Doublet, p. 287, describes as the "premiere partie du Chœur" (viz., the part between the jubé and the crossing) and, p. 1256, as the "milieu du Chœur." Both the Matutinal Altar and the tomb of Charles the Bald must therefore have been within, not without the enclosure of the monks' choir. The only question is whether the altar was to the west or to the east of the tomb. Since the altar was dismantled in 1610 (Crosby, p. 185; Conway, p. 112), and since the "Cross of Charlemagne" which Suger had set up between (*inter*) the altar and the tomb (*Adm.* XXXIII A, 70, 23) was removed in the same year (Conway, p. 141), this question cannot be answered with absolute certainty. But Doublet, writing only fifteen years after the altar's destruction, is positive that it was to the east of the tomb. Describing, on p. 286, the "premiere partie du Chœur" from west to east, he first discusses the jubé; then, the tomb slab of Charles the Bald; and, finally, the "Autel dedié à la saincte Trinité, dit aussi Matutinal" as having been located "au bout de ceste premiere partie," that is to say, in the end near the crossing. The Altar of the Trinity, separated from the tomb of Charles the Bald by the "Cross of Charlemagne," was therefore to the east of both. It should be noted that this arrangement agrees to perfection with the ninth-century story of the blind woman Doctrudis of Anjou who, on being refused some oil from the Main Altar ("before the tomb of Saint Denis") as a cure for her ailment, "turned round" (*conversa*) to the Altar of the Trinity and there received what she needed by dint of a miracle (*Miracula Sancti Dionysii*, II, 32 [quoted above, p. 156], p. 323; referred to by Crosby, p. 185, note 84).

66, 20-25. QUIA CUM VETUSTATE . . . RENOVARE EXCEPIMUS. From this sentence Millet, p. 34 (followed by Conway, p. 107), has drawn the conclusion that the Matutinal Altar had been reconstructed by Suger in its entirety: "Suger fit aussi refaire tout de nouveau l'Autel qui estoit fort vieil, et le fit bastir de marbre noir et enrichir de personages de marbre blanc, representant la passion du sainct Denis." However, this description is hardly suggestive of twelfth-century work; Doublet, p. 287, does not yet insist on Suger's responsibility, and the continuation of Suger's own text as well as the parallel passage in *Ord.*, 130, 9 f., make it perfectly clear that he merely restored the wooden, gold-covered framework of the altar stone and not the altar as a whole.

66, 29-68, 3. Cujus concavi . . . interius perorabat. This shows that the relics of Sts. James, Stephen, and Vincent had never been "attached to" the altar and were never "reset" by Suger (so Conway, p. 107), but that they had always been hidden in the hollow framework of the altar stone. Suger merely opened up this framework, had the relics inspected, and repaired the old receptacle *auro pretioso et opere approbato* (*Ord.*, 130, 10). From the same account we also learn that the arm placed in the front part of the altar belonged to St. James the Less ("Brother of the Lord"), and not to St. James the Great. The phrase *pervia candidissimi cristalli apertio* denotes those pieces of crystal, frequently found in medieval reliquaries, which permit the reading of a short description of the relics (*titulus*, as Suger calls it) while the relics themselves remain invisible.

68, 10 f. octavo scilicet idus octobris. The Feast of Saint Denis is on October 9.

68, 14-17. archiepiscopi scilicet Lugdunensis . . . Venetensis. The date of the inspection of Charles the Bald's relics, and thereby the identity of the dignitaries involved, can be established with some accuracy. Since the event is recorded in *Ord.* —which was enacted between July 14, 1140 and January 22, 1142—the latest possible date is October 9, 1141. On the other hand, Suger would not have waited many years to go on record with an incident like this, and to institute the reforms suggested thereby (see shortly below); we can thus presume that it had taken place fairly recently. Now, among those present was the Archbishop of Reims, and the See of Reims had been vacant for two full years, from 1138 to 1140. Consequently, the choice is narrowed down to a date prior to 1138, on the one hand, and to the years 1140 and 1141, on the other; and there can be little doubt that the second of these alternatives is preferable. The Archbishop of Reims, then, was probably not Renaud de Martigné, who died on January 13, 1138, but Samson de Mauvoisin who reigned from the earlier half of 1140 (he was present at the Synod of Sens on June 2, of this year) to September 22, 1161 and witnessed *Ord.*, the very document in which the inspection of the relics was officially recorded; some four years later he also participated in the consecration of Suger's new chevet. The Archbishop of Lyons was, accordingly, Faucon de Bothéon (1139-1142); the Archbishop of Tours, Hugues de la Ferté (1133-1147); the Bishop of Soissons, Jocelin de Vierzy (1126-1152); the Bishop of Rennes, either Hamelin (1127-February 2, 1141) or Alain (1141-1156); the Bishop of St.-Malo, Donald (1120-1144); the Bishop of Vannes, Ivès (Evenus, 1137-1143). The Archbishop of Rouen and the Bishops of Beauvais, Senlis, and Meaux were Suger's old friends Hugues d'Amiens, Eudes II, Peter, and Manasseh II, already mentioned above, pp. 151, 154.

68, 33. MEDIUM. Since the altar had been in the central nave all the time, the word *medium* must here be understood as "into our midst," connoting the official and public character of the proceedings as in the phrases "rem in medium proferre" or "rem in medio ponere."

70, 4 f. KAROLUS . . . QUI EIDEM ALTARI SUBJACET. As appears from *Ord.*, 130, 6, where Charles the Bald is spoken of as *prope altare sepultus*, and from the statement that the "Cross of Charlemagne" was placed *inter altare et tumulum ejusdem Karoli* (p. 70, line 23), his grave was at some distance from the Matutinal Altar. But the distance must have been so small that the verb *subjacere* (cf., e.g., Pliny, *Epistolæ*, v, 6, 2) seemed permissible, and that the Emperor could feel himself protected by the relics deposited in the framework of the altar stone.

⟨For the tomb of Charles the Bald, see further de Montesquiou-Fezensac, Bib. 123; and the inventory description of 1634 published by *id.*, Bib. 125, p. 195 no. 161 and *passim.*⟩

70, 6. THECA. For the significance of the word, see Ducange, VIII, p. 95. Cf. the parallel passage in *Ord.*, 128, 29, which has *de theca imperiali capellæ.*

70, 10. LAMPADES IN VASIS ARGENTEIS. According to *Ord.*, 130, 17-20, Suger not only renewed the silver vessels of these lamps (see Conway, p. 139) but also had them relit and made provisions for their being kept burning ever after. They should not be confused with the seven candlesticks (*candelabra*) likewise given by Charles the Bald but apparently belonging to the Main Altar (see below, p. 216 f.). The lamps, as well as the candlesticks, are lost.

70, 14 f. ANNIVERSARII SUI, ET SUORUM REFECTIONI. As we learn from *Ord.*, 128, 16-21, Charles the Bald had ordained that his death be commemorated every month by a funeral service and a solemn repast (*honesta refectio*) of the brethren, and that these observances were supposed to take place *pridie nonas*, that is to say, strictly speaking, on the sixth day of March, May, July, and October, and on the fourth day of the other months; but since Charles had died in October, we may assume that they were always held on the sixth. Suger reinstated them after they had been discontinued for a long time. *Anniversarium* is not necessarily an annual celebration but can denote "quodlibet officium pro defunctis quocumque tempore" (Ducange, I, p. 258).

70, 15. QUÆ DICITUR RUOILUM. For this donation, and the various observances entailed thereby, see A. Giry, "La Donation de Rueil à l'Abbaye de Saint-Denis," *Mélanges Julien Havet*, Paris, 1895, p. 683 ff. (quoted in Crosby, p. 184, note 81).

70, 17 f. MAGNI ET HONESTI CEREI SEX. According to *Ord.*, 130, 20-22, the memory of Charles the Bald was further honored by the fact that the one candle which always burned for him in front of the Main Altar—as opposed to the six which were periodically lit for him in front of the Matutinal Altar—was supplemented by a second one.

70, 22. CRUCEM ETIAM MIRABILEM. This "man-sized" cross, formerly known as "*Croix de Charlemagne*" (Conway, pp. 131, 140 f.), disappeared after 1610; see above, pp. 195, 197.

⟨For the "Cross of Charlemagne," cf. further Elbern, Bib. 46, p. 121 f.; de Montesquiou-Fezensac, Bib. 125, p. 64.⟩

70, 24-26. MONILE NANTILDIS REGINÆ, UXORIS DAGOBERTI . . . ALIUD VERO IN FRONTEM SANCTI DIONYSII. On the authority of Doublet, p. 245, these two *monilia*—one fastened to the "*Croix de Charlemagne*," the other to the reliquary of the head of Saint Denis—are commonly referred to as "a pair of bracelets" (Conway, p. 127). However, since they had disappeared before the inventories were drawn up, Doublet had to base his description exclusively upon the present passage in Suger's *De Administratione* (thus Conway himself, p. 131), and obviously misinterpreted it. In the first place, Suger stresses the symbolical relationship between the *monilia* and the iron collar that had "circled the most sacred neck" of Saint Denis while he was kept in the *carcer Glaucini* (for this, see Crosby, pp. 25, 47) and this parallel would not have much point had those *monilia* been bracelets. In the second place, Suger emphatically states that they were not only of different workmanship but also of different size and that even the smaller one could be affixed, apparently as a kind of wreath or diadem, to the "brow" (*frons*) of the reliquary supposedly containing the head of Saint Denis, that is to say, to the "brow" of a life-sized bust (replaced in the thirteenth century; see Félibien, pp. 209, 256, 540 and pl. II, A). It seems therefore justifiable to interpret the word *monile* in its narrower and more legitimate sense, viz., as "collar" or "necklace." For Queen Nanthilda and King Dagobert (reigned 629-638), see recently R. Barroux, *Dagobert Roi des Francs*, Paris, 1938. ⟨For the necklace of Queen Nanthilda, see further Schramm in Bib. 153, p. 58 f.⟩

70, 31-72, 2. ABBAS VENERABILIS CORBEIÆ . . . TABULAM ARGEN-TEAM . . . FIERI FECIT. Abbot Robert of Corbie, who had signed the *Ordinatio* of 1140 or 1141 and may have made his donation on this occasion, is here called *bonæ memoriæ* because he had died on January 22, 1142. Originally a monk at St.-Denis, he had been elected, on Suger's recommendation, in 1127. The panel given by him—now lost—was not a retable, as assumed by Conway, p. 107, but an altar frontal. That Suger "beset it with gems" (Conway, *ibidem*) is reported by Doublet, p. 245, but not borne out by Suger's own statements.

XXXIV

72, 3. CHORUM ETIAM FRATRUM. Nothing remains of either Suger's wooden choir stalls or their chilly predecessors which must have occupied about half of the central nave (see Crosby, pp. 117 f., 162).

72, 9-16. P<small>ULPITUM ETIAM ANTIQUUM, QUOD, AMMIRABILE TABU-</small>
LARUM EBURNEARUM . . . ERIGI FECIMUS. After the rebuilding
of the church in the thirteenth century the pulpit was on the
gallery of the jubé which separated the monks' choir from the
nave (Crosby, p. 162; Conway, p. 106). It was destroyed by
the Huguenots, but Conway has rightly pointed out that the
famous "ambo" given by Emperor Henry II to the Cathedral
of Aix-la-Chapelle—likewise composed of late-antique and
Early Christian ivories—may give some idea of its original
appearance. Cf. S. Beissel, *Kunstschätze des Aachener Kaiser-
domes*, München-Gladbach, 1904, pls. VII, VIII; *Die Kunstdenkmäler der Rheinprovinz*, x (*Die Kunstdenkmäler der
Stadt Aachen*, 1), Düsseldorf, 1916, p. 114 ff., with further
references. Since Suger was in Mayence in 1125 (Cartellieri,
p. 133, nos. 46, 47), it is not impossible that he had occasion
to see the pulpit of Aix-la-Chapelle in person.

72, 17. IMPEDIMENTUM QUODDAM. Crosby, pp. 108, 118 has made
it very probable that this "dark wall" was the enclosure of the
original monks' choir. ⟨Cf. *id.*, Bib. 26, p. 54; Formigé, Bib.
56, pp. 62, 101 f.; Vieillard-Troïekouroff, Bib. 173, p. 351 f.;
Crosby, Bib. 40, p. 43 f.⟩

72, 20. NOBILEM GLORIOSI REGIS DAGOBERTI CATHEDRAM. For this
famous piece, now in the Cabinet des Médailles, see Conway,
p. 120 f. and pl. v, 2 (our *fig.* 22). The back piece and the
ajouré scrollwork of the arms have been ascribed to Suger. The
chair itself is now considered a Carolingian work rather than a
Merovingian or Roman one; cf. J. Hubert, "Le Fauteuil du
Roi Dagobert," *Demareteion*, I, 1935, p. 17 ff. (quoted in
Crosby, p. 72, note 49).

⟨For an extensive discussion of the bronze gilt *faldistorium*,
see now Schramm, Bib. 152, 1, p. 326 ff., where the following
statement ought to be corrected: on p. 331 note 1 Schramm
quotes Panofsky as having concluded in the second edition
[recte "second printing"] of 1948 of the present book, on p.
262 [*sic*] "more than likely that it [i.e. the Dagobert Throne]
was placed in the apse on axis with the nave and was used by
the monastic bishop or abbot, or by the king when he was

COMMENTARY UPON "DE ADMINISTRATIONE"

present,"—a passage, taken instead from Crosby, p. 162 [not "p. 262" f.]. Cf. further Swarzenski, Bib. 164, p. 54 no. 92, pl. 92 fig. 213; Mütherich, in Bib. 153, p. 137 no. 57; Lasko, Bib. 111, p. 20 f.; and the inventory entry of 1634, recently published by de Montesquiou-Fezensac, Bib. 125, p. 291 no. 362. The chair is now generally considered a Carolingian work with only some restoration or repair done by Suger.〉

72, 26. Aquilam vero. This Eagle lectern, which was in the middle of the monks' choir (Crosby, p. 162; Conway, p. 106 f.), has disappeared.

72, 28-76, 6. Vitrearum etiam novarum præclaram varieta-tem . . . littera mortificat. For Suger's famous stained-glass windows see particularly Martin-Cahier, pp. 122-127 and pls. "Etudes vi and vii"; furthermore, Mâle, i, pp. 91 ff., 161 ff., 253 ff., and ii, p. 152 ff. (as to the question of priority in relation to the school of Chartres cf., however, Y. Delaporte, *Les Vitraux de la Cathédrale de Chartres*, 1926, p. 4); F. de Lasteyrie, *Histoire de la Peinture sur Verre*, Paris, 1857, pp. 26-34, pls. iii-vii; N. H. J. Westlake, *A History of Design on Painted Glass*, i, London, 1881, pp. 27-33; and, most recently, A. Watson, *The Early Iconography of the Tree of Jesse*, London, 1934, pp. 81 f., 112-120, 160, pls. xxiv, xxv.

〈See further, in addition to the literature quoted on the following pages, Aubert, Bib. 3, p. 7 ff., esp. p. 14 f.; *id.*, Bib. 5, p. 152 ff.; Crosby, Bib. 26, p. 46 ff.; v. Simson, Bib. 158, p. 120 ff.; of paramount importance the various publications by Grodecki, to list only the most comprehensive: Bib. 78, p. 14 ff.; Bib. 80-82; Bib. 83, p. 38 ff.; Bib. 84; Bib. 87, esp. p. 105 ff.; Bib. 90, 91, and above all Bib. 93.〉

What had been left of Suger's historiated glass in 1793 was brought to the "Musée des Monuments Français" which was abolished in 1816. After that, the remnants were returned to St.-Denis and were installed, with restorations and in an arbitrary arrangement, in the Chapels of the Virgin (*plan*, 5) and of St. Eugene (*plan*, 7). From 1848 to 1858 they were once more restored, supplemented and rearranged—under the supervision of Viollet-le-Duc, and apparently with due consideration of the Suger text—by Alfred (not Henri) Gérente[7] and finally installed in their present places. Prior to this, drawings and tracings were made and published by Martin-Cahier and de Lasteyrie (whose lithographs are little short of caricature but have the advantage of showing two of the windows in their entirety whereas the much better lithographs in Martin-Cahier show only isolated medallions and details). With the exception of the *Tree of Jesse* window, and a small part of the *"Life of the Virgin* Window" (see shortly below), all the later illustrations that have come to the translator's knowledge, including the two in C. J. Connick, "Windows of Old France," *The International Studio*, LXXVIII, 1924, p. 327 ff., are more or less embellished versions of the lithographs in either Martin-Cahier or de Lasteyrie. Westlake, writing as late as 1881, describes the general arrangement of the windows on the basis of de Lasteyrie, apparently without realizing that the latter records it as it was before Viollet-le-Duc; de Lasteyrie's otherwise so excellent son republished, in 1912, one of the two windows illustrated in the work of his father (pl. III) as "Vitrail du Temps de Suger" although it is a medley composed of four Suger medallions—but from two different windows— and two medallions of the thirteenth century (R. C. de Lasteyrie, *L'Architecture Religieuse en France à l'Epoque Romane*, Paris, 1912, fig. 566); and this, in turn, has misled as astute and accurate an author as R. Grinnell, "Iconography and Philosophy in the Crucifixion Window at Poitiers," *The Art Bulletin*, XXVIII, 1946, p. 171 ff., part. pp. 175 note 22, 185. Thus our illustrations (*frontispiece, figs.* 11-18) and a brief summary of the present situation, largely based upon the notes of Professor W. F. Stohlman, might be welcome.

⟨As L. Grodecki has kindly pointed out to me, it was only in 1799/1800 that Suger's stained glass windows were brought to the "Musée des Monuments Français," and it was in 1818/19 that the remnants were returned to St.-Denis. When restora-

---

[7] See Thieme-Becker, *Allgemeines Lexikon der Bildenden Künstler*, XIII, 1920, p. 449. Henri Gérente died as early as 1849 when the work had hardly begun, and was succeeded by his brother Alfred. It is Alfred's, and not Henri's, monogram that can be seen, juxtaposed with that of Viollet-le-Duc, in our *fig.* 15.

tion began in 1847, it was Henri Gérente who completed the *Tree of Jesse* window and who started work on the *Life of the Virgin*, or rather *Infancy of Christ* window before his death in 1849. In 1916/17 as well as in 1920, the medieval windows underwent further restorations. In 1939, at the beginning of World War II, they were removed by J. J. Gruber and taken into storage, and in 1946/47 they were installed in their present setting at St.-Denis.⟩

Suger describes specifically the following three windows: First, the "*Tree of Jesse Window*" (*fig.* 12). It is now where it was probably installed by Suger himself, viz., in the southern bay of the Chapel of the Virgin (*plan,* 5) but its—comparatively—genuine parts are limited to about one-third of its area. Second, what may be called, in Suger's own phraseology, the "*Anagogical Window*" of which he says that it "urges us onward from the material to the immaterial" (*figs.* 14, 16). It is now in the southern bay of the Chapel of St. Peregrinus (*plan,* 4; the place assigned to it by Suger is not known) and comprises five medallions four of which are described by Suger and will be discussed presently. However, only the two medallions at the top and at the bottom are—comparatively—genuine; the former represents the "*Arca Fœderis*" as the foundation of the Christian altar; the latter, the only one not individually described by Suger but wholly in keeping with his interpretation of Christ as the Revealer of the Meaning of the Law (cf. p. 74, line 11), shows the Saviour Crowning the Church and Unveiling the Synagogue, His figure "charged" with seven doves, time-honored symbols of the *Dona Sancti Spiritus* (Martin-Cahier, pl. "Etude vi," D; Mâle 1, p. 102 and 11, p. 166; our *fig.* 16, lower medallion). Third, the "*Moses Window*" (*fig.* 13). It is now in the northern bay of the Chapel of St. Cucuphas (*plan,* 6; the place assigned to it by Suger is not known) and comprises five scenes in roundels all of which are described by Suger and will be discussed presently; they are all—comparatively—genuine, though the medallion at the bottom is more heavily restored than the rest.

⟨For the genuine parts of the "*Tree of Jesse Window*," see below, p. 210.

The five medallions of the *"Anagogical Window"* have been rearranged in 1946/47, so that, unlike the photograph reproduced in *fig.* 14, the *"Arca Fœderis"* is now at the bottom and "Christ Crowning the Church and Unveiling the Synagogue" at the top (cf. *fig.* 8). On this window, see further Grodecki, Bib. 91, esp. p. 174; in particular on the iconography of "Christ Unveiling the Synagogue," see *id.*, Bib. 90, esp. p. 32 ff. In connection with the fragmentary inscription of this medallion Grodecki has argued, "Panofsky a proposé *Arca velat, mensa revelat*; c'est peu vraisemblable . . . ," a conjecture, however, not to be found in the present book, but having been based on oral communication. For a different iconographic interpretation, see Blumenkranz, Bib. 11, esp. p. 1146 f. Cf. further Hoffmann, Bib. 98, esp. p. 69 ff.

The *"Moses Window"* is in the northern bay of the Chapel of St. Peregrinus (*plan*, 4; *not* in the Chapel of St. Cucuphas), where it has been installed since 1852.)

Of the windows mentioned by Suger only in general terms, this writer knows, apart from purely decorative designs, only the following items: First; small portions of a *"Life of the Virgin Window"* (*fig.* 11) two stray medallions of which—the *Annunciation* and the *Adoration of the Magi*—are found in de Lasteyrie, *l.c.*, pl. III, while part of the lower section and a piece of the border are reproduced from photographs in L. Magne, *Décor du Verre (L'Art Appliqué aux Métiers)*, Paris, 1913, *figs.* 83 and 84 (the "Apocalypse Window" illustrated *ibid.* is probably by A. Gérente and Viollet-le-Duc). The *"Life of the Virgin Window"* is now in the northern bay of the Chapel of the Virgin (*plan*, 5), and this would seem to be its logical and therefore original place; moreover its bottom picture contained the donor's portrait of Suger (*frontispiece*) which was presumably intended to be displayed in the most prominent part of the chevet. This window, apparently dismantled and mostly destroyed as early as the thirteenth century when it had to make way for a *Crusade* window described and illustrated by de Montfaucon,[8] is almost entirely modern

---

[8] The window with ten scenes from the First Crusade which Bernard de Montfaucon (*Les Monumens de la Monarchie Françoise*, vol. I, Paris, 1729, p. 384 ff.)

except for portions of the *Annunciation* (*fig.* 15, the genuine portions fortunately including the head and hands of Suger's portrait as well as the inscription SVGERIVS ABA), some details of the *Nativity* (second picture from bottom), and the *Angel Visiting St. Joseph* (lower right-hand corner). Second, a medallion with the *Martyrdom of St. Vincent* one of whose

---

saw in the Chapel of the Virgin ("à l'extrémité du rond-point derriere le grand Autel") and ascribed to Suger must have been executed and put in place long after Suger's death, probably displacing what was and now is the *Life of the Virgin*. In the first place, there is no evidence that Suger's series included any secular subjects; had he devised the *Crusade* window, its inscriptions would have been well-turned *versiculi* instead of the simple prose lines transmitted by Montfaucon. In the second place, the style of the *Crusade* window, sufficiently recognizable even in Montfaucon's engravings, distinctly indicates the third quarter of the thirteenth century. The lost originals must have been very similar to three roundels in the Philadelphia Museum of Art which so closely agree with those reproduced by Montfaucon—and also with the medallion in de Lasteyrie, *l.c.*, pl. III, lower right-hand corner—that they have been thought to come from St.-Denis themselves (*Pennsylvania Museum Bulletin*, March 1931, no. 140, p. 20; a better illustration, *ibidem*, March 1923, no. 75, cover). Montfaucon's *Crusade* window, then, must have been executed and installed near the end of the period of remodelling that lasted from 1231 to 1281, probably in connection with an event important enough to justify the removal of one of Suger's earlier windows; it is a fair assumption that this event was the burial, on May 22, 1271, of the remains of Saint Louis, the Crusader king *par excellence*.

This is contested by L. Grodecki ("A Stained Glass *Atelier* of the Thirteenth Century," *Journal of the Warburg and Courtauld Institutes*, XI, 1948, p. 87 ff., part. p. 92 note 1; ⟨*id.*, Bib. 84; Bib. 87, p. 105; Bib. 91, esp. p. 172 f.⟩). He believes that this window and its parallel (*Charlemagne's Journey to the Holy Land*) are of Suger's time. However, Suger was *not* "passionately interested in the Second Crusade," but Grodecki may be right, that Montfaucon's "à l'extrémité du rond-point" does not mean the Chapel of the Virgin, as I had assumed, but one of the chapels at the beginning of the ambulatory.

⟨Since the lost *Crusade* window must be placed either in the northern Chapel of St. Osmanna (*plan*, 2) or in the southern Chapel of St. Hilary (*plan*, 8), but not in the Chapel of the Virgin, it is no longer necessary to assume that the *"Life of the Virgin Window"* (or more properly the *"Infancy of Christ Window"*) had to be dismantled in the thirteenth century (cf. below, p. 206 f.).

A date of ca. 1150 for the *Crusade* window is also assumed by Loomis, Bib. 115, esp. p. 78 ff. On Suger's involvement in the Second Crusade as well as on the memory of Charlemagne's legendary journey cherished at St.-Denis during the twelfth century, see Folz, Bib. 52, pp. 134 ff., 179 ff., and *passim*; *id.*, Bib. 53, p. 253 f.; v. Simson, Bib. 158, pp. 81 ff., 84 ff., 90, 236 f.; Vieillard-Troïekouroff, Bib. 173, p. 344 note 41; Hohler, Bib. 99, pp. 37 f., 68 f., suggesting again a date as late as the early thirteenth century for the St.-Denis window; Greenhill, Bib. 76, esp. p. 97 ff., emphasizing the role of Eleanor of Aquitaine in the Carolingian *renovatio*; cf. further below, p. 250 f.

A fragment of a coronation scene, possibly from the *Charlemagne* window and now in the Museo Civico at Turin, has been published by Grodecki, Bib. 82, p. 50 f.

The provenance of three roundels in the Philadelphia Museum of Art has since been identified as from the Ste.-Chapelle in Paris by Harrison-Caviness and Grodecki, Bib. 94.⟩

arms was preserved in the Matutinal Altar (cf. *Adm.* XXXIII A, 68, 2 f., and *Ord.*, 130, 1). This medallion (*fig.* 17) is now in the south-east corner of the crypt (window facing east) and may have belonged to one of the windows in this crypt (*inferius*). Apart from a portion of the hearth and from the sector between the two sticks or poles manipulated by the executioners, it is in very good condition and has some special interest in two respects. On the one hand, it illustrates the stylistic affinity which exists between the glass and some of the stone sculpture in St.-Denis: the St. Vincent in *fig.* 17 is almost identical, in the treatment of form as well as in posture, with the Caryatid in *fig.* 6 (left), reversed and turned to a horizontal position. On the other hand, the composition constitutes an important piece of iconographical evidence. Datable between ca. 1140 and ca. 1144, the window of St.-Denis ushers in a whole series of High Romanesque and Early Gothic representations of the Martyrdom of St. Vincent as exemplified, for instance, by the windows in Angers and Rouen of ca. 1180 and ca. 1240, respectively (see L. Farcy, *La Cathédrale d'Angers*, 1, Angers, 1916, pl. facing p. 152, c; G. Ritter, *Les Vitraux de la Cathédrale de Rouen*, Paris, 1926, pl. XXVII). Compared with this close-knit tradition, on the one hand, and with an earlier composition such as the fresco of 1007 in Galliano (P. Toesca, *La Pittura e la Miniatura nella Lombardia*, Milan, 1912, p. 47), on the other, the much-debated St. Vincent relief in Basel Cathedral is clearly a work of the second half of the twelfth century (thus, e.g., H. Beenken, *Romanische Skulptur in Deutschland*, Leipzig, 1924, p. 252 ff.; J. Gantner, *Kunstgeschichte der Schweiz*, Frauenfeld and Leipzig, 1936, p. 239 ff.), and not a work of ca. 1000 as has recently been contended by H. Reinhardt, *Das Basler Münster*, Basel, 1939, p. 11.

⟨The *"Life of the Virgin Window"* should more properly be designated the *"Infancy of Christ Window"* as its iconography has been reconstructed by Grodecki, Bib. 91. The window remained intact and was never dismantled until after the very end of the eighteenth century, when it was still re-

corded in the Chapel of the Virgin. Several new fragments of
the *"Infancy of Christ Window"* have been identified since the
first edition of this book was published in 1946: for parts of
the ornamental border, now in the Metropolitan Museum,
New York, and in the crypt of St.-Denis, see Grodecki, Bib. 81,
esp. p. 55 ff.; *id.*, Bib. 83, p. 38 f. no. 2; for the scene of the
"Presentation in the Temple," now in the parish church of
Twycross, Leicestershire, see *id.*, Bib. 88, esp. p. 167; for the
half-medallion representing "Herod and His Counselors" and
the related panel with "The Three Magi before Herod," both
still in storage with the Monuments Historiques at the Château de Champs-sur-Marne (1973), see Bib. 172; further
Bib. 135, p. 48 f. nos. 100-101; for the prophet "Jeremiah,"
see Wentzel, Bib. 177, p. 247 ff.

In August of 1973, L. Grodecki very generously communicated *avant-la-lettre* further findings concerning the *"Infancy
of Christ Window"*: in the parish church of Wilton, Wiltshire,
four fragments, once belonging to the panels of the "Adoration
of the Magi," the "Flight into Egypt," and the "Presentation
in the Temple" as well as in the house of the glass painter
Dennis King at Norwich the scene of the "Adoration of the
Shepherds" (which from 1828 to 1964 had been at Highcliffe
near Brighton), cf. Grodecki, Bib. 92.

According to the information kindly provided by L. Grodecki, the medallion with the *Martyrdom of St. Vincent* was
installed, together with thirteenth-century windows from St.-
Germain-des-Prés, in the Chapel of St. Eustace (*plan,* 3) between 1834 and 1848 (cf. F. de Lasteyrie, *Histoire de la
Peinture sur Verre*, Paris, 1857, I, p. 35; Fr. de Guilhermy,
handwritten notes in Paris, Bibl. Nat., MS nouv. acq. Fr. 6121,
fol. 84). Removed by Viollet-le-Duc in 1848, the medallion
remained in storage at St.-Denis until 1896, when it was re-
installed in the crypt by the architect Darcy. In 1956, it was
again removed by the architect J. Formigé and taken into
storage with the Monuments Historiques at the Château de
Champs-sur-Marne. For this medallion, see further Lafond,
Bib. 108, p. 154 (maintaining that the provenance of the

St. Vincent roundel was St.-Germain-des-Prés, not St.-Denis);
Grodecki, Bib. 83, p. 39 f. no. 3; *id.*, Bib. 87, p. 94 fig. 64;
id., Bib. 91, p. 177.

To the "windows mentioned by Suger only in general
terms" should be added: the grisaille panes, fragments of
which are still extant in the ambulatory (cf. Crosby, Bib. 26,
p. 47; Grodecki, Bib. 80; *id.*, Bib. 91, p. 174; v. Simson, Bib.
158, p. 111 ff., esp. note 70). Further, the *Signum Tau*
roundel (our *fig.* 18) was installed in 1854 in the northern
bay of the Chapel of St. Cucuphas (*plan*, 6). As it depicts
the Vision of *Ezekiel* ix, 2-4, it might originally have formed
part of a typological *Passion* window (cf. Grodecki, Bib. 91,
pp. 174 ff., 184 f.; *id.*, Bib. 90, esp. p. 41 [with a reproduction
in color]; Verdier, Bib. 169, p. 34). In addition, there are five
scenes from the "Life of St. Benedict," which might have
come from the northernmost chapel of the crypt. Two of them
have been in the parish church of Twycross, Leicestershire,
since 1840; one of them since 1958 in the Musée de Cluny,
Paris; and two more have been discovered in the parish church
of St.-Léonard at Fougères, Mayenne (cf. Bib. 172; Grodecki,
Bib. 88).)

72, 29. STIRPS JESSE. See now, in addition to Mâle i, p. 253 ff. and
II, p. 168 ff., the interesting discussion in Watson's *Early Iconography of the Tree of Jesse, l.c.* As can be seen from the
outside (Watson, pl. xxv) even more clearly than from the
inside (Watson, pl. xxiv; our *fig.* 12), the old portions comprise the central strip (minus the square at the bottom) and the
four half-medallions on the right; the illustration in L. Magne,
Décor du Verre, fig. 82, shows very little of the genuine
portions. The "donor's portrait" in the lower right-hand
corner, showing Suger presenting the *Tree of Jesse* window
itself, is entirely modern. Has it perhaps taken the place of a
genuine one? De Montfaucon, quoted p. 204, note, repeatedly
informs us that Suger "s'est fait peindre *plusieurs fois* dans les
vitres du chevet," and Doublet, p. 247, even explicitly attests
the presence of Suger's portrait in the *Tree of Jesse* window:
"Il est dépeint en ceste vitre auec son habit de Religieux, pros-

terné en terre, tenant sa crosse, & cest escrit, *Suggerius Abbas*."
But the trouble with this description is that it literally agrees
with the portrait now seen at the feet of the Mary Annunciate
in the *Life of the Virgin* window and demonstrably not taken
out of context by Alfred Gérente and Viollet-le-Duc. De
Lasteyrie, *l.c.*, pl. III, shows the Annunciation medallion in
much the same form as it appears today (our *fig.* 15); Félibien, p. 531, speaking of the "chapelle de milieu," records
"dans une vitre de la même chapelle l'image de l'abbé Suger
prosterné aux pieds de la mere de Dieu avec ces deux mots au
dessous, SUGERIUS ABBAS"; and in Mabillon's *Annales
Ordinis S. Benedicti*, VI, E. Martène ed., Paris, 1739, p. 493,
we find a highly amusing engraving which shows Suger as seen
in the Annunciation medallion (and previously illustrated in
de Montfaucon, *l.c.*, pl. XXIV) in an imaginary, pseudo-medi-
eval chapel, adoring a likewise imaginary but distinctly modern statue of the Madonna, and the accompanying text avers
that this little personage, "ad pedes beatissimæ Virginis provolutus," could be seen "in sacello beatæ Mariæ in vitrea
fenestra." This evidence confronts us with three choices.
Either, the portrait seen by Doublet in the *Tree of Jesse*
window was practically a duplicate of that described by
Félibien, de Montfaucon and Mabillon-Martène and now
extant in the Annunciation medallion. Or, Doublet confused
the *Tree of Jesse* window with another one. Or, finally, the
Annunciation medallion had actually been transferred from
the *Life of the Virgin* window to the *Tree of Jesse* window
(whose bottom strip, as has been mentioned, is entirely modern)
after the former had been dismantled in the thirteenth century
(cf. above, pp. 204 f., 206 f.). Of these choices the third seems
preferable because it makes it possible to reconcile the statement of de Montfaucon, who saw his *Crusade* window in the
Chapel of the Virgin, with the statement of Doublet, who saw,
in the same chapel, the portrait of Suger "prosterné en terre"
in the *Tree of Jesse* window; and with the statements of
Félibien and Mabillon-Martène, who saw, still in the same
chapel, the portrait of Suger, "prosterné aux pieds de la mere

de Dieu" or "ad pedes beatissimæ Virginis provolutus," in a window not specified but certainly not identical with the *Crusade* window. This being so, the question whether or not the *Tree of Jesse* window had originally included another portrait of Suger cannot be answered with certainty. A palmette from the original border of the *Tree of Jesse* window has found its way into the Victoria and Albert Museum in London; see B. Rackham, *A Guide to the Collections of Stained Glass*, London, 1936, p. 31 (with slightly incorrect dates), and pl. 2, B.

⟨Concerning the iconography of the *Tree of Jesse* window, ". . . Mâle seems to have come nearer to the truth than anyone else. Watson has succeeded in showing that there were Trees of Jesse before Suger's window; but so far as I know he has not proved that these pre-Sugerian windows included the *Kings* of Israel (more or less equated with those of France). So far as I know the material . . . we have, before Suger, either Trees minus the Kings or the Kings minus the Trees, and Mâle would still seem to be right in thinking that Suger, who first introduced the Kings and Queens into a façade was also the first to include them into the Tree of Jesse." (letter from E. Panofsky to L. Grodecki, dated June 1, 1961); see further Katzenellenbogen, Bib. 103, p. 34, and above all Thérel, Bib. 167.

For the repeated restorations of the *Tree of Jesse* window, see Grodecki, Bib. 91, p. 174 ff. The genuine portions consist of five figures (two of the Kings, the Virgin, Christ, and one of the prophets) as well as parts of the third King, and of three other prophets.

Concerning the question of Suger's portrait, the last of the three choices discussed above has been superseded by recent scholarship (cf. above, p. 206 f.). Doublet apparently confused the *Tree of Jesse* window with the *Life of the Virgin*, or rather *Infancy of Christ* window in the same Chapel of the Virgin, so that his crucial passage would in fact refer to the extant Annunciation medallion, in its original context though; see Grodecki, Bib. 91, p. 177 f.⟩

72, 29. IN CAPITE ECCLESIÆ. For the comparison of the choir of the church with the head of the body (hence also the French term "chevet"), see J. Sauer, *Symbolik des Kirchengebäudes*, 2nd ed., Freiburg, 1924, pp. 111, 128; and, for its cosmological implications, F. Saxl, *Verzeichnis Astrologischer und Mythologischer Illustrierter Handschriften des Lateinischen Mittelalters (Sitzungsberichte der Heidelberger Akademie der Wissenschaften, Philos.-Histor. Klasse, 1925/26)*, II, *Die Handschriften der National-Bibliothek in Wien*, Heidelberg, 1927, p. 40 ff. In *Ord.*, 134, 6 f., Suger uses the phrase "superioris ecclesiæ *pars capitalis*." ⟨See further Fingesten, Bib. 50, p. 12 ff.⟩

72, 30 f. TAM SUPERIUS QUAM INFERIUS. In contrast to Suger's general usage (*Adm.* XXVIII, 48, 9-13; *Adm.* XXXI, 54, head-line-24; *Ord.*, 134, 6-12), and in spite of the *usque ad* in line 29, this antithesis can hardly refer to the upper choir as opposed to the transept and nave; for, since Suger planned to rebuild the latter as soon as the chevet was completed he would hardly have troubled to provide it with new windows. He would here seem to distinguish between two zones within the chevet itself, either between the clerestory and the chapels, or between the whole upper choir and the crypt. As the second usage is clearly attested by *Adm.* XXVIII, 48, 28; *Cons.* VII, 118, 4 and 22; ⟨*Cons.* VII, 120, 2 f.⟩ (while the first can only be inferred from *Adm.* XXXI, 54, 28), the translator has assumed (p. 206) that the *inferius* here refers to the crypt. This seems all the more plausible as the fact that even the crypt received stained-glass windows was more noteworthy than the self-evident circumstance that this was true of the clerestory as well as of the chapels.

74, 5-8. TOLLIS AGENDO MOLAM . . . NOSTER ET ANGELICUS. See Mâle I, p. 167; II, p. 206. The medallion seen in our *fig.* 14 (third medallion) is modern.

⟨Originally, the medallion representing "St. Paul turning a Mill" seems to have been at the bottom of the *"Anagogical Window,"* for which see above all Grodecki, Bib. 90, esp. pp. 22 ff., 34 f.; further Hoffmann, Bib. 98, esp. p. 71 ff.⟩

74, 11 f. QUOD MOYSES VELAT . . . QUI SPOLIANT MOYSEN. The

scene, described in *Exodus* xxxiv, 33-35, is interpreted by
Suger as expressing the contrast between Jewish Law and
Christian Revelation ("Vetus testamentum velatum, Novum
Testamentum revelatum"; for the interpretation of the same
scene in the *Bible Moralisée* cf. shortly below, p. 214). In
Suger's distich this antithesis—intimately connected with the
contrast between light and darkness, day and night, sunrise and
sunset, clear-sightedness and blindness (cf. E. Panofsky,
Studies in Iconology, New York, 1939 (and 1962), p. 111 ff.)
—is expressed by a sophisticated and almost untranslatable
play upon the words *revelare, spoliare* and *denudare*, all of
which mean "to uncover" but carry sharply different connotations. *Revelare* means the positive process of "revealing,"
spoliare and *denudare* the negative process of "despoiling." In
Christ, Suger intimates, God is revealed to all men. But Moses
must remain veiled in the presence of human beings, and those
who would presume to uncover *him* would commit an offense.
The medallion seen in our *figs.* 14 (second from bottom) and
16 (upper medallion) is modern.

⟨Though in Suger's time the "Unveiling of Moses" was
probably the second medallion from bottom as seen in photographs taken before World War II, it was placed second from
top when in 1946/47 the windows were taken out of storage
and reinstalled at St.-Denis. For Suger's exegesis of this scene,
see v. Simson, Bib. 158, p. 121, and Grodecki, Bib. 90, esp. pp.
24, 26; for the iconography, see further Hoffmann, Bib. 98,
esp. p. 59 ff.⟩

74, 14 f. Fœderis ex arca ... vult ibi vita mori. See Martin-
Cahier, pls. "Etudes vi, f and vii, a"; de Lasteyrie, pl. vii;
Mâle ii, p. 182; our *fig.* 14 (top), showing a restoration prior
to Alfred Gérente and Viollet-le-Duc. For the *sistitur*, cf. the
classical phrase *fana sistere*, "to establish a temple or sacred
shrine."

⟨As stated above, p. 204, in 1946/47 this medallion was
shifted to the bottom of the window. Originally, it was apparently neither the top nor the bottom roundel, but the third
one in the center of the entire composition. Cf. Grodecki, Bib.

91, esp. p. 174; *id.*, Bib. 90, esp. p. 26 ff.; less convincing Hoffmann, Bib. 98, esp. p. 65 ff. On the iconography of the Quadriga of Aminadab, see also Panofsky, Bib. 134.⟩

74, 17 f. Qui Deus est magnus ... fit caro juncta Deo. The subject is taken from *Revelation* v, 1-vi, 1. It should be noted that this text does not speak of two separate animals unsealing the book but identifies the Lamb Himself as the "Lion of the tribe of Judah" (*Rev.* v, 5). In the distich this spiritual identity is brought out by the conjunction *sive* and by the singulars *solvit* and *fit*. The *solvunt* and the *et* in the preceding line, however, would seem to indicate that the glass painting actually showed the Lion and the Lamb as two separate animals —as was indeed necessary unless Suger and his designer wished to resort to a still less Biblical crossbreed. The medallion seen in our *fig.* 14 (second from top) is modern.

⟨This medallion, now second from bottom, was originally perhaps the second from top as before 1939. Cf. Grodecki, Bib. 90, esp. p. 30 ff.; further Hoffmann, Bib. 98, esp. p. 59 ff., who links the iconography with Touronian Bibles of the Carolingian period.⟩

74, 20 f. Est in fiscella ... quem fovet Ecclesia. The play upon the words *Puer* and *puella* cannot be adequately rendered in any modern language. The comparison between the Finding of Moses by the Daughter of Pharaoh and the Reception of Christ by the Church was almost literally appropriated in the *Bible Moralisée*, where the interpretation of *Exodus* ii, 5 begins: "Filia Pharaonis significat Ecclesiam." In the latter half of the fourteenth century, however, the editors of the *Bible Moralisée* significantly replaced the impersonal "Church" by a "pious person" (*deuote persone*) whose "compassion and devotion" was depicted under the guise of the Virgin Mary Adoring the Infant Jesus (de Laborde, pl. 143).

C. R. Morey has rightly stressed the compositional relationship which exists between the original, thirteenth-century *Bible Moralisée*—each of its pages showing eight medallions which are arranged in two vertical columns of four and are set off against a mosaic background—and Early Gothic windows

(C. R. Morey, *Mediæval Art*, New York, 1942, p. 272); there can be no doubt that its iconography, too, often draws from the same source. Yet cases of a correspondence as perfect as that of the Daughter of Pharaoh are comparatively rare. The spirit of the *Bible Moralisée*—composed almost a hundred years after Suger—is more rationalistic and, if one may say so, more professional than that of Suger's *allegoriæ*, as when the Veiling and Unveiling of Moses is interpreted as meaning that the simple-minded and the laymen (*simplices* and *laici*) cannot understand the *subtilitatem* of Holy Scripture (de Laborde, pl. 56), and that "the wise preacher or prelate (*sapiens prædicator vel prælatus*) must expound to them the words of God in crude fashion (*grosse*)" (de Laborde, pl. 57). In certain cases (see also above, p. 187) the more human symbolism of Suger is therefore more closely akin to that of the *Speculum Humanæ Salvationis* and the *Biblia Pauperum*. The medallion (Martin-Cahier, pl. "Etude VII, B") is still extant though less well preserved than the others in the same window; our *fig.* 13 (bottom). ⟨Cf. Grodecki, Bib. 90, esp. p. 35 f.⟩

74, 24 f. SICUT CONSPICITUR . . . AB IGNE, NEC ARDET. The *Bible Moralisée* (de Laborde, pl. 40) interprets the incident (*Exodus* III, 2, 3) in precisely the opposite way: the unconsumed foliage of the burning bush represents "the wicked (*pravos homines*) who cannot be inflamed with love through the grace of Holy Scripture." Yet a relationship is obvious in that, in both cases, the incident from the Old Testament is paralleled with a subjective experience, and not with an event from the Gospels. In the *Speculum* (ch. VII, Lutz-Perdrizet, I, p. 16/17; II, pl. 13), the Burning Bush incident is compared with the Annunciation, in the *Biblia Pauperum* (Cornell, p. 253, pl. I) with the Nativity. The medallion (Martin-Cahier, pl. "Etude VII, B") is moderately well preserved; our *fig.* 13 (second from bottom). ⟨Cf. Grodecki, Bib. 90, esp. p. 36.⟩

74, 28 f. QUOD BAPTISMA BONIS . . . CAUSAQUE DISSIMILIS. The distich expresses the idea that the same "form" or means (immersion) can serve opposite "causes" or ends: destruction in the case of Pharaoh's horsemen, and salvation in the case of a person being baptized. Both in the *Bible Moralisée* (de Laborde, pl. 48) and in the *Speculum* (ch. xli, Lutz-Perdrizet, i, p. 84/85; ii, pls. 81/82) the incident (*Exodus* xiv, 23) is paralleled with the Casting of the Sinners into Hell. The *Biblia Pauperum*, however, compares (or, rather, contrasts) it, like Suger, with the Baptism (Cornell, p. 263, pl. 5). The medallion (Martin-Cahier, pl. "Etude vii, e") is moderately well preserved; our *fig.* 13 (third medallion). ⟨Cf. Grodecki, Bib. 90, esp. p. 36 f., who for the parallel between the Crossing of the Red Sea and the Baptism quotes also St. Paul, I *Corinthians* x, 1 ff.⟩

76, 2 f. Sɪᴄᴜᴛ sᴇʀᴘᴇɴᴛᴇs . . . ɪɴ ᴄʀᴜᴄᴇ Cʜʀɪsᴛᴜs. For this parallel, one of the most popular and earliest ones, see Mâle i, p. 100 f.; ii, p. 159. It occurs in the *Biblia Pauperum* (Cornell, p. 277, pl. 10) but not in the *Speculum*; and in the *Bible Moralisée* the incident (*Numbers* xxi, 9) is, characteristically, not compared with the Crucifixion itself but with the exorcism of demons by means of the Cross (de Laborde, pl. 81: "Hoc significat quod gloriosi confessores Christi de obsessis corporibus demonia eiecerunt per virtutem et signum sancte crucis"; in the miniature, however, the exorcism is performed with a crucifix so large that the whole still looks like a Crucifixion at first glance). The medallion (Martin-Cahier, pls. "Etudes vi, a and vii, d, g, f, h"; Mâle i, p. 97 and ii, p. 156) is moderately well preserved; our *fig.* 13 (top). ⟨Cf. Grodecki, Bib. 90, esp. pp. 37 f., 46 note 170. Until 1848 the *Brazen Serpent* medallion had been the second from top, and was only then exchanged with the *Giving of the Law* medallion, for which see below.⟩

76, 5 f. Lᴇɢᴇ ᴅᴀᴛᴀ Mᴏʏsɪ . . . ʟɪᴛᴛᴇʀᴀ ᴍᴏʀᴛɪꜰɪᴄᴀᴛ. In the *Speculum* (ch. xxxiv, Lutz-Perdrizet, i, p. 70/71; ii, pls. 67/68) and in the *Biblia Pauperum* (Cornell, p. 291, pl. 13) the scene (*Exodus* xxxi, 18 and xxxiv, 28 ff.) is paralleled with Pentecost. According to the *Bible Moralisée*, however, Moses signifies the preachers and theologians (*prædicatores et theologos*), and his two horns denote the Old and the New Testament. The medallion (Martin-Cahier, pl. "Etude VII, 1") contrasts the Giving of the Law with the scene described in *Exodus* XXXII, 4-6 (the Molten Calf and the Jews "sitting down to eat and to drink") and is moderately well preserved; our *fig.* 13 (second from top). ⟨Cf. Grodecki, Bib. 90, esp. pp. 38, 41, 46 note 170.⟩

76, 8. VITRI VESTITI. The translator has assumed that the term *vitrum vestitum* refers to glass covered with pigments ("painted glass" in the narrower sense) as opposed to glass stained in the pot ("pot-metal"), the pigments "covering" the glass as do *vestes* the human body. For an analogous use of *vestitus* without adverbial adjunct, see Cicero's *montes vestiti atque silvestres* ("mountains covered [with verdure] and wooded") in *De Natura Deorum*, II, 53, 132.

76, 8. SAPHIRORUM MATERIA. See above, p. 171.

76, 9 f. ORNAMENTIS AUREIS . . . AURIFABRUM. Although *peritus* can take the ablative as well as the genitive, it appears more reasonable (because tautology is avoided) to construe the *ornamentis aureis et argenteis* as a dative depending, like *tuitioni et refectioni*, upon *constituimus*.

76, 13. ET AB EORUM PROVIDENTIA NUMQUAM SE ABSENTENT. Assuming that this part of the sentence does not continue the relative clause beginning with *qui* but constitutes a new principal sentence referring back to *fratrum*, it would enjoin the brethren always to look after the two "curators" instead of enjoining the two "curators" always to look after the *objets d'art*. It seems more natural, however, to connect the subjunctive *absentent* with the same *qui* that governs the subjunctive *suscipiant*; if Suger had intended to begin a new sentence governed by "the brethren" he would probably have written: "et ab eorum providentia *fratres* numquam se absentent."

76, 14. SEPTEM QUOQUE CANDELABRA. According to Doublet, p. 1259 (and, after him, Conway, pp. 134, 139), Charles the Bald's original candlesticks had been of silver like the lamps mentioned above, p. 197 f. Even if this apparently unsupported statement were true, the two sets should not be confused

(Crosby, p. 185). The lamps belonged to the Matutinal Altar, the candlesticks apparently to the Main Altar.

[XXXIV A]

76, 22. CALICEM AUREUM SEPTIES VIGINTI UNCIARUM. This chalice was apparently of solid gold (for the expression *septies viginti* instead of *centum quadraginta*, cf. the *quater viginti* in *Cons.* IV, 98, 14; 102, 21, and *Ord.* 134, 1, the latter surviving in modern French "quatre-vingt") and was, probably for this very reason, lost at so early a time that nothing further is known about it. It can, of course, not be identical with the so-called *"Coupe des Ptolemées,"* that beautiful classical sardonyx cup which still exists in the Cabinet des Médailles (E. C. F. Babelon, *Catalogue des Camées Antiques et Modernes de la Bibliothèque Nationale*, Paris, 1897, p. 201 ff., no. 366, pl. XLIII [with many references]; Conway, pp. 119 f., 143 f., fig. 1), and which had been made into a chalice by being mounted on a foot of gold beset with gems; Félibien, pl. IV, facing p. 542, F and pl. VI, facing p. 545; our *figs.* 26, 27 (cf. also C. Rohault de Fleury, *La Messe . . .* , Paris, 1883-1889, IV, pl. CCXCVI). This setting—destroyed on the occasion of the notorious theft of 1804—is generally ascribed to Suger, and this hypothesis is all the more plausible as the inscription, two-thirds of which are transmitted by Félibien and an eighteenth-century drawing, can be restored into a distich in Suger's manner which glorifies his special hero, Charles the Bald (here explicitly characterized as the "third ruler *of the French*"):

"Hoc vas, Christe, tibi [devota] mente dicavit
Tertius in Francos [sublimis, or sublatus] regmine Karlus."

Suger himself, however, makes no reference to this.

⟨For the so-called *"Coupe des Ptolemées,"* see now the catalogue entry by Mütherich, in Bib. 153, p. 133 no. 50 ("Kelch Karls des Kahlen"), where the sardonyx cup is identified as Alexandrian, 2nd/1st century B.C., but the lost gold setting as Carolingian from the time of Charles the Bald with

perhaps only the inscription added by Suger. The entry cites a
hitherto unpublished source from 1644, but omits a reference
to Colin, Bib. 17, esp. p. 107. Colin, following E. Babelon,
suggested that the mounting of the sardonyx cup had been a
Byzantine goldsmithwork of the ninth century, when the
chalice might have been sent as a present of the Emperor at
Constantinople to Charles the Bald. Cf. further Elbern, Bib.
45, p. 10, where the inscription too is thought to have been
Carolingian and merely restored by Suger; Lasko, Bib. 111,
pp. 66, 271 note 39. For the appertaining paten, an antique
serpentine dish with inlaid gold dolphins and a similar Carolingian mounting of gold, precious stones, and pearls, still preserved in the Louvre, see Mütherich, Bib. 153, p. 133 no. 49,
and Lasko, Bib. 111, p. 66 f., the latter defining the goldsmiths' technique as Byzantine. Both, chalice and paten are
extensively described in the inventory of 1634, for which see
now de Montesquiou-Fezensac, Bib. 125, p. 163 f. no. 69 and
passim.)

76, 26-78, 2. ALIUD ETIAM VAS . . . AD FORMAM NAVIS EXSCULP-
TUM . . . CUM QUIBUSDAM FLORIBUS CORONÆ IMPERATRICIS . . .
INCLUSORIO SANCTI ELIGII OPERE. A gondola or "boat" was,
and is, employed for holding the grains of incense. The gondola here under discussion—probably carved of jade rather
than of prase—is sketchily illustrated in Félibien, pl. IV, facing
p. 542, CC, and is circumstantially described in the inventories.
It was stolen from the Cabinet des Médailles in 1804 and has
never been heard of since (see Conway, p. 126 f.). A jade gondola still preserved in the Cabinet des Médailles and listed as
"*Navette de St. Eloi*" in Babelon, *l.c.*, p. 211 f., no. 374, cannot be identical with the one described by Suger because it bears
no resemblance to Félibien's engraving and shows no traces of
ever having been adorned with *verroterie cloisonnée*. Moreover the stolen gondola is not mentioned among the objects
recovered after the theft (Babelon, *l.c.*, p. 135). A reconstruction by C. de Linas, *Orfèvrerie Mérovingienne; Les Œuvres
de Saint Eloi et la Verroterie Cloisonnée*, Paris, 1864, p. 60
ff., is also illustrated in Conway, pl. IX, 1. A second gondola

which originally belonged to the Treasury of St.-Denis (Féli-bien, pl. IV, facing p. 542, BB) is still in the Cabinet des Mé-dailles (Babelon, p. 209 f., no. 373, pl. XLIV; Conway, p. 153 and pl. XVIII, 2). This is, however, of sardonyx and is not men-tioned by Suger (cf. below, p. 221).

⟨For the latter sardonyx gondola, cf. Schramm, Bib. 152, II, p. 405 ff. and Pl. 43; id., Bib. 153, p. 68 note 370; and the recently published inventory entry of 1634 (de Montesquiou-Fezensac, Bib. 125, p. 165 no. 73; for the jade gondola, see ibid., no. 74).

The *imperatrix* must be the famous Empress Matilda or Maud (cf. O. Rössler, *Kaiserin Mathilde*, Berlin, 1897; The Earl of Onslow, *The Empress Maud*, London, 1939). Born in 1102 as daughter and heiress of Henry I Beauclerc of Eng-land, she married the German Emperor Henry V in 1114. After the Emperor's death in 1125, and married to Geoffroy of Anjou in 1127, she spent most of her life in France until 1139 when she returned to England and temporarily asserted herself against Stephen of Blois (see above, p. 180). In 1147 she was forced to return to France where she died in 1167. Since Suger redeemed the *"Navette de St. Eloi"* while Louis VI was still alive, that is to say, prior to 1137, her little gift must have been made before her period as *"Domina Anglo-rum."* Quite late in life, in summer 1150, Suger wrote her a letter asking her and her husband to come to terms with King Louis VII and to protect the possessions of St.-Denis in Nor-mandy (Lecoy, p. 264; Migne, col. 1419 c; Cartellieri, p. 162, no. 298).

For the technique of *verroterie cloisonnée* (or "cold *cloi-sonné*"), see C. de Linas, *l.c.*; for the term *opus inclusorium*, cf. Ducange, IV, p. 329, referring, among other examples, to the present passage.

78, 4. INSTAR JUSTÆ. A *justa*—hence old French "juste," the "right" measure for a good man to drink at a time—was ap-proximately the equivalent of a "pinte de Paris," viz., 0.93 litres or about twice as much as an American pint (see Du-cange, IV, p. 471; La Curne de Sainte-Palaye, *Dictionnaire Historique de la Langue Française*, VII, p. 124). Suger's gift

(Félibien, pl. iv, facing p. 542, z) is preserved in the Louvre. It is now regarded as "probably Egyptian work of the fourth or fifth century A.D." See C. J. Lamm, *Mittelalterliche Gläser und Steinschnittarbeiten*, Berlin, 1929-1930, i, p. 187 and ii, pl. 64, no. 1; further Guibert, pl. vi; Conway, p. 142, pl. xv, 2; our *fig.* 28.

⟨For Queen Eleanor's Vase, see further Lasko, Bib. 111, p. 227, where the original vessel is considered a Fatimid rock-crystal vase of the tenth or eleventh century; and the inventory entry of 1634, recently published by de Montesquiou-Fezensac, Bib. 125, p. 166 no. 75.⟩

78, 5-12. AQUITANIÆ REGINA . . . SANCTISQUE SUGERUS. Eleanor ("Aanor") of Aquitaine married Louis VII, in Suger's presence, on July 25 or August 1, 1137. She accompanied her husband on the Second Crusade but was divorced by him for good and sufficient reasons in 1152. In the same year she married Henry II of England and died in retirement in 1204. The "Mitadolus" who had given the original crystal vessel to her grandfather is otherwise unknown. For the more general aspects of the medieval practice of resetting "heathenish" vases, gems, etc., for ecclesiastical use, see the interesting article by W. S. Heckscher, "Relics of Pagan Antiquity in Mediæval Settings," *Journal of the Warburg Institute*, i, 1938, p. 204 ff.

⟨For Eleanor of Aquitaine's royal patronage of St.-Denis, see the recent article by Greenhill, Bib. 76, to which Carl Nordenfalk has kindly called my attention.⟩

78, 13 f. CALICEM PRECIOSUM, DE UNO ET CONTINUO SARDONICE. This precious chalice was long believed to be lost and to be transmitted only through an engraving in Félibien (pl. iii, facing p. 540, R) and a beautiful drawing from the "Cabinet Peiresc" (Guibert, p. 27 ff., pl. iii; Conway, p. 143 f., pl. xvi, 1). It was, however, rediscovered in 1922, acquired by Mr. Widener in Philadelphia and recently given to the National Gallery of Art in Washington (our *fig.* 29); see Seymour de Ricci, "Un Chalice du Trésor de St.-Denis," *Académie des Inscriptions et Belles-Lettres, Comptes-Rendus*, 1923, p. 335 ff., and M. Rosenberg, "Ein wiedergefundener Kelch," *Festschrift zum Sechzigsten Geburtstag von Paul Clemen*, Bonn,

1926, p. 209 ff. (with excellent illustrations of details). Of the five medallions on the foot only that showing the bust of Christ is original; the bust portraits in the four other roundels, presumably representing the Four Evangelists, were replaced after 1633 by the present set of Eucharistic symbols (clusters of grapes alternating with sheaves of ears).

⟨On Suger's chalice, since 1942 in the National Gallery of Art, Washington, D.C., see further Seymour, Bib. 156, p. 10 f.; Bib. 176, pp. 5 f., 30; Wentzel, Bib. 178, p. 73 ff.; Bib. 16, pp. 70, 353 f. no. III, 13; v. Euw, Bib. 47, p. 256; Lasko, Bib. 111, p. 227; as well as the recently published inventory text of 1634 (de Montesquiou-Fezensac, Bib. 125, p. 164 f. no. 71 and *passim*), which still describes the foot with "cinq ronds garnis de cinq demy images de demy bosse."

While Byzantine influence has been generally assumed for the over-all shape of the chalice, John D. Cooney has recently established the provenance of the agate cup as Egyptian, perhaps Alexandrian, second century B.C. (Bib. 20: the unpublished typescript the author very generously made available for this edition).⟩

78, 18. VAS QUOQUE ALIUD, HUIC IPSI MATERIA, NON FORMA PERSIMILE. This is the *"Aiguière de Suger"* preserved in the Louvre. See Félibien, pl. IV, facing p. 542 E; Guibert, pl. V; Conway, p. 142 f., pl. XIII, 1; our *fig.* 30.

⟨Cf. the 1634 inventory entry in de Montesquiou-Fezensac, Bib. 125, p. 150 no. 27.⟩

78, 22-24. LAGENAM QUOQUE PRÆCLARAM . . . TRANSMISERAT. This vessel, now lost, must have been much larger than the others. A *lagena* (more correctly *lagona*) amounts to about a gallon (see Ducange, V, p. 13; also J. H. Baxter and C. Johnson, *Medieval-Latin Word-List*, Oxford, 1934, p. 240), and the word "gallon" probably derives from it. It is therefore impossible to identify Suger's *lagena* with one of the tiny vessels marked L in Félibien, pl. II, facing p. 538, as was vaguely suggested by Conway, p. 142. An earlier attempt to identify it with the sardonyx gondola no. 373 in the Cabinet des Médailles (cf. above, p. 218 f.) has been justly refuted by Babelon (quoted *ibidem*), p. 211. M. Rosenberg, *l.c.* p. 211, erroneously describes and captions Queen Eleanor's *justa* as *lagena*. The King of Sicily was Roger II (1101-1154).

78, 26. VASCULA ETIAM CRISTALLINA. It is obviously with these little vessels, and not with the *lagena*, that the vases marked L in Félibien's pl. II ("donnez par l'abbé Suger; l'un est de crystal de roche, & l'autre de béril taillé en pointe de diamant") are identical. See *text illustration.*

⟨Cf. the inventory entries of 1634, published by de Montesquiou-Fezensac, Bib. 125, p. 161 f. nos. 64, 65.⟩

78, 28-31. NEC MINUS PORPHYRITICUM VAS . . . IN AQUILÆ FORMAM TRANSFERENDO . . . ADAPTAVIMUS. This is Suger's famous Eagle Vase (Félibien, pl. IV, facing p. 542, EE), now in the Louvre. See Guibert, pl. XI; Conway, pp. 118, 144, pl. XVII, 2; our *fig.* 31. For more specific information cf. R. Delbrück, *Antike Porphyrwerke*, Berlin, 1932, p. 30 ff., and J. Evans, "Die Adlervase des Sugerius," *Pantheon*, x, 1932, p. 221 ff. Suger's idea of "converting" an antique vase "into the shape of an eagle" was imitated, probably at St.-Denis itself, in an incense boat transmitted only through a drawing from the "Cabinet Peiresc" (Guibert, pl. x; Conway, p. 145, pl. XVI, 2).

⟨For the Eagle Vase, see further Swarzenski, Bib. 164, p. 65 no. 152, plate 152 fig. 336, plate 153 fig. 337; Déer, Bib. 44, p. 98 f.; Schramm, in Bib. 153, p. 68 note 370; v. Euw, Bib. 47, p. 256; Lasko, Bib. 111, p. 227, as well as the inventory entry of 1634, recently published by de Montesquiou-Fezensac, Bib. 125, p. 150 no. 28.⟩

80, 2 f. SANCTISSIMO ALTARI . . . OFFERRI VOLUIT. Cf. above, p. 185.

80, 6-9. PALLIORUM . . . IN ANNIVERSARIO. *Pallia* has been translated as "textiles" because Suger seems to use the word as a generic term for precious fabrics in contradistinction to metal objects and jewelry. In *Adm.* 1, 40, 10 f., he contrasts *pallia* with *aurum, argentum et pretiosissimæ gemmæ,* and in his "Testament" of 1137 (Lecoy, p. 338; Migne, col. 1442 A) he requests the brethren to lay out, on his anniversary, *sive palliorum sive auri et argenti ornamenta;* in the *Life of Louis le Gros* (Lecoy, p. 143; Migne, col. 1337 C) he even speaks of *cappæ de pallio,* "copes of precious material." According to Suger's "Testament" (Lecoy, p. 335; Migne, col. 1441 D), the *anniversarium* is the anniversary of his exequies and not, as would be terminologically possible, of his benediction.

COMMENTARY UPON THE "LIBELLUS ALTER DE CONSECRATIONE ECCLESIAE SANCTI DIONYSII"

I

82, 1-5. DIVINORUM HUMANORUMQUE DISPARITATEM . . . CON-COPULAT. For the neo-Platonic implications of this sentence, as well as of the rest of the chapter, cf. above, p. 24.

82, 7-9. IN SOLIO MENTIS ARGUTÆ QUASI PRO TRIBUNALI . . . CON-TRARIORUM INVENTIONI ET JUDICIO. In the context of a simile in which the processes of reason are likened to those of the law we are justified in rendering *contrariorum* and *inventioni* in terms of legal language. For *inventio* and *invenire* as law terms see Ducange, IV, p. 409.

II

86, 1-5. REX FRANCORUM DAGOBERTUS . . . PATRIS SUI CLOTHARII MAGNI . . . CATULLIACUM VICUM. Clothaire II, born posthumously in 584, died in 629. For the Roman village variously spelled Catulliacum, Catulacum, Catolacum, etc., see Crosby, p. 37 f.

86, 5-7. SANCTORUM MARTYRUM . . . EFFIGIES . . . TANQUAM PUL-CHERRIMOS VIROS NIVEIS VESTIBUS COMPTOS. This tale is based on the *Gesta Dagoberti* which describe how Dagobert falls asleep while worshiping Saint Denis and his Companions, and how these appear to him as "tres viri et corporum liniamentis et vestium nitore conspicui" (*Monumenta Germaniæ Historica, Scriptores Rerum Merovingicarum*, II, Hanover, 1898, p. 403).

86, 10-17. QUAM CUM MIRIFICA MARMOREARUM COLUMNARUM VARIETATE . . . INÆSTIMABILI DECORE SPLENDESCERET. As Gall, p. 101, has shown, this description of the old church allegedly constructed by Dagobert is taken over almost *verbatim* from the *Gesta Dagoberti, l.c.*, pp. 406 and 407 (except for the marble columns which held no interest for the Carolingian writer but were important for Suger in view of what follows on p. 90, line 15 ff.): "Dagobertus denique . . . eorum-

que memorias auro puro et preciosissimis gemmis exornavit . . .
Nam et per totam ecclesiam auro textas vestes, margaritarum
varietatibus multipliciter exornatas in parietibus et columnis
atque arcubus suspendi devotissime iussit, quatinus aliarum
ecclesiarum ornamentis præcellere videretur, et omnimodis
incomparabili nitore vernans, omni terrena pulcritudine compta
atque inæstimabili decore inradiata splendesceret."

86, 22 f. PROPINQUITATI ARRIDENTIUM OCULORUM . . . REFUN-
DENDO. Literally translated, the phrase would read: "reflecting the splendor of gleaming gold and gems to the nearness
of the admiring [or: "the admirers' "] eyes more keenly and
delightfully."

86, 31-88, 12. VIDERES ALIQUANDO . . . CUNCTIS DESPERANTIBUS,
ANHELARE. Cf. the parallel passages in *Adm.* xxv, 42, 23 ff.,
and *Ord.*, 134, 11-23 (already mentioned above, p. 148). In
Ord. the cloisters, here called *pratum* (see Ducange, vi, p.
478), are explicitly designated as *claustrum*.

88, 14 f. PER FENESTRAS CUM RELIQUIIS MULTOTIES EFFUGERUNT.
For the fact that these windows were probably those of the
cripta later remodelled by Suger (*Cons.* iv, 100, 7-14 and
below, p. 238; *text illustration*, p. 239) rather than those of
the church proper, see Crosby, p. 178. For the relics of the
Passion, see Crosby, p. 177; and Conway, pp. 104, 130 f., with
further references ⟨esp. Folz, Bib. 52, p. 179 ff.⟩

88, 16. EXTRA. Allusion to the time when Suger, as a *juvenis*, was
absent from St.-Denis, first 1104-ca. 1106 when he was study-
ing in Burgundy, probably in St.-Benoît-sur-Loire; then ca.
1107-1112 when he was *præpositus* of Berneval-le-Grand and
Toury (Cartellieri, p. 126 f., nos. 5, 9, 10).

88, 27-30. AB AQUILONE, PRINCIPALI INGRESSU PRINCIPALIUM
VALVARUM PORTICUS ARTUS HINC ET INDE . . . TURRIBUS ANGE-
BATUR. For the phrase *ingressus principalium valvarum*, cf.
Adm. xxv, 44, 10 ff.: *valvarum introitus* and *introitus valvarum.* For the reconstruction of the Carolingian west front as a
whole, see the excellent exposition in Crosby, pp. 118-127,
150-152, based upon his recent excavations and marred only
by the fact that he translates the word *artus* ("narrow") as
"arched"; furthermore R. Krautheimer, *American Journal of*

Archaeology, XLVIII, 1944, p. 220, and *ibidem*, XLIX, 1945, p. 117. While Crosby assumes that the flanking towers were higher than the central section of the façade, Krautheimer arrives at the opposite conclusion because, as he rightly points out, the front wall of this central section is thicker than that of the flanking bays which formed the substructures of the two towers. There is, however, agreement about the fact that the entire façade, except for the little porch protecting the tomb of Pepin the Short, was flush; and that Suger's *porticus artus* must be identical with the inner entrance hall between the towers— indeed a "narrow" room, and one "squeezed in on either side."

It is therefore hard to see how Suger could refer to this entrance hall, located right in the center of the original west façade, as being *ab aquilone*, viz., "in, or facing, the north." Now Crosby, p. 123, has called attention to the fact that a similar problem is raised by the *Pilgrims' Guide* to Santiago de Compostela which contains the following passage: "In majori navi, triginta unus minus pilares habentur, quatuordecim ad dexteram, totidemque ad levam, et unus est inter duos portallos deintus, *adversus aquilonem*, qui ciborios separat"—"In the principal nave, there are twenty-nine piers, fourteen on the right and as many on the left; and one is between the two portals inside, facing the north, and this one separates the vaulted bays [of the two portals]" (J. Vieillard, *Le Guide du Pélerin de Saint-Jacques de Compostelle*, Mâcon, 1938, p. 88). Here, too, the architectural feature referred to as standing *adversus aquilonem* unquestionably faces the west and not the north. Taking up a tentative suggestion of K. J. Conant (*The Early Architectural History of the Cathedral of Santiago de Compostela*, Cambridge, Mass., 1926, p. 50), Crosby proposes to solve the difficulty by interpreting, in both cases, the word *aquilo*, not as "the north" but as "the north wind" or "bad weather"; then both the inner portal of Santiago and the entrance hall of St. Denis would have been designated as a "protection against the weather." However, while *aquilo* as such may in fact denote something like "tempest," the phrases *ab aquilone* and *adversus aquilonem*, without an explicit reference to protection, can only mean what they say, namely, "in the north" or—what amounts to the same thing—"facing the north"; moreover, in the case of Santiago the idea of protection from the weather is at variance with the context. In the *Pilgrims' Guide* the *adversus aquilonem*, corresponding as it does to the *ad dexteram* and to the *ad levam*, does not refer to the inner portal as a whole but merely serves to define the location of that odd pier, which separates the inner portal's bays, in contradistinction to that of the piers in the nave arcades; needless to say, this twenty-ninth pier needed and afforded no more "protection against the weather" than did the twenty-eight others. We are thus confronted with an alternative. Either Suger as well as the author of the *Pilgrims' Guide* wrote *aquilo* by mistake (as, in the latter case, was assumed by Vieillard, *l.c.*); or the term *aquilo* was used in a yet different sense. And since it seems somewhat improbable—though of course not impossible—that two approximately contemporary but absolutely independent writers should have committed precisely the same and not too common error (we often confound the west with the east, and the north with the south, but rarely the west with the north), the second of these alternatives deserves to be considered, all the more so as a possible clue is found in Suger's treatise itself.

In *Cons.* v, 104, 5-7, he metaphorically refers to his new chevet as "mount Zion," describing it, in the exact words of *Psalm* XLVII, 3, as "mons Syon, *latera aquilonis*, civitas Regis magni." Since mount Zion, viz., the site of the Early Christian Zion church and, later on, of the so-called tomb of David, is the southernmost spur of the mountain range on which Jerusalem is built, it was unanimously assumed that *latera* here means, not so much "on the sides of" as "opposite to": "contrarius solet esse aquilo Sion," to quote from St. Augustine's *Enarratio in Psalmos* (Migne, *Pat. Lat.*, vol. 36, col. 534). And in view of such passages as *Isaiah* XIV, 13, where Lucifer says of himself that he will exalt his throne above the stars of God and will sit upon the mount of the congregation *in lateribus aquilonis*, all patristic and medieval writers were agreed that, as mount Zion signifies the Church, so *aquilo*, lying in the "opposite" direction, signifies the devil and, indirectly, his adherents, the Jews and the Gentiles. However, by the grace of God these infidels can be, and in part have been, converted to the true faith and "aligned with the City of God." This was the accepted explanation of the verse quoted by Suger, as summarized, with admirable clarity, by Cassiodorus: "*Mons* vero *Sion*, sicut sæpe dictum est, designat Ecclesiam. . . . *Latera* autem *aquilonis* significant populos infideles, in quibus diaboli regnabat iniquitas. . . . Sed quia peccatores. . . . Deo miserante conversi sunt, modo *mons Sion*, et *latera aquilonis*, id est natio Judæorum et populi gentium, facta est *civitas Regis magni*, hoc est Ecclesia catholica, quam de universo mundo constat esse collectam"—"*Mount Zion*, as has often been mentioned, means the Church . . . *The sides of the north*, however, signify the unbelieving peoples among whom the iniquity of the devil held sway . . . But because the sinners . . . have been converted by the mercy of God, now *mount Zion* —and *the sides of the north*, viz., the nation of the Jews and the Gentile peoples—has come to be *the city of the great King*, viz., the Catholic Church which is known to have been collected from the whole world" (*Expositio in Psalterium*, Migne, *Pat. Lat.*, vol. 70, col. 337; for other analogous interpretations of *aquilo*, cf. J. Sauer, *Symbolik des Kirchengebäudes*, 2nd ed., Freiburg, 1924, pp. 88, 90-92).

Prof. George Kubler kindly called the translator's attention to an interesting passage from St. Gregory's *Homiliæ in Ezechielem* (Migne, *Pat. Lat.*, vol. 76, col. 1021): "Pateat porta ad Aquilonem, ut hi qui post inchoationem caloris et luminis in peccatorum suorum frigore et obscuritate dilapsi sunt per compunctionem pœnitentiæ ad veniam redeant."

Thus the term *aquilo* had come to assume a symbolical or theological significance quite independent of its geographical or topographical one. It had come to denote the region or habitat of those who, living "in opposition to" mount Zion, viz., to the Christian faith, can nevertheless be transformed into members thereof by conversion. And since, as evidenced by Suger himself, mount Zion is specifically symbolized, even represented, by the sanctuary or chevet of any actual church, we can easily see how, in the same architectural terms, the word *aquilo* could come to denote the region or habitat of those who, living in and approaching the church from a direction "opposite to" the sanctuary, can nevertheless be welcomed therein as worshipers. Assuming that both Suger and the author of the *Pilgrims' Guide* to Santiago employed the term in this symbolical or theological sense, their phrases *ab aquilone* and *adversus aquilonem* would make good sense: they would denote, not "that which faces the north" but "that which faces the secular world," in other words, the congregational or front side of the church in contradistinction to its chevet. From the point of view of medieval symbolism such a substitution of a word normally meaning "the north" for what is really the west was much less strange than it would seem to us; for, the west, too, bore unfavorable connotations in a symbolical sense. As the region of the setting sun, it, too, was associated with the Old Law as opposed to the New Testament ("Pia gratia surgit in ortu, lex tenet in occasum," as it says in the famous Crucifixion miniature in the Uta Gospels) and was, more generally, conceived of as the realm of "imperfect faith"; cf. especially R. Salomon, *Opicinus de Canistris* . . . (Studies of the Warburg Institute, vol. I, A), London, 1936, pp. 271, 286.

⟨Recent excavations of the Carolingian narthex, conducted and published by Crosby (Bib. 25, esp. p. 357 ff.; *id.*, Bib. 26, p. 15) seem to indicate that Suger's description *ab aquilone* could indeed be understood as "in, or facing, the north": the main entrance was apparently "toward the north" of the "porch," or rather the polygonal apse protecting the tomb of Pepin the Short (for which cf. above, p. 149: 44, 10), i.e. squeezed in between this apse and the north tower. Hard to comprehend is the relevant interpretation by Formigé which reads: "une entrée principale aurait été au nord de la nef, à l'extrémité orientale du bas-côté entre deux 'tours basses' dont il est difficile de se faire une idée, à moins que ce mot 'tour' signifie autre chose; on se demande quoi" (Bib. 56, p. 63).⟩

88, 30 f. DIRECTÆ TESTUDINIS ET GEMINARUM TURRIUM. The adjective *directus* means "straight" or "unbroken," and at first glance the phrase might be thought to refer to the fact that Suger's new façade formed one plane surface, whereas from the old one there had protruded the little porch with the tomb of Pepin the Short; this seems to be the view of Gall, p. 94, who paraphrases Suger's statement by "eine von 2 Türmen flankierte, in gerader Flucht verlaufende Halle." However, what Suger really meant was that the entire west structure was carefully aligned with the old nave on one "straight" axis, whereas there was a considerable deviation between the axes of the old nave and the original east part. In the first place, the word *testudo* (cf. above, p. 151) does not denote, in Sugerian usage, a mere "hall" between towers (this, we remember, is designated as *porticus*, and Gall's translation according to which the *geminæ turres* "flanked" the *testudo* is arbitrary). In the second place, we know from Suger himself that he considered axial alignment as a real problem the successful handling of which he thought worth mentioning (cf. below, p. 239f.). In the third place, the word *directus*, capable of being construed with the dative, was a technical term in geometry, meaning precisely what it means here, viz., that two or more quantities form one continuous straight line: "erit igitur ΔΓ latus ΓΗ lateri *directum*" ("thus the side ΔΓ will be the straight continuation of the side ΓΗ"), to quote a recurrent phrase from Chalcidius's Commentary on Plato's *Timæus*. ⟨For "the little porch with the tomb of Pepin the Short" cf. again above, p. 149: 44, 10.⟩

90, 15-17. APPRIME DE CONVENIENTIA . . . COLUMNAS. These columns, probably eight in number, must have been those in the link between the new narthex and the Carolingian nave (cf. above, p. 150); the narthex itself is not supported by monolithic columns but by compound piers of masonry (*fig.* 2). The situation is clearly described in *Ord.*, 132, 29 ff. ("ipsoque novo antiquo operi pulchra novarum columnarum et arcuum convenientia apte unito"), where the columns and arcades are explicitly characterized as that which "connects" the new part with the old.

90, 20-25. AB URBE . . . PER MARE MEDITERRANEUM . . . CONDUCTU HABEREMUS. The imaginary Odyssey of these columns would seem to have been patterned on the real Odyssey, probably well-known to Suger (cf. above, p. 169), of those which

had been brought from Rome to Montecassino by Abbot Desiderius in 1066: ". . . ipse interea Romam profectus est, et
quosque amicissimos alloquens, simulque larga manu pecunias
oportune dispensans, columnas, bases ac lilia, nec non et diversorum colorum marmora abundanter coemit; illaque omnia *ab
Urbe* ad portum, a portu autem Romano *per mare* usque ad
turrem de Gariliano, *indeque* ad Suium navigiis conductis ingenti fiducia detulit. *Abinde* vero usque in hunc locum plaustrorum vehiculis non sine labore maximo comportavit" (Leo
of Ostia, *Chronicon Monasterii Casinensis*, Migne, *Pat. Lat.*,
vol. 173, col. 746, and J. von Schlosser, *Quellenbuch zur
Kunstgeschichte des Abendländischen Mittelalters* [Quellenschriften für Kunstgeschichte, new series, vol. VII], Vienna,
1896, p. 202 f.). Another interesting, though less close parallel—Heiricus's description of the transportation of antique
marbles from Marseille to Auxerre—was pointed out to the
translator by Dr. Meyer Schapiro (J. von Schlosser, *Schriftquellen zur Geschichte der Karolingischen Kunst* [Quellenschriften für Kunstgeschichte, new series, vol. IV], Vienna,
1892, p. 193). For *conductus* as "passage money," see Ducange, II, p. 492: "quod pro rerum quæ exportantur securitate
Domino exsolvitur." The Saracens held the Straits of Gibraltar, with one brief interruption in the fourteenth century, up
to 1462 ⟨cf. Panofsky, Bib. 132, p. 120.⟩

90, 30-33. UNDE QUANTO . . . CONFERRE, TANTO MAJORES GRATI
ARUM ACTIONES . . . REFERRE. The play upon the rhyme *conferre-referre* and upon the twofold significance of *gratiarum
actiones* ("acts of grace" and "acts of gratitude") cannot be
adequately rendered in English.

92, 8 ff. NOBILES ET INNOBILES . . . VICE TRAHENTIUM ANIMALIUM
EDUCEBANT. If Suger's account could be taken literally these
incidents, which would have taken place several years before
1140, would mark the beginning of the so-called "cult of the
carts" in France. This cult (cf., e.g., Kingsley Porter *Medieval
Architecture*, New Haven, II, 1912, p. 151 ff., and G. G. Coulton, *Art and Reformation*, New York, 1928, p. 338 ff.) is
described, in an already formalized and officially regulated
form, in a famous letter of Hugues d'Amiens, Archbishop of

Rouen, to Thierry, Bishop of Amiens, and in an equally famous treatise by Haymo, Abbot of St.-Pierre-sur-Dives in Normandy, both of which are datable about 1145 and represent the custom as an entirely new manifestation of piety originating in Chartres and having developed into a mass movement in Normandy. This view seems to have been accepted by most modern scholars; but it should not be overlooked that similar phenomena are recorded before and in other places, especially in connection with the construction of the abbey church of Montecassino in 1066: "Et ut magis fervorem fidelium obsequentium admireris, primam hic columnam ab ipso montis exordio sola *civium* numerositas *colli brachiique* proprii virtute imposuit" (Leo of Ostia, directly following the passage quoted above, p. 231). The most remarkable fact about this incident is that it gives the impression of a symbolical rather than practical action: only the *first* column is carried up by the faithful laymen—and this, it seems, at Desiderius's instigation—much as today a group of citizens drives the first bus over a new bridge. Be that as it may, Hugues d'Amiens and Haymo do not take cognizance of this and other precedents. But neither do they mention St.-Denis, and Hugues's silence in this respect is all the more significant as he was a very intimate friend of Suger and participated in nearly all the memorable events in St.-Denis between 1140 and 1144 (consecration of the west structure on June 9, 1140; disclosure of the relics in the Matutinal Altar on October 9, 1140 or 1141; consecration of the chevet on June 11, 1144). In addition, the following section of *Cons.* makes it perfectly clear that the quarrying and transportation of the stones at Pontoise was not an *opus pietatis* but a perfectly workmanlike job, with hundreds of honest ox-drivers (*bubulci*) and laborers (*operarii*) toiling and grumbling as their forebears and descendants had done and will do at all times. Of course the good people of Pontoise and vicinity—there could hardly have been a real conflux of *nobiles*—may have been very helpful on given occasions; but one cannot help feeling that Suger, writing precisely in 1145 or very shortly after, apparently familiar with Leo of Ostia (whose *Narratio de Consecratione et Dedicatione Ecclesiæ Casinensis* [Migne,

Pat. Lat., vol. 173, col. 997 ff.] may well have been the modest model of *Cons.*, even in that it, too, enumerates the many dignitaries present at the dedication ceremonies), and certainly informed of the developments in Normandy, colored his account somewhat so that St.-Denis might not seem to fall short of Chartres and Rouen.

92, 10 f. PER MEDIUM CASTRI DECLIVIUM DIVERSI OFFICIALES, RE-LICTIS OFFICIORUM SUORUM INSTRUMENTIS. No doubt *castrum* means here "town" and not "castle" (cf. p. 147f.), and *officium* "craft" or "trade" and not "office" (cf. Ducange, VI, p. 38).

III

94, 8 f. TABULATIS. This term has been well explained by Crosby, p. 133. *Tabulatum, -i*, from which Suger's ablative is derived, is (in contrast with the later *tabulatus, -us*) a good classical word occurring already in Caesar and Virgil.

94, 9-12. MAGNOQUE DEPOSITO . . . TIMORE . . . DEAPTARE SOLLI-CITABAMUR. From this brief retrospective account we learn that, while the walls of the old nave had been temporarily restored before the new west structure was started (cf. *Adm.* XXIV, 42, 12 ff.), the apparently not too serious damages in the capitals and bases of the old columns were not repaired until the new structure was finished (with the exception of the timber work) and had been joined to the old nave.

⟨For Suger's repairs of the Carolingian column bases, cf. Vieillard-Troïekouroff, Bib. 173, p. 346.⟩

94, 19 f. A MATUTINARUM OBSEQUIO REGRESSUS. Matins is the night office, generally said at midnight.

94, 24. AD SILVAM QUÆ DICITUR IVILINA. For the Abbey's posses-sions in the Valley of Chevreuse and for the Forest "Ivilina" (originally "Æqualina," today "Forêt de Rambouillet"), see *Adm.* X, Lecoy, p. 165 f.; Migne, cols. 1216 D - 1217 C. The forest, except for such parts as had been given to other abbeys specifically named, had been donated to St.-Denis by Pepin the Short in 768 (J. Tardif, *Monuments Historiques*, Paris, 1866, no. 62; *Monumenta Germaniæ Historica, Diplomat. Karol.*, I, M. Tangl, ed., Hanover, 1906, p. 39 f.). But this did not prevent the later kings from granting woodcutting and grazing privileges, tithes and even pieces of the land itself to other ecclesiastical institutions and private persons (see, for instance, Tardif, *l.c.*, no. 240; further A. Luchaire, *Etudes sur les Actes de Louis VII*, Paris, 1885, nos. 71, 93, 105, 227, 281, 426, 439, 453, 714, and *idem, Histoire des Institutions Monarchiques de la France sous les Premiers Capétiens*, 2nd ed., Paris, 1891, I, p. 105 ff.); nor did it restrain some of the nearby noblemen from all sorts of infringement. Suger put an end to these abuses and revived—"non levitate, sed pro jure ecclesiæ reparando"—even the hunting rights of the Abbey wherever they had been illegally usurped.

94, 31-33. MILO CAPREOLENSIS . . . QUI MEDIETATEM SILVÆ A NOBIS CUM ALIO FEODO HABET. Milon II de Montlhéry, Castellan of Bray-sur-Seine and Vicomte de Troyes, is mentioned on several occasions—always, to quote from Waquet, as "gémissant ou fondant en larmes"—in Suger's *Life of Louis le Gros*.

From the account in *Adm.* x, just quoted, it is evident that the *alio* in our passage cannot refer to another person as was assumed by Gall, p. 96 ("Milo . . . , der mit einem anderen die Hälfte des Waldes von uns zu Lehen hatte") but must be construed with *feodo*. Apart from the fact that a fief held by two noblemen at the same time would be a rather odd thing in itself, Suger explicitly states that the Lords of Chevreuse held *two* ancient fiefs of the Abbey, viz., first, the *advocatio* (for this term, see below, p. 252) of the Abbey's domains and, second, the *medietas silvæ*. Milon thus held in fact "one half of the forest in addition to another fief." For the use of *medietas* in this sense (as opposed to that of "moiety" in *Ord.*, 126, 5 f.), see the little collection of documents in M. Brussel, *Nouvel Examen de l'Usage Général des Fiefs en France pendant le XI. le XII. le XIII. et le XIVᵉ Siècle*, Paris, 1727, I, p. 43, where a gentleman is enfeoffed with "one half" of the "banvin" (here: wine tax) of La Ferté-sur-Aube, and a lady with "one half" of "the swarms of bees and other useful things" that might be had from a near-by forest. Milon himself was reduced by Suger to his two ancient and legitimate fiefs, viz., the *medietas silvæ* and the *advocatio*, but he had to be paid ("although he was our liegeman") an appeasement bonus of 100 shillings per year lest he again resort to exaction and oppression.

94, 34. AMALRICO DE MONTE FORTI. Amaury III, Seigneur de Montfort from about 1101 to 1137, Comte d'Evreux. As brother of Bertrade l'Angevine—the second, slightly bigamous wife of Philip I—he was an uncle of Louis le Gros.

96, 9 f. NOVI OPERIS OPERTURÆ SUPERPONI. Evidently the big beams were needed as tie-beams for the roof of the central nave of the new west structure and were therefore more than thirty-five feet long; assuming that the roof, covering the whole *novum opus*, extended over the narthex proper as well as over the link between the latter and the Carolingian nave (cf. above, p. 150), they would have been spaced at intervals of ca. nine feet. The only difficulty is presented by the phrase *superponi operturæ*; for, pending the publication of Crosby's second volume, we do not know whether the link was already vaulted in order to harmonize with the narthex, or still provisionally covered with a flat wooden ceiling in order to harmonize with the old nave then still extant. In the first case, the word *opertura* would merely be another way of expressing a continuous series of vaults; in the second, it would be a kind of common denominator both for the vaults of the narthex and the flat ceiling of the link. Unless there is evidence to the contrary, the translator would be inclined to prefer the second alternative, first, because a patron so anxious to "harmonize" his new "addition" with the old nave that he thought of importing conformable columns from Rome (*Cons.* II, 90, 20-25) may also be presumed to have insisted on a uniform covering; second, because Suger, when speaking of vaults pure and simple, invariably refers to them as *voltæ*. The fact that he preferred the word *opertura* ("covering") would seem to indicate that he was searching for a neutral term that would be applicable to a ceiling partly vaulted and partly flat. The verb *superponere*, too, would make good sense in either connection. While nothing is more natural than to describe the tie-beams of a roof as being placed "upon" or "on top of" a series of vaults, they could equally well be described as being placed "upon" or "on top of" a flat, wooden ceiling which would have been fastened to them from underneath. ⟨Crosby (Bib. 26, p. 42) is convinced that the bays of Suger's link were covered "en charpente, comme celles de la vieille nef."⟩

IV

96, 24-26. QUI IN MEDIO NOVI INCREMENTI PRIOREM IN CONSISTENTE DOLIO BENEDICENTES AQUAM. The word *priorem* would seem to refer to the fact that the "Gregorian" water prepared and blessed for the dedication here described (June 9, 1140) and held by a vessel placed in the middle of the link between the new narthex and the Carolingian nave was to be reused—with or without a second benediction—for mixing the mortar when the foundations of the new chevet were laid on July 14, exactly five weeks later (*Cons.* IV, 100, 27 f.). This water, then, is here called *prior*, not as something belonging to the past while being viewed from the standpoint of the present (as when Suger, in *Adm.* xxv, 44, 9 f., speaks of the "former" or "previous" west façade as "prior valvarum introitus"), but as something belonging to the present while being viewed from the standpoint of the future (as when a historian speaks of "Dionysius prior" with reference to a subsequent "Dionysius minor" or "Dionysius filius"). The word has therefore been translated as "first."

96, 26-98, 9. PER ORATORIUM SANCTI EUSTACHII . . . PER PLATEAM QUÆ "PANTERIA" . . . VOCITATUR . . . ET GLORIAM DEI OMNIPOTENTIS. For the arrangement of the procession, the problem of the *porta atrii* (here *quæ in sacro cimeterio aperitur*) and the discrepancies as to the participants and the designation of the lower right-hand chapel, see above, p. 151 f. The etymology of the name "Panteria" (according to Suger deriving from Greek παν, "all" or "everything," and Latin *terere*, "to grind," "to wear down") is of course just as fantastic as most other medieval etymologies. The name probably derives from *panis*, "bread."

96, 34-98, 1. IN HONORE SANCTÆ DEI GENITRICIS . . . ET SANCTI MICHAELIS ARCHANGELI. See above, p. 151. For other examples of chapels in high places dedicated to the Angels and Archangels, cf. K. Conant, "La Chapelle Saint-Gabriel a Cluny," *Bulletin Monumental,* LXXXVII, 1928, p. 55 ff., especially p. 59, and, with ampler documentation, W. Effmann, *Centula,* Münster, 1912, p. 90 f.

98, 4-7. INFERIUS VERO IN DEXTRO LATERE . . . PERHIBETUR HIPPOLITUS. See above, p. 151 f.

98, 11. QUASI PRO DOTE. For the "dowry" of a newly erected church or chapel (*dos ecclesiæ,* referred to as *dos catholica* in *Ord.,* 132, 35-134, 1), see Ducange, III, p. 187. In theory no ecclesiastical structure was permitted to be consecrated unless an adequate "dowry" had been settled upon it for its upkeep.

98, 12-15. PLATEAM QUANDAM . . . JUXTA ECCLESIAM SANCTI MICHAELIS, QUAM QUATER VIGINTI LIBRIS A WILLELMO CORNILLONENSI EMERAMUS. For this property—located across the cemetery at the southeast corner of what Anselin's plan of 1704 in Félibien, before p. 1, lists as the Rue Petit Piechet—cf. *Ord.,* 134, 1-3, *Adm.* 1 (Lecoy, p. 157 f.; Migne, col. 1213 c), and below, p. 258. As we learn from *Ord.,* its previous owner had sold it to St.-Denis with the consent of his parents and children. But concerning the identity of this previous owner there is considerable confusion. In the passage here under discussion and in *Adm.* 1 he is called Willelmus, or Guillelmus, *Corneilensis,* which would mean Guillaume de Corneilha, and Lecoy (p. 157, footnote, and Index) has, apparently without documentary basis, conjectured *Cormeilensis,* thereby connecting him with Cormeilles-en-Parisis, one of the possessions of St.-Denis. In *Ord.,* however, he is called Willelmus *Cornillonensis,* which means Guillaume de Cornillon, and is thus separately indexed by Lecoy who seems to have been unaware of the fact that the two properties, and therefore the two Willelmuses, are identical. Since *Ord.* is transmitted in the original, the latter reading must be accepted, all the more so as it is confirmed by another original document, viz., the Release Order of 1125 (Lecoy, p. 322; Migne, col. 1449 D; cf. above, p. 150), where Guillelmus *de Cornelione* and his son of the same name appear among the witnesses. Moreover a "Guillelmus *Cornillon*," but no Guillaume de *Corneilha* or de *Cormeilles*, is mentioned in the Obituary of St.-Denis (p. 323 of the edition quoted above, p. 163), and a later member of what would seem to be the same family, Renaud de Cornillon, had dealings with St.-Denis in 1202 in his capacity of "Prévôt de Paris" (G. Lebel, p. 170). For the *quater viginti*, cf. above, p. 217.

98, 17. SI TAMEN NON OBSCURETUR. To translate this as "unless it has become effaced" implies the preposterous notion that Suger, writing at St.-Denis about 1145, was not quite sure whether or not his inscription of 1140 was still legible. *Si tamen* is here used as an equivalent of *utinam*, which is good classical usage in the more elevated style.

98, 25. CIRCA SANCTUM SANCTORUM. Duchesne's text omits the *Sanctum*, and Brial (adduced by Lecoy, p. 224) has conjectured *ipsa cura Sanctorum*. However, this conjecture can be dismissed because *Ord.*, 134, 12, supplies the much better reading *Sanctum Sanctorum* (cf. below, p. 258).

100, 3 f. PROPRIA ET MANUALI EXTENSIONE . . . BENEDICTIONEM. See above, p. 148.

100, 7-14. CONSULTE SIQUIDEM . . . OBTUTIBUS DESIGNARET. According to Panofsky, the *altiori inæqualis volta* is simply the old Carolingian apse (for the term *volta* cf. above, p. 172) which was, of course, lower than Suger's new upper choir. Freely paraphrased, the sentence means: "It was decided to remove the apse which formed the upper part of the sanctuary wherein were kept the relics of our Patron Saints. This apse, lower than the present one, was removed all the way down to the top surface of the crypt to which it was attached. . . ."

100, 14-20. PROVISUM EST ETIAM SAGACITER . . . ADAPTARETUR. It should be noted that Suger makes a linguistic distinction between the problem of the side-aisles, on the one hand, and the problem of the central nave, on the other. In the former case he describes the harmonization of the *quantitas alarum* (*"dimensions* of the side-aisles"), in the latter the harmonization of the *medium* (here "central nave") pure and simple. According to Panofsky, this can be accounted for by the fact

ST.-DENIS, LONGITUDINAL SECTION OF THE CAROLINGIAN CRYPT
ENLARGED BY SUGER, AND OF SUGER'S NEW UPPER CHOIR in a pre-
liminary reconstruction by S. McK. Crosby (Drawing lent by S. McK.
Crosby)

that the correct planning of the central nave, with the Carolingian apse still standing, posed a problem, not only with
respect to the dimensions but also with respect to axial alignment. Suger must have realized that that "crypt which offered
its top as a pavement" to the new upper choir was heavily out
of alignment with the nave (cf. above, p. 230), and saw to it
that the axis of his new chevet was determined afresh "with the
aid of geometrical and arithmetical instruments." This done,
the planning of the side-aisles was in fact only a matter of
quantitas.

⟨For the "geometrical and arithmetical instruments" possibly applied in the planning of Suger's new crypt and choir,
see Crosby, Bib. 27, esp. p. 87 ff.; *id.*, Bib. 31 (for résumé see

Bib. 33); v. Simson, Bib. 158, p. 101; for similar problems in aligning a new choir with an older nave, cf. Forsyth, Bib. 57.

That Suger's new choir had a gallery over the inner ambulatory, as formerly assumed by Panofsky in the first edition of this book, p. 221 (cf. Frankl, Bib. 60, pp. 34, esp. 276 note 4), has been questioned by Crosby, Bib. 24, p. 15; id., Bib. 26, p. 46; cf. also id., Bib. 28, p. 64 (against the renewed proposal of galleries over the inner side-aisles of the nave by Formigé, Bib. 56, pp. 68, 104); further Grodecki, Bib. 86, p. 728 f.; v. Simson, Bib. 158, pp. 99 ff., 115 ff. (see *text illustration*, p. 239). For the partial rebuilding of Suger's choir under Abbot Eudes Clément (1230-1245), see Branner, Bib. 13, pp. 45 ff., 143 ff.)

100, 20-22. EXCEPTO ILLO . . . IN CIRCUITU ORATORIORUM INCREMENTO, QUO TOTA . . . LUCE MIRABILI ET CONTINUA . . . ENITERET. It is tempting to render *circuitus* by the technical term "ambulatory" and to translate: "except for that . . . extension, in [the form of] an ambulatory with chapels, by virtue of which . . ." However, the expression *circuitus oratoriorum* (instead of *circuitus cum suis oratoriis*, or the like) would seem to refer to the grouping of the chapels themselves rather than to something to which they are attached. Moreover, it is not so much the ambulatory—whose width does not exceed that of the side-aisles—as the hemicycle of the chapels proper which constitutes the *incrementum* described by Suger; the relative clause *quo . . . eniteret*, with its reference to the stained-glass windows, also connects a little more logically with the fenestrated chapels than with the ambulatory. For the neo-Platonic connotations of this relative clause and for the specific meaning of the *continua* (referring to the radical reduction of all masonry which would have "interrupted" the light), cf. Panofsky. To supply a *pictura* after *tota* (Lecoy, p. 225) would spoil rather than improve the sense of the passage; the *tota* refers back to the *ecclesiæ* in the first half of the sentence.

⟨For twelfth-century masons' marks on stones of the radiating chapels, see Crosby, Bib. 32.⟩

100, 27. REGIS FRANCORUM LUDOVICI. Louis VII, reigned 1137-1180.

100, 27 f. PRIDIE IDUS JULII. July 14, 1140.

102, 2 f. EX AQUA BENEDICTA DEDICATIONIS FACTÆ PROXIMO
QUINTO IDUS JUNII. Cf. above, p. 236.

102, 16 and 25. GAZOFILACIO . . . GAZOFILACII. The money chest
or collection box (*gazophilacium*, from Greek γάζα, "treasure," and φυλάκειον, "guard-house") was attached to the
Main Altar (see Crosby, pp. 104, 184).

102, 17. IN INDICTO. Cf. above, p. 148.

102, 18. IN FESTO SANCTI DIONYSII. October 9.

102, 19. VILLANA. Cf. the parallel passage in *Adm.* XI, Lecoy, p.
169 f.; Migne, col. 1219 B.

102, 21. QUATER VIGINTI. Cf. *Cons.* IV, 98, 14, and above, p. 217.[1]

V

104, 5 f. EXULTATIONI . . . LATERA AQUILONIS . . . REGIS MAGNI.
Cf. above, p. 225 f.

104, 6-9. CUIUS IN MEDIO DEUS NON COMMOVEBITUR . . . COM-
MOTUS . . . DEDIGNABITUR. Note the play upon the words
medium and *commovere*. While, according to *Psalm* XLV, God
will not be "moved" in the "midst" of the real Zion, He will
be "moved" (to mercy) in the "midst" (viz., the central nave
with the chief altars) of the new choir of St.-Denis, which
choir is Zion in a symbolical sense.

104, 13-21. JAM NON ESTIS . . . IN SPIRITU SANCTO EDOCEMUR. In
his desire to justify his magnificent architectural enterprises
Suger made three significant changes. In *Ephesians* II, 20, he
inserted, after *Christo Jesu*, the relative clause *qui utrumque
conjugit parietem*, a metaphorical allusion to the two natures
in Christ which, in turn, signify the material and the immaterial spheres. In *Ephesians* II, 21, he replaced, even more
boldly and explicitly, the word *constructa* by *sive spiritualis
sive materialis*. The verse *Ephesians* II, 22, the Sugerian paraphrase of which reiterates this antithesis with the accent
reversed, reads in the original: "In quo et vos coædificamini in

---

[1] As has been mentioned on p. 141 f., the whole section from p. 100, line 25 (*col.
lecto virorum illustrium . . .*) to the end of the chapter (*. . . omnino honorifice compleantur*), has been taken over from *Ord.*, Lecoy, p. 358, line 5 - p. 359, line 7 from
bottom.

habitaculum Dei in Spiritu." ⟨Bandmann, Bib. 7, pp. 64 ff., 73
f., understands the above passus as Christ being likened not to
the cornerstone of the church but to the keystone of the rib
vaults.⟩

104, 30-106, 3. ET DEFORIS QUIDEM . . . PRÆPARAVIMUS. For the
construction of the new tomb of Saint Denis and his Companions see above, p. 172 ff.

106, 11-15. QUÆ NUNQUAM IBIDEM FUERAT, ERIGEREMUS ARAM
. . . TABULAM AUREAM. Cf. above, p. 173.

106, 21. VALDE PRETIOSAM TAM OPERE QUAM MATERIA. Cf. the
remarks on *Adm.* XXVII, 46, 26, and XXXIII, 60, 30.

106, 32 f. AFFEREBANTUR . . . OFFEREBANTUR. The play upon
these words cannot be adequately rendered in English.

108, 8-19. CUM NECDUM PRINCIPALES ARCUS SINGULARITER VO-
LUTI VOLTARUM CUMULO COHÆRERENT . . . PRÆFATOS ARCUS
NULLO SUFFULTOS PODIO, NULLIS RENITENTES SUFFRAGIIS IM-
PINGEBAT. This is the *locus classicus* for that characteristically
Gothic method of vault construction according to which the
erection of a virtually self-sufficient "skeleton," consisting of
transverse arches and diagonal ribs, preceded the construction
of the webs. The *principales* clearly implies a distinction between "main" or "major" and "secondary" or "minor" arches.
At first glance one might be inclined to believe that this distinction refers to the transverse arches as opposed to the diagonal ribs; so that, at the time of the "miracle," the latter
would not yet have been in place (except for their springings
which used to form an integral part of the *tas de charge* of the
former). Such an assumption militates, however, against the
fact that the *podium* (scaffolding) and the *suffragia* (props,
here in all probability to be interpreted in the specific sense of
"centering") had already been removed. This can only be done
after the mortar has had time to harden, which takes several
months; and it would have been an incredible waste of energy
and time—especially in a structure erected at record speed—to
spring the transverse arches alone, to wait for them to settle, to
remove their centering, and then to repeat the whole procedure
with the diagonal ribs. We must therefore assume that the
entire "skeleton," viz., the transverse arches as well as the

diagonals, was constructed and freed from its centering at one and the same time; in other words, the term *arcus principales* must here denote, not the transverse arches in contradistinction to the diagonals but the whole arch-and-rib system of the "main," viz., central, nave in contradistinction to that of the side-aisles, ambulatory and chapels (for the use of the term *fornices arcuatæ* for rib vaults as opposed to groin vaults see Gervase of Canterbury, recently quoted by P. Frankl in *The Art Bulletin*, XXVI, 1944, p. 200). At the time of the "miracle," then, the central nave of Suger's chevet must have offered an aspect similar to that of the famous ruin of Ourscamp (except for the fact that the sky did not shine through the arches and ribs because the roofing, *operturæ*, was already in place): everything was completed with the exception of the webs which were to be superimposed upon the "isolated" (*singulariter voluti*, later *solis*) ribs and arches and would thus "hold them together." It is these webs that are denoted by Suger's *voltarum cumulus*, the word *cumulus* here being used, not in the sense of "crown" or "summit" (thus Gall, p. 100, and L. Levillain, "L'Eglise Carolingienne de Saint-Denis," *Bulletin Monumental*, LXXI, 1907, p. 253) but, as in our expression "cumulus clouds," in the sense of "body," "mass" or "bulk"; M. Aubert, "Les Plus Anciennes Croisées d'Ogives," *Bulletin Monumental*, XCIII, 1934, p. 216, is perfectly right in paraphrasing the term with "les *compartiments* de la voûte." Thus interpreted, Suger's phrase reveals a remarkable insight into the *reciprocal* relationship between the "skeleton" and the webs: he knew that, while the ribs and arches precede and, in a sense, support the webs, it is the webs that make the ribs and arches "cohere."

That the roof had been built before the vaulting started is not surprising; it served to protect the work and the workmen from the weather, especially since the operations were not to be interrupted in winter (*Cons.* v, 104, 2: *æstate et hieme*). But when the big storm came this very roof was probably a source of danger rather than of comfort. As pointed out to the translator by his friend George H. Forsyth, Jr., the "isolated arches" would have been less seriously affected by the wind had they not been "protected" by the roof; whereas, as it was, the roof was bound to transmit its own vibration to their springings. ⟨For the construction of medieval scaffoldings, consisting of *podia* and *suffragia*, see the extensive discussion by Frankl, Bib. 59, p. 13 ff. and pl. 2; for a different interpretation of *arcus principales* as flying buttresses and *arcus superiores* as ribs, see Fitchen, Bib. 51, p. 289 ff., a reference kindly brought to my attention by Mrs. Edith Zuckerman.⟩

108, 14 f. ANNIVERSARIO GLORIOSI DAGOBERTI REGIS. This anniversary fell on January 19. Since the foundations of the chevet were laid on July 14, 1140, and since, as we know from *Adm.* XXVIII, 48, 27, the building operations proper lasted only "three years and three months" (cf. above, p. 168), the "miracle" must have taken place on January 19, 1143.

108, 15 f. CARNOTENSIS EPISCOPUS GAUFREDUS. Geoffroy II de Lèves, Bishop of Chartres 1116-1149.

108, 16-24. MISSAS GRATIARUM PRO ANIMA EJUSDEM IN CONVENTU . . . BRACHIUM SANCTI SENIS SIMEONIS . . . OPPONEBAT. The phrase *in conventu* characterizes the Mass as a High or Conventual Mass (*Magna Missa, Missa conventualis*). The *gratiarum* may either mean that the Mass was offered as an act of gratitude for the many benefactions which the Abbey had received from Dagobert, or it may refer to the fact that Masses *pro anima* fell into three classes: if the deceased had been "very good," and could be presumed to be saved, the Mass was considered an expression of gratitude; if he or she had been "not very bad" it was considered a means of propitiation; if he or she had been "very bad" it was considered a consolation for the living (Julianus Pomerius, *Prognosticon Futuri Sæculi*, 1, 22, quoted in Ducange, V, p. 414). It is quite possible that Suger considered Dagobert as "a very good man" whereas Félibien, p. 19, was to interpret the continuance of the custom as "la preuve de l'incertitude où l'on a toûjours esté jusqu'à cette heure, qu'il soit dans un état à n'avoir plus besoin des suffrages de l'Eglise." For the arm of St. Simeon, see Doublet, p. 291; Félibien, p. 537 and pl. 1, G.

110, 14 f. DE FRATRIBUS ALBIS MONACHUS. The Order of the Premonstratensians or Norbertines was founded in Prémontré near Laon in 1119. Its members are still known as "White Canons."

110, 26. RELIGIOSORUM FRATRUM DEPORTATIONE. In medieval usage *deportatio* could also mean "assistance" or "favor" (Ducange, III, p. 70); it would thus be possible to render the phrase as "through the courtesy of the pious brethren." The translator has made his choice, first, because the literal interpretation was more common (cf. *Cons.* III, 96, 9: *deportatas*) and, second, because *deportatio*, when taken to mean "to bring hither," makes a much neater contrast with *quærendo*, "to search for."

VI

112, 1. SECUNDA JUNII DOMINICA, VIDELICET III IDUS. Sunday, June 11, 1144.

112, 10. MATER EJUS. Adelaide of Savoy, married to Louis le Gros in 1115 and, after his death, to Matthieu de Montmorency. She died in the Convent of Montmartre, founded by her in 1134, in 1154.

112, 12. MILITUM ET PEDITUM TURMIS. For the use of *milites* as an equivalent of "knight" in contradistinction to ordinary soldiers, see Ducange, V, p. 377.

112, 14-24. SAMSON REMENSIS . . . PETRUS SILVANECTENSIS EPISCOPUS. The dignitaries not yet mentioned previously are the following: Hugues (not Guy) de Toucy, Archbishop of Sens, 1142-1168; Geoffroy III du Louroux, Archbishop of Bordeaux, 1136-1158; Theobald, Archbishop of Canterbury, 1139-1161; Simon de Vermandois, Bishop of Noyon, 1123-1148; Elias, Bishop of Orléans, 1137-1146; Hugues de Mâcon, Bishop of Auxerre, 1137-1151; Alvise, Bishop of Arras, 1131-1148; Guy II de Montaigu, Bishop of Châlons-sur-Marne, 1144-1147; Algare, Bishop of Coutances, 1132-1150 (1151); Rotrou de Beaumont-le-Roger (Warwick), Bishop of Evreux, 1139-1165; Milon I, Bishop of Térouanne, 1131–1158. As appears from the end of the last chapter, p. 118, 8–34, there was also present Nicholas I de Chièvres, Bishop of Cambrai, 1137 (or 1138)-1167. In the manuscript Bibl.

Nat., MS. Lat. 5949 A (cf. above, p. 144) his name has been added to the present list.

114, 3 f. PERNOCTANTES . . . SYNAXI. On special occasions, particularly on the eve of the great feasts, the night Office (Matins) could be expanded into an all-night service (*pervigilium*).

114, 8. PERSONALITER ADESSE DIGNARETUR. Apparently Suger had hoped for a repetition of the miraculous consecration of 636 cf. above, p. 148).

114, 12. DOLIUM PRO CONSECRATIONE AQUARUM. Unless we wish to change the position of the words to *dolium aquarum pro consecratione* (in which case the translation would read: "the vat with the [holy] water for the consecration"), we must consider *aquarum* as an instrumental, and not as an objective, genitive. Holy water is never "consecrated" (which is the case only with buildings, altars, altar stones, chalices, and patens) but merely "blessed," "exorcized," or, at the utmost, "sanctified"; cf. Ducange, I, p. 338 ff., and Suger's own *aqua benedicta* in *Cons.* IV, 102, 2, and *Cons.* VI, 114, 24.

114, 13. SANCTI SALVATORIS ALTARE. From the fact that the vessel with the holy water for the consecration was placed "between" the new tomb of the Patron Saints and the *altare Salvatoris*—or, as it is called on p. 118, line 10 f., the altar which *Salvatori nostro et sanctorum choro Angelorum et sanctæ Cruci assignatur*—we can infer that the latter was near the western opening of the new upper choir, probably appropriately close to Suger's Great Cross.

114, 17. CIRCINATIS AURIFRISIIS. The verb *circinare*, like the verb *rotare*, means, primarily, "to make, to move in, or to arrange in, a circle or circles." It would seem, therefore, that Suger's somewhat *recherché* expression *circinata aurifrisia* is synonymous with the more customary term *vestes rotatæ*, viz., textiles embellished with circular ornaments (cf. Ducange, VII, p. 222: "Rotatus: figuris rotularum ornatus, distinctus, ubi de pannis sermo est"). More specifically, these terms would seem to denote those Eastern fabrics, highly appreciated in the West, that show an overall pattern of roundels, each enclosing a conventionalized figure or group. This interpretation seems preferable to another one which might be based upon the phrase *caligas circinare*, "to lace one's boots" (Ducange, II, p. 30), in which case the verb would refer to the loops and interlacings of the thread in needlework, and the translation would have to read: "orphreys embellished with embroidery."

VII

114, 31-116, 1. NEQUE ENIM ADHUC DE LOCO SUO MOTA ERANT. This does not mean, of course, that the Relics had never been moved from their place in a purely technical sense; we know, for instance, from Suger himself that they were temporarily exhibited on the Main Altar in 1124 when Louis le Gros assembled his armies against the invasion threatened by Emperor Henry V (*Life of Louis le Gros*, Lecoy, p. 120; Migne, col. 1318 B). But it does mean that they had never been *translated*, and that the "confessio" which had been their resting place until June 11, 1144 (cf. above, pp. 172, 178), could not have been subject to major architectural alterations before this day; see Crosby, p. 147 f., and Panofsky.

116, 3. ISTO APERTO. According to Brial (referred to by Lecoy, p. 235) *isto operto* should read *ostio aperto*. The reading *isto* can be defended as referring back to the *loci* in the preceding line; *aperto*, however, seems inevitable and has been accepted by the translator as well as by the editors of the *Acta Sanctorum, Octobris IV*, Brussels, 1856, p. 942. With reference to the hypothesis proposed on p. 178 it would be tempting to read *cista aperta* ("after the chest [containing the three chasses] had been opened"); but the translator does not quite dare to pile a philological conjecture upon an archaeological one. ⟨Cf. Panofsky, Bib. 132, p. 120.⟩

116, 3 f. SCRINIIS REGE DAGOBERTO FABRICATIS. Cf. above, p. 172 ff. The chasses were commonly ascribed to St. Eloy who had served King Dagobert as goldsmith and Treasurer.

116, 16 f. EQUULEI EXTENSIONEM, CLIBANI SUCCENSIONEM. The rhyme cannot be adequately rendered in any modern language.

116, 24. SEPTIMA MANUS. Brial (referred to by Lecoy, p. 236) conjectures *sceptrigera manus*, meaning the "scepter-bearing" hand of the King. But according to Panofsky the reading *sep-*

tima may be saved if *septima manus* is taken as an allusion to the medieval law terms "secunda, tertia, etc. manu jurare," which refer to oaths taken in such a way that one, two or more cojurors (*conjuratores, consacramentales*) placed their hands on the same sacred object—frequently relics—as did the juror himself; cf. Ducange, IV, p. 453 ff. Then Suger's phrase may mean that the space was so confined, and the onrush of those present so violent, that no seventh *consacramentalis* would have been able to lay his hand upon the sacred chasses.

116, 29 f. IN ANTIQUA CONSECRATIONE CŒLESTIS EXERCITUS. Another allusion to the miraculous consecration of 636 (cf. above, p. 148).

116, 33 f. AD EBURNEUM OSTIUM . . . PER CLAUSTRUM. It seems that, while the King and his retinue carried the chasses of the Patron Saints from the "confessio" up into the crossing, all the other relics to be transferred to the new chevet—previously placed in "draped tents" near the exit of the monks' choir—were simultaneously taken up by the lesser dignitaries and moved so as "to meet" those of the Patron Saints at the "ivory door." Whether this (Carolingian?) "ivory door" led into the cloisters—in which case it would have been identical with the "door of St. Eustace" (cf. above, p. 157 f.)—or, much more probably, from the "confessio" into the crossing is as yet undetermined. Certain it is that the two separate processions met inside the church and then proceeded into the cloisters as a unified cortege, the King with the Patron Saints taking due precedence over the others.

⟨In the 1930's, Dr. Johann Joseph Morper, Bamberg, and Professor Bernhard Bischoff, Munich, independently discovered a copy of a manuscript from 799, containing a description of the Carolingian basilica at St.-Denis in which mention is made of at least three doors in ivory and silver. Unfortunately, as Prof. Bischoff has kindly informed me, the publication of this text of paramount importance is still pending (see the short announcement by Morper, Bib. 128).⟩

118, 3-5. REVERTENTES IGITUR . . . SUPER ANTIQUUM ALTARE PIGNORIBUS SANCTORUM REPOSITIS. After having made the round of the cloisters, the whole procession reentered the

COMMENTARY UPON "DE CONSECRATIONE"

church, presumably again through the "door of St. Eustace," and the archbishops and bishops entrusted with the consecration of the twenty new altars in the new chevet had, of course, partly to ascend the twin stairs to the upper choir and partly to descend the central stair so as to reach the enlarged and remodelled crypt behind the old "confessio." But until the consecration of the altars was completed the relics had to be temporarily deposited in a worthy place (cf. J. Hastings, *Encyclopædia of Religion and Ethics*, IV, New York, 1912, p. 62). Therefore the chasses of the Patron Saints were provisionally placed upon the *antiquum altare*, viz., the Main Altar, whereas the other relics were presumably returned to their "draped tents." All the ceremonies were calculated to stress the prerogatives of the Patron Saints who, from the point of view of St.-Denis, were to all other saints, however worthy, as the king of France was to all his subjects, however great.

118, 8-34. AGEBATUR ETIAM DE ALIIS . . . ARIS VIGINTI CONSE-CRANDIS . . . ODONI BELVACENSI EPISCOPO CONSECRANDAM AS-SIGNAVIMUS. The expression *aliis . . . aris viginti* is somewhat ambiguous because there were not twenty new altars *in addition* to the "new main altar in front of the new tomb" but twenty new altars *in all*, eleven in the upper choir and nine in the crypt. With the aid of Suger's description and Félibien's plan the location of these twenty altars has been correctly ascertained by L. Levillain, *Bulletin Monumental*, LXXI, 1907, pp. 257-262, except for the fact that he erroneously identifies the place of the *altare Salvatoris* with that of the Matutinal, or Trinity, Altar (cf. above, p. 194 ff.). Those in the crypt were disposed as follows: the Altar of the Virgin was beneath its counterpart in the upper choir (*plan*, 5); the Altar of St. Christopher, beneath that of St. Peregrinus (*plan*, 4); that of St. Stephen, beneath that of St. Eustace (*plan*, 3); that of St. Edmund, beneath that of St. Osmanna (*plan*, 2); that of St. Benedict, beneath that of St. Innocent (*plan*, 1); that of Sts. Sixtus, Felicissimus and Agapitus, beneath that of St. Cucuphas (*plan*, 6); that of St. Barnabas, beneath that of St. Eugene (*plan*, 7); that of Sts. George and Walburga, beneath that of

[249]

St. Hilary (*plan*, 8); and that of St. Luke, beneath that of Sts. John the Baptist and John the Evangelist (*plan*, 9). Since Suger counts the altars in the radiating chapels from that in the Chapel of the Virgin, viz., from the *easternmost* point of the central axis, he here employs the terms *dexter* and *sinister* in the opposite sense as he does in *Cons.* IV, 98, 4 ff. (cf. p. 152): *dexter* for the Gospel, or southern side; *sinister* for the Epistle, or northern, side. For the fact that one of the nineteen archbishops and bishops here mentioned is omitted from the list given in *Cons.* VI, 112, 14-24, see above, p. 245 f.

120, 14 f. ETIAM PRÆSENTEM. In writing *præsentem* instead of *præsens*, Suger apparently anticipated, in his fast-working mind, the word *rempublicam* which follows three lines farther down.

122, 7-11. HIS SIQUIDEM SIGNATUM EST . . . ET QUÆCUMQUE MO-
LESTA. The reference is to *Exodus* XXVI, 14 and XXXVI, 19
where, however, the double covering of the "tent" (not the
Ark proper) is said to consist of rams' skins dyed red and of
"violet"—more correctly: "badgers' "—skins (*de pellibus
arietum rubricatis* and *de ianthinis pellibus*).

122, 11. IN QUO IDEM IPSI EXPRIMUNTUR. *Idem* stands here, as
sometimes even in classical Latin, for *iidem* or *eidem*.

122, 15 f. MANDATORUM DEI PRÆVARICATOR. For this expression,
cf. *Cons.* I, 84, 7, where Suger uses the term *prima prævari-
catio* with reference to Original Sin, implying as it did not only
disobedience but also evasion (*Genesis* III, 8 ff.).

122, 19 f. IRRELIGIOSUS . . . RELIGIONEM . . . RELIGIOSORUM. In
order to appreciate this play upon words we have to bear in
mind that *religiosus*, as a noun, means both "a religious person" and "a monk," and that the second of these connotations
has much more force in Latin than is the case with its equivalent in modern English.

122, 25. DE PRÆPOSITURA SIQUIDEM VILCASSINI. The more important domains of St.-Denis were administered by an official
who acted as deputy of the Abbot, and fell into two classes:
præposituræ ("Prévôtés") which were administered by a *præpositus*, and *cellæ* ("Prieurés") which were administered by a
prior (for the difference see Cartellieri, p. 100 f.). The "Pré-
vôté du Vexin" was a sizable territory between the rivers Epte
and Oise, in the vicinity of Pontoise and Mantes. Given to St.-
Denis at a very early time, it had been enfeoffed to a family
of counts but had become a part of the Royal Domain under
Philip I (reigned 1060-1108). As Count of Vexin the King of
France became the "first vassal" of St.-Denis (cf. *Adm.* IV,
Lecoy, p. 161 f.; Migne, col. 1215 C), and it was in this capacity that Louis le Gros assumed the "banner of St.-Denis"
in 1124 (see Lecoy, p. 442; Conway, p. 116; Crosby, p. 50 f.;
C. J. Liebman, Jr., "Un sermon de Philippe de Villette, Abbé
de Saint-Denis, pour la levée de l'Oriflamme (1414)," *Ro-*

mania, LXVIII, 1944-1945, p. 444 ff. More recently, L. H. Loomis, "The Oriflamme of France and the War-Cry 'Monjoie' in the Twelfth Century," in *Studies in Art and Literature for Belle da Costa Greene*, 1954, p. 67 ff., has convincingly shown that the identity of the banner of St. Denis with the famous "Oriflamme" was not claimed until some time after Suger's death). ⟨See further, Barroux, Bib. 9 (without knowledge of the article by Loomis, just quoted), and the refutation thereof by van de Kieft, Bib. 105, p. 419 ff.; v. Simson, Bib. 158, pp. 71, 75 f., 87, 89. For the actual relic of the "Oriflamme," cf. de Montesquiou-Fezensac, Bib. 125, p. 229 no. 201.⟩

122, 26 f. COTIDIANUM FRATRUM GENERALE. In a Benedictine monastery dinner (simply called *prima*, scil., *refectio*, by Suger) was served about 11 o'clock a.m., and consisted, according to the *Rule of St. Benedict*, XXXIX, of one main course, supplemented by a *pulmentum* (see below, p. 253). This main course, which comprised two different dishes "so that he who cannot eat of the one may make his meal of the other," was known as the *generale*.

122, 29 f. AB OPPRESSIONE ADVOCATORUM ET ALIORUM MALE-FACTORUM. The *advocati*—here translated as "bailiffs"—were local noblemen invested by the Abbey with the military and, to some extent, juridical custody of its outlying possessions, in return for which they received a part of the fines (*forisfacta*) and a fixed tax "for protection" (*tensamentum*). In the course of time the *advocationes* had become hereditary, and the incumbents, instead of protecting the immediate officials of the Abbey and its tenants, tended to limit themselves to collecting the revenue or even resorted to exploitations of their own (see Cartellieri, p. 86 ff.; Lebel, p. 66 ff.). So far as the possessions of St.-Denis were concerned, Suger gradually succeeded in putting an end to these abuses, and it may have been on his suggestion that the Synod of Reims (March 21, 1148), which he attended in his capacity of representative of the Crown, adopted a general resolution against them; see C. J. Hefele, *Conciliengeschichte*, V, 2nd ed., Freiburg, 1886, p. 514.

124, 4-11. ALIIS SIQUIDEM DUOBUS DIEBUS . . . IN ALIA ORDINA-
TIONE . . . CONSTARE DINOSCITUR. An Ordinance, by which the
weekly observances on Thursdays and Saturdays and an increase of the meal allowance for these occasions were instituted,
was issued about 1130 (Lecoy, p. 328; Migne, col. 1446 D).
There is, however, an arithmetical problem. In the present
Ordinance, the tenor of which is repeated in *Adm.* IV (Lecoy,
p. 162; Migne, col. 1215 D-1216 A), Suger states that the allowance for the *generale* on ordinary days had been five shillings and was to be increased to ten, while the allowance for
the *generale* on Thursdays and Saturdays had already been
raised to fourteen shillings in a previous Ordinance. In the
document of about 1130, however, he says that the normal allowance was, and apparently remained, six shillings and was
to be increased to ten on Thursdays and Saturdays. This difficulty can be solved only by two conjectures: First, that the
normal allowance had already been increased from five to six
shillings prior to the Ordinance of about 1130; second, that
the special allowance for Thursdays and Saturdays, and this
alone, had already been increased from ten to fourteen shillings
some time between the Ordinance of about 1130 and the present one. These two conjectures are in keeping with the fact
that, according to *Adm.* IV, the sum of five shillings had been
the rule "temporibus *antecessorum* nostrorum" (from which
we may conclude that it had been increased to six at the very
beginning of Suger's abbacy); and that the present Ordinance
especially sanctions everything "previously allowed beyond
five shillings" (from which we may conclude that there had
been unofficial increases which had to be "regularized").

124, 15 f. DE PULMENTO AUTEM . . . SUBTRAHEBATUR. The *pulmentum* is a light additional dish which, again according to
the *Rule of St. Benedict*, consisted of "fruit or young vege-
tables." Later on, however, such delicacies as "tender fish"
were included in this category (see Ducange, VI, p. 563). The
octabæ beati Dionysii are, in a narrower sense, the Feast of
October 16 and, in a wider sense, the whole week between
October 9 and that day. For *Indictum* see above, p. 148.

124, 19 f. CENSUM NOVUM NOVORUM QUOS HOSPITARI FECI. For
the various conditions, from enfeoffment down to métayage,
under which land could be held of St.-Denis, see Lebel, p.
79 ff. The *hospites* (Lebel, p. 87), who held comparatively
small plots of land (generally for life or even hereditarily)
paid a fixed rent (*census*) either in cash or kind or both, were
strictly supervised as to their agricultural or horticultural efficiency, and could not sell or trade their holdings except to a
person in the same village who could be trusted to cultivate the
land in equally orderly fashion.

124, 26. DE SECUNDA VERO, QUÆ CŒNA DICITUR. Supper was
served after Vespers, that is to say, normally about half past
five p.m. in winter and about half past six p.m. in summer.

124, 29. SANCTI LUCIANI DECIMIS, QUÆ AD NOS PERTINEBANT. For
the domain of St.-Lucien near St.-Denis, cf. *Adm.* 1 (Lecoy,
p. 158; Migne, col. 1213 c) and the Ordinance of about 1130
(Lecoy, p. 329; Migne, col. 1447 c). The vigorous injunctions of many Councils and Synods notwithstanding (see Hefele, *Conciliengeschichte, l.c.,* Index, *s.v.* "Zehnten"), the
tithes, originally destined exclusively for ecclesiastical purposes, had gradually lost their special character; they could be
sold, bartered or otherwise ceded like any other kind of doma-
nial revenue (see Lebel, p. 148), and had thus frequently
passed into the hands of laymen. Therefore Suger mentions
explicitly that the tithes of St.-Lucien "belonged to the Abbey"
and, later in *Ord.* (132, 19 f.), refers to the tithe from another
possession as having been "bought"—meaning "bought back"
—from the then holder. The Synod of Reims (see above, p.
252) was among those which ruled that no tithes be held by
laymen.

124, 31-126, 6. ANNONA ETIAM QUÆ NOBIS DE PETRAFICTA RED-
DEBATUR . . . AD MEDIATORES PERTINET VINEARUM. If the
revenue of an individual domain, or a part thereof, was allocated to a specific office these assets were managed by the
"obedientiary" in charge of this office. Thus, when the tithe of
St.-Lucien, just mentioned, was appropriated for the improvement of the brethren's supper, this tithe was handled by the
cœnator or *cœnarius* (French "Cenier") who was responsible

for that meal. This is explicitly stated in the Ordinance of about 1130 (Lecoy, p. 329; Migne, with a bad clerical error, col. 1447 c), and it is to this arrangement that the otherwise unintelligible *ejusdem* in the phrase "ejusdem monachi cœnatoris deliberatione" alludes. From our passage it appears that, in addition to the tithe of St.-Lucien, there had already been appropriated for the same purpose a part of the revenue (viz., the grain) from another domain, Pierrefitte-sur-Seine, and that Suger now extended this partial appropriation to the entire rent from this possession. The whole domain of Pierrefitte thus became specifically and permanently attached to the office of the "Cenier" who—and this applies to other officials and other possessions as well—gradually acquired the rights of a secondary landlord, including the use of the manor (see Lebel, p. 14). Suger makes only one exception: the yield of the vineyards is not to be turned over to the "Cenier's" department but is to be withheld for general use; and he is careful to remind his monks that these vineyards were operated on the métayage system according to which the tenants (*mediatores*) were provided by the landlord with all the necessary implements, seeds, saplings, livestock, etc., and paid their dues, not in the form of a fixed rent in kind and/or cash but by surrendering one half of the *expensæ* ("that which is weighed out," here freely rendered as "produce") while keeping the other for themselves (*medietas* in the sense of "moiety," not to be confused with *medietas* as used in *Cons.* III, 94, 32). For further details about the métayage system, as opposed to the *hospitium* system, see Lebel, p. 90.

126, 7-10. INFIRMORUM CURAM GERERE . . . CONTRARIA CONTRARIIS. For this passage, including the quotation from *Matthew* xxv, 36, cf. the *Rule of St. Benedict*, xxxvi: "Infirmorum cura ante omnia et super omnia adhibenda est, ut sicut revera Christo ita eis serviatur, quia ipse dixit: *Infirmus fui et visitastis me.*"

126, 11 f. QUI OVEM MORBIDAM . . . IN HUMERIS REPORTAVIT. The reference is, of course, to *Matthew* xviii, 12 ff. and *Luke* xv, 4 ff. But in both passages mention is made of a "lost sheep," and not of a sick one.

126, 21 f. QUI QUACUMQUE DE CAUSA JUSSU CUSTODIS ORDINIS IN

DOMIBUS INFIRMORUM CESSERINT. When used in plural, the term *custos Ordinis* can be applied to all the officials responsible for the order in the house (F. A. Gasquet, *English Monastic Life*, 4th ed., London, 1912, p. 122). When used in singular, it seems to denote the Sub-Prior (Ducange, II, p. 682). The verb *cedere*, construed with *in* and ablative, would seem to refer to such brethren as were confined to the infirmary without being actually bedridden, and therefore deserved consideration in a lesser degree than the seriously ill, yet "in the same spirit."

126, 34 f. SENIORUM. For the Seniors—"monks of advanced age and distinguished by knowledge, as well as by an exemplary way of life," their number varying from two to twelve according to the size of the convent—see Ducange, VII, p. 422.

128, 1 f. TENSAMENTUM GARSONIS VILLÆ NOSTRUM, QUI DE IPSA VILLA EORUM ERAT. If not ceded to an *advocatus*, the *tensamentum* (cf. above, p. 252) went, of course, directly to the landlord. The purport of the present sentence seems to be that the *tensamentum* from Garsonis Villa (a possession not mentioned by Suger in any other connection) had always been used for the heating of the Seniors' rooms as a matter of custom, but that this custom was now sanctioned as a statutory right.

128, 3. PORRO, QUONIAM PARVITATIS NOSTRÆ. This opens the second main section of the Ordinance which—apart from the brief appendix, p. 132, lines 17-23—deals with the revival of the observances for Charles the Bald and the disclosure of the relics hidden in the woodwork of the Matutinal Altar. This section thus parallels the account in *Adm.* XXXIII A, 66, 17-70, 21; most of it has already been commented upon on p. 194 ff.

128, 13 f. VILLAM RUOILUM CUM APPENDICIIS SUIS ET AQUARUM FORESTE. According to the study by A. Giry (quoted above, p. 198), the document referred to by Suger had been falsified, perhaps by Abbot Vivien (1008-1049), by the insertion of several items originally not included in the donation of Rueil. This is especially true of the fisheries, referred to as *forestis aquatica* in what Suger believed to be the authentic diploma of Charles the Bald (Giry, p. 696).

130, 29 f. OCTABIS BEATI DIONYSII. See above, p. 253.

130, 30 f. CAPICIARIO SACRISTÆ. For the office of the Sacrist, "to whom was committed the care of the church fabric with its sacred plates and vestments, as well as of the various reliquaries, shrines and precious ornaments," see Gasquet, *l.c.*, p. 66 ff. One of his four assistants was the *capiciarius* (French "Chevecier"); but as often as not the *sacrista* and the *capiciarius* were the same person (see Ducange, II, p. 137 "capicerio id est Sacristæ"). That this was so in St.-Denis is evident from Doublet, p. 430: "Le Cheuecier, ou Sacristin."

132, 17–23. MATRICULARIIS ETIAM QUATUOR CLERICIS . . . A PAGANO DE GISORTIO IN FRANCORUM VILLA . . . ASSUMITUR. *Matricularii* (old French "Marreliers," modern French "Marguilliers") were indigent persons—either laymen or, as in our case, clerics—whose names were on a church's list of dependents (*matricula*), and who repaid their stipends by such services as bell ringing, guard duty, etc. (see Ducange, V, p. 307 f.) There does not seem to be an adequate word for this peculiar situation in either English or German; "church-warden"—the translation given in the usual Dictionaries and corresponding to Cartellieri's "Kirchenvorsteher" (p. 140, no. 108)—is as unsatisfactory as "sexton" or "verger." The tithe of Franconville (near Pontoise) was one of those which had been ceded to a layman (cf. above, p. 254) but had been bought back by Suger. The layman in this case was Thibaut Payen I de Gisors et Neaufles, mentioned on several occasions in Suger's *Life of Louis le Gros.* The whole transaction referred to in our passage—including the "withholding" of the vintage, as in the somewhat analogous case of Pierrefitte (see p. 255)—is set down in *Adm.* V (Lecoy, p. 163; Migne, col. 1216 B). The term *clausum* survives, e.g., in "Clos Vougeot."

132, 24. SUPEREST SIQUIDEM ET ALIUD PROBABILE CAPITULUM. This opens the third and last section of the Ordinance which deals with the rebuilding of the west part of the church and with the laying of the foundations for the new chevet. This section thus parallels, in part *verbatim*, the accounts in *Cons.* II and IV (pp. 86 ff., 96 ff.) and in *Adm.* XXV, XXVI, XXVIII and XXIX (pp. 42 ff., 48 ff.) most of it has already been commented upon on pp. 148 ff., 168 ff., 224 ff., 236 ff.

132, 25. EXSECUTIONE RERUM POLLICITARUM TERMINABILE. Suger means to say that the last *capitulum* of his Ordinance, in contrast to the preceding ones, refers to the prospects of the future rather than to the accomplishments of the past. In 1140 or 1141 the completion of the west façade as well as the erection of the newly founded chevet were in fact contingent upon the performance (*exsecutio*) of promises (*res pollicitæ*), viz., upon the continuous availability of specified revenue as predicated upon the continued favor of the king, the continued generosity of the faithful, and the efficiency and good will of future abbots (*Cons.* IV, 102, 10-29). Yet Suger hopes that this good work too, however far from completion at the time of his writing, will be credited to him on the day of reckoning.

134, 1-3. TERRAM REGIÆ DOMUS . . . A WILLELMO CORNILLONENSI . . . LOCANDAM ET HOSPITANDAM. The ungrammatical plural *locandas et hospitandas* as transmitted both by Doublet and Félibien is, in a sense, justified by the circumstances: the property consisted of five separate dwellings (*mansiones*) which could be leased or rented (*locatio* being on ordinary lease, for *hospitium*, see above, p. 254) individually. When *Adm.* was written, three of these dwellings were occupied while two were still vacant (Lecoy, p. 157 f.; Migne, col. 1213 c). For Guillaume de Cornillon, see above, p. 237 f. For the term *regia domus*, see Ducange, III, p. 118: "Domum regis dicimus, ubicumque in regione sita sit, cuiuscumque feudum vel mansio sit"; for the *quater viginti*, see above, p. 217.

134, 12. INFRA SANCTI SANCTORUM LOCUS. The *Sancti Sanctorum locus* (cf. above, pp. 98 note 33, 238) is the monks' choir which enclosed both the Main Altar and the Altar of the Trinity (cf. p. 194 f.). The *infra*, therefore, refers here, not to the crypt but to the nave and transept as opposed to the chevet, called *ecclesiæ superioris pars capitalis* in the preceding sentence. The pavement of the nave and transept was in fact about two meters lower than the floor of the Carolingian apse, and about 3.70 meters lower than that of Suger's new upper choir (cf. Crosby, pp. 132, 146 ff. and *passim*).

⟨For fragments of the Carolingian limestone pavement found in situ, see Crosby, Bib. 40.⟩

134, 19. PROMTAS MULIERCULAS. The negligent spelling *promtus* for *promptus* ("ready," "eager," "resolute") occurs not only in the Middle Ages (Ducange, VI, p. 530: *promta pecunia*) but occasionally even in classical times.

136, 4-11. SIGNUM MILONIS . . . ROBERTI, ABBATIS CORBEIÆ. All the dignitaries who acted as witnesses have already been mentioned except for Guérin de Châtillon-St.-Paul, Bishop of Amiens 1127-1144.

GLOSSARY

absis, "apse" as term for "chevet" or "sanctuary" as a whole, comprising crypt as well as "apse" in the narrower sense: 100, 9.

advocatus, bailiff (nobleman "protecting" ecclesiastical domain in return for revenue): 122, 29 f.

ala, side-aisle: 52, 8; 100, 19; 104, 11.

anaglifum (opus), chased relief: 60, 31.

anniversarius (dies) [more frequently *anniversarium*] commemoration of the dead whether held annually or otherwise: 70, 14; 80, 8 f.; 108, 14; 128, 18; 130, 24.

aquilo, region of infidels, therefore direction opposite to the sanctuary of a church: 88, 27.

asciscere (erroneously for *accire*), to summon, to invite: 42, 14; 64, 11; 68, 24 f. and 33.

atrium, cemetery: 46, 1.

aula, church: 50, 9.

aurifrisium, orphrey: 114, 17.

capiciarius, treasurer, either assisting or identical with the *sacrista:* 130, 30.

castrum [*castellum*], town not having the *jus Episcopatus:* 40, 28; 92, 10.

census, rent paid by tenants: 98, 15 and *passim.*

circinatus, adorned with circular ornaments: 114, 17.

cœna, monks' supper: 124, 26.

cœnator [more frequently *cœnarius*], monk in charge of monks' supper: 126, 3.

conductus, passage money: 90, 25.

crux collateralis, transept wing: 50, 19.

custos Ordinis, Sub-Prior: 126, 21.

dos, endowment settled upon church or chapel for upkeep: 98, 11; 132, 35.

forestis aquarum, fisheries: 128, 14.

gazofilacium, money chest, collection box: 102, 16 and 25.

generale, main course of monks' dinner: 122, 27; 124, 2 and 14.

homo, vassal: 94, 32.

hospitare, to install as, or to rent property to, permanent tenant: 124, 20; 134, 3.

inclusorium (opus), "verroterie cloisonnée," cold "cloisonné": 78, 2.

justa, pint bottle: 78, 4.

lagena, gallon vessel: 78, 22.

materies [*materia*] *saphirorum,* sapphire glass: 52, 12; 76, 8.

matricularius, dependent of church receiving stipend in return for small services: 132, 17.

mediator, métayer: 126, 5.

medietas, moiety (half of produce shared by métayer and landlord): 126, 5.

medium, central nave as opposed to side-aisles: 96, 24; 100, 17 f.; 104, 7 and 9; 118, 10.

medium, middle part of church as opposed to narthex and chevet: 50, 9.

monasterium, church: 44, 1.

monile, necklace: 70, 24.

musivum (opus), mosaic: 46, 12.

natio, region, district, territory: 54, 14; 74, 1; 112, 11.

officiales, officium, craftsmen or tradesmen, craft or trade: 92, 10 f.

pallia, textiles: 40, 11; 80, 6; 126, 32.

pignora, relics: 118, 5; 130, 7 f.

platea, plot of land with dwelling or dwellings built thereon: 98, 12.

podium, scaffolding: 108, 18.

portio, part of oblations transferred from church or chapel to other ecclesiastical purposes: 60, 4.

præpositura, domain of abbey headed by *præpositus* instead of by Prior: 122, 25.

pratum, cloisters: 88, 11.

prima, monks' dinner: 124, 25.

propugnacula, crenelations: 46, 13 f.

pulmentum, light additional dish supplementing monks' dinner: 124, 15 and 22.

regnum, dominion whether ruled by the king or a "great vassal": 54, 13; 112, 11.

sacrista, monk in charge of church as physical structure and of liturgical objects, frequently acting also as *capiciarius*: 130, 31.

saphirus, see *materies saphirorum*.

secunda, monks' supper: 124, 26.

septima manus, hand of sixth cojuror in oath sworn on relics, etc.: 116, 24.

smaltire, to make, or adorn with, enamel work: 58, 28.

suffragia, props, centering: 108, 19.

tabulatum, floor, story: 94, 8 f.

tensamentum, protection tax: 128, 1.

testudo, nave: 44, 24 f.; 50, 25 f.; 88, 30 f.; 100, 17 f.

vitrum vestitum, painted glass: 76, 8.

volta, "vault" as synonym of "apse" in the narrower sense: 54, 24; 100, 10.

BIBLIOGRAPHIC ABBREVIATIONS

Apart from the symbols *"Adm.," "Cons."* and *"Ord.,"* which refer to the texts reprinted and translated in the present volume (cf. p. 141), the following abbreviations have been used:

Cartellieri: O. Cartellieri, *Abt Suger von Saint-Denis* (Historische Studien, vol. XI), Berlin, 1898.

Conway: W. Martin Conway, "The Abbey of Saint-Denis and its Ancient Treasures," *Archaeologia or Miscellaneous Tracts Relating to Antiquity*, LXVI, 1915, pp. 103-158.[1]

Cornell: H. Cornell, *Biblia Pauperum*, Stockholm, 1925.

Crosby: S. McK. Crosby, *The Abbey of St.-Denis*, 1, New Haven, 1942.[2]

Doublet: J. Doublet, *Histoire de l'Abbaye de S. Denys en France*, Paris, 1625.

Ducange: Dom DuCange, *Glossarium Mediæ et Infimæ Latinitatis*, new ed., Niort, 1883-1887.

Félibien: M. Félibien, *Histoire de l'Abbaye Royale de Saint-Denys en France*, Paris, 1706.

Gall: E. Gall, *Die Gotische Baukunst in Frankreich und Deutschland*, I, Leipzig, 1925.

Guibert: J. Guibert, *Les Dessins du Cabinet Peiresc au Cabinet des Estampes de la Bibliothèque Nationale*, Paris, 1910.

de Laborde: A. de Laborde, *La Bible Moralisée Illustrée*, Paris, 1911.

Lebel: G. Lebel, *Histoire Administrative, Economique, et Financière de Saint-Denis* (Publications de la Faculté des Lettres d'Alger), Paris, 1934.

Lecoy: A. Lecoy de la Marche, *Œuvres Complètes de Suger* (Société de l'Histoire de France, Publications, no. 139), Paris, 1867. ⟨Ed. Paris, 1886; Reprint by Georg Olms, Hildesheim, in press.⟩

Luchaire: A. Luchaire, *Études sur quelques manuscrits de Rome et de Paris (Université de Paris, Bibliothèque de la Faculté des Lettres*, VIII), Paris, 1899, pp. 1-5.

---

[1] This excellent article, apparently overlooked by Crosby, p. 162, note 116, supersedes such earlier essays as that by L. Goudallier, "Travaux Artistiques de Saint Eloi et de l'Abbé Suger à l'Abbaye de Saint-Denis," *Revue de l'Art Chrétien*, V, 1909, pp. 235-244; cf., furthermore, J. J. Marquet de Vasselot, *Bibliographie de l'Orfèvrerie et de l'Emaillerie Française*, Paris, 1925, pp. 86-88. Attention should also be paid to the fact that the *Diary* of John Evelyn, under November 12 ff., 1643, contains a very detailed and, in part, highly entertaining description of the treasury.

[2] This volume covers the period from the foundation of St.-Denis in 475 to Suger's accession in 1122. A full account of Suger's activities and of the later history of the Abbey will be given in vol. II.

Lutz-Perdrizet: J. Lutz and P. Perdrizet, *Speculum Humanæ Salvationis*, Mühlhausen, 1907-1909.

Mâle I: E. Mâle, "La Part de Suger dans la Création de l'Iconographie du Moyen-Age," *Revue de l'Art Ancien et Moderne*, XXXV, 1914/15, pp. 91-102, 161-168, 253-262, 339-349.

Mâle II: E. Mâle, *L'Art Religieux du XIIe Siècle en France*, Paris, 1922, pp. 151-185.

Martin-Cahier: A. Martin and C. Cahier, *Monographie de la Cathédrale de Bourges, Première Partie, Vitraux du XIIIe Siècle*, Paris, 1841-1844.

Migne: J.-P. Migne, *Patrologia Latina*, vol. 186, Paris, 1854.

Millet: S. G. Millet, *Le Trésor Sacré ou Inventaire des Sainctes Reliques . . . de S. Denis en France*, 2nd ed., Paris, 1638.

Panofsky: E. Panofsky, "Note on a Controversial Passage in Suger's *De Consecratione Ecclesiæ Sancti Dionysii*," *Gazette des Beaux-Arts*, 6th series, XXVI, 1944 (*Mélanges Henri Focillon*, published in 1947), p. 95 ff.

ADDITIONAL BIBLIOGRAPHY
SINCE 1945

Compiled by Gerda Panofsky-Soergel

1. *Aachen, Rathaus. Karl der Grosse, Werk und Wirkung* (ed. by Wolfgang Braunfels), Düsseldorf, 1965.
2. Aubert, Marcel, "Têtes de statues-colonnes du portail occidental de Saint-Denis," *Bulletin monumental,* CIII, 1945, p. 243 ff.
3. ———, *Le vitrail en France,* Paris, 1946.
4. ———, *La Sculpture Française au Moyen-Âge,* Paris, 1947.
5. ———, *Suger,* Rouen (Abbaye S. Wandrille), 1950.
   ———, see Bib. 136.
6. ———, "La construction au moyen âge," *Bulletin monumental,* CXIX, 1961, p. 181 ff.
7. Bandmann, Günter, *Mittelalterliche Architektur als Bedeutungsträger,* Berlin, 1951.
8. Barbieri, Franco, "Vincenzo Scamozzi, studioso ed artista," *Critica d'Arte,* VIII, 1949, p. 222 ff.
9. Barroux, Robert, "L'Abbé Suger et la vassalité du Vexin en 1124. La levée de l'oriflamme, la Chronique du Pseudo-Turpin et la fausse donation de Charlemagne à Saint-Denis de 813," *Le Moyen Âge,* LXIV, 1958, p. 1 ff.
10. Bauch, Kurt, "Kunst des 12. Jahrhunderts an Rhein und Maas," in *Rhein und Maas II,* Cologne, 1973, p. 151 ff.
    Beaulieu, Michèle, see Bib. 136.
    Blum, Pamela Z., see Bib. 43.
11. Blumenkranz, Bernhard, "Géographie historique d'un thème de l'iconographie religieuse: les représentations de 'Synagoga' en France," in *Mélanges offerts à René Crozet,* Poitiers, 1966, II, p. 1141 ff.
12. Borries, Johann Eckart von, "Die Westportale der Abteikirche von St.-Denis. Versuch einer Rekonstruktion," unpublished PhD. Diss., Universität Hamburg, 1955.
13. Branner, Robert, *St. Louis and the Court Style in Gothic Architecture,* London, 1965.
    Braunfels, Wolfgang, see Bib. 1.
14. Bricket, Robert, "Fouilles et travaux récents à la basilique de Saint-Denis," *Construction moderne,* LXXVII, 1961, p. 60 ff.
15. Brière, Gaston, and Paul Vitry, *L'abbaye de Saint-Denis* (*Petites Monographies des Grands Edifices de la France*), Paris, 1948.
    Christensen, Erwin O., see Bib. 176.

16. *Cleveland, Museum of Art. Treasures from Medieval France* (William D. Wixom), Cleveland, 1967.

17. Colin, Jean, "La plastique 'gréco-romaine' dans l'empire Carolingien," *Cahiers Archéologiques*, II, 1947, p. 87 ff.

18. Collon-Gevaert, Suzanne, *Histoire des Arts du Métal en Belgique (Académie royale de Belgique, Classe des Beaux-Arts, Mémoires, Series 2, vol. VII)*, Brussels, 1951.

19. Colombier, Pierre du, *Les Chantiers des Cathédrales*, Paris, 1953.

20. Cooney, John D., "The Agate Bowl of the Chalice of the Abbé Suger," unpublished paper, read at the CAA Meeting at Cleveland, Ohio, 1967.

21. Crosby, Sumner McKnight, "New Excavations in the Abbey Church of Saint Denis," *Gazette des Beaux-Arts*, 6th series, XXVI, 1944 (*Mélanges Henri Focillon*, published in 1947), p. 115 ff.

22. ———, in *Bulletin de la Société nationale des Antiquaires de France*, 1945-1947 (published in 1950), p. 253.

23. ———, "Fouilles exécutées récemment dans la basilique de Saint-Denis," *Bulletin monumental*, CV, 1947, p. 167 ff.

24. ———, "Early Gothic Architecture—New Problems as a Result of the St. Denis Excavations," *Journal of the Society of Architectural Historians*, VII, 1948, p. 13 ff.

25. ———, "Excavations in the Abbey Church of St.-Denis 1948. The Façade of Fulrad's Church," *Proceedings of the American Philosophical Society*, XCIII, 1949, p. 347 ff.

26. ———, *L'Abbaye royale de Saint-Denis*, Paris, 1953.

27. ———, "Abbot Suger's St.-Denis. The New Gothic," in *Studies in Western Art (Acts of the Twentieth International Congress of the History of Art, New York, 1961)*, Princeton, N. J., 1963, vol. I, p. 85 ff.

28. ———, "The Inside of St.-Denis' West Façade," in *Gedenkschrift Ernst Gall* (ed. by Margarete Kühn and Louis Grodecki), Munich-Berlin, 1965, p. 59 ff.

29. ———, "The Creative Environment," *Ventures (Magazine of the Yale Graduate School)*, Fall 1965, p. 10 ff.

30. ———, "An International Workshop in the Twelfth Century," *Cahiers d'histoire mondiale (Journal of World History)*, X/1, 1966, p. 19 ff.

31. ———, "Crypt and Choir Plans at Saint-Denis," *Gesta*, V, 1966, p. 4 ff.

32. ———, "Masons' Marks at Saint-Denis," in *Mélanges offerts à René Crozet*, Poitiers, 1966, vol. II, p. 711 ff.

33. Crosby, Sumner McKnight, "Plan de la crypte et du choeur de l'église de Suger à Saint-Denis," *Bulletin de la Société nationale des Antiquaires de France*, 1967, p. 230.

34. ———, "Sous le dallage de l'abbaye royale de Saint-Denis," *Archeologia*, XIV-XV, 1967, pp. 34 ff., 71 ff.

35. ———, "The Plan of the Western Bays of Suger's New Church at Saint-Denis," *Journal of the Society of Architectural Historians*, XXVII, 1968, p. 39 ff.

36. ———, "Le plan et l'élévation des baies ouest de l'église abbatiale de Suger," *Bulletin de la Société nationale des Antiquaires de France*, 1968, p. 175 f. (Résumé of Bib. 35).

37. ———, "Excavations at Saint-Denis—July 1967," *Gesta*, VII, 1968, p. 48 ff.

38. ———, "A Relief from Saint-Denis in a Paris Apartment," *Gesta*, VIII/2, 1969, p. 45 f.

39. ———, "La sculpture des portails occidentaux à Saint-Denis et le style dionysien," *Bulletin de la Société nationale des Antiquaires de France*, 1969, p. 236 ff.

40. ———, "A Carolingian Pavement at Saint-Denis. Preliminary Report," *Gesta*, IX/1, 1970, p. 42 ff.

41. ———, "The West Portals of Saint-Denis and the Saint-Denis Style," *Gesta*, IX/2, 1970, p. 1 ff.

42. ———, *The Apostle Bas-Relief at Saint-Denis* (*Yale Publications in the History of Art*, 21), New Haven and London, 1972.

43. ———, and Pamela Z. Blum, "Le portail central de la façade occidentale de Saint-Denis," *Bulletin monumental*, CXXXI, 1973, p. 209 ff.

Davies, Martin, see Bib. 114.

44. Déer, Josef, "Adler aus der Zeit Friedrichs II.: VICTRIX AQUILA," in Percy Ernst Schramm, *Kaiser Friedrichs II. Herrschaftszeichen*, Göttingen, 1955, p. 88 ff.

45. Elbern, Victor H., *Der eucharistische Kelch im frühen Mittelalter*, Berlin, 1964.

46. ———, "Liturgisches Gerät in edlen Materialien zur Zeit Karls des Grossen," in *Karl der Grosse. Lebenswerk und Nachleben* (ed. by Wolfgang Braunfels), vol. III, 3rd ed. Düsseldorf, 1966, p. 115 ff.

47. Euw, Anton von, in Bib. 49, p. 256 ff.

48. Evans, Joan, *Magical Jewels of the Middle Ages and the Renaissance particularly in England*, Oxford, 1922.

49. Fillitz, Hermann, *Das Mittelalter I* (*Propyläen-Kunstgeschichte*, vol. V), Berlin, 1969.

50. Fingesten, Peter, "Topographical and Anatomical Aspects of the Gothic Cathedral," *The Journal of Aesthetics and Art Criticism*, XX, 1961, p. 3 ff.

51. Fitchen, John, *The Construction of Gothic Cathedrals. A Study of Medieval Vault Erection*, Oxford, 1961.

52. Folz, Robert, *Le Souvenir et la Légende de Charlemagne dans l'Empire germanique médiéval*, Paris, 1950.

53. ———, *Le couronnement impérial de Charlemagne*, Paris, 1964.

54. Formigé, Jules, "Travaux de mise en valeur à l'église abbatiale de Saint-Denis," *Les Monuments Historiques de la France*, nouv. série I, 1955, p. 106 ff.

55. ———, "Les travaux récents de la basilique de Saint-Denis," *Académie des Beaux-Arts*, 1956-1957, p. 77 ff.

56. ———, *L'Abbaye royale de Saint-Denis. Recherches nouvelles*, Paris, 1960.

57. Forsyth, Jr., George H., "A Problem of Surveying in Mediaeval Architecture. 'Geometricis et Aritmeticis Instrumentis,'" *Archaeology*, III, 1950, p. 74 ff.

58. Francastel, Pierre, "Suger et les débuts de l'âge gothique," *Annales*, VII, 1952, p. 237 ff.

59. Frankl, Paul, *The Gothic. Literary Sources and Interpretations through Eight Centuries*, Princeton, N. J., 1960.

60. ———, *Gothic Architecture (The Pelican History of Art, Z 19)*, Baltimore, Md., 1962.

61. Freund, Walter, *Modernus und andere Zeitbegriffe des Mittelalters (Neue Münstersche Beiträge zur Geschichtsforschung, IV)*, Köln, 1957.

62. Gaborit-Chopin, Danielle, "La croix de l'abbé Suger," *Bulletin monumental*, CXXVIII, 1970, p. 243 ff.
    ———, see Bib. 125.

63. Gall, Ernst, review of S. McK. Crosby, *L'Abbaye royale de Saint-Denis*, Paris, 1953, in *The Art Bulletin*, XXXVII, 1955, p. 137 ff.

64. Gauthier, Marie-Madeleine, *Émaux du moyen âge occidental*, Fribourg, 1972.

65. Gerson, Paula Lieber, "The West Façade of St.-Denis, an Iconographic Study," unpublished PhD. Diss., Columbia University, New York, 1970.

66. ———, "The Lintels of the West Façade of Saint-Denis," *Journal of the Society of Architectural Historians*, XXXIV, 1975, p. 189 ff.

67. Giesau, Hermann, "Stand der Forschung über das Figurenportal des Mittelalters," in *Beiträge zur Kunst des Mittelalters. Vorträge der*

Ersten Deutschen Kunsthistorikertagung auf Schloss Brühl 1948, Berlin, 1950, p. 119 ff.

68. Glaser, Hubert, "Beati Dionysii qualiscumque abbas. Studien zu Selbstbewusstsein und Geschichtsbild des Abtes Suger von Saint-Denis," unpublished PhD. Diss., Munich, 1957.

69. ———, "Sugers Vorstellung von der geordneten Welt," *Historisches Jahrbuch,* LXXX, 1961, p. 93 ff.

70. ———, "Wilhelm von Saint-Denis. Ein Humanist aus der Umgebung des Abtes Suger und die Krise seiner Abtei von 1151 bis 1153," *Historisches Jahrbuch,* LXXXV, 1965, p. 257 ff.

71. Goldscheider, Cécile, "Les Origines du Portail à Statues-Colonnes," *Bulletin des Musées de France,* XI, nos. 6-7, 1946, p. 22 ff.

72. Gosebruch, Martin, review of H. Sedlmayr, *Die Entstehung der Kathedrale,* Zürich, 1950, in *Göttingische Gelehrte Anzeigen,* CCVIII, 1954, p. 232 ff.

73. Grabois, A., "The St. Denis Jews and their Role in the Development of the Monastery during the Twelfth Century," *Zion. A Quarterly for Research in Jewish History,* XXX, 1965, p. 115 ff.

Grand, Roger, see Bib. 100.

74. Green, Rosalie B., "Ex Ungue Leonem," in *De Artibus Opuscula XL. Essays in Honor of Erwin Panofsky* (ed. by Millard Meiss), Zürich, 1960—New York, 1961, vol. I, p. 157 ff.

75. Greenhill, Eleanor S., "French Monumental Sculpture," in *The Year 1200,* New York (The Metropolitan Museum of Art), 1970, vol. II, p. 33 ff.

76. ———, "Eleanor, Abbot Suger, and Saint-Denis," in *Eleanor of Aquitaine. Patron and Politician,* ed. by William W. Kibler (Symposia in the Arts and the Humanities, no. 3, University of Texas), Austin and London, 1976, p. 81 ff.

77. Grinnell, Robert, "Iconography and Philosophy in the Crucifixion Window at Poitiers," *The Art Bulletin,* XXVIII, 1946, p. 171 ff.

78. Grodecki, Louis, *Vitraux des églises de France,* Paris, 1947 (published in 1948).

79. ———, "A Stained Glass *Atelier* of the Thirteenth Century. A Study of Windows in the Cathedrals of Bourges, Chartres and Poitiers," *Journal of the Warburg and Courtauld Institutes,* XI, 1948, p. 87 ff.

80. ———, "Suger et l'architecture monastique," in *L'architecture monastique (Actes et travaux de la rencontre franco-allemande des historiens d'art),* numéro spécial du *Bulletin des Relations Artistiques France-Allemagne,* Mayence, 1951.

81. ———, "Fragments de vitraux provenant de Saint-Denis," *Bulletin monumental*, CX, 1952, p. 51 ff.

82. ———, "Vitraux exécutés par ordre de Suger pour l'abbatiale de Saint-Denis," *Bulletin de la Société nationale des Antiquaires de France*, 1952-1953, p. 48 ff.

83. ———, *Vitraux de France du XIᵉ au XVIᵉ siècle* [Paris, 1953].

84. ———, "Les vitraux de Saint-Denis; le programme iconographique et son exécution," *Bulletin van de Koninklijke Nederlandse Oudheidkundige Bond*, 6th series, VI, 1953, col. 93 ff.

85. ———, review of W. S. Stoddard, *The West Portals of Saint-Denis and Chartres*, Cambridge, Mass., 1952, in *Bulletin monumental*, CXI, 1953, p. 312 ff.

86. ———, "L'abbaye de St.-Denis-en-France," *Critique*, 75-76, août-septembre 1953, p. 723 ff.

87. ———, in *Paris, Musée des arts décoratifs. Le vitrail français*, [Paris], 1958, pp. 39 ff., 95 ff.

88. ———, "Une scène de la vie de Saint Benoît provenant de Saint-Denis au Musée de Cluny," *La Revue des arts, Musées de France*, VIII, 1958, p. 161 ff.

89. ———, "La 'première sculpture gothique.' Wilhelm Vöge et l'état actuel des problèmes," *Bulletin monumental*, CXVII, 1959, p. 265 ff.

90. ———, "Les vitraux allégoriques de Saint-Denis," *Art de France*, I, 1961, p. 19 ff.

91. ———, "Les Vitraux de Saint-Denis. L'Enfance du Christ," in *De Artibus Opuscula XL. Essays in Honor of Erwin Panofsky* (ed. by Millard Meiss), Zürich, 1960-New York, 1961, vol. I, p. 170 ff.
———, see Bib. 94.

92. ———, in *Bulletin de la Société nationale des Antiquaires de France*, 1972 (published in 1975), p. 104 ff.

93. ———, *Les Vitraux de Saint-Denis*, vol. I, *Histoire et restitution* (*Corpus Vitrearum Medii Aevi*, France "Études" I), Paris, 1976 (vol. II in press).

94. Harrison-Caviness, Madeleine, and Louis Grodecki, "Les vitraux de la Sainte-Chapelle," *Revue de l'Art*, I-II, 1968, p. 9 ff., esp. p. 13 ff.

95. Heckscher, William Sebastian, "Spiritualia sub metaphoris corporalium," review of E. Panofsky, *Abbot Suger*, Princeton, N.J., 1946, in *University of Toronto Quarterly*, XVI, 1947, p. 210 ff.

96. Hinkle, William M., "The Iconography of the Four Panels by the

Master of Saint Giles," *Journal of the Warburg and Courtauld Institutes*, XXVIII, 1965, p. 110 ff.

97. Hirschfeld, Peter, *Mäzene. Die Rolle des Auftraggebers in der Kunst* (*Kunstwissenschaftliche Studien*, XL), Berlin-Munich, 1968, p. 48 ff.

98. Hoffmann, Konrad, "Sugers 'Anagogisches Fenster' in St. Denis," *Wallraf-Richartz-Jahrbuch*, XXX, 1968, p. 57 ff.

99. Hohler, Christopher, "A Note on *Jacobus*," *Journal of the Warburg and Courtauld Institutes*, XXXV, 1972, p. 31 ff.

100. Hubert, Jean, Comte Blaise de Montesquiou-Fezensac and Roger Grand, in *Bulletin de la Société nationale des Antiquaires de France*, 1945-1947 (published in 1950), p. 119 ff.

101. Hubert, Jean, in *Bulletin de la Société nationale des Antiquaires de France*, 1945-1947 (published in 1950), pp. 137 ff., 176 f.

102. ———, "L' 'escrain' dit de Charlemagne au trésor de Saint-Denis," *Cahiers archéologiques*, IV, 1949, p. 71 ff.

103. Katzenellenbogen, Adolf, *The Sculptural Programs of Chartres Cathedral*, Baltimore, Md., 1959.

104. Kerber, Bernhard, *Burgund und die Entwicklung der französischen Kathedralskulptur im zwölften Jahrhundert* (*Münstersche Studien zur Kunstgeschichte*, IV), Recklinghausen, 1966.

105. Kieft, C. van de, "Deux diplômes faux de Charlemagne pour Saint-Denis, du XIIe siècle," *Le Moyen Âge*, LXIV, 1958, p. 401 ff.

106. Kötzsche, Dietrich, in *Rhein und Maas I*, Cologne, 1972, p. 254 no. G 17.

107. ———, "Zum Stand der Forschung der Goldschmiedekunst des 12. Jahrhunderts im Rhein-Maas-Gebiet," in *Rhein und Maas II*, Cologne, 1973, p. 191 ff.

108. Lafond, Jean, "The Stained Glass Decoration of Lincoln Cathedral in the Thirteenth Century," *The Archaeological Journal*, CIII, 1946, p. 119 ff.

109. Landais, Hubert, "Essai de groupement de quelques émaux autour de Godefroid de Huy," in *L'art mosan* (ed. by Pierre Francastel), Paris, 1953, p. 139 ff.

110. Lapeyre, André, *Des Façades Occidentales de Saint-Denis et de Chartres aux Portails de Laon. Études sur la sculpture monumentale dans l'Ile-de-France et les régions voisines au XIIe siècle*, Mâcon, 1960.

111. Lasko, Peter, *Ars Sacra 800-1200* (*The Pelican History of Art*, Z 36), Harmondsworth, 1972.

112. Leclercq, Dom Jean, O.S.B., tr., *Suger. Comment fut construit Saint-Denis* (*La Clarté-Dieu*, XVIII), Paris, 1945.
Lecoy de la Marche, Richard Albert, see BIBLIOGRAPHIC AB-BREVIATIONS, p. 262.

113. Loenertz, Raymond J., O.P., "La légende parisienne de S. Denys l'Aréopagite, sa genèse et son premier témoin," *Analecta Bollandiana*, LXIX, 1951, p. 217 ff.

114. *London, National Gallery Catalogues. Early Netherlandish School* (Martin Davies), 3rd ed. revised, London, 1968.

115. Loomis, Laura Hibbard, "The Oriflamme of France and the War-Cry 'Monjoie' in the Twelfth Century," in *Studies in Art and Literature for Belle da Costa Greene* (ed. by Dorothy Miner), Princeton, N. J., 1954, p. 67 ff.

116. Misch, Georg, *Studien zur Geschichte der Autobiographie, IV. Die Darstellung der eigenen Persönlichkeit in den Schriften des Abtes Suger von St. Denis* (*Nachrichten der Akademie der Wissenschaften in Göttingen, I. Philologisch-Historische Klasse*), 1957/4, p. 93 ff.

117. ———, *Geschichte der Autobiographie*, vol. III/2, 1, Frankfort, 1959, p. 316 ff.

118. Montesquiou-Fezensac, Comte Blaise de, in *Bulletin de la Société nationale des Antiquaires de France*, 1945-1947 (published in 1950), pp. 80, 128 ff.
———, see Bib. 100.

119. ———, "Le chapiteau du pied de croix de Suger à l'abbaye de Saint-Denis," in *L'art mosan* (ed. by Pierre Francastel), Paris, 1953, p. 147 ff.

120. ———, " 'In sexto lapide,' l'ancien autel de Saint-Denis et son inscription," *Cahiers archéologiques*, VII, 1954, p. 51 ff.

121. ———, "A Carolingian Rock Crystal from the Abbey of Saint-Denis at the British Museum," *The Antiquaries Journal*, XXXIV, 1954, p. 38 ff.

122. ———, "Les derniers jours du crucifix d'or de Suger," in *Études et documents sur l'art français du XIIe au XIXe siècle* . . . (*Hommage à Gaston Brière*), *Archives de l'art français*, nouvelle période, XXII, Paris, 1959, p. 150 ff.

123. ———, "Le tombeau de Charles le Chauve à Saint-Denis," *Bulletin de la Société nationale des Antiquaires de France*, 1963, p. 84 ff.

124. ———, "Nouvelles observations sur la croix de saint Éloy du trésor de Saint-Denis," *Bulletin de la Société nationale des Antiquaires de France*, 1967, p. 229 f.

ABBOT SUGER

125. Montesquiou-Fezensac, Comte Blaise de, *Le Trésor de Saint-Denis. Inventaire de 1634*, avec la collaboration de Danielle Gaborit-Chopin, Paris, 1973, vol. I (vols. II and III in press).

126. Moretus Plantin, Henri, S.J., "Les passions de saint Denys," in *Mélanges offerts au R. P. Ferdinand Cavallera*, Toulouse, 1948, p. 215 ff.

127. Morgan, Nigel, "The Iconography of twelfth century Mosan enamels," in *Rhein und Maas II*, Cologne, 1973, p. 263 ff.

128. Morper, Johann Joseph, "St. Denis," *Kunstchronik*, I, 1948, Heft 10, "Deutscher Kunsthistoriker-Tag 1948," p. 11.
Mütherich, Florentine, see Bib. 153.

129. Ostoia, Vera K., "A Statue from Saint-Denis," *The Metropolitan Museum of Art Bulletin*, XIII, 1955, p. 298 ff.

130. Oursel, Raymond, "Pierre le Venerable, Suger et la lumière gothique," *Annales de l'Académie de Mâcon*, XLIV, 1958 (published in 1964), p. 53 ff.

131. Panofsky, Erwin, *Abbot Suger on the Abbey Church of St.-Denis and its Art Treasures*, Princeton, N. J., 1946, pp. 1-37, reprinted in E. Panofsky, *Meaning in the Visual Arts*, Garden City, N. Y., 1957, p. 108 ff. (paperback edition Harmondsworth, Middlesex, England, and Victoria, Australia, 1970, p. 139 ff.); Italian translation (by Renzo Federici) in E. Panofsky, *Il significato nelle arti visive*, Torino, 1962, p. 107 ff.; French translation (by Pierre Bourdieu) in E. Panofsky, *Architecture gothique et pensée scolastique*, Paris, 1967, p. 7 ff.; Polish translation (by Paulina Ratkowska) in E. Panofsky, *Studia z Historii Sztuki* (ed. by Jan Białostocki), Warsaw, 1971, p. 66 ff.
Pp. 43 ff., 47 ff., 55 ff., 73 ff., 87 ff., 105 ff. of the first edition were reprinted in *A Documentary History of Art* (ed. by Elizabeth G. Holt), vol. I, Garden City, N. Y., 1957, p. 22 ff.

132. ———, "Postlogium Sugerianum," *The Art Bulletin*, XXIX, 1947, p. 119 ff.

133. ———, *Renaissance and Renascences in Western Art*, 2nd ed. Uppsala, 1965 (paperback edition New York, 1969).

134. ———, *Problems in Titian, Mostly Iconographic* (*The Wrightsman Lectures*, II), New York, 1969, p. 61 f.
Paris, Musée des arts décoratifs. Vitraux de France du XIᵉ au XVIᵉ siècle, see Grodecki, Louis, Bib. 83.
———, *Le vitrail français*, see Grodecki, Louis, Bib. 87.

135. ———, *Les trésors des églises de France* (Jean Taralon), 1965.

136. *Paris, Musée national du Louvre. Description raisonnée des sculptures* . . . , vol. I, *Moyen Âge* (Marcel Aubert and Michèle Beaulieu), Paris, 1950.

137. ———, *Cathédrales* (Pierre Pradel), 1962.

138. ———, *L'Europe Gothique* (Pierre Pradel), 1968.

Pradel, Pierre, see the two entries above.

139. Pressouyre, Léon, "Une tête du Louvre prétendue dionysienne," *Bulletin de la Société nationale des Antiquaires de France*, 1967, p. 242 ff.

140. ———, "Réflexions sur la Sculpture du XIIᵉ Siècle en Champagne," *Gesta*, IX/2, 1970, p. 16 ff.

141. *Providence, Rhode Island, Museum of Art Rhode Island School of Design. The Renaissance of the Twelfth Century* (Stephen K. Scher), Providence, Rhode Island, 1969.

142. Quarré, Pierre, "La sculpture des anciens portails de Saint-Benigne de Dijon," *Gazette des Beaux-Arts*, 6th series, L, 1957, p. 177 ff.

143. *Rhein und Maas, Kunst und Kultur 800-1400*, 2 vols., Cologne, 1972-1973.

Rhode Island School of Design, see Bib. 141.

144. Rockwell, Anne, *Glass, Stones & Crown. The Abbé Suger and the Building of St. Denis*, New York, 1968.

145. Sauerländer, Willibald, "Die Marienkrönungsportale von Senlis und Mantes," *Wallraf-Richartz-Jahrbuch*, XX, 1958, p. 115 ff.

146. ———, "Cathédrales," *Kunstchronik*, XV, 1962, p. 225 ff.

147. ———, "Cathédrales," *Art de France*, III, 1963, p. 210 ff.

148. ———, "Sculpture on Early Gothic Churches: The State of Research and Open Questions," *Gesta*, IX/2, 1970, p. 32 ff.

149. ———, *Gothic Sculpture in France 1140-1270*, English translation (by Janet Sondheimer), London-New York, 1972.

150. ———, review of S. McK. Crosby, *The Apostle Bas-Relief at Saint-Denis*, New Haven and London, 1972, in *The Art Bulletin*, LVI, 1974, p. 438 f.

Scher, Stephen K., see Bib. 141.

151. ———, " 'The Renaissance of the Twelfth Century' Revisited," *Gesta*, IX/2, 1970, p. 59 ff.

152. Schramm, Percy Ernst, *Herrschaftszeichen und Staatssymbolik (Schriften der Monumenta Germaniae historica*, 13), 3 vols., Stuttgart, 1954-1956.

153. ——— and Florentine Mütherich, *Denkmale der deutschen Könige und Kaiser. Ein Beitrag zur Herrschergeschichte von Karl dem Grossen bis Friedrich II. 768-1250*, Munich, 1962.

154. Sedlmayr, Hans, *Die Entstehung der Kathedrale*, Zürich, 1950.

155. ———, "Die Wende der Kunst im 12. Jahrhundert," in *Probleme des 12. Jahrhunderts, Reichenau-Vorträge, 1965-1967 (Vorträge und Forschungen*, XII), Konstanz-Stuttgart, 1968, p. 425 ff.

156. Seymour, Jr., Charles, *Masterpieces of Sculpture from the National Gallery of Art*, New York, 1949.

157. Simson, Otto G. von, "The Birth of the Gothic," *Measure*, I, 1950, p. 275 ff.

158. ———, *The Gothic Cathedral*, 2nd ed. revised, New York, 1962 (paperback ed. revised, New York, 1964).

159. Smith, E. Baldwin, *Architectural Symbolism of Imperial Rome and the Middle Ages*, Princeton, N. J., 1956.

160. Springer, Peter, "Ikonographie und Typologie hochmittelalterlicher Kreuzfüsse," unpublished Ph.D. Diss., Freie Universität, Berlin, 1972.

161. Steingräber, Erich, *Antique Jewelry*, New York, 1957.

162. Stern, Henri, "Mosaïques de pavement préromanes et romanes en France," *Cahiers de civilisation médiévale X^e-XIIe siècles*, V, 1962, p. 13 ff.

163. Stoddard, Whitney S., *The West Portals of Saint-Denis and Chartres. Sculpture in the Île de France from 1140 to 1190. Theory of origins*. Cambridge, Mass., 1952.

164. Swarzenski, Hanns, *Monuments of Romanesque Art*, London, 1954; 2nd ed. University of Chicago Press, [1967].

165. ———, "The Song of The Three Worthies," *Boston Museum of Fine Arts Bulletin*, LVI, 1958, p. 30 ff.

Taralon, Jean, see Bib. 135.

166. Theophilus, *The Various Arts*, translated from the Latin with Introduction and Notes by C. R. Dodwell, London and New York, 1961.

167. Thérel, Marie-Louise, "Comment la patrologie peut éclairer l'archéologie. À propos de l'Arbre de Jessé et des statues-colonnes de Saint-Denis," *Cahiers de civilisation médiévale X^e-XIIe siècles*, VI, 1963, p. 145 ff.

168. Vanuxem, Jacques, "The Theories of Mabillon and Montfaucon on French Sculpture of the Twelfth Century," *Journal of the Warburg and Courtauld Institutes*, XX, 1957, p. 45 ff.

169. Verdier, Philippe, "A Mosan Plaque with Ezechiel's Vision of the Sign Thau (Tau)," *The Journal of the Walters Art Gallery*, XXIX-XXX, 1966-1967, pp. 17 ff., 67.

170. ———, "La grande croix de l'abbé Suger à Saint-Denis," *Cahiers de civilisation médiévale, X^e-XIIe siècles,* XIII, 1970, p. 1 ff.

171. ———, "What do we know of the Great Cross of Suger in Saint-Denis," *Gesta,* IX/2, 1970, p. 12 ff.

172. Verrier, Jean, in *Les Monuments Historiques de la France,* IV, 1958, p. 95 f.

173. Vieillard-Troïekouroff, May, "L'architecture en France du temps de Charlemagne," in *Karl der Grosse. Lebenswerk und Nachleben* (ed. by Wolfgang Braunfels), vol. III, 3rd ed. Düsseldorf, 1966, p. 336 ff.

174. ———, "Les zodiaques Parisiens sculptés d'après le Gentil de la Galaisière astronome du XVIIIe siècle," *Mémoires de la Société nationale des Antiquaires de France,* neuvième série, IV, 1968, p. 161 ff.

Vitry, Paul, see Bib. 15.

175. Volbach, Wolfgang Friedrich, in Jean Hubert, Jean Porcher and W. F. Volbach, *L'Europe des invasions,* Paris, 1967, pp. 241 ff., 364 f.

176. *Washington, D. C., National Gallery of Art. Objects of Medieval Art from the Widener Collection* (Erwin O. Christensen), Washington, D. C., 1952.

177. Wentzel, Hans, "Unbekannte mittelalterliche Glasmalereien der Burrell Collection zu Glasgow (3. Teil)," *Pantheon,* XIX, 1961, p. 240 ff.

178. ———, "Abseitige Trouvaillen an Goldschmiedearbeiten," in *Studien zur Buchmalerei und Goldschmiedekunst des Mittelalters. Festschrift für Karl Hermann Usener zum 60. Geburtstag am 19. August 1965,* Marburg an der Lahn, 1967, p. 65 ff.

Wixom, William D., see Bib. 16.

INDEX

Eleutherius, Saint, see Denis, Saint, and Companions

Elias, Bishop of Orléans (1137-1146), 113, 119, 245

Eloy, Saint, Bishop of Noyon (640-659), 189 f.; see also St.-Denis, Abbey of, Carolingian treasury, silver chasses of St. Denis and Companions, "Cross of St. Eloy," incenseboat; see further *Vita Sancti Eligii*

Emmelina, sister-in-law of Suger, 30

Engelberti, Ulric, see Ulric Engelberti of Strassburg

Erasmus, Desiderius, of Rotterdam (1465/66-1536), 33

Erigena, Johannes Scotus, see John the Scot

Essonnes, Notre-Dame-des-Champs, possession of St.-Denis, 9

Etienne de Garlande, Seneschal of Louis VI, 10 f.

Eudes (Odo) II, Bishop of Beauvais (1133-1144), 69, 97, 113, 119, 131, 137, 154, 197

Eudes Clément, Abbot of St.-Denis (1230-1245), 240

Eugenius III, Pope (1145-1154), 30, 59-61, 183

Evelyn, John (1620-1706), *Diary*, 262

Evenus, see Ivès

Evodos, 190

Evrard de Breteuil, 142

Exordium Magnum Ordinis Cisterciensis, 14

Ezekiel, quoted by Suger, 63, 121, 191

Faucon de Bothéon, Archbishop of Lyons (1139-1142), 69, 131, 197

Ferté, Hugues de la, see Hugues de la Ferté

Ferté-sur-Aube, La, 234

Ficino, Marsilio (1433-1499), 36

Fontevrault, 59

Formigé, Jules, architect (1879-1960), 207

Fougères, Mayenne, St.-Léonard, stained-glass, 208

Franconville, possession of St.-Denis, 133, 257

Fulrad, Abbot of St.-Denis (750-784), 153, 159

Galliano, San Vincenzo, fresco, 206

Garlande, Etienne de, see Etienne de Garlande

Garsonis Villa, possession of St.-Denis, 129, 256

Gellius, Aulus, *Noctes Atticae*, 188

Genesis, quoted by Suger, 182, 251

Geoffroy of Anjou and Normandy, 4, 219

Geoffroy de Lèves, Bishop of Chartres (1116-1149), 8, 109, 113, 117, 119, 137, 244

Geoffroy III du Louroux, Archbishop of Bordeaux (1136-1158), 113, 119, 245

Gerard, nephew of Suger, 30

Gérente, Alfred (1821-1868), 202, 204, 209, 212; Henri (-1849), 202 f.

Gervase of Canterbury (c.1141-c.1210), *Tractatus de Combustione et Reparatione Cantuariensis Ecclesiae*, 243

Gesta Dagoberti, 87, 224 f.

Gibraltar, Straits of, 231

Gisors, Payen I de, see Payen I de Gisors et Neaufles

Glasgow, Burrell Collection, stained-glass, 207

Glaucin, prison of, 71, 199

Gregory the Great, Saint, Pope (590-604), *Homiliæ in Evangelia*, 191; *Homiliæ in Ezechielem*, 228; *Moralia*, 191

Grosseteste, Robert (c. 1175-1253), 36

Gruber, J. J., 203

Guérin de Châtillon-St.-Paul, Bishop of Amiens (1127-1144), 137, 259

Guido, see Hugues, Archbishop of Sens

Guilhermy, Fr. de, 207

Guillaume (Willelmus) de Cornillon, 99, 135, 237 f., 258

Guy, brother of St. Bernard, 12

Guy (Guido) II de Montaigu, Bishop of Châlons-sur-Marne (1144-1147), 113, 119, 245

Hannah, mother of Samuel, see Suger

Hamelin, Bishop of Rennes (1127-1141), 69 (?), 131 f. (?), 197

Haymo, Abbot of St.-Pierre-sur-Dives, 232

Heiricus of Auxerre, *De Miraculis S. Germani*, 231

Helinandus, father of Suger, 30

Héloise (1101-1164), Prioress of Argenteuil, 8

Henry II, Emperor (1002-1024), 200

St.-Denis, Abbey of (*cont.*)
St. Hippolytus and others, 45, 99, 133-135, 152 ff.; of St. Romanus, St. Michael and others, 45, 99, 133-135, 151, 154, 237

Suger's chevet incl. crypt, 16, 27 ff., 36 f., 103, 105, 135, 141, 148, 168, 172, 180, 238, 248 f., 258, *plan* following p. 285, *figs.* 8, 9; foundations, 28, 49, 101-103, 141 f., 168, 236, 257 f.; alignment, 36, 101, 238 f.; columns, 20 f., 37, 105; elevation, 240, *text ill.* p. 239; masons' marks, 240; rib vaults, 27 f., 109, 242 ff.; roof, 109, 243 f.; consecration ceremony, 14, 22, 34, 49-51, 85, 111-115, 119-121, 141 f., 157, 168, 197, 232, 249 f.; signifying Mount Zion, 105, 227, 241;

stained-glass, 14, 25, 36 f., 53, 73-77, 101, 168, 172, 182, 201 ff., 240; "Anagogical" window, 20, 75, 203 f., 211 ff., *figs.* 14, 16; Apocalypse window, 204; Charlemagne window, 205; Crusade window, 204 f., 209 f.; grisaille windows, 208; Life of St. Benedict window, 208; Life of the Virgin (Infancy of Christ) window, 29, 202 f., 204 ff., 209 f., *text ill.* opposite p. 1, *figs.* 11, 15; Martyrdom of St. Vincent medaillon, 205 f., 207 f., *fig.* 17; Moses window, 75-77, 203 f., 213 ff., *fig.* 13; Passion window ("Signum Tau" roundel), 208 *fig.* 18; Tree of Jesse window, 73, 202 f., 208 ff., *fig.* 12;

new Altar and Tomb of St. Denis and Companions, 15, 55-57, 105-109, 115, 119, 172 f., 176 ff., 246, 249, *text ill.* pp. 174, 175; antependium, 27, 33, 55, 107-109; see also Denis, Saint and Companions, translation of relics; Altar of the Saviour and the Holy Cross, 115, 119, 246, 249; altars in chapels and crypt, 119, 249 f.; choir stalls, 13, 73; Holy water basin, 115, 228; stone relief of "Twelve Apostles," 176; wrought-iron grille, 184;

treasury (for Carolingian works, see above), 13 f., 36, 168, 171 f.; Suger's Great Cross, 15, 29, 57-61, 180 ff., 188, 246; silver panel, given

by Abbot Robert of Corbie, 71-73, 199; altar vessels, 77, 79, 172, 221 f., *text ill.* p. 222; golden chalice, 77, 217; sardonyx chalice, 25, 79, 220 f., *fig.* 29; porphyry eagle vase, 36, 79, 222, *fig.* 31; sardonyx ewer, 79, 221, *fig.* 30; rock-crystal vase ("*Justa*"), 79, 219 f., 221 f., *fig.* 28; *lagena*, 79, 221 f.; incenseboats, 218 f., 221, 222; headreliquary of St. Denis, 71, 198 f.; reliquary of St. Louis, 176; candlesticks of Louis le Gros, 61, 186; enamelled candlesticks, 77, 172, 202; flowers from crown of Empress Matilda, 77, 219; textiles, 14, 41, 81, 127, 222 f.

Thirteenth century structure, Chapel of St. Hippolytus, 152 f.
St.-Denis-de-l'Estrée, see St.-Denis, town of
St.-Denis-en-Vaux, Priory of St.-Denis, 4
St.-Lucien, possession of St.-Denis, 125, 254 f.
St.-Maur, Abbey of, 143 f.
St.-Omer, Musée de la Ville, pedestal of cross from Abbey of St.-Bertin, 181 f., *fig.* 23
St.-Pierre-sur-Dives, Abbey of, 232
St.-Victor, former Abbey of, see Paris
Samson de Mauvoisin, Archbishop of Reims (1140-1161), 69, 113, 117, 119, 131, 137, 196 f.
Santiago de Compostela, Cathedral, 226 f., 229; *Pilgrims' Guide* to, *ibid.*
Scamozzi, Vincenzo (1552-1616), 158 f.
Scharfenberg, Albrecht von, see Albrecht von Scharfenberg
Sens, Synod of, 18, 196
Simeon, Saint, arm of, see St.-Denis, Abbey of, Carolingian treasury
Simon, nephew of Suger, 30
Simon Chièvre d'Or (Capra Aurea), Canon Regular of St.-Victor, 33
Simon de Vermandois, Bishop of Noyon (1123-1148), 113, 119, 245
Soissons, Bernard de, see Bernard de Soissons
Speculum Humanæ Salvationis, 180, 187, 214 f.
Stephen, Saint, arm of, see St.-Denis, Abbey of, Carolingian treasury
Stephen II, Pope (752-757), alleged *Revelatio*, 160

ILLUSTRATIONS

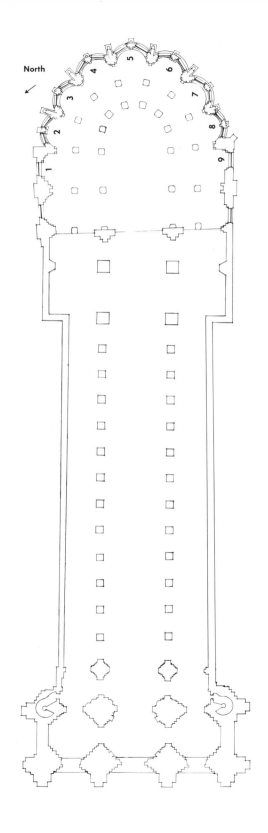

North

St.-Denis, Plan of the Carolingian nave and transept as reconstructed by S. McK. Crosby, and of Suger's still extant narthex and choir (Drawing lent by S. McK. Crosby)

1. Chapel of St. Innocent (later of St. Firminus, now of St. Michael)

2. Chapel of St. Osmanna (now of St. Joseph)

3. Chapel of St. Eustace (later of St. Maurice, now of the Holy Cross and All Saints)

4. Chapel of St. Peregrinus (now of St. Philip)

5. Chapel of the Virgin (now also of St. Hilary)

6. Chapel of St. Cucuphas (now of St. John the Baptist)

7. Chapel of St. Eugene (now of St. Geneviève)

8. Chapel of St. Hilary (now of St. Benedict)

9. Chapel of Sts. John the Baptist and John the Evangelist (later of St. Romanus, now of St. Louis)

1. St.-Denis, West Façade prior to 1837. Engraving

2. St.-Denis, Interior of Narthex

3. St.-Denis, West Façade, central portal

4. Destroyed Jamb Figure, formerly on the West Façade of St.-Denis. Drawing. Paris, Bibliothèque Nationale

5. Head of a Jamb Figure, formerly on the West Façade of
St.-Denis. Baltimore, Md., The Walters Art Gallery

7. St.-Denis, West Façade, southern portal, reliefs showing February and January

6. St.-Denis, West Façade, southern portal, reliefs showing November and December

8. St.-Denis, Exterior of Chapels on Ambulatory

9.   St.-Denis, Interior of Choir

10. Statue of a King, formerly in the Cloister of St.-Denis. New York, The Metropolitan Museum of Art

11. St.-Denis, Chapel of the Virgin. Life of the Virgin (Infancy of Christ) Window in northern bay

12. St.-Denis, Chapel of the Virgin. Tree of
Jesse Window in southern bay

13. St.-Denis, Chapel of St. Peregrinus.
Moses Window in northern bay

14. St.-Denis, Chapel of St. Peregrinus. "Anagogical" Window (before 1946/ 47) in southern bay

16. St.-Denis, Chapel of St. Peregrinus. "Ana-gogical" Window (before 1946/47) in south-ern bay. Detail of Fig. 14

15. St.-Denis, Chapel of the Virgin. Life of the Virgin (In-fancy of Christ) Window in northern bay. Detail of Fig. 11

18. St.-Denis, Chapel of St. Cucuphas. Roundel with the "Signum Tau" in northern bay

17. St.-Denis, "Martyrdom of St. Vincent." Roundel from a destroyed window. In storage

19. Master of St. Giles, "The Mass of St. Giles." Painting.
London, National Gallery

20. Master of St. Giles,
"The Mass of St.
Giles." Detail of Fig.
19

21. Fragment of the
"Cross of St. Eloy."
Paris, Bibliothèque
Nationale, Cabinet des
Médailles

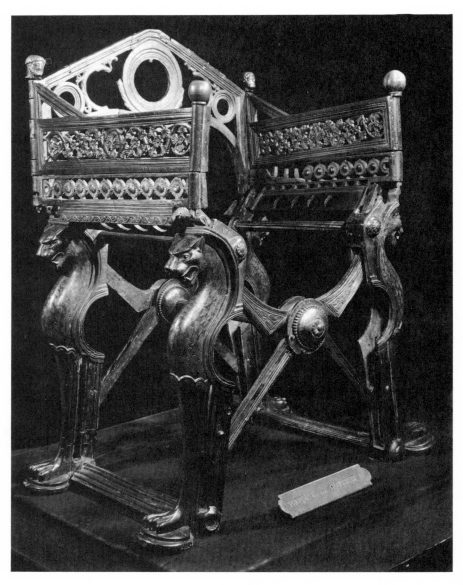

22. "Throne of Dagobert." Paris, Bibliothèque Nationale, Cabinet des Médailles

23. Pedestal of a Cross from St.-Bertin. St.-Omer, Musée de la Ville

24. Destroyed "*Escrin de Charlemagne*" ("*Crista*"). Drawing. Paris, Bibliothèque Nationale, Cabinet des Estampes

25. Crest Jewel of the former "*Escrin de Charlemagne*" ("*Crista*"). Paris, Bibliothèque Nationale, Cabinet des Médailles

27. "*Coupe des Ptolemées.*" Paris, Bibliothèque Nationale, Cabinet des Médailles

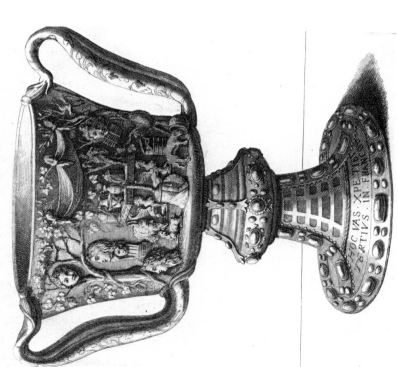

26. "*Coupe des Ptolemées*," before 1804. Engraving

28. Rock-Crystal Vase ("*Justa*"). Paris, Louvre

29. Sardonyx Chalice. Washington, D.C., National Gallery of Art, Widener Collection

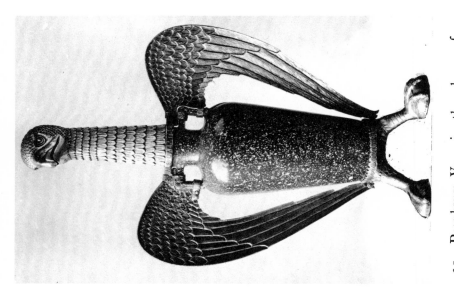

31. Porphyry Vase in the shape of an
Eagle. Paris, Louvre

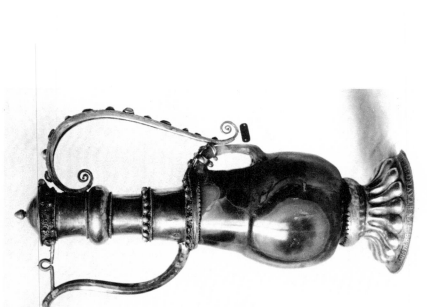

30. Sardonyx Ewer. Paris, Louvre

Library of Congress Cataloging in Publication Data

Suger, Abbot of Saint Denis, 1081-1151.
    Abbot Suger on the Abbey Church of St.-Denis and its
art treasures.

        Latin and English.
        Bibliography: p.
        Includes index.
        1.   Saint-Denis, France (Benedictine abbey)
2.   Architecture—Early works to 1800.   3.   Art—Early
works to 1800.   I.   Panofsky, Erwin, 1892-1968.
II.   Panofsky-Soergel, Gerda   III.   Title.
NA5551.S2S8   1978   726'.5'0944362   78-51186
ISBN 0-691-03936-4
ISBN 0-691-00314-9 pbk.